Praise ...

COMMITTING THEATRE

"A remarkable book. Filewod's meticulous research draws on the archive and repertoire of Canadian activist performance since the mid-nineteenth century to trace a history of radical, interventionist theatre in Canada, from individual acts of protest to established companies. In the process he recuperates a broad spectrum of performers and performance practices that have been marginalized, erased, or ignored in previous theatrical histories. *Committing Theatre* challenges traditional paradigms and should be required reading in any study of Canadian theatre."

— **Jerry Wasserman**, professor of English and Theatre, University of British Columbia

"*Committing Theatre* is an unprecedented study of radical theatre and per-formative political activism in Canada since the nineteenth century. It interweaves a historical and theoretical analysis with juicy anecdotes, candid stories, and engaging script excerpts, many of which are treasures from the pre-digital era. Filewod's lucid, brisk writing style makes this book a compelling read, validating and instigating much needed theat-rical political intervention."

— **Aida Jordão**, popular theatre artist and scholar

COMMITTING THEATRE

Theatre Radicalism and Political Intervention in Canada

ALAN FILEWOD

BETWEEN THE LINES

Toronto

Committing Theatre: Theatre Radicalism and Political Intervention in Canada

First published in 2011 by
Between the Lines
401 Richmond Street West, Studio 277
Toronto, Ontario M5V 3A8
Canada
1-800-718-7201
www.btlbooks.com

Library and Archives Canada Cataloguing in Publication

Filewod, Alan D. (Alan Douglas), 1952–

Committing theatre : theatre radicalism and political intervention in Canada / Alan Filewod.

Includes bibliographical references and index.
Issued also in electronic format.
ISBN 978-1-926662-76-3

1. Theater–Political aspects–Canada–History–19th century. 2. Theater–Political aspects–Canada–History–20th century. 3. Actors and actresses–Political activity–Canada–History–19th century. 4. Actors and actresses–Political activity–Canada–History–20th century. I. Title.

PN2303.F54 2011   792.097109'034   C2011-905005-6

Front cover photo: Unemployed demonstration, Edmonton, October 1933 (Glenbow Archives NC-6-13068b). Back cover/spine photo: From the only performance of *Eight Men Speak* (L.W. Conolly Theatre Archives, McLaughlin Library, University of Guelph). Cover and text design by David Vereschagin/Quadrat Communications
Printed in Canada

Between the Lines gratefully acknowledges assistance for its publishing activities from the Canada Council for the Arts, the Ontario Arts Council, the Government of Ontario through the Ontario Book Publishers Tax Credit program and through the Ontario Book Initiative, and the Government of Canada through the Canada Book Fund.

 Canada Council   Conseil des Arts
for the Arts   du Canada   Canadä    ONTARIO ARTS COUNCIL
CONSEIL DES ARTS DE L'ONTARIO

Contents

Preface and Acknowledgements

If theatre is a human language that constantly finds expression in changing cultural forms and spectatorial practices, it follows that any attempt to write a comprehensive account of a given aspect of theatre is an application of particular cultural schematics. But a study that attempts to penetrate the outer boundaries of those schematics, where theatre dissolves as form or fails to emerge into artistic professionalism, must be defeated by the sheer immensity of the subject. With this issue in mind I am aware that readers who pick up this book are likely to note its many absences. Every example I cite and every case study I choose exclude many more.

In this study of the ways in which activists have used theatre as a method of political intervention, I have chosen, wherever possible, to draw on material I have seen myself; sometimes I was a participant in the work I describe. I have known many of the people whose work I mention. In dealing with the work of the last thirty years, I have tried to follow my own connective path, from performance to meeting to festival. In this sense, I am practising historiography from within. Still, it is history, not memoir. Often in my encounters with theatre activists over the decades I was taking notes, collecting documents, and trying to find ways of theorizing and describing the work I was seeing.

Readers may well note that because of this personal history my analysis is oriented towards hegemonic normatives: of cultural geography in Toronto, of demographics in whiteness, of gender in hetero-straightness, of language in English. In part this reflects the trajectory of my own experience; I write from within the formations that have shaped me and my fields of participation. But it also arises from a commitment to the local. If this book seems heavily tilted in the direction of Toronto, for example, it is because of the positionality of what I think of as "hundred mile research." Whenever possible I have drawn on examples that are local for me, spiralling outwards from my home in Guelph. In theatre studies, I firmly believe, we are always practising standpoint scholarship. If theatre is everywhere, then I begin with the theatre I have seen and the people I have met.

This book is my attempt, then, to synthesize the particularity of my experiences with activist theatre into historical principles, and to reclaim marginalized and delegitimized performance practices as the legacy of generations of theatrical radicals and innovators. In the 1980s I was one of the founders of the Canadian Popular Theatre Alliance, which drew up the manifesto of the activist theatre network that I describe in chapter 8. The manifesto began, "We believe that theatre is a means and not an end. We are theatres which work to effect social change." As a theatre historian, I believe that principle applies to scholarship as well.

Acknowledgments

This book was made possible by a Standard Research Grant from the Social Sciences and Humanities Research Council of Canada. Because of that grant I have been fortunate to work with gifted and committed graduate research assistants. I extend thanks and respect to Kelsie Acton, Tony Berto, Siscoe Boschman, Vanessa Falsetti, Kim Nelson, and Kailin Wright. Thanks also to the Editing Modernism in Canada collaborative research project, which supported research assistance for work on *Eight Men Speak*. I owe a special debt to Lee Baxter for her help in preparing the manuscript.

I am deeply thankful to Amanda Crocker and Between the Lines, who welcomed the proposal for this book and were always encouraging and helpful. And I thank them for giving the manuscript to Robert Clarke to edit. His painstaking line-by-line work on the text and his many pages of notes and queries have helped me immeasurably to clarify ideas, eliminate ambiguity, and break long-held habits developed over a career of writing for academic journals. The copy editor, like the dramaturge who helps the playwright shape the play for performance, labours to make someone else look good. We who benefit from that labour know how much effort it takes.

I have also benefited from the work of numerous librarians and archivists across the country. They are the unsung heroes of scholarly research. I am particularly grateful to the staff of the Glenbow Museum Archives in Calgary and to the librarians and archivists at the McLaughlin Library at the University of Guelph. In particular, I extend thanks to Kathryn Harvey, Bev Buckle, Pam O'Rielly, Paul Stack, and Darlene Wiltsie.

Many conversations over the years have influenced the shape of this book. I could not have written it without the thinking, advice, contestation, and solidarity of Phil Allt, Don Bouzek, Julie Salverson, Mike Sell, Jan Selman, Jerrard Smith, and Dave Watt.

I owe more than thanks to my partner Linda Warley and my son Clem Filewod. I give them this book with love.

I dedicate this project to the memory of four fighters for activist theatre whose lives touched mine: George Luscombe, Rhonda Payne, Toby Gordon Ryan, and Oscar Ryan.

1

Purposeful Performance and Theatrical Refusals

Dissonant spectatorship: the Guelph
Old Boys parade, 1908.
Guelph Public Library Archives

In my home, sitting on a mantle, is an old wooden carving that I would not part with for anything. My grandfather brought it back to Canada from Japan almost a century ago. He was a petty officer in the Canadian navy in its earliest years, having left his working-class family to join the Royal Navy in England at the age of sixteen. The two-foot-high carving depicts an old man with a staff. But what has always fascinated me is that my grandfather turned it into a lampstand.

I began to see a cultural practice at work in that carving-turned-into-a-lamp only years later when I bought my father – himself a naval officer – an antique print of an eighteenth-century sea battle. I was disconcerted when, instead of framing it, he turned it into a lampshade. I came to understand that for both men art was to be appreciated and enjoyed – but if it could also be useful, so much the better.

From this lesson I also came to understand my own deep interest in a theatre that works to be useful, that has purposeful intent. My focus on the instrumentality of theatre as a social practice is conditioned by a cultural tradition that has its sources in the utilitarianism of British working-class culture. Still, I am interested not so much in the thematics of politically conscientious artists and workers as in how some of these people have tried to implement theatrical action to produce political results. When we begin to look for theatre activism in this manner, we discover it all around us. For the most part this activity is ignored and dismissed because it does not lead to reproducible and marketable texts.

This inquiry into how theatre in Canada has not just expressed but participated instrumentally in radical dissent begins with the fundamental premise that when we speak of "theatre" we are always balancing a historically defined set of performance and spectatorial routines against a vaster set of practices that cannot be easily defined, or even discerned. When we speak of nineteenth-century theatre, for example, we are always negotiating a reconciliation of what the word "theatre" meant at that time and what it means now. This would seem to be a simple exercise, but it becomes complex when we start to draw boundaries between kinds of performances. Even if we start with the dubious proposition that theatre is what happens on a stage in a playhouse, does that mean we include *everything* that happens on the stage? And if we find this same performance outside of the theatre, does that mean we need to approach a definition on the basis of practice, and not place? These are the methodological questions that theatre historians are constantly testing.

Since the late nineteenth century, theatre has been one of the most public sites of social activism, dissent, and controversy. Popular convention posits that the introduction of cinema in the early years of the twentieth century killed the theatre as playhouses across North America converted to film houses and theatre producers left New York for the year-round location shoots of California. As it turns out, film no more killed theatre than television killed film, or home video killed cinemas, or video killed the radio star. As new technologies opened up and new cultural fields expanded, the "old" never lost social purchase. Theatre lost its pre-eminence as a mass entertainment, but by the end of the twentieth century North America had more live theatre than ever before. And theatre had chaotically developed into a vast and unclassifiable number of forms and practices that were a pervasive presence in the consumer entertainment society.

I take it as axiomatic that most theatre occurs locally, is seen by only a few, and leaves few traces. Although many people might identify theatre as dramatic literature – that is, plays – most theatrical performances, even if they can be called plays, are never published. Most human performances are unrecorded. They pass by unremarked. Theatre history, then, is for the most part a history of the forgotten and unremarked, traced through the survival of the exceptional. Perhaps the most familiar example of this might be the theatricality of a buskers festival, in which street performers use character, comedy, and skill to catch and compel an audience. These are not dramatic plays, but they are theatrical performances. The distance between them and Shakespeare is not great, but for every Shakespeare there are tens of thousands of jugglers, stand-up comics, buskers, and clowns. Most of them labour and live in obscurity.

In our consumer entertainment world we think of theatre as "the theatre," a particular disciplinary practice (actors, stage, playhouse, scenery) in a larger entertainment industry: the institutionalized theatre. Those who pay attention to theatre may divide it into roughly defined sectors differentiated by cultural economy, taste, and audience. Mega-musicals, legitimate theatre, the classics, alternative theatre, the fringe: these are concentric spheres through which theatre workers and audiences navigate.[1]

All of these spheres of theatre work can witness a desire to articulate social visions, to express political conviction, and advocate social change. It could not be otherwise, because theatre in the end is about creating feelings in the body of the spectator, and theatre people never forget Molière's much-quoted dictum that all you need to make theatre is two planks and a passion. Sometimes in the theatre we see moments of true social courage as artists play against censorship, repression, and violence.

While the domain of "the theatre" is the most visible and iconic manifestation, it is still only one small part of theatre culture. Historically, most theatre work has happened outside of the institutionalized theatre. In particular, while the boundaries are porous, theatre that participates in radical politics tends to refuse the institutionalized theatre's aesthetics and conventions. Local, unremarked, and artistically invisible, the theatre of political intervention is impossible to trace in any complete way. How then is it possible to write a history of it?

Traditional theatre history emerged as a discipline in the interstices of archaeology and literary history; it developed investigative techniques that sought evidence in both material and written sources. Whether counting the remaining stones at the Theatre of Dionysus in Athens, examining the records of payments to players in ducal account books, or reading the diaries of playgoers, theatre historians look for traces of performances. Until fairly recently, much of theatre history in Canada consisted of building detailed performance calendars and reconstructing conditions of performance. That labour has proved to have been a productive enterprise, but it has been subject to one major restriction: it can only outline the histories of theatres and performances that left such traces. "Theatre" thus becomes that which is findable by theatre historians.

A Bouquet and Some Caterpillars

In June 1919 a rather unremarkable story appeared in the Vancouver newspaper *The Province*:

PROTESTS BY WAY OF A LIVING BOUQUET

Mayor Gayle's secretary, Mr. Charles Read, was presented with a bouquet on Friday afternoon. The central effect of the bouquet consisted of green tips cut from vacant property bushes in some part of the city. The green tips, however, were almost entirely smothered by huge bunches of tent caterpillars at the young agile age when they hang to the tree by their tail and wriggle the rest of their body lustily in the air, anxious to migrate to greener pastures.

The bouquet was presented by a determined looking citizen, who said his object was to show the city how wealthy corporations look after their property – to the detriment of the small man trying to raise fruit and vegetables in his garden plot. The wriggling mass had been cut, he said, from some vacant railroad property adjoining his own.

Not able to tender his living protest to the mayor in person, the determined citizen left in search of Ald. Owen, who has charge of caterpillar extermination energies.[2]

Here, behind the scrim of journalistic bombast, we can discern an event so ordinary that it is barely reportable. A man walks into an office in City Hall and thrusts a bouquet of caterpillars at a bureaucrat. He does not get past the secretary, so he leaves. As an act of political protest, this is about as local and ordinary as it can get. But something else is happening in this event. The unnamed "determined citizen" did not just enter and throw down a cutting covered with caterpillars. By presenting it as a bouquet, in a parody of courtly formality, he chose to turn it into what Bertolt Brecht would call a *gest*, a theatricalized action that embodies, enacts, and watches a social critique.[3] He was performing a theatrical intervention, although he probably did not understand his actions in those terms. But he knew he wanted to be seen, and wanted others to spectate. In fact, all we know about this man is his performance.

Considered as a theatrical performance, this event would seem to be the polar opposite of what most people understand as political theatre – of theatre that takes its formal principles and aesthetics from its engagement with political activism. The most famous and celebrated "political" performances are generally the most institutionalized, produced in peak theatre facilities by consummately trained professionals. Tony Kushner's adaptation of Brecht's *Mother Courage*, mounted in 2006 for the New York Public Theatre and starring Meryl Streep, is an example. So too is Judith Thompson's play *Palace of the End*, which was honoured by Amnesty International, and in which three actors in turn deliver (invented) harrowing monologues from three ("real") people touched by or complicit in the invasion of Iraq. Yet another example is David Hare's widely produced *Stuff Happens*, a behind-the-scenes docudrama about Tony Blair and George W. Bush in the prelude to that invasion. Plays on this scale, offered for public consumption, can utilize the fullest resources of the theatre industry and still lay claim to a process of political engagement. This is the case with Théâtre du Soleil's massive *Le Dernier Caravansérail*, a play developed in a documentary research process involving migrant refugees in France. The creators fed real-life narratives to the troupe, which processed them through the author (Hélène Cixous) and textual collaborators and embodied them in the cast, which modelled French metropolitan interculturalism. The play, having thus gathered its migrant sources into aesthetic order, deployed the fullest technical resources of the theatre and toured internationally. Tracing the migrations of the informants, the play travelled from platform to platform, always landing in a theatre apparatus capable of installing it, including the Villa Borghese in Rome, Lincoln Center in New York, Berlin Arena, and Royal Exhibition Building in Melbourne.

However far removed these performances seem from a man walking into an office carrying a bouquet of caterpillars, they are located on a grid that plots along two axes, of institutionalism and professionalism. These peak performances occupy the very visible space delineated by the highest degree of both conditions; the solo protester desperately inventing theatrical performance in an office stands, with countless others, in the much more crowded sector of unprofessional, non-institutionalized theatre. They stand outside of what the British activist scholar and director Baz Kershaw has defined as the disciplinary regime of the "theatre estate" – the complex of industry, professionalism, economy, and canonicity that constitutes "the theatre."[4] Like any social estate, "the theatre" has clear, if porous, borders. It legitimizes a particular understanding of theatre, which developed in the nineteenth and twentieth centuries as a simulacrum of the nation-state.

Mapping Canadian Theatre

Although Canada today has more theatrical performance than at any point in its history, we are experiencing a crisis in the historical relationship of nation, theatre, and literary canon that has sustained the master narrative of the theatre as a disciplinary regime and has invested cultural significance in playwrights and plays despite the theatre's minority position against economically more powerful art forms. (We always need to remember that more people saw *Avatar* in its first week in the movie theatres than went to all the plays in the country in a year.) The crisis of nationhood in an era of globalized corporate economics and cultural imperium produces a dilemma for the institutionalization of national cultures and destabilizes fundamental assumptions of aesthetic and cultural value. Historically nations such as Canada have reinforced their claims to autonomy and indeed their occupation of territory with canonical structures of value in literature and art. Today we see this relationship weakening at both ends, as the boundaries of nation and of cultural aesthetics begin to dissolve under external pressures: of empire, hybridities, cultural mobilities, and the migration of forms and practices.

This tendency leads to the suggestion that rather than continue to question ideas of identity and national culture we need to understand theatre and drama as operations of power and presence in the cultural networks that constitute auxiliary nationhood in the modern empire. The historical relationship in which theatre and drama are metonymic of the nation may no longer be viable. The idea of national theatre as an institutionalized industry that announces and enacts the historical presence of the nation through a canon of performed texts is a historical artifact originating in nineteenth-century movements of popular nationhood. In Canada this model was embedded in the Massey Report, the 1951 document that established the basis of public arts in the country. For Vincent Massey, the chair of the Royal Commission on National Development in the Arts, Letters and Sciences and a lifelong patron of the arts, the theatre was "not only the most striking symbol of a nation's culture but the central structure enshrining much that is finest in a nation's spiritual and artistic greatness." A typical passage that represents the mid-century humanist belief of cultural maturation states: "There is undoubtedly in Canada a widespread interest in the theatre.... A first-rate company of players could probably maintain themselves profitably in Canada for as long as they wished to stay.... It seems apparent that there is in Canada a genuine desire for the drama."[5] This comment may seem sound and logical, even self-evident. But if we make one small substitution, suddenly it is much less coherent: "There is undoubtedly in Resource Extraction Colony 'C' a widespread interest in the theatre.... A first-rate company of players could probably maintain themselves profitably in Resource Extraction Colony 'C' for as long as they wished to stay.... It seems apparent that there is in Resource Extraction Colony 'C' a genuine desire for the drama."

We speak of national theatre, national literature, or national cinema with the assumption that we can identify a reciprocally constitutive relationship between the nation as the site of cultural expression and cultural production as the experience and practice of living of the nation. Debates on interculturalism extend the reach of these constitutive terms, negotiating wider concepts of nation, and broader understandings of cultural forms and practices, but they are still held in mutual suspension. We do not speak of the national video game, or the national massive multi-player role-play game. To speak of "Canadian gaming" seems as absurd as speaking of "Resource Extraction Colony Theatre." The simulated worlds of these games are on the one hand vast and rhizomorphic – in the sense, that is, of an evolving, adaptive network – and they cross boundaries of nation, culture, class, race, and gender. But on the other hand they are specific products of cultural industries located in the material world, and as such replay their cultural origins.

The problem is that in computer gaming those origins are difficult to discern. Moreover, they invert the traditional understanding of cultural metonymy that sunders the significance of art from its social practice, and which justifies the critical examination of elite artistic works over mass cultural entertainments. In this sundering, a single performance of *Hamlet* is held to be more significant than all of *The Lion King*, and five hundred copies of a new book of poems are held to be more important than five hundred thousand copies of the latest detective novel. But in computer game culture, the digital world only exists to the extent that it is used, and whatever cultural significance a game may have is entirely a condition of its popular reception. If we do not speak of "national computer gaming" or "Canadian gaming," that is because game culture has not historically produced reproducible textual artifacts that survive the moment of play. That has, however, begun to change as technology enables gamers to edit staged sequences from the game world, add dialogue and music, and release the result on the Internet. The proliferation of video-game dramaturgy is as sudden and dazzling as the proliferation of secular humanist theatrical drama in the sixteenth century. But even as new textual forms emerge from game culture, they cannot be understood as expressions of national culture because, in gaming, national experience speaks through the systems of playing rather than through the game texts. In an online role-play game like *World of Warcraft,* which requires gamers to form into "guilds" to gain access to high-end content in group play, the content is the same whether the guild is located in Korea or Canada. But national and cultural differences significantly alter both how the game is played and the function of the player guilds.

The concept of theatrical nationhood is a useful way of looking at how performance models, enacts, and constitutes the nation, and it attempts to reconcile a fundamental contradiction of metonymy and popular participation: less than 20 per cent of the Canadian population go to the theatre, but the theatre is the nation only to the extent that the nation goes to the theatre.[6]

In the twentieth century the humanist vision of a self-sustaining theatre culture was a response to American economic colonialism and the spread of monopoly capitalism. The theatre industry had been one of the first sectors in the Canadian economy to be penetrated by U.S. capital, and during the great rush of monopoly empire-building in the 1890s it became one of the first sites of resistance. The idea of Canadian theatre originally surfaced as a trope of resistance, as the aspiration of national autonomy deferred by U.S. cultural expansion. This phenomenon produced an overdetermined concept of Canadian theatre – with theatre perceived as being both a cultural and an economic field of possibility.

The objection to American theatre in anglophone Canadian cultural nationalism was both practical and ideological. On the practical level the deep circulation of American popular culture, then as now, presented a powerful argument that Canadians really are Americans, and that far from locking Canadians out of their own systems of representation, American theatre was a field in which Canadian artists and audiences were deeply complicit. Along with the popularity of touring U.S. productions (and British companies booked through New York), a large number of local minstrel shows and *Uncle Tom's Cabin* companies consisted of Canadian performers playing to Canadian audiences. The ideological objection that followed from this pattern was that despite affinities of race and history, American theatre culture circulated republican values that were foreign to monarchist anglo-Canadians. For the anglo-Canadians, the absent Canadian theatre would be marked by its "freedom" from American themes and forms. In this regard, critics tended to agree that British models would be useful. In francophone Quebec, where a professional theatre industry developed later than in anglophone Canada (primarily because of the rigid anti-theatrical position of the Catholic Church), the many literary nationalist dramas of the nineteenth century were influenced by the French classical tradition.

The absent Canadian theatre became more material but no less imagined over the course of the twentieth century, in large part because of the efforts of Vincent Massey. A diplomat and politician, Massey not only devoted much of his life to the cause of a national drama and a national theatre culture, but also led the Royal Commission that recommended the establishment of a national arts council. Most histories of Canadian theatre follow a narrative derived from Massey's analysis. This narrative argues that the cause of Canadian playwriting was artificially inhibited by the absence of a professional theatre system until the postwar years, at which point the introduction of public funding established a "mainstream" that generated a radical "alternative" theatre movement in which Canadian playwriting came into its own.

This narrative was historically dubious, but it provided a critical genealogical sequence that allowed for the maturation of a professional theatre in which the drama and the theatrical system function as reciprocating engines of growth: new dramatic "voices" encourage new forms of theatrical production; new theatres enable new drama, and so on through the generations. In this positivist account, the theatre "evolves" in stages that supersede colonialism; every accomplishment is a step closer to deferred autonomy. Eugene Benson and Leonard Conolly reiterate this thesis in their *English-Canadian Theatre* when they write: "It has been one of the purposes of this study to show that the factors militating against an indigenous Canadian theatre were cultural and political, not climatic, and that Canadians were long denied – or denied themselves – full imaginative expression in drama and theatre."[7]

Theatre in Canada is a disparate set of practices scattered across a great amount of space. Throughout history, the phrase "Canadian theatre" has always meant an imagined theatre contained within (and often inhibited by) the material theatre of the day. It is a phrase that has expressed longing for a sense of national community and has been the site of severe contestation (especially in the 1970s). The idea of a Canadian theatre carries the necessary corollary of a non-Canadian, or a not-yet Canadian, theatre, the theatre of the moment, which had variously been defined as alien, colonial, foreign, Other. Theatre and nation collapse into each other at the point of imagined authenticity: the "real" nation is out there, the "real" theatre is its articulation.

In the middle of the twentieth century, when the idea of a Canadian theatre industry capable of drawing audiences to the works of Canadian playwrights was still an aspiration, writer Robertson Davies made the satirical comment:

> Every great drama, as you know, has been shaped by its play-house.... Now what is the Canadian playhouse? Nine times out of ten ... it is a school hall, smelling of chalk and kids, and decorated in the Early Concrete style. The stage is a small, raised room at one end. And I mean room. If you step into the wings suddenly you will fracture your nose against the wall. There is no place for storing scenery, no place for the actors to dress, and the lighting is designed to warm the stage but not to illuminate it. Write your plays, then, for such a stage. Do not demand any procession of elephants, or dances by the maidens of the Caliph's harem. Keep away from sunsets and storms at sea. Place as many scenes as you can in cellars and kindred spots.[8]

As Davies playfully argued, the formal principles of dramatic literature derive not from aesthetic theory or critical tradition but from the material and economic conditions of theatre work. Playtexts circulate as markers of theatrical processes, although they are rarely studied as such. Twentieth-century liberal humanism perceived such processes as ideologically neutral, and expressed a belief in the "capacity development," or technological capacity, of the professionally equipped playhouse. By capacity development I mean an analysis that sees, for example, that a symphonic hall has the architectural and acoustic form necessary to fulfil the capacity of performing a symphony perfectly, or that a theatre playhouse has the necessary conditions for the performance of a fully realized play. This is an argument that requires continual reinvestment in a tradition of classic mastery, and as such explains the endurance of the Shakespeare industry. It assumes that although a Canadian and German symphonic hall may speak to different cultural contexts, they will both be capable of hosting the Berlin Philharmonic.

In the canonical theatre we can speak confidently of dramatic literature, and identify value: a good play is one that fulfils spectatorial desire by using the performance resources of the theatre to stage reproducible stories. This is more or less the same point made by Aristotle. But as we expand our understandings of the theatre, the plays that fulfil them expand as well, so that we can have avant-garde performance in alternative spaces, processional performances in forests, outdoor performances on farms, urban street performances – all expanding the set of aesthetic principles that define "good" dramaturgy. We can bring in external conditions, of class, culture, ethnicity, and gender, and expand our aesthetics to incorporate the particularities of culture specificity. In Canada as in other Western nations, theatrical diversity has been contained and regulated by the narratives of artistic mastery of the theatrical profession and its economy, centred around the idea of genius and tradition, usually made concrete in the classic repertoire.

The logic of public funding in the arts, as it was introduced in the 1950s, was that a cultural system of disciplinary mastery would organize around elite exemplary companies. But Canadian theatre did not quite develop that way. Rather than developing coherently with regional theatre companies performing repertoires of provocative dramas to discerning citizens, it grew into a rhizomorphic chaos, which gradually formed very general and overlapping sectors. The chief reason for this particular evolution is that the theatre economy in Canada has long been fundamentally subsidized by the artists themselves.

The four major sectors of the theatre economy in Canada – the public, commercial, amateur, and fringe sectors – overlap and change, but they are reinforced by a web of contractual and taxation practices. The public sector includes what is generally known as the professional theatre, which is what most people refer to as "Canadian theatre." It comprises several hundred theatre companies incorporated as not-for-profit and thus eligible for arts council funding.[9] Most are members of the Professional Association of Canadian Theatre, and they sign agreements with the Canadian Actors' Equity Association or the Union des artistes, as the case may be. This sector includes everything from the Stratford Shakespeare Festival to Native Earth Performing Arts, and is further subdivided into "large theatre" and "small theatre" sectors, although, this being Canada after all, these differentiations are regionally variable. A "small theatre" in Toronto may be larger than a "large theatre" in Saskatchewan. Then too, while this sector is commonly referred to as subsidized, a typical theatre company receives no more than 20 per cent of its revenue from public sources.

Historically the public theatre has been held in balance by the commercial and amateur sectors. These binaries, of professional/amateur and public/commercial, have been stabilized by the narrative of disciplinary mastery, and they explain why the Stratford Festival functions as a simulation of a national theatre. Indeed, Stratford *does* what national theatres do, and in its mandate to perform Shakespeare and other plays for a mass audience it has a built-in reason to avoid the commitment to a national dramatic literature that one might expect of a national theatre; in Canada, dramatic literature functions to divide, not unify, the nation. For a brief period in the 1970s, Stratford did call itself the Stratford National Theatre in Canada. The amateur theatre today is a vast and diverse sector because it is anywhere and everywhere, and it becomes increasingly difficult to define and categorize. Similarly, commercial theatre ranges from local dinner theatres to massive multinational corporate productions, and increasingly operates in partnership with subsidized theatres.

In the final sector, the fringe, anything goes. This entity manifests itself in the network of Fringe Festivals across the country every summer, and includes hundreds, perhaps thousands, of troupes. In fringe theatre, as in rock music, groups form and reform constantly, working on a project-to-project basis. Most of this work is unpaid and unsubsidized. We can no more quantify fringe theatre than we can quantify rock bands. We can count the numbers of shows produced or songs released, but we have no idea how many rock bands are out there.

The fundamental condition underlying the systemization of Canadian theatre is that all cultural organizations operate in a permanent state of financial emergency. Several features follow from this, and they have a direct impact on the ways in which Canadian playwrights tell their stories. The first is that incomes for artists in Canada are very low, a factor that leads to a general migration of artists and workers from the theatre at an early age. The average income for an actor in Canada is $17,866, and a significant drop occurs in the number of working actors between the ages of thirty and forty. In effect this pattern amounts to a deficit of age and experience, and we lose the possibilities of the artistic work that might have been. The second feature is that theatres cannot afford to spend money on development, which in practice means very short rehearsal periods compared to European or even Québécois standards.[10]

A significant material result of this state of affairs is that most plays never move beyond their first production, and most playwrights do not have the opportunity to work at length with an ensemble familiar with their work. To answer this need, we have a system of playwriting workshops and new play development programs in which playwrights work with dramaturges. This process generally leads to script-in-hand public readings. For some large theatres this practice fulfils their obligation to develop new playwrights. The results can be productive, but they can also trap playwrights. Take, for example, Lorena Gale, whose play *Angélique* is one of the most powerful expressions of a new wave of African-Canadian playwrights. It received eight separate workshop readings before its first professional production in 1999.

The plays that circulate through this system – at least, the plays that do manage to find their way to publication and reproduction – do not enter the canon strictly because of narrative power but because they satisfy the needs of the theatre economy that spawned them. This is why philological and formalist criticism fails when it comes to the study of Canadian drama. In the end the concept of the dramatic canon is an operation of power, not of aesthetics or national culture. Canadian drama cannot be understood in terms of theme or reduced to formal categories of genre because the formal aspects of play texts are the markers of the conditions of a generally panic-stricken production. Short rehearsal times and dispersed theatres mean that in Canadian theatre texts circulate more than theatrical processes do, and this more than any other factor explains the tendency towards dramatic realism and theatrical simplicity in anglophone Canadian drama.

The fundamental logic in the Canadian theatrical development system is that of the entrepreneurial marketplace, and it is a logic that represents how discourses of public funding have been rendered acceptable in an era of neo-conservative economics. Theatrical production is organized around a hierarchical scale of value that is pyramidal in shape because, like the wealth economy, it requires an unequal allocation of reward and a wide competitive resource base. There can only be one actor playing King Lear on the Stratford stage. The axis of professionalism and the nature of institutionalization define a space that can be remapped as an economic and creative pyramid. At the top, peak professional and institutional theatres command the largest share of resources and economic integration (to the point at which some, like the Stratford Festival, sustain regional economies). As the pyramid descends into the crowded, vastly diverse, and economically poor fringe, where inexperienced and self-subsidized artists strive for recognition, aesthetics and sociology meet.

Because Canadian arts organizations exist in financial crisis, and desperately attempt to retain declining audiences, their programming becomes increasingly conservative as they become more institutional. Most large theatres in Canada produce season programs that are virtually identical – which in itself reveals two basic principles of operation. The principle of inverse differentiation states that the more institutionalized and capitalized a theatre company is, the more it resembles other companies. Conversely, as we work down the pyramid, we see increasing diversity in theatres, styles, mandates, and aesthetics. The corollary here is that the more culturally specific a theatre is, the less institutionalized it will be. The principle of inverse creativity makes the same point in the domain of aesthetics. The more institutionalized a theatre is, the more money it has and the less creative it can be. Its primary mission is to retain its audience, and consequently theatres such as Stratford attempt to market a product with broad appeal. In effect this means that they market experience, not content; they sell not plays but the experience of going to plays in elite theatres. With the possible exception of Stratford – which functions as the regional public-sector economic pump – all theatres exist in precarious danger of financial collapse. The more they have, the greater the risk, and the more cautious the programming. They compensate for this dilemma with a reliance on the idea of cultural excellence, which again means selling experience.

In contrast, the diverse vastness of the unfunded bottom of the pyramid is the place in which theatrical creativity flourishes. This bottom ground replenishes the pyramid with the assistance of the arts councils and of artists and critics in search of new material and talent. The bottom-line reality is that the theatre industry draws its creativity and innovation from outside its borders.

The Nature of Politically Engaged Theatre

In the end, both the irate gardener and a production of a play like *Palace of the End* are "political theatre." Clearly, however, they are distinct in their assumptions of social effect and performance efficacy. Plays like *Palace of the End* address the community, working to fulfil the Enlightenment vision of the theatre as a moral institution. At the turn of the twentieth century the idea of the theatre as a privileged place of assembly and speech was a powerful response to the loss of the mass audience. The term "political theatre" was coined by Brecht's mentor Erwin Piscator, who aligned his theatre with the German Communist Party (KPD) in the Weimar Republic. Piscator staged technically complex plays that modelled social issues and ideological investigations, introduced new techniques to the theatre (including projected animations), and devised new dramaturgical forms, including what became the template for documentary theatre. As a committed communist and theatrical visionary, Piscator dedicated his work to an activist theatre for a proletarian audience. Before they both left Berlin for exile, Brecht wrote of him:

> For 3000 marks a month
> He is prepared
> To put on the misery of the masses
> For 100 marks a day
> He displays
> The injustice of the world.[11]

Piscator gave up his Political Theatre in 1928, with the embittered conclusion that "like a red thread running through this book, through the history of my undertakings runs the realization that the proletariat, whatever the reason may be, is too weak to support a theatre of its own." For Piscator, a political theatre that modelled and explained history from within required a politicized audience that could absorb this experience critically and apply it. The authority of the theatre derives from its critical analysis. Piscator himself noted, "That we could not stop fascism with our theatre was abundantly clear to us all from the outset. What our theatre was supposed to do was communicate critical responses, which, translated into practical politics, might possibly have stopped fascism."

In an age of mass political movements, this led him to the conclusion that an audience of the masses must be a mass audience, and this in turn drove him to seek increasingly larger stages and venues. His unrealized vision for a "total theatre" as sketched by Gropius bears a startling similarity to a modern high-tech football stadium. The modernist assumption of cultural access – if you build it, they will come – failed. The masses did not come. "We had gone as far as financially possible to enable the proletariat to come to the theatre," he said. "Are we to blame if they failed to make better use of the opportunity?"[12] Well, yes.

Throughout the twentieth century, as mass communications enabled mass political movements, politicized theatre artists sought ways of solving this fundamental paradox. For Brecht, perhaps the most influential theatre artist of the century when measured by the global impact of his plays, directorial methods, and theorizations, the answer was simple: theatre must address itself to the specific audience, not a metonymic nation. Brecht's plays were devised as entertaining puzzles that exercise the critical mind. But they were for the most part large and expensive to produce, and therefore needed the resources of a peak theatre.

In the end, theatre artists have contented themselves with a ripple-effect thinking: a play that stirs the minds and conscience of its audience is better than one that does not; a play that creates a space of truth or speaks a counter-narrative, or brings attention to an important story, is part of the constant jostling of the public sphere. It may touch only a few, but it can touch them profoundly; a great reckoning in a little room may be part of a larger process of social change. The alternative was to take the theatre outside and celebrate community in carnivalesque pageantry. This approach has become a common and popular form of engaged theatre, not least because it is affirmative and festive.

For others, including many of the artists and theatre workers that I speak of in this book, Piscator's failure was not a failure of the audience, but of the theatre itself. Piscator had been a soldier in the First World War, and as a stage director he encouraged the tactical agitprop troupes that waged theatrical warfare in the streets of Berlin. His disappointment was really about his inability to make his theatre politically effective at a time when more than critical reflection was needed.

The difference between the irate gardener and street agitprop on the one hand and Piscator and *Palace of the End* on the other is not just a matter of artistic professionalism and cultural economics. These two manifestations of theatre are fundamentally different in how they conceive of audience and the act of spectatorship – and here this key term of "spectatorship" is meant to embrace more than familiar terms such as "audience" or "viewing" might suggest. The moment of performance creates a relationship between performer and spectator; it summons these categories into being and grants them licence. For the duration of the performance the performer is licensed to violate social distance and transgress propriety, and the spectator is licensed to gaze without reservation, shame, or apology. Each acts on the other. Normally we understand spectatorship in the context of the playhouse theatre, which awaits a self-selected audience. But the gardener targeted his audience and took his performance to it. The distinction is crucial because it addresses the core questions of how politically engaged theatre can produce the change it seeks.

Intervention theatre, then, can be located at any point in the grid of the theatre estate, and can express any ideological value (although there are definable reasons as to why most intervention theatre emerges from the left). As I see it, a study of political intervention theatre as a cultural field, and based on a historical perspective, rests on three fundamental hypotheses.

1. Radical theatre refuses the theatre estate

My analysis of the history of radical theatre in English Canada begins with a recognition that such a history is impossible to define because radical theatre is diverse, rhizomorphic, and for the most part unrecorded and undocumented. Hence "history" here is used not in the recuperative, narrative sense, but in the sense argued by Raphael Samuel as the assembled practices of memory and production.[13] A grounding principle is that most political theatre has always happened outside of the paradigm of the theatre as a national structure, although it engages with the radical edges of the professional theatre estate. Most radical theatre goes unnoticed by the professional theatre establishment, and when it is noticed it is usually devalued. We need to think of political theatre as a decentred network of practices that migrate through various domains. The network extends into the world of professionalized theatre but is not defined or contained by it.

Any history of intervention performance can only gesture to its complexities, in nineteenth-century working-class labour ceremonies, in lumber-camp mock trials, in women's suffrage mock parliaments at the turn of the century, in Mayday parades and street protests, and in the festivals and local performances of migrant communities. My first principle is to make a fundamental distinction between the theatrical performances of radical activism and the politicized, occasionally radical work that takes place within the theatre as an institution and disciplinary regime.

2. Radical performance is a process of networks, not structures

The most powerful and seductive icons of the twentieth-century dream of a politically activist people's theatre are also the most deceptive and atypical. What draws us to the images of political theatre as modernist hero-combat drama for the industrial age? Think of Brecht in his leather-jacket posture as Bolshevik thug, of the machine-gun aesthetics of the workers' theatre agitprops, the regimented mass rallies of the Popular Front, and, recurrently, the guerrilla artist: masked, confrontational, poised in the ecstasy of combat. The field of politically engaged radical theatre in its actual operations defies categorizations and refuses these militarized images. Political theatre is not an archive of forms and genres, but a shifting and situated articulation of radicalism working through the entire ecology of theatre cultures. Most political theatre ventures are local and grounded in the communities they construct and enact. They are participatory and interventionist, and they enact the contingent social and ideological processes that produce them.

Still, there is a temptation to think of theatre as a weapon in the struggle of the people, of the theatre artist as a guerrilla cadre, of the theatre itself as an insurrectionary front. In recent years we have seen this kind of theatre revived in the streets of the anti-globalization protests. The most disturbing thing about the persistence of these images is the lingering appeal of militarism in radical theatre, and the entrenched (to use a military word) hold of the combat figure as the "real" moment of political engagement. This entrenchment mirrors the wider hold of insurrection as the "real" moment of revolutionary politics. My second principle, then, is that radical theatre reflects the continuity of local practices aimed towards the generation rather than the display of power. This leads to the point that political performance can be seen as the ceremonial enactment of the social processes it activates.

3. Networks enter history as "movements" when they are captured by structures of control and regulation

The formalizing "movements" of political theatre in the first half of the twentieth century were notable for their obsession with scale, professionalism, and theory. In the years prior to the submergence of radical discourse in the recuperation of national culture that was the Popular Front – the international alliance of Communist, radical, and socialist elements that was ascendant in the second half of the 1930s – political theatre was understood as a category of power: that is, as a counter-theatre that mirrored the bourgeois theatre in all of its complexes and operations. This was the Leninist model of mobilization. Like the bourgeois stage it countered, it was a movement oriented towards texts, textuality, and authorship and secured by the authority of theory and structures of legitimation. In its clearest moments, this principle suggests that "political theatre" may be most effective as a political strategy when there is very little theatre work to contradict the categorization.

Political theatre has been narrated as a property of the left, in the modernist binary of socialist left and imperialist-capitalist right that defined the twentieth-century political ground. The postmodern refutations of this binary, coming from within struggles against oppression and led by feminist, queer, and postcolonial activists, enable us to recast the binary with the proposition that theatrical practices identified with statist political programs and masculinist heroism straddle the ideological divide.

In this recasting I suggest the continuity of a tradition of radical refusal. This tradition is characterized by local interventions, the production rather than the demonstration of power, a refusal of masculinist and military performance models, and, most critically, a repudiation of the theatre economy.

Spectatorship, Historical Periods, and Practices

If political intervention theatre, as an application of theatre performance for purposeful ends, is contingent on local conditions, cannot be categorized, and leaves few traces, its history is not to be seen in an archive of forms but in a collection of practices. There is, however, a methodological danger in this approach, because once we leave the ambit of the canonical or legitimate theatre culture, "theatre" begins to encounter a wider concept of "performance" as proposed by the relatively new discipline of performance studies. As formulated by Richard Schechner, performance is a universal human practice embracing "restored behaviours" and can include any intentional action intended to be viewed. In this model, a football game is as much a performance as a play in a theatre.[14]

There is much to be said for this analytical approach, but it can lead to methodological chaos: because any act that excites response can be performance, a consideration of political intervention performance must necessarily be a history of all politics, which must expand to be an impossible history of everything. If we accept that theatre is a particular organization of performance to be understood in terms of particular practices and the meaning of practices, we are placing weight on the reciprocal contract of actor and spectator. Spectatorship is a state constituted in the moment of performance, but it is conditioned by subjectivity and by address. Performance "speaks" to and constitutes particular ways of spectating. The field of address can be inclusive and multiple, or specific and exclusive.

Theatrical performance, whether *Hamlet* or our caterpillar man, always exists in the doubled phenomenal world of what Augusto Boal calls "the aesthetic space," in which laws of time, space, and representation can be manipulated, in which simulation overlays real bodies and produces what Raymond Williams called "structures of feelings."[15] It is the real effect of the invented world that marks theatrical performance as particular in the wider field of social performances. In the theatre, a chair is always more than a chair. It is the apprehension of everything the chair might become in the hands of the actor.

If theatre is, then, a committed action projected onto the bodies and into the heads and sensoria of the audience, a history of practices must also be a history centred on spectatorship. But if spectatorship can never be empirically documented, how can we speak of a spectator-centred historiography? How can we periodize ways of seeing? This problem can be approached in two ways, both of them leading to the same structure of periodization.

The first way of approaching the problem has to do with technological changes that have an impact on how we spectate, or alter how we view the performing body. The progression from the playhouse pictorial illusion stage to cinema, radio, military communications, television, and the Internet offers stages in the constant reformation of spectatorship.[16]

It does this by expanding the fields of entertainment experience and thereby relocating the phenomenological sense of "normal" viewing. Each new dimension of media experience denaturalizes the previous dominant form by extending the horizon of the "real." Theatre, for example, can still be "magic" and scenographically astonishing, but it can never again claim the literal pictorial illusion that thrilled audiences through the nineteenth century. Old special effects are always cheesy at the horizon of the new. These technological eras become the "decades" of political intervention theatre because each phase of technological development opens new possibilities for theatrical radicalism and offers new cultural vocabularies and theatrical methods. Each stage brings reformations of theatre practice and new understandings of audience.

The second way of approaching this question of periodization is, appropriately to theatre, personal and local. It considers the social experience of these changes. If widespread changes have occurred in ways of spectating, the traces of those changes must be resident in cultural memory. In my own case I can trace these changes over four generations: from my grandfather to my son. In each of these generations I discern very different understandings of theatre, and different ways of spectating.

I see these differences first in the changing nature of theatre culture in the century spanned by these four generations. My grandfather was born in 1896, and in the first week of December of that year (a week chosen arbitrarily), at the bottom of its second page, under the heading of "Amusements," the Toronto *Globe* listed three performances taking place in town. This particular listing does not mean that the performances noted were all there was to be seen in Toronto; the items were paid advertisements, and did not include amateur theatricals and musical entertainments. But the listing does provide a rough sense of what was available, and what consumers were paying for. The Toronto Opera House offered a show called *McSorley's Twins*, which judging from the title's reference to a popular Irish song of the day was a dialect comedy. The Grand Theatre featured the celebrated British-American Shakespearean actor Robert Mantell in his historical romance *The Face in the Moonlight*, touring from New York. The Bijou offered *The Booming Town*, which we can assume was either a melodrama or a comedy, given that the Bijou was a variety house that presented "continuous vaudeville."

In 1924, the year my father was born, film had widened the field of selection considerably, and yet the first week of December had even more live vaudeville on offer. Sometimes the forms went together. At Pantages, the movie *Dante's Inferno* was framed by "regular vaudeville fare." Shea's Victoria Theatre and Loew's on Yonge Street also featured "drop in" vaudeville along with movies, and the Royal Alexandra hosted Beatrice Lillie and Gertrude Lawrence in a Broadway revue. The great ballerina Karsavina, "Queen of Russian dancers," was headlined at Massey Hall, and at the Princess, Tyrone Power (father of the movie star of later decades) was playing in "the new modern drama" *Take and Pay*. In the space of a generation, a major shift had taken place. Theatre had been uplifted from slightly disreputable amusement to both leisure and fine art, although this shift was more evident in the amateur sphere, in the Little Theatres, the Arts and Letters Clubs, the Women's Alumnae Dramatic Society, and especially the Hart House Theatre, which had already produced its first season of all-Canadian drama. Vincent Massey was tirelessly advocating the cause of the Canadian drama, but it was still an amateur aspiration. The movies had taken over most of the playhouses, but this merely encouraged a notion of theatre as intimate and elite.

In 1952, the year of my birth, and one that marked the inauguration of television broadcasting in Canada, that same December week offered a vast increase in film selections and a smaller choice of legitimate theatre: a touring production of *Call Me Madam* at the Royal Alex, and Tyrone Power (the younger) and Raymond Massey (Vincent's brother) in Charles Laughton's staged reading of Steven Vincent Benét's epic poem *John Brown's Body*. Again, this coverage excludes the busy amateur theatre scene, which was both recycling the bourgeois affectations of the Dominion Drama Festival and breaking out towards "semi-professional" status. In the 1950s, theatre was competing for audiences with film and TV, but a cadre of determined artists was establishing the ground for a professional theatre culture. In the year after I was born, the Stratford Shakespeare Festival raised its tent; four years later the Canada Council offered its first funding grants to newly professional theatres. "Culture" was now perceived as a national property, and indeed a form of national defence, and the theatre had acquired a new social identity as a marker of middle-class taste and prosperity. My grandfather went to the theatre rarely if at all, but my parents saw it as an excursion, an entree into the middle-class way of life made possible by the social mobility of the war. I grew up to the songs of *My Fair Lady*.

By 1995, the year of my son's birth, the theatre industry in Toronto had proliferated beyond the wildest expectations of previous generations; the *Globe and Mail*'s Saturday entertainment section ran to fifteen pages, and dozens of theatres catered to a widely diverse range of tastes and experiences. Most of that work was created and produced locally. Toronto's theatre culture was national and metropolitan, and the economy of that culture was self-sustaining. Theatres differentiated and marked divergent communities. They had become a critical means of announcing the public assertion of marginalized identities.

In each of these four generations, cultural, technological, and demographic change wrought immense changes in how audiences watched theatre performances, and the physical spaces and social contexts in which they watched them. Theatre is a bodily, sensual experience, and the ways in which people gather, sit together, laugh, and respond changed as well. The physical experience of theatre-going today is vastly different than it was a century ago. Theatre decorum too has changed – a century ago no audience member would sit in silent agony rather than disrupt the show to crawl along the row to gain the aisle and proceed to a washroom. In the variety theatres loud raucous behaviour was the norm, and a dense cloud of tobacco smoke was omnipresent, if not in the auditorium itself then certainly in the foyers, loges, and smoking galleries. Modern sensibilities would recoil at the spittoons.

If for my parents theatre was a pleasure afforded by class advancement, for me as a young man it was place of rebellion and refusal. The theatres that I gravitated to were collective, loudly political, leftist, and naively proletarian. More importantly, I understood theatre as a sector of life, as a possibility of living a different kind of life. Although we talked endlessly about seeking audiences and working with the people, our real object was to live a creative working life. (Of course we didn't understand that then; our politics were naive but deeply felt.) But for my son, who has grown up seeing theatre, real entertainment is in the vast world of online digital play. Theatre is something that he enjoys and appreciates, but I doubt that he will ever see it as deeply important – at least, not as a form of art consumption. Still, he will undoubtedly live in a world in which theatre not only proliferates but also fully emerges as the most common, accessible, and perhaps useful medium of political intervention.

2

Class, Spectatorship, and the Unruly

The Nineteenth Century

J.W. Bengough's self-caricature of his chalk-talk performance.

WHAT HAS A WORKING MAN TO DO WITH ART?
– Labor Advocate, *March 20, 1891*

Huge playhouses, crowd-pleasing melodramas, engin-
eered special effects, and spectacular illusions: this was the theatre of
the nineteenth century. It was the era in which the theatre became an
industry and a profession that played to a mass audience. Much of the
culture of the theatre profession today – its languages, folklore, traditions
and memories, and even its sense of professionalism – has been handed
down from the nineteenth-century theatre.[1]

What came together as "the theatre" of the time would prove to be
a vast, diverse, and plural culture in its forms and practices. In Canada
the nineteenth century started with small playhouses built into inns and
assembly halls, with amateur theatricals played against rough scenery.
By the end of the century electricity and rail transport had transformed
both the technical capacity of the playhouse and the economics of the
business. The century began with oratory and ended with film, feminism, and a new modernist concept of theatre as a fine art. Indeed, rather
than "killing" theatre in the early twentieth century, film would occupy
theatre spaces. The audiences and playhouses remained, but theatre
migrated, spatially, socially, and discursively.

In the wide diversity of forms and practices in the nineteenth century one significant absence stands out: there was little in the way of what
the next century would call political theatre. We do see the development
of a polemical "problem play" that touches on the politics of living in the
modern world (as in Ibsen's *A Doll's House*) and argumentative drama
that provokes public discussion of social issues (as in George Bernard
Shaw's work). Britain and the United States saw tentative attempts to
use theatre to represent the actual conditions of the working classes, but
Canada had significantly less of this sort of thing.

That does not mean that no interventionist theatre existed in the nineteenth century; it means only that this other theatre cannot be found in the canons and performance calendars of the "legitimate" theatre.

Theatrical Ambivalence

On the busy stages of the nineteenth century, audiences saw a great variety of performance forms. In a single week in any North American city (in, say, the 1880s), a spectator could take in a visiting Shakespearean actor, a medicine show, a mile-long circus parade, a minstrel show, a music hall variety show, a pantomime, a ballet, a comic hypnotist, a scientific phrenologist, a satiric dialect lecturer, a military re-enactment spectacle, a temperance melodrama, and a chalk-talk lecture. (Today many of these forms still exist, having migrated to television studios.) Balloon ascensions, firework extravaganzas, *Uncle Tom's Cabin* troupes ("Tom" shows, big and small) – all appealed to the appetite for spectacle and sensation. Where crowds had money to spend, entertainers were there to collect it. Even certain respectable "moral" entertainments, such as mock parliaments, temperance dialogues, and chautauquas, revelled in the public delight in theatricality and show.[2] Legitimate theatre, especially when it featured touring actors from Britain, gave the middle and upper classes occasion for social display. Theatre, like alcohol, was pervasive in society, both deeply loved and widely condemned. It was a place of pleasure and an opportunity for sin. For much of the century it appealed to mainly male audiences. It was invariably eroticized, whether only by nuance and implication or by salacious teasing.

In the middle of the nineteenth century, when theatre troupes could use the railways to spread out across the continent, theatrical performances were the stuff of popular culture, characterized by vulgar populism, urban rowdyism, and mainly working-class male audiences. But over the second half of the century, particularly in the large Eastern cities, a dramatic change occurred: the theatre business became institutionalized and gentrified. Corporate centralization by New York booking syndicates bought up and tamed the playhouses. The industry trafficked in the celebrity of star actors and the prestige of European modernism, and took aim at middle-class women. As Richard Butsch points out in his history of American audiences, "By the 1890s, legitimate theater was a woman's entertainment."[3] On the frontiers, though, theatre continued to share social (and often physical) space with gambling dens, saloons, and brothels.

The emerging middle-class culture had a deep love of theatrical acts, but disapproved of the unruly theatre industry and the vulgar populism of melodrama. Mark Blagrave, in his work on temperance soiree performances in nineteenth-century Nova Scotia, cites the opening address of the musical *Cadets of Temperance,* in which audiences were told: "Our entertainment is not intended to affect you like a show, which excites momentary pleasure and is then forgotten."[4] The nineteenth-century spectator faced a dilemma: if theatre could be moral and instructive, it could also be – and usually was – immoral and harmful, not least because it brought young men into the ambit of alcohol, prostitution, and gambling. Theatre culture as a whole was ambivalent. Theatricality was pervasive, but even as late as 1891 the Ministerial Association of Toronto declared theatre evil and theatregoing a sin. *The Labor Advocate* took offence:

> Verily we should be grateful to our censors for settling this momentous question for us, but matters of such moment demand serious consideration. It is a pity that their time is so occupied with such serious things, as it would be nice to be told what to do to prevent girls being driven to lives of shame by two and three dollars a week salaries; to get a little information on the question "Have one part of humanity a right to own the planet and charge the rest of us for the use of it"; to be shown some remedy other than charity, for a state of things under which able-bodied men search in vain for work to enable them to provide for the wants of their loved ones.[5]

Still, although theatre was a sin for some, the pleasure of dramatics was understood to be an important part of effective proselytizing. In 1850 a report in the Guelph *Herald* described in detail the visit of one John Gough, a temperance lecturer, while taking care to note, "It were vain to attempt to give an idea of Mr. Gough's peculiar style and manner of address." The townspeople had previously "listened with long-remembered delight" to visiting actors who "embodied in appropriate tone, and look, and gesture, the immortal conceptions and sublime language of Shakespeare." Audiences had "laughed till our sides ached under the wonderful powers of mimicry" that the entertainers had brought to the city's stage. "But Gough, while unlike any of these, possesses some of the highest qualities of each, while moreover he is the author of his sentiments he utters and not merely the representative of the conceptions of another mind."[6]

The language of performance adapted itself to fit moral boundaries. On the respectable side of the boundary, theatre was not "theatre" but rather entertainments, soirees, concerts, recitals, even "theatricals." (Home theatricals, mixing tableaux and charades, were common in middle-class families.) Schools, temperance societies, and churches produced instructive dramas, usually offered as "dialogues" to distance them from the disrepute of the popular stage. Drama was respectable, the more so the farther it was removed from the stage. But "the theatre" itself remained a place of deception and temptation. Language marked social place, which is why so many nineteenth-century playhouses, whether standing alone or built into the upstairs of a hotel or a town hall, were called "opera" houses. The theatre industry was quick to capitalize on these distinctions. A poster for a touring *Uncle Tom's Cabin* show (one of the hundreds that crisscrossed the continent for fifty years) pronounced:

> Little Miss Ethel, Smallest Child Actress as EVA will appear in each performance with the Newest Song Specialties.
> Our Uncle Tom is nine feet high, the tallest on earth.
> Every Christian mother should see that her children do not miss the opportunity to see this grand production of the greatest of moral dramas.[7]

In 1883 *The Labor Union* offered a sarcastic review of P.T. Barnum's book *The Art of Money Getting*, inadvertently providing, for later generations, a taste of the problematic social positioning of theatre as an adaptive business practice:

> Get up some kind of show likely to tickle children: – get a few Canadians, bleach their hair, call them Albinos from the African kingdom at Muskatingo; get a very fat woman – tattoo or paint her arms, call her a cannibal ... who has been raised on roasted children; get an elephant that England has got tired of, publish

10,000 lies about him; get a happy family and drug it well; get some spotted horses which will canter around in a ring, and a few low and painted women who can ride on them naked.

Call this a *Great Moral Show*, send free tickets to the clergy, plaster every wall with gaudy pictures, blow a steam calliope about the town, have the schools all adjourn: – do this and keep doing it, and you can get every half dollar in a town, so that the inhabitants can't pay the grocer's bills for months to come.[8]

In the robust and religion-bound Canada of the nineteenth century, theatre stood as a potential threat not just to morality but to the very social order that it generated. At mid-century the theatre was suspect because of its rough working-class masculinism; by the end of the century it was less unruly but even more suspect because of its entrepreneurial opportunism, its American republicanism, and its racial influences. Later, in 1922, Vincent Massey would express his wariness of the New York syndicates run by "New York gentlemen with Old Testament names."[9] The introduction of modernist theatre, brought in by New York syndicates and endorsed by educated critics like Hector Charlesworth (who was one of the first Canadian advocates of Ibsen) spread the new idea that theatre was a fine art but increasingly linked the medium to the idea of the nation. For the generation of early twentieth-century theatre intellectuals like Charlesworth, Bernard Sandwell, and Vincent Massey, theatre was both a fine art and a condition of nationhood, in which theatre work and the dramatic canon would consolidate in the disciplinary regime of "the profession." The idea of an artistic political theatre would emerge out of this statist concept as theatre artists took up their positions in the ideological wars of the twentieth century.

What we do not appear to see in this milieu is theatrical performance as an expression of dissent or an occasion of intervention. In the extremely busy theatre culture in Canada, particularly after the building of the railways, the emerging business was clearly a property of the entrepreneurial middle class, even as it drew largely on the working classes for its labour and audiences. It could, and often did, editorialize on the politics of the day; then as now, audiences had a great appetite for political satire, such as William Henry Fuller's 1880 *H.M.S. Parliament*, which riffed the ever-popular Gilbert and Sullivan opus to satirize the policy of the federal government of the day.[10]

The Theatricals of Political Reform: Performances of Integration and Order

In the growth of nineteenth-century democratic reform movements, advocacy theatricals outside of the legitimate theatre were a popular and effective means of generating attention and occupying social space. A number of reformist social movements negotiated rights and voice in the dominant political bloc: political reform (especially in the first half of the century), temperance, labour, and women's suffrage. The theatricalities deployed by these movements fall into a spectrum of practices covering journalistic and literary polemical drama, pedagogical paratheatre (especially temperance dialogues, fraternal ceremony, and parades), and, at the end of the century, mock parliaments.

Journalistic drama

Not surprisingly, the first people in Canada to turn to dramatic form as a political forum were the editors and typographers who had access to the printing press. For the most part the dramas they created were editorial position statements that used the theatrical form to model a new understanding of a public sphere. Throughout the nineteenth century the pages of newspapers featured journalistic dramas, although as the business consolidated and changed towards the end of the century – driven by increased urban circulation and telegraph news services – these dramatic sketches tended to appear in smaller or more localized newspapers.

A typical example, "Measure by Measure, or the Coalition in Secret Session," published in *The New Dominion and True Humorist* in 1871, was an intervention in a public debate over a non-sectarian bill that led to a non-confidence vote and a coalition government. According to the New Brunswick theatre historian Mary Elizabeth Smith, "The ninth and final scene of 'Measure by Measure' would be printed in *The New Dominion* four days before George King actually introduced the school bill on 12 April for what was to be a remarkably calm passage considering the public debate that preceded it."[11] In her research Smith found a number of such plays in New Brunswick, starting with the Loyalists in the late eighteenth century.

The most volatile arena for political dramas in the newspapers was Quebec, where dramatic sketches were the sharp end of heated debates, especially in the 1830s. In Quebec in that decade the first theatre troupe with a labour affinity, Les Amateurs typographes, led by the Swiss-born editor and Patriote Aimé-Nicolas "Napoleón" Aubin, performed polemical and nationalist plays, including Voltaire's *Death of Julius Caesar*. But the real drama of partisan engagement was played out in the pages of newspapers and pamphlets. Len Doucette's translated anthology of plays from nineteenth-century Quebec includes the five "Status Quo comedies," which he refers to as "political paratheatre." Even though they were not written for performance, Doucette sees those pieces as the first expressions of a political dramaturgical tradition of satiric burlesque and monologues that continued well into the twentieth century with Gratien Gélinas's popular *Les fridolinades* in the 1930s and 1940s.[12] In part because of the intellectual tradition of literary nationalism in Quebec, and in part because theatre gives subordinated languages a public voice, drama has always had a more iconic power in Quebec than in anglophone Canada.

Doucette suggests that in the absence of a popular theatre culture early Quebec had no dramatic models for journalistic dialogues, but nevertheless the work began to appear as soon as printing presses became available. He offers the fascinating suggestion that the first plain dialogues may have been written to be read aloud at public assemblies. The Status Quo comedies were written by former seminarians who, as Doucette reminds us, would have been exposed to "paradramatic teaching methods" and would have seen drama as "a vehicle for adversarial argument and debate." Doucette notes that when the first of these comedies appeared in the pages of *Gazette de Québec* on April 26, 1834, it "represented a real escalation in current political tension" – which would erupt in revolution three years later.[13] The comedies contributed to the radicalization of the intelligentsia in the Patriote cause. The first two were written in support of the Patriote "resolutionaries," the third, published in *Le Canadien*, was a counterbarrage from the other side, and the final two – the last of which was published as a pamphlet – continued from the first two. They were written in the manner of light prose comedies, satirizing politicians and journalists with barely disguised names. They seemed politer and lighter than they actually were.

These editorial plays raise at least a couple of questions. What advantage did dramatic form offer in these contexts? And how can they be understood as theatre? In one sense the dramatic form was a method of deflecting, by framing criticism in dialogic debate. It was a fast way of reducing complex political arguments to partisan stereotypes, and even on the page it theatricalized the situation by privileging the readers as a spectator. Typographically, dramatic form stood out against the busy column of the newspaper. These playlets were not devised for performance, but they were performative.

The newspaper editorial sketch was a remarkably resilient form, and perhaps only faded away as journalism began to present itself as a profession founded upon objectivity and reportage, rather than polemics. A good example of these playlets appeared in the November 10, 1883, issue of *The Palladium of Labor*, published in Hamilton:

THE LEGAL TRADE-UNION

How Circumstances Alter Cases
A Legal Gent Who Does Not Believe in Grading Wages Except for Mechanics
SCENE --- a Lawyer's office, the occupant writing at his desk.
--- Enter client.
Client. --- Good morning, Mr. Briefless.
Lawyer. --- Ah, good morning sir. --- Anything new?
Client. --- Oh, nothing. Those rascally strikers interfering terribly with businesses. The insolence of the lower classes is getting unbearable. What do you think the rascally fellows have the audacity to propose?
Lawyer. --- Can't say --- Perhaps they think they ought to have a share in the profits. Hang 'em --- Half of them are better off than I am.
Client. --- It will come to that, by and bye no doubt, but in the meantime they insist that good and bad workmen shall receive the same rate of wages. --- I am actually not allowed to pay any man less for his work than the price fixed by the union.
Lawyer. --- There is no objection to your paying him more, I suppose.
Client. --- Of course not. --- But isn't it a rascally shame that I shouldn't be at liberty to engage a man at any price for which he is willing to work? It's an interference with the

liberty of the subject. These unions, sir, are the curse of the country. They should be put down by law.

Lawyer. --- Yes, if it were only possible. But unfortunately the scoundrels have votes, and they really believe that they have so little principle but if such a thing were attempted they would vote against their own party to punish the government that did it. But I should like to see it tried for all that. The growing spirit of insubordination must be checked at any cost. Every man ought to be at liberty to work for what he can get, and no man should be compelled to pay more to one than another would do the work for.

Client. --- Your enlightened sentiments sir, do you credit --- You are just the kind of man I had been looking for. I wish to trust you with a case for the next court. It's a simple case involving a matter of a few hundred dollars. Most of you lawyers are terrible fellows for running up big bills of cost. Now I don't want to be stuck too heavily if the case goes against us, so I'll tell you what I'll do --- I'll foot all actual outlay and give you $10 for your own trouble in managing the case. Is it a bargain?

Lawyer. --- Sir, your proposition is such that I cannot for a moment entertain it. I must charge you the full amount fixed by the legal tariff for my services, were I to do otherwise I should be guilty of grossly unprofessional conduct.

Client. --- Oh I know that you have a fixed rate and all that --- I know it too well. --- Of course if I had to hire a first-class lawyer like Blake or Dalton McCarthy, I expect he would stick by the regular tariff. But you see you are only a new beginner in the business and you ought to work cheap at first. Your time isn't as valuable as that of a leading professional man. Why, I don't believe you've had a case for the last six months.

Lawyer. --- Sir, allow me to tell you that I consider your comparisons insulting. As a professional gentleman I cannot demean myself by "working cheap," I must refuse your case upon any other than the usual terms.

Client. --- All right --- You're a great fool to stand in your own light. Ten dollars is better than nothing, and if you won't take it to put the case through there are other lawyers [who]

will. I'll go over to young Hardup, he'll be only too glad to
take hold of it.

Lawyer. --- (indignantly.) --- I never heard of anything so deroga-
tory to the dignity of the profession in my life. I don't believe
Hardup will touch it on your terms.

Client. --- Never fear. He is a young fellow of some sense. He'll
get on, that man will. He's had several cases for old Griper,
the [rate]-shaver because he was willing to take about half
the regular fees. He's only a one horse lawyer, but in a case
where it's all plain sailing he'll do well enough.

Lawyer. --- Oh that's how he's been managing to make a living
is it. Well, we'll soon put a stop to that. I can tell Mr. Hardup
that his professional career will be cut very short. --- I'm
very glad sir to have had this conversation with you for I
shall at once take proceedings to have Hardup's unprofessional conduct brought to the notice of the Law Society in
order that he may be struck off the roll and deprived of
his gown.

Client. --- Why, Mr. Briefless, I'm amazed. Haven't you just now
said that a man had a right to sell his labor for whatever
he could get for it? Would you interfere with the liberty of
the subject by preventing me and Hardup fixing our own
rates? For all I can see your Law Society is no better than
a Trade Union!

Lawyer. --- Ah --- um --- the analogy does not hold good. --- Don't
you see that there is a difference between a professional
gentleman and a mere mechanic?

Client. --- I see just this, that you professional chaps are always
ready to swear that black is white with your own interests
come in. Why there's no consistency about you. You'd abol-
ish Trade Unions would you? Well if that day ever comes
about, I hope they'll begin with the Law Society. --- Good
day (Exit).[14]

In this sketch the anonymous author – probably the publication's editor –
takes a column and a half (almost one thousand words) to make a point
that could easily have been stated in a two-sentence editorial. Even by
the prolix verbosity of nineteenth-century journalism this item would

be a waste of copy space if the point was that simple. But by staging the point in dialogue, the author develops the point as an exercise in critical thinking. The reader, of course, is in on the joke from the beginning and recognizes the client's language as ironic parody. In its satiric personification of the class enemy, its use of ridicule and debate, this skit is not all that different from the agitprops of the 1930s or the guerrilla street theatre of the 1960s.

It is obviously different from those later forms in that it was not published to be performed, but this condition does not disallow it as theatre. It has a dramatic coherence and integrity that offers a situational modelling of a problem, and it works its argument through a simple plot with an ironic reversal. It is worth bearing in mind that in the nineteenth century literary drama was something to be read – indeed, for many, better read than watched. Instead, this piece introduces a recurring principle of agitational theatre – that it is expressive of and shaped by the conventions of mass communication. Agitprop in the 1930s could not have developed without radio, nor could guerrilla theatre have worked without television. In this case, the skit is a theatricalization of the dominant medium of mass communication of its day. It was not written to be performed because the theatrical conditions that could have been used to do so did not yet exist. But the reading becomes a self-performance, and perhaps we can think of them as scripts for conversations, designed to be told and retold, circulating through shared laughter.

Polemical drama and burlesque

The theatrical drama of the ninetheenth century was an active forum of political comment and critique and, like the editorial dramas, tended to express the positions of the entrepreneurial and professional urban classes. Many of them were written for publishers rather than for theatre companies, using template dramatic forms to circulate partisan critiques and advocacy. The historical term for these efforts, "closet drama," is perhaps too firm in its rejection of theatrical possibility. Most stage plays of the time, especially before the introduction of copyright and performance royalties, were published after they had been introduced on the stage; a play that reached its public by way of publication may not have been originally "intended" to be read rather than staged, as the idea of a "closet drama" proposes. Rather it was intended to circulate through a different public than a theatrical performance might attract.

For several decades the consensus among Canadian theatre historians was that the proliferation of unstaged patriotic melodramas and verse tragedies in the second half of the century reflected the absence of a theatre culture committed to "Canadian" drama; the creators were "playwrights in a vacuum," as Michael Tait describes them in his influential 1964 essay. "For want of even a minority demand for the performance of a native play," he wrote, "these would-be dramatists were compelled willy-nilly to write for the closet rather than the stage."[15] We know now that this was not so: many stock companies produced local plays until the great U.S. theatrical syndicates absorbed most Canadian playhouses into their contractual distribution circuits in the 1890s. Theatre managers and audiences had an insatiable appetite for new plays, and then, as now, the dominant taste was for melodrama ("action") and comedy.

Polemical playwrights tended to more gravid forms, the five-act Shakespearean tragedy in verse being particularly favoured by conservative nationalists such as Charles Mair, whose *Tecumseh* proposed Isaac Brock as the founding father of a British-Canadian nation imbued with aboriginal authenticity, and Sarah Anne Curzon, whose *Laura Secord: The Heroine of 1812* similarly locates Ontario's experience of U.S. invasion as the founding moment of the Canadian nation.[16] Both plays incorporate elements of "low" theatricality: Mair depicts the invading Americans as Shakespearean buffoons, and Curzon mixes in memes of *Uncle Tom's Cabin* and minstrel shows. But like many similar playwrights they wrote for a like-minded elite and sought literary salon celebrity rather than vulgar theatrical applause.

A more telling example of polemical drama comes from the mid-century, in what may be one of the most unusual plays in the canon of Canadian drama. *The Female Consistory of Brockville* is a prose comedy in five short acts, written in the template of the eighteenth-century comedy of manners (Sheridan's *The School for Scandal* [1777] was the enduring favourite for a century). The title of the play refers to a mock consistory, or ecclesiastical court.

Published privately in Brockville in 1856 by "Caroli Candidus, Esq., a Citizen of Canada," the play is a savage comment on recent events in the Brockville Presbyterian church, when actions taken by congregants forced the ecclesiastical trial of a local minister, John Whyte. (Whyte had been sent to Canada by the Church of Scotland and had been the minister of the new St. John's Presbyterian Church for five years.) The play details the conniving plots of a cabal of well-established women to bribe servants to give false testimony that the minister had beaten his wife. The anonymous author's bitter dedication to the play states:

> To the Ladies of Brockville
>
> My Dear Ladies –
>
> To you who are so distinguished in the Province as patrons of the Drama, or Preaching, and Horticulture, – I dedicate this little work.
>
> Your judgment of it will at once seal its condemnation or open to it the door of popular favor. In either case, I shall have the satisfaction of knowing that I am judged by discerning and impartial judges. None know better than you whether it is true to nature. None know better whether it be true to fact. None know better whether the portraits are drawn from life. None know better whether they are daubs or photographs.
>
> Therefore with implicit confidence in your usual, good taste, fine feelings, and liberal sympathies, I commit it to your patronizing care.
>
> And that you may never lose your partonizing [sic] celebrity of waxflowers, preachers, and playactors, is the fervent hope of
>
> Your very humble Servant
>
> Caroli Candidus
>
> Glentattle February, 1856.[17]

The wit of the play is in large part derived from the parody of the actual people involved in the case that led to John Whyte's dismissal from the ministry. They are coded in the script with comic names – Sir George and Lady Mulish, Madam Noheart, Miss Prim Proboscis, Lady Dowager Mooress, and Sally Rubknocker – and the author, whether it was Whyte or a loyal friend, clearly expected readers to associate these figures with their real-life counterparts. Interestingly, the character of the maligned preacher (maligned in the play, at least) does not appear on stage until he is brought in at the end as a corpse who rises from the dead to scatter his enemies. Vitriolic, angry, and funny, *The Female Consistory of Brockville* is a rare example of a play written to channel social rage, although again, as in the case of so many of the editorial playlets, it is the anger of class privilege. Indeed, the action of the play turns on the willing complicity of the female servants, who are easily bribed to perjure themselves. In its gender and class politics, *The Female Consistory of Brockville* articulates angry conservative reaction. At the same time its theatricality is the first example of a form that would come to be identified with reformist suffrage a generation later. In effect scenes of the conspiring women serve to parody male procedures of law and governance:

> *The Consistory discovered in Session – Lady Mulish in the Chair*
>
> LADY D. MOORESS: Ladies! I hold in my hand the draft of a petition to venerable Delectables, which, with your permission, I shall read.
> LADY MULISH: Proceed.
> LADY D. MOORESS: The Prayer of the Petition is to bring our rebellious subject before the Court of Capables, to answer for his revolt against our time-honoured jurisdiction.[18]

The author's starting point is the ridiculous distortion of proper order; the dramatic plot is the embellishment necessary to bring the idea into dramatic realization. A generation later, activist women would construct a similar theatrical image in the mock parliaments that gave the suffrage movement its performative identity in Canada.

Like the polemical dramas, the satiric burlesques that were so popular in the late nineteenth century represented the tradition of political satire performance that would move into revues in cabarets and touring shows in the mid-twentieth century (*Spring Thaw*, for example) and migrate to television later in the century (with shows such as *Wayne and Shuster*, *The Royal Canadian Air Farce*, and *This Hour Has 22 Minutes*).

In the late nineteenth century these burlesques typically offered mild political comment in musical parodies of popular works. The works of Gilbert and Sullivan provided a popular model, and in Canada the most famous of these burlesques was Fuller's *H.M.S. Parliament*, a satire of Prime Minister John A. Macdonald's protectionist National Policy. Fuller was a retired banker who turned his hand to comedy. He wrote several theatrical comedies satirizing the Conservative Macdonald government, and in his 1873 *The Unspecific Scandal* he had the prime minister singing in words that resonate today:

Prorogation, Prorogration
That's the dodge for the situation;
It will cause the Grits vexation
And save ourselves great botheration.
When in the House I take my station
I know I shall meet great objuration;
Blake will make a fierce oration
And hold me up to detestation.
I rather dread an appeal to the nation
In its present state of fermentation
So I think upon consideration
I'd better go in for prorogation.
Prorogation, Prorogation, &c.[19]

H.M.S. Parliament, or, The Lady that Loved a Government Clerk was, as its title suggests, a faithful parody of Gilbert and Sullivan, and may only have received a professional production because Eugene McDowell, the U.S. manager of a stock company operating out of Montreal, saw an opportunity to cash in on the current popularity of *H.M.S. Pinafore*, which had opened in London two seasons earlier. He billed the resulting show as the "Canadian Sensation of 1880," with "magnificent scenery" including a "correct view of the Parliament buildings by moonlight, and the interior of the Parliament library at Ottawa" and "new costumes and mechanical effects."[20] *H.M.S. Parliament* was merely the most lavish of the many similar light operas, operettas, and burlesque musical comedies that mixed light political satire with patriotic themes (and underneath the hyperbole it was probably not very lavish at that). It has come to be remembered not for its political or dramatic merits, but through its identification as the most successful professional production of a Canadian play in the nineteenth century. According to Robert Lawrence, it had "the longest theatre tour ever undertaken in Canada" to that time, travelling from Saint John to Winnipeg in the winter and spring of 1880.[21]

Temperance performance

In 1869 an Ottawa publisher pulled together a collection of temperance dialogues, among them a pointed conversation between a distiller and an unwelcome visitor.

DISTILLER: Good morning, Mr. Conscience; though I know you to be one of the earliest risers, especially of late, I hardly expected to meet you here at day-dawn.

CONSCIENCE: I am none too early, it seems, to find you at your vocation. But how are you going to dispose of this great black building?

DISTILLER: Why, I do not understand you.

CONSCIENCE: What are you doing with these boiling craters, and that hideous worm there?

DISTILLER: Pray explain yourself.

CONSCIENCE: Whose grain is that? and what is bread called in the Bible?

DISTILLER: More enigmatical still.

CONSCIENCE To what market do you mean to send that long row of casks? And how many of them will it take upon an average to dig a drunkard's grave?[22]

For close to a century the temperance movement was the most active domain of theatrical performance outside of the playhouse economy. The temperance movement was a vast social phenomenon, a popular front that touched all aspects of life in North America, reconciling opposing factions in pursuit of a common goal. It sought fundamental reforms in the structure of domestic life and in policies of social welfare. At issue was not just the consumption and trade in alcohol but the debilitating effects of tavern culture on women and families in the absence of social security.

Over the course of the nineteenth century the temperance movement became largely secularized. In addition to the primary push from churches and religious organizations, it attracted social welfare reformists whose principle motivations were not especially religious. In one case, for instance, the Dominion Women's Enfranchisement Association partnered with the Women's Christian Temperance Union (WCTU) in the production of suffrage mock parliaments. For temperance crusaders, women's suffrage was a link that would help to carry the day if and when prohibition came to the vote, as it did unsuccessfully in 1898.

Embracing a spread of social practices, class locations, and ideologies, the theatricalities of temperance were as diverse as the movement itself. They ranged from fully developed melodramas on the legitimate stage to a wide variety of private parlour and domestic performances. They spanned the fullest extent of social spaces: the playhouse stage, with its tiered simulation of the public sphere, the church nave and Sunday school hall, school rooms, streets, and private houses. The resulting explosion of theatrical practices defies categorization, but the one thing that stands out as a common principle is the reliance, once again, on theatrical pleasure. Temperance performance, even when it emerged from stoutly anti-theatrical sources, always also entailed the satisfaction of spectatorial desire – the craving for the uninhibited licence of spectatorship.

Given this ambivalence, the language of performance was adapted to fit moral boundaries. On the side of respectability and morality, theatre was not "theatre" but rather entertainments, soirees, concerts, and recitals. Schools, temperance societies, and churches produced instructive dramas, usually offered as "dialogues" to distance them from the disrepute of the popular stage. As Blagrave argues, "The temperance soireés, although they might abjure the intent, at least made use of the conditions of 'a show,' and thereby planted in audiences and performers alike an appetite for more."[23]

The numerous anthologies of temperance recitations and parlour tableaux that can still be found in small-town second-hand stores attest to the scale of organization. An example is the conversation between the distiller and his conscience, which appeared under the title *A Collection of Temperance Dialogues for Divisions of Sons, Good Templar Lodges, Sections of Cadets, Bands of Hope, and Other Temperance Societies.* Like the editorial playlets in the popular press, many of these dialogues were intended for reading, whether singly or aloud in a group.

If it is possible to offer a general characterization of temperance performance it is that its conventions and genres primarily involved rhetorical devices – whether the events took place on the legitimate stage or in organized amateur societies such as the "Dramatic Company" of an Ontario lodge of the Sons of Temperance, which produced the celebrated melodrama *The Little Brown Jug* in 1879. Performances tended towards the non-dramatic and fell into two broad categories: the pageant and the platform.[24]

The term "pageant" – used broadly here – has a convoluted and still evocative history. The nineteenth century saw pageants elevated into a highly contrived art form that persists today in commercialized remnants, in beauty pageants and Santa Claus parades – in which the outward form of pageantry remains, though emptied of allegorical meaning. The historical pageant as we now know it in numerous outdoor summer community performances marking civic, patriotic, or religious events was perfected by a small group of British producers clustered around the person of Louis Napoleon Parker, who advocated that communities mobilize to stage their histories in episodic dramatic sequences.[25] Parker's vocabulary was a deliberate citation of the medieval craft biblical pageants from which Elizabethan drama arose, and he was influenced by the rustic conservatism of the arts and crafts movement. From Parker and in particular his protégé Frank Lascelles came the grand imperial pageants of the early twentieth century, of which the Quebec tercentenary may be the most well known.[26]

Before Parker and company codified pageantry in a form that continues to this day, the term generally signified any performance that produced meaning through a sequence of visual images. Pageants were framed in a spectacle logic of iconic rather than causal movement – that is, their effect did not tend to proceed from the internal logic of a plot, or the working out of an argument through a simulated problem (as in the dramatic "fable"), but from the spectacular effect of visual imagery and emotive rhetoric. Those characteristics differentiate drama from pageantry. Both forms share a repertoire of theatrical and dramatic devices – plays can have pageant elements, and vice versa – but the fundamental distinction is that pageants advance meaning by presenting sequences of images and icons that create powerful emotional triggers to parlay their message. As in the case of mock parliaments, collective participation and organization are more important than the actual performance. In that sense, pageants are performance ceremonies that celebrate their own social process.

Pageantry could appear both on a large public scale and in private domestic intimacy. A good example of the public is an immense metadramatic (containing plays within plays, and drawing attention to its theatricalities) soiree that Blagrave describes in detail. Produced in Halifax in 1859, the event had a text published under the grandiose title (typical of the emotive rhetoric of the movement) *Scenes and Dialogues Entitled Harvest Queen Coronation Prepared and Presented for the Halifax "Cold Water Army" and Intended to Benefit the Cause of Temperance and Intelligence.* The script contains florid passages of stand-and-deliver recitation ("The tender foliage, soon, will no longer adorn the meadows ..."), iconic procession of allegorical figures (The Harvest Queen and the four seasons), dramatic episodes, and songs. Blagrave notes that the pageant requires at least twenty performers, and that the female roles are all mute, suggesting that the show was an educational experience for young male temperance cadets. He concludes that its "chief benefit is to be to the performing group, who will be improved by the activity itself."[27]

Harvest Queen is representative of a corrective performance that alludes to theatrical conventions, with painted scenery, and a seated audience, yet in its structures it sidesteps the vulgarity of the theatre. We see this in miniature in the domestic parlour pageants that enabled theatrical pleasure in respectable, controlled conditions. The most common of these was the "parlour tableaux vivants," which translated the new aesthetic of scenic realism and pictorial staging to the domestic living room. Tableaux usually depicted famous historical, patriotic, or moral images, often drawn from theatre or painting (Washington crossing the Delaware was a favourite). These were meant to be instructive not just because of their uplifting content but because, as explained in one book of recitations, readings, etiquette, and home entertainment published in the United States but clearly reaching to Canadian readers as well, "The affair is sure to be a failure unless the actors not only have the most perfect command of feeling, but are able to enter completely into the spirit of the subject they attempt to depict."[28] Such home theatricals were exercises in "self-culture," as defined by the widely influential *Girl's Own Paper* in 1899: "The man or woman of culture is the man or woman whose nature has been cultivated in such a way as to develop all its capabilities in the best possible direction; whose education has been adapted skillfully to taste and capacity, and who has been taught the art of self-instruction."[29] That these ideas circulated widely can be seen in the surviving program of the Self Culture Club in the boom town of High River, Alberta, dating from 1908. The monthly meetings of the club were devoted to readings and analysis of *King Lear* and *The Tempest*. On March 25, for example, Mrs. Ballantyne made a presentation on Act III of *The Tempest*, and Miss Jackson spoke on "Ariel – the intellectual element; Caliban – the animal nature."[30] At the end of the season the club held its social meeting at which members were invited to "represent any character in Shakespeare." This idea of social welfare through exposure and "access" to classic humanism was also at this time the tenet of the cultural policy, such as it was, of the Second International.

Whether comprising three people on a living-room sofa, or a hundred in an outdoor spectacle, the pageant form immersed its participants in a virtual reality. Pageants had particular power in affirming social and ideological norms, but they were quickly adapted by the reformist and revolutionary left in the early twentieth century (following the precedent of the French Revolution). The Paterson Strike Pageant, produced by John Reed at Madison Square Gardens, Piscator's *Despite All!* (the first documentary pageant), produced for the German Communist Party in 1926, and the immense re-enactment pageants of the pre-Stalinist USSR and fascist Italy all adhered to the principle of iconographic staging and ideological conditioning.

If pageantry sought to be immersive, drawing performers and spectators into a sense of a shared community and historical moment, the other performance category – the platform – emphasized dynamic and emotionally charged performances that used theatre stages to frame polemics as entertainment. The line between "speaking" and performing was never clear or stable, and the pages of nineteenth-century newspapers are filled with ads for theatrical routines by comical "Professors." Parody lectures in stage dialect, whether African-American or Irish, were a staple of minstrel and vaudeville shows; stage illusionists, medicine-show hucksters, mesmerists, and pyrotechnicians routinely billed themselves as "Professor" to give their performances a patina of educational respectability. But even foursquare temperance lecturers could be enjoyed as theatre, as witnessed in the case of John Gough's 1850 visit to Guelph.

Like today's motivational speakers and evangelical preachers, temperance crusaders knew that public speech was show business. That meant meeting an insatiable audience demand for novelty. North American audiences were extremely receptive to new performance forms and practices, and performers invented numerous theatrical entertainments that supplied theatrical delight under the pretense of public pedagogy. One such was the cartoonist J.W. Bengough, editor of the satiric magazine *Grip*. Bengough's caricatures of Canadian politicians made him a national celebrity; in the pages of the *Globe* the poet Wilfred Campbell called him a genius.[31] Bengough was a vocal adherent of several causes, including temperance, women's suffrage, and the quasi-socialist single tax.

Bengough had a high-profile sideline as a public speaker specializing in "chalk talks," during which he would illustrate his lectures with cartoons drawn on stage. Shortly before his death in 1923 he published a volume of his favourite talks, with just enough illustrations to convey a sense of his technique. As he describes in his prefatory memoir, he would arrive in a town and chat up the locals before his talk so that he could – like CBC Radio's *Vinyl Cafe* today – incorporate spoofs of local characters and events into his material. His brilliance as a stage performer lay in his ability to improvise and in how he used the actual technique of drawing before an audience to develop his argument. In his talk on "Women Suffrage," for example, he ridiculed the proposition that "in the sphere of human rights the half is equal to the whole" with a parodic demonstration of a Euclidian proof, in which the whole of a diagrammed (ABCD) is equal to the half-circle (ABC). By the end of the "proof," by filling in the circle with the face of a pig he reaches his conclusion that "man has monopolized all the governmental power, and has thus displayed a hoggish disposition."[32]

Chalk talks were more than theatricalizations of information; they were the precedents for what would become (and still are) a popular aesthetic technique for politicized theatre artists who want to establish a non-fictive, phenomenal presence to authenticate their material. Chalk talks came again to the fore in the 1930s, when the artist Avrom Yanovsky delivered them as part of the Workers' Experimental Theatre in Toronto. In later decades artists would turn to projections and digital media in place of chalk, and the drawn cartoon performance would find another home on children's television.

Suffrage: mock parliaments

The nineteenth century's most visible and effective form of intervention theatre was the mock parliament, although its political capacity was not fully realized until the very end of the century and in the early years of the next. The form was made most visible by Nellie McClung's several accounts of the *Parliament of Women* staged in Winnipeg in 1914.[33] This work was the peak performance of the final surge that led to the enfranchisement of women in Manitoba, and for that reason entered the public imagination – even becoming the subject of a television "Heritage Minute" re-enactment.

The mock parliament was a powerful and ambivalent form of performance that both was and was not perceived as theatre, and was capable of shifting between public and private spaces of reception. The best known of these performances – because they were the most

theatricalized and politically effective – were the woman's suffrage parliaments, including McClung's. In her study of these performances,
Kym Bird identifies nine mock-parliament scripts and thirteen stagings
of these pieces between 1893 and 1914. That date span means that for
many women (and their male supporters) the mock parliament was a
familiar convention for much of their political lives.[34]

With incisive analysis and archival research, Bird reconstructs the
actual performance conditions of the two most notable parliaments, the
WCTU 1893 performance in Toronto (featuring Emily Stowe), and the
1914 Winnipeg performance. Bird analyses them as the expression of
a liberal feminism that "challenged women's traditional social sphere."
She notes that the organization of the performances "proved women's
acuity in campaign strategy. They were organized to raise the profile of
suffrage, to supply its coffers, and develop greater public support. They
provided forums for discussions and lobbying, pamphlet distribution,
and signature collection."[35] Bird thus implicitly recognizes a recurring
principle: that the performance event often functions as the social enunciation of a larger political process. In this context the performance is the
ceremonial enactment, not the agent, of political change.

Because of their public advocacy function, the women's parliaments
were staged publicly in well-known performance venues, including the
1,798-seat Walker Theatre in Winnipeg and the Allan Gardens Pavilion in Toronto. That the women's groups could command prestigious
venues indicates their class and social positioning. The 1914 Winnipeg
performance was preceded by a recital of suffrage songs and the famous
British suffrage play *How the Vote Was Won*, adapted to local names and
references and directed by Hattie Walker, wife of the theatre's proprietor. On the day before the performance McClung had led a delegation of women to petition the Premier for the right to vote, knowing
he would refuse. She incorporated his remarks into her own speech as
mock-premier in the play. The collection of those remarks seems to have
been the actual purpose of the delegation.

The Winnipeg play was a particularly public statement of emergent
power and hegemonic negotiation by women who could ask for and
receive an audience with a provincial premier. Led by eminent, wealthy,
and educated women, the suffrage movement demanded access, not to
radical change, but to the structures of political power. Even as they were
negotiating space in one hegemonic structure, they reinforced another.

This tendency is notable when we see the names involved in the Winnipeg performance. In one of the most ethnically diverse cities in Canada, all of the participants were British in origin.

That these mock parliaments were in this sense not expressions of social change but of the consolidation of power within hegemonic blocs and social elites becomes clear when they are placed in a wider context. The mock parliament became a common performance structure in the 1880s, and continues today primarily as a teaching method in school civics classes. In the nineteenth century it was popular as both a method of public discussion and a form of parody, and it was frequently both. Such parliaments are public and secular manifestations of the parliamentary proceedings of the fraternal societies, but their spread was in all likelihood linked to the 1884 publication of John George Bourinot's *Parliamentary Procedure and Practice with an Introductory Account of the Origin and Growth of Parliamentary Institutions in the Dominion of Canada.* Margaret Banks notes that both in 1884, with the first edition, and 1892, following the second edition, Bourinot received many requests from outside groups seeking procedural advice. She cites frequent correspondence with the principals of a mock parliament society in Montreal.[36]

Reports in local newspapers indicate the range and usage of mock parliaments. The March 16, 1900, issue of the *Globe* contains an account of a mock parliament held by the North Toronto Young Men's Liberal Club in one of its fortnightly meetings. The mock parliament was apparently "arousing considerable interest among the members" and was "likely to be a beneficial feature of the club." This particular debate – which had to do with the involvement of Canadians in Britain's war in South Africa – was, the *Globe* reported, "conducted with a great deal of spirit and no little humor."[37]

In that event the parliament debated an issue of current interest, but with an apparent clubby joviality. Just over two years later came another report: "The largest mock Parliament ever attempted in this city will take place April 10 in Broadway Hall, Spadina avenue, four literary societies joining in it. The subject will be Imperial federation, and the Saturday Night and Ruskin Societies will be the Government and introduce the bill, and the Opposition will be composed of the Broadway Liberal Society and the Carlton Street Young Men's Club."[38]

Both of these parliaments were in effect simulations or rehearsals of hegemonic power by groups claiming space in public discourse.

Similarly, a mock parliament by the Moose Jaw Literary and Debating Society in 1903 appears to have been a forum in which new social ideas could be tested. ("A Bill will be introduced for the adjustment of all capital and labor disputes by a Board of Arbitration"; "A measure will be introduced placing women on an equal social and political basis with men.")[39] In that respect they are like the suffrage parliaments, but they lack the fundamental stance of parody that Bird identifies as a signal feature of the women's parliaments.

The parody featured in the women's parliaments was not a function of the citing of the parliamentary form but of the regendering of it. But the parliamentary form lent itself to other, less reformist, parodies. In 1908 the students of the Ontario Agricultural College (OAC) in Guelph conducted a mock parliament whose bills included an act "to provide legislation for the restocking of the Speed River with trilobites," plus "an act respecting the enfranchisement of women" and "a bill to amend the regulations governing pie-makers and home-seekers at Macdonald Hall."[40] At the same time, in their college across the green, the young women of Macdonald Institute, the women's domestic science college affiliated with the OAC, developed their own alternative to the mock parliament by inventing a satiric mock society. As the *OAC Journal* described it, "the Spinsters' Convention" was "a short entertainment on behalf of the Y.W.C.A.":

> Eighteen of the oldest maids imaginable, having banded themselves together as the Young Ladies' Single Blessedness Debating Society, are doing their utmost to secure for themselves all those blissful joys attended upon the possession of a husband. The scene produced was one of the regular meetings of the Society, and it certainly gave a fairly thorough knowledge of the methods employed by these damsels in the pursuit of their desires. Perhaps the most useful piece of information provided was the exact state of the matrimonial market up to date. As the Secretary read this report, each Spinster took down carefully such items as seemed particularly fitted to her special need.
>
> Toward the close of the Session, Professor Make-over entered, bringing his marvelous remodeloscope with the aid of which he undertook to transform each member of the Society, in turn, into their heart's desire. The only obstacle was the fact

that before entering the machine each maiden was required to give her exact age. In the first two instances this was reluctantly, yet more or less successfully done; and the results fully justified our expectations: but the third candidate for beautification was so hopelessly ancient that she came out absolutely unaffected, while the fourth so completely forgot her dignity as to insist that her fleeting blushes arose out of her timid inexperience of twenty years of sheltered youth. Alas! In spite of the Professor's protests, she rushed madly to her doom, her innocent frame was ground limb from limb, and the precious remodeloscope utterly destroyed.

This put an effectual stop to any further effort, and the ensuing consternation and frenzied panic may better be imagined than described.[41]

Like the mock parliaments, the "Spinsters' Convention" enacted a parodic simulation of public life to frame theatrical pleasure. In it we see another principle that characterizes politically engaged theatre: the meaning of the event lies not so much in the text as in the context and conditions of performance. Only someone in the room would have found the remodeloscope funny, but to those who were there, who knew the players and the social subtext, it was, by this account, absolutely hilarious.

Labour: spectating performers

In 1883, at the climax of a failed strike by telegraph operators that shut down wireless communications across North America, a notice appeared in *The Palladium of Labor*: "A benefit concert in aid of striking telegraphers was held at the camp pavilion in Toronto on Wednesday evening. Mr. F. Jenkins, of this city, was present and sang a couple of solos."[42]

In the later nineteenth century and into the twentieth, countless events of that sort occurred – whether celebratory dinners, concerts, smokers, picnics – all of which had an element of performance, all of which appear to have expressed and produced a pleasurable sense of spectatorial engagement among the members of an ideological or political community, and all of which must have contributed to a sphere of class-porous political domesticity. A "splendid banquet" held by the Regina local of the Bricklayers' and Masons' International Union in 1910, for instance, followed a "sumptuous repast" with a program that included the chairman's address and various toasts, three speeches, a recitation, and twenty-six songs and duets by the members present.[43] In Toronto one Friday evening in 1891, the usually quite earnest Single Tax Association decided to drop its weekly meeting's standard speech and discussion and instead provide "a literary, musical and artistic entertainment." Entitled "An Evening with Tom Hood," the meeting included a list of five "leading participants" reciting from the works of the celebrated British humorist. As a report noted, "The presentation of Hood's whimsical and pathetic creations was greatly appreciated by the audience."[44]

At dinners, recitals, parodies, and concerts, the performance of the public self, even when satiric, legitimized the entertainments as something other than theatre; but at the same time the popular stage and the assembled, collaborative anthology performances of the minstrel show and its vaudeville successors gave them performance templates. *The Labor Advocate* carried an advertisement for a series of books that suggests the reach of these forms: *Wilford's Original Dialogues and Speeches for Young Folks, Ritter's Book of Mock Trials, Rowton's Complete Debater, Burdett's Dutch Dialect Recitations and Readings* ("selected gems of Humorous German dialect pieces"), *Brudder Gardner's Stump Speeches and Comic Lectures* ("The newest and best book of Negro comicalities").[45]

The ambivalent theatre worked at a certain distance from the circulation of social practices that it produced – as particularly reflected in two constants: mobility and spectating performers. A typical theatricalized subject, say, a striking telegrapher, would readily move from the cozy performative enclosure of public life fellowship to two other spaces of performance.

The first space reflecting this mobility was that of the craft union parades that began in the 1880s and served as predecessors and models for the later Labour Day parades. These craft union events mobilized the growing civic power of skilled labour in the industrial cities and superimposed class interests on already established sectarian and ethnic identities. Historians Craig Heron and Steven Penfold look at craft union parades and Labour Day parades in Canada as street performance. They argue: "The 'art' involved in these events was simple, sometimes crude, but always colorful and engaging. While borrowing heavily from many familiar forms of public celebration, it created the most visible, persistent, and widespread form of collectively produced working-class cultural production that Canada has ever seen."[46] This

new claim to public space variously followed on, referred to, or continued the celebratory traditions of civic festivals and military parades.
The craft union parades mobilized a working-class presence on streets
and routes that hosted numerous parades of different kinds. In Toronto
the annual Orange Parade was a major event for close to a hundred
years. King Billy on his white horse may be the longest-running role in
Canadian political theatre.

The craft union parades were notable for their inclusion of civic and
military authority, as overlapping spheres of male social organization.
As described by *The Globe*, somewhere between three thousand and four
thousand "men" participated in the Toronto parade of 1882, marching in
union formations with distinctive props and costumes, some with allegorical or illustrative floats, including the shoemakers' traditional patron,
King Crispin.[47] With them marched four regimental bands (Grenadiers,
Governor-General's Horse Guard, The Queen's Own Rifles, and Garrison Battery) and the band of the Loyal Orange Lodge, representing
Protestant civic power, and the Emerald band, representing Irish labour.
The parade was a public display of the convergence of power blocs and
at the same time a performance of the overlapping spheres of masculinist
and ethnic participatory hegemony.

As Heron and Penfold demonstrate, working women were generally excluded from the craft parades, and racial minorities were locked
out entirely except in the form of parody and a surrogate. The regimental and cultural society bands did not just represent power blocs in
civic society; they were also the spheres between which performing men
passed on a daily basis. A wage-earning typographer, for instance, may
also be a sergeant in the militia; he could be an Orangeman; he is probably a Knight of Labor, and he could be a Mason, Oddfellow, Forester,
or Knight of Temperance.

The second space of performance was not on the street but hidden
from it, in the highly theatrical world of fraternal societies in which millions of men in North America worked their way through a manifold of
degrees, rituals, and ceremonies, to the point that, as Mark Carnes notes,
"the writing of rituals was a major growth industry."[48] The spawn of fraternal ritual societies reproduced the template formula of freemasonry,
which itself saw a massive proliferation of subsects and affiliated rites; the
1907 *Cyclopaedia of Fraternities* lists more than six hundred such societies
in North America.[49] The template of costumed ritualists, secret signs,

ornate levels of achievement, binding oaths, and initiation into mysteries was a performance practice that covered the immense cultural range between the Masonic Lodges, Ku Klux Klan, Mormon church, Knights of Labor, and temperance movement. The Knights of Labor in particular come into the frame of discussion because they were instrumental in the formation of the craft unions and a claim to public space.

The fraternal societies themselves reflect a multitude of possible disciplinary positions: emergent middle-class homosocialization, the negotiation of class transformation in modernism, the interpellation of aspirant middle-class subjectivity into imperial discourse, or a theatricalized way of getting away from the women. They were a form of theatre; not just *theatrical* but theatre, as much as J.W. Bengough's single tax chalk talks or a temperance mock parliament, discernible along an axis of performance and spectating. They also became in essence the first real multi-player role-play games, in which progress through a virtual world offers prestige and the satisfaction of meaningful work. Observers often noted that the main business of fraternal lodges was writing, staging, and participating in initiation ceremonies for constantly proliferating rites and degrees; or, in the language of gamers, levelling up.

At the same time the rituals and offices were serious business. The Knights of Labor's ritual manual, *Adelphon Kruptos*, consisted of forty-two pages of descriptions of offices, rules, rituals, secret signs, and oaths. The Knights had a political advocacy platform for workers' rights, the eight-hour day, graduated income tax, arbitration, and equal pay for equal work for women, but this work was to some extent impeded by the amount of time spent on what seemed to some to be needless ceremony. But as the Masons had firmly established, the ceremonies were indeed meaningful, if not in their content then in their social dimension as a performance that shapes the field of reception.

Fraternal associations enveloped social life in masculinist performance. The career of Henry Robertson of Collingwood, Ontario, serves as an example. His entry in a historical register of the Supreme Grand Masters of the Knights Templar, which office he held in 1891–92, shows the range of civic fraternal and political associations that marked male success and literally staged the persona of power. He was in public life variously a lawyer, Queen's Counsel, chairman of the high-school board, chairman of the public library board, president of the local golf and curling clubs, reeve, president of the West Simcoe Reform Association of the Liberal Party, and a member of a provincial royal commission on law reform. He joined the Masons at the age of twenty-one and rapidly ascended as Worshipful Master, Deputy District Grandmaster, Grand Steward Junior Warden, Deputy Grand Master, and Grand Master of the Grand Lodge of Ontario. He was "exalted" in the York rite. In Capitular Masonry he was a founding member of the Manitoba chapter, and he was Grand First Principal of the Grand Chapter of Royal Arch Masons in Ontario. In the Knights Templar, he was a charter member and Presiding Preceptor of the Ontario Preceptory in Collingwood. He was elected as Provincial Grand Prior for Toronto district in 1890 and elected Supreme Grand Master of the Sovereign Great Priory of Canada in 1891. He was also a 33° Scottish Rite Mason and a Grand Master Oddfellow.[50]

In this typical profile of a high-ranking Mason of the time, virtual identity is sustained in a network – indeed, a kind of web – of affiliations and alliances that cross over civic, family, and recreational boundaries. Robertson's career shows the particular network of the political elite – all that is missing is a military commission – and may mark the consolidation of civic power by the professional middle class; but its fluidity was essentially the same as for the wage-earning typographer who moves between his class-specific identities. For both the bourgeois civic leader and the working-class typographer, performance and spectatorship, and the reciprocal constitutive relation of the two that we call theatre, were instrumental in the creation of social and political identity. This double exposure has a disconcerting implication for those who turn to labour parades to seek evidence of a potent working-class cultural movement. What they find is the working-class instance of a masculinist performance culture that serves to unlock social strata. In her detailed examination of social life in nineteenth-century Petrolia, Ontario, Christina Burr argues, "The fraternal order was an ideal way of responding to class differences while at the same time making possible a limited degree of class action and class expression."[51]

Moving between these theatricalized locations, of concert fellowship, public parades, and fraternal virtuality, the nineteenth-century man was in effect using performance to construct systems of order and attainment. In these varied locations performance expresses a form of emergent power by activating its capacity not just to transform public space but to invoke spectatorship. The great craft parades, the Orange July 12 processions, and the ceremonial movements of the fraternal societies were performances devised to generate order, mobilization and organization, and power. Hegemonic power has a wider field of resources: in fact, the state itself is the largest and most public of these performance organizations, renewed and made known through its manifold performances on all levels of social life.

The parading craft workers and the fraternal ritualists participated in overlapping performances. Regardless of their degree of social affinity (a Mason might be a mason, or he might be an employer of masons) their performances shared a significant feature: they were both performer and spectator. Spectatorship was situated within performance, with the audience looking out through the performance: to perform the public self in a theatricalization of social space meant that on the one hand the physical geography of the performance situated each participant as the chief spectator of his fellows, and it reflected one's own self-performance. The *Adelphon Kruptos* offers an instruction for opening a service, with the specific spots assigned to various officers:

> Precisely at the hour for opening, allowing five minutes for difference in time pieces, the Master Workman, standing at the Capital. [sic] Shall give one rap and say; "All persons not entitled to sit with us will please retire." The Worthy Inspector then takes the Globe and Lance and proceeds to mark the Inner and Outer Veils with them. Previous to that time all persons were at liberty to enter the room, but the Veils are then closed and none can enter without giving the Password. When the Worthy Inspector goes to the Outer Veil to put the Globe in its place, the Outside Esquire takes position in the anteroom, and when the Worthy Inspector enters the Inner Veil, the Inside Esquire takes position at the Inner Veil.[52]

Once the Veils are "secured," the instruction continues, "The Master Workman will give three raps. Officers and members will form a circle around the centre, Officers in front of their stations as near as possible."

All are fixed within the gaze of the performing members; each is given the best seat in the house. Masonic rituals, with their dramatic scenarios and backdrops, placed members within a theatrical narrative of which they were both actor and audience. As such they appear to have been distanced from the increasingly controlled division of performance and reception of the legitimate theatre of the later nineteenth century. Electric light, modernist dramaturgy, and changing decorum in a regendered theatre culture calmed the participatory unruliness of the old playhouse culture (women had been present before that, but the institution as a whole became a more feminized space); while outside the playhouse, theatrical culture continued to depend on the simultaneity and convergence of performance and spectatorship.

Performances of Disorder: Unruly Crowds, Mobs, and Mummers

The performances of the knockabout farce on a makeshift stage or of the market-square busker and street-corner comedian may not be art – they are unruly, beyond discipline – but they are the most common forms of theatrical performance, and it is with these performances that theatrical dissent both appears and usually escapes. In Canada instances of the unruly are many; they can be discerned whenever nineteenth-century masculinity erupted into performance. One such event was reported in the *Labor Advocate* in February 1891: "On Wednesday of last week two or 300 unemployed laborers assembled in St. Andrew Square and formed a procession, carrying a black flag with the legend, 'Work or Bread.' They marched by West King Street to the City Hall where a large crowd had gathered." Tending to go unreported was the crowded history of charivaris (or shivarees), calithumpian parades, and mumming, which often expressed working-class anger given licence through the use of costume, although that anger was more often incited by religion and ethnicity than by class conflict.[53]

But in our search for a tradition of organized, aestheticized political theatre in nineteenth-century Canada we can find very few examples. Perhaps the most obvious, or visible, is Les Amateurs typographes. Formed by members of the Union typographique de Québec in the 1830s, the group presented a repertoire of nationalist and republican plays. If we widen our scope and look at organized theatricality, we can see a rich culture of politically and socially assertive performance as the working class marched into its place in hegemonic civic life, and middle-class women staged themselves into political discourse. But even these – the craft parades, fraternal orders, social reform theatricals – were the performances of hegemonic negotiation in the class positions of industrial democracy, and their pervasive masculinism reinforced a deeper gender hegemony. The issue, then, is not just one of disciplinarity, nor is the binary at play here a simple one of enclosed playhouse and public street. Both stage and street performed to promote a social order in which working-class aspirations wore middle-class garb and striking telegraphers drank tea at concert recitals. To seek traces of theatricalized dissent, we need to look past the record, into the unrecorded, the unremarked, and the unruly.

Ironically, theatrical spectatorship from below was most commonly from above, in the highest and cheapest tiers of the playhouse, known still as "the gods." As playhouses increased in size to meet popular demand for sensationalist performance, they became focal points of urban politics and factionalism. Nineteenth-century theatre history in Europe and the United States is filled with stories of theatre riots. In Canada, riotous behaviour took place on a smaller scale. One of the earliest records of a theatre event in Toronto, when it was still the town of York, is an 1825 legislative Select Committee hearing into the transgressive rowdyism of an all-male audience of parliamentarians at the performance of a touring U.S. troupe of players on New Year's Eve. The small tavern theatre was almost deserted, the all-male audience was drunk, and fists flew over a perceived insult to the Crown. But as theatres increased in size, so too did the riots. In a typical example, a mob armed with clubs stormed a theatre in Saint John in 1845 to disrupt the premiere of Thomas Hill's local political satire, *The Provincial Association.*[54]

The playhouse was a meeting place in which social and cultural boundaries were tested, often violently. In his history of theatre on the western frontiers, Chad Evans includes an account of a violent race riot in the Colonial Theatre in Victoria in 1860, when American miners protested the presence of Black spectators in better seats. A year later a Black family in gallery seats was showered with flour and vegetables from above.[55] The Victoria theatre was a convergence zone of very different spectating communities: naval officers and ratings from the British fleet, U.S. miners, immigrant prospectors, English settlers, and, relegated to the cheapest seats, First Nations people. In mid-century Victoria, the Colonial Theatre may have been the most politically volatile space in town.

Evans also gives us a detailed account of the "box-house" theatres of the mining towns of the Kootenay, including the Theatre Comique in Kaslo, which was a variety theatre and a saloon with two bars and a staff of eighty "box rustler" bar girls. Evans describes the box-house theatre as a "perfectly designed trap" (and the predecessor of today's casinos).[56] In the box-house theatre, spectatorship spilled into the brothel rooms and out into the street. The actual theatrical performance is incidental; it functions as an occasion of spectating and a place of public display because it is axiomatic that a theatre audience watches the show and each other. Amidst the theatricality and spectacle of the place itself, the audience too becomes the show.

Perhaps the most notorious of such places was Joe Beef's Canteen in Montreal. Joe Beef, whose real name was Charles McKiernan, is one of the most notorious folk heroes in Quebec history. He was an Irish veteran of the British army, and his canteen was a four-storey waterfront tavern, hostel, soup kitchen, zoo, and theatre. Beef became famous for providing free meals and support for striking canal and mill workers. He was himself a self-created persona who advertised:

> Joe Beef, the Son of the People.
> He cares not for Pope, Priest, Parson, or King
> William of the Boyne; all Joe wants is the Coin.
> He trusts in God in the summer to keep him
> from all harm; when he sees the first frost and
> snow poor old Joe trusts to the Almighty Dollar
> and good old maple wood to keep his belly warm.[57]

His canteen was a must-see stop for out-of-town visitors, for whom it was evidence of a dissipation that only Montreal could achieve. According to one *New York Times* writer:

> I was introduced to Beef, and he showed me some of his curiosities, as a special mark of his favor. Most of them were too disgusting to look at, too indecent to describe. He had snakes done up in glass jars, and toads, and a variety of other articles. In a small dark room, just back of the bar-room, an enormous black bear was chained, and by his side were fastened a score or more of ferocious dogs. The next room was the "theatre," where, on

Sundays, religious services are held. A half-drunken clown and a black monkey were performing on the stage for the edification of half a dozen tramps, who were stretched on the benches.[58]

Similarly *Montreal by Gaslight*, a muck-raking pamphlet from 1889 (after McKiernan's death), which ostensibly documents the perfidy of Montreal's nightlife but in so doing offers a detailed catalogue of brothels, along with their locations, identifying features, and specialties, gives a lurid description of the canteen, dwelling in detail on its filth and concluding, "But let one thing be remembered – many a tired head has here found rest; many a hungry mouth has here been filled."[59] Indeed, many good citizens did find entertainment. If there was any place in Canada that could be described as a dissenting, insurgent working-class theatre, this was it. It was an intensely performative space, and Joe Beef himself was a theatricalized character. Peter DeLottinville points out that McKiernan "eagerly debated topics of the day, or amused patrons with humorous poems of this own composition. He had a remarkable ability to ramble on for hours in rhyming couplets."[60] But to the middle classes the canteen was only spoken of as a space of disruption, filth, and danger. We can only imagine the performances that erupted there, but the presence of striking workers, performing bears, parrots, a rhyming landlord, indigent tramps, petty criminals, and a "half-drunken clown" suggests the possibility of a politicized theatre that was so unruly as to be inconceivable to anyone not present.

If the box-house theatres were venues that move away from the decorum of "the theatre," and if Joe Beef's canteen was in effect a box-house theatre with only the sketchiest of stages, what are we left with if we move out of the premises altogether, onto the street – without form, without discipline, with nothing but unruly performance in public space? We are left with mummers and their equivalents, however named. Here basic elements of disguise and grotesquerie exist to give licence to unruly behaviours, often but not exclusively on festive occasions.

Mummers are most commonly associated with Newfoundland, where the (much-changed) tradition continues to the present day, but mumming also continues elsewhere, on Hallowe'en, on festive holidays, and in the public, disguised or masked, performances of sports fans. And as with sports fans today, the routines could often turn violent. In Newfoundland mumming in disguise was banned in 1860 after the death of a protestant mummer in a religious riot in Bay Roberts. In St. John's, as one witness later recalled, rival Irish gangs of mummers slugged it out in costumes. "Men were often beaten badly for old grievances by the fools. I remember, as a boy, how proud I used to be to shake hands with the fool.... Each company had one or more hobbyhorses, with gaping jaws snapping at people."[61] Scholarly historical accounts of mumming – most of them written by folklorists and anthropologists – have tended to examine performance traits and characteristics to establish typologies. They seek to identify the patterned activity – evidence of order and a kind of disciplinarity – with the result that they see mumming as manifested in structure (like the mummers' plays or ritualized house-visiting) and decomposing in riot. But the heart of mumming is a delight in unruly public disorder.

The determined gardener who presented his caterpillar bouquet to City Hall was in his own way a mummer. He was masked in gesture, and his unruliness was his activism. For the most part such unruliness went unremarked because it could only be seen as disorder and disruption. This phenomenon more than anything else explains the apparent but deceptive absence of "working-class political theatre" in the nineteenth century. That deceptive absence forces us to ask whether we have been looking at the question from the wrong end. Seeking performances of dissent and political theatre in the nineteenth century, we find less than we expect, and our genealogical mechanism, which seeks antecedents for the agitprop and interventionist theatre of the twentieth century, is disrupted (until we realize that their sources are mass communication, not theatre). The peculiar case of Joe Beef reminds us of the need to think again – it reminds us not to assume that the theatre culture of his time was framed in artistic disciplinarity and sanitized from political activism and dissent. If we start with the hypothesis that all theatre in the nineteenth century was "political," tending to the unruly in location, in spectatorship, or in the simulations of the public self, we can then go on to ask how it transpired that theatrical modernism became disciplined and socially calmed.

3

Mobilized Theatre and the Invention of Agitprop

Inventing agitprop: unemployed demonstration,
Edmonton, October 1933.
Glenbow Archives

If the audience can be made to feel the speaker's
genuine cordiality, the very atmosphere will
vibrate with stimulating good feeling.
   – *William Aberhart*

When Nellie McClung took her historic mock parliament to Winnipeg in January 1914 she was fortunate enough to have the new Walker
Theatre as her dream venue. The huge and opulent theatre had opened
just a few years earlier, in December 1906, with its nearly eighteen hundred seats. But it was only one of many new theatrical palaces in the
country. At the close of the nineteenth century the first theatrical film
screenings in Canada had increased the public appetite for spectacular
entertainment and completed the transition of the playhouse into social
respectability.

   In the opening decades of the new century the construction of theatres for live performance was expanding at an increasing rate, with larger and more lavish playhouses springing up across the land. In 1907
in Toronto the Royal Alexandra Theatre, sponsored by a syndicate of
extremely wealthy investors led by Cawthra Mulock, opened with fifteen hundred seats. In those years too the Greek immigrant seaman
Alexander Pantages, who entered the business as proprietor of a burlesque house in the Klondike, was expanding his theatre-building habit
to an eventual chain of over one hundred playhouses across the continent. The Winnipeg Pantages, built in 1907, was the centre of a circuit that
had its eastern terminus in Toronto.

   All of these playhouses, with their palatial decor, smoking loges,
red velvet fittings, and chandeliers, were connected by an immense web
of circuits and road contracts, which invariably locked them into one of
a small number of booking agency syndicates based in New York. Of
these, the most powerful were the Theatrical Syndicate and the Shuberts. The Theatrical Syndicate controlled some five hundred theatres

across the continent, but by the end of the 1910s its rivals, the Shuberts, had won the agency wars to dominate the theatre market (including in their contractual stable the Royal Alexandra). The booking syndicates invented the production and distribution system that later went west to Hollywood. With revolutions in transportation and electrical communication enabling new forms of centralized distribution, just as in manufacturing industries, these businesses were the inevitable application of the expansionist economics of the age of monopoly capital to theatrical production.

The monopoly wars of the American theatre established the material conditions for the advent of Canadian theatre as a deferred aspiration. Liberal nationalist critics such as Bernard Sandwell in *Saturday Night* and Hector Charlesworth in the Toronto *Mail and Empire* identified U.S. control of Canadian playhouses as a form of cultural colonialism that was retarding the anticipated maturation of national culture. In a series of famous talks, Sandwell spoke at length about "our adjunct theatre" and the "annexed stage," pointing out the results of the erasure of the border on the theatrical map of North America: "Canada is the only nation in the world whose stage is entirely controlled by aliens."[1] Vincent Massey, like Charlesworth, saw a certain promise in the new art theatre movement that championed small theatres, realist and methodic acting, interior dramaturgy, and psychological realism. Pioneered in Europe by avant-garde modernist artists including August Strindberg, in his later Intimate Theatre stage, Henrik Ibsen, and the French director André Antoine, founder of the experimental Théâtre Libre, this new discourse of "theatre art" offered a practical and intellectual reclamation of the theatre in what became known as the Little Theatre Movement.

In Canada this largely amateur movement was the starting point for a decades-long conversation about the need for a national theatre and its ancillary, a national dramatic literature. That conversation was invariably moderated by Massey in his various roles as founder and mentor of Hart House Theatre at the University of Toronto, as editor of anthologies of Canadian plays and author of critical articles about them, as organizer of the Dominion Drama Festival, as chair of the Royal Commission on the arts that bore his name, and as Governor General and silent patron of the Stratford Festival. For Massey and the rest of the club of affluent, university-educated, and largely anglophiliac intellectuals who debated the coming arrival of a theatre culture that would monumentalize the nation and prove its historical presence, the problem was binary: the only alternative to large, splashy, U.S.-controlled sensationalism had to be local, small, refined, and Canadian; and for that reason the country's theatre deserved to have the patronage of the state. Massey was quick to acknowledge that "there are several Canadas," but with the exception of francophone Quebec, most of the Canadas he had in mind appeared to speak English.[2]

The combination of large commercial show-business and non-commercial artistic theatre was to be the foundation of what became known as "Canadian theatre," with its success measured equally in audience numbers and new plays – that is, by consumption and production. But, again, these indices only seemed to matter if they were in English. Even as Massey was writing articles about the "need" for Canadian drama and the possibilities of a popular theatre culture, the first wave of "Canadian theatre" was well under way, with immigrant and displaced communities using the stage as a means of consolidation, of preserving cultural memory, and political affirmation. For most of the twentieth century this rich legacy of performance would be dismissively categorized as "multicultural theatre" and separated from the nation-building enterprise that was seeking out "the Canadian playwright."

By the 1920s various phenomena of engaged theatre were for very different reasons separated from or refusing the emergent discourse of "Canadian theatre" and were instead taking steps to provoke social action. One such case would prove to be the first solid articulation of radical leftist theatre in Canada. Others were asserting a conservative or reactionary politics, and in this regard Canada may have been unique: both documentary theatre and agitprop emerged as theatrical discoveries from the right.

Unremarked and Marginal Theatricalities

Of all the ethnic cultures that contributed to the development of Canada, the British were arguably both the least theatrical and the most anxious about the lack of a theatre culture that they could identify as such. The puritan traditions that came into Canada from Great Britain and the American colonies mitigated against theatre as a showcase of the nation, but the resistance to theatre that Massey and his liberal-nationalist compatriots saw as an impediment to nationhood derived from their own cultural sources and was largely confined to their own ethnic community (which always identified itself as congruent to the nation).

Elsewhere, where English was spoken with accents from around the world, theatre flourished. Traces of this theatre can be seen in archival photographs of costumed drama groups, in the tattered scenic backgrounds in old community halls, and more recently in deep research by historians who are rebuilding the lost, suppressed, or dismissed histories of their communities.

A Winnipeg example

The use of theatre and drama as a process of cultural preservation, a means of negotiation with forces of assimilation, and an organizational strategy of ideological resistance was in play across Canada, but nowhere can it been seen more clearly than in Winnipeg.

In 1983 the Multicultural History Association undertook a preliminary survey and discovered archival evidence of organized theatrical activity and playwriting amidst Canada's early-twentieth-century immigrant peoples from Finland, Ukraine, Poland, China, Macedonia, and Hungary.[3] Winnipeg in particular provides a notable example of how an immigrant community – in this case, Ukrainian – used theatre as a form of cultural organization and mobilization, and moreover used it especially to claim position in difficult factional disputes, usually between conservative nationalists and socialists.

While Nellie McClung was in downtown Winnipeg staging her mock parliament to secure political rights for (bourgeois, white) women, across the tracks in the immigrant North End other theatrical performances were enacting the cultural memory and political demands of people whom McClung saw as alien to British Canada, and whom she barely mentions in her memoirs. In 1914 Winnipeg was the boomtown launching point for the final push to open the Western prairies for economic development. It was the third-largest city in Canada, and approximately 35 per cent of its new population consisted of immigrants from non-anglophone cultures. Of them, the majority were Ukrainians, Poles, and Yiddish-speaking Jews from Eastern Europe. Among them they created a unique theatre culture that was largely invisible to the anglophone majority. The nourishing of this culture was not just because of the relatively large percentage of foreign-born immigrants, but also because the city was little more than a generation away from its Red River settlement origins and displaced Métis history. The anglo majority was itself relatively new. The rapid growth of the city was a result of modern transportation technology and agricultural capitalism, and it was synchronous with the emergence of socialism and syndicalism in Canada. Politically and culturally Winnipeg was one of the most radical cities in the country. It was a place where the fractures of class and ethnicity were particularly acute and visible.

The immigrants who swelled the working class in Winnipeg had brought with them the drama, poetry, and music of their homelands. For some, their sense of nationhood was already deeply formed by literary nationalism; the poetry of Taras Shevchenko and the dramas of Adam Mickiewicz were virtual monuments of Ukraine and Poland respectively. Mickiewicz, exiled from his native Lithuania, had written his epic dramatic poem *Forefather's Eve* in France, for a Poland that did not exist in his lifetime, but his play announced and enacted an idea of a Polish nation that would come into realization in 1918. Romantic literary nationalism in imperial Europe posited that the nation survives and persists even if it exists only in literature.

For the Ukrainians and other Slavic peoples who came to Western Canada to clear land and develop property value for the railroads, nationalism and cultural memory fused with politics, whether conservative nationalism or socialism. When transported to the new land these literatures had talismanic force. They were a way of preserving identity through language and memory, of expressing a nationalist sentiment that had been outlawed in the old country, and of sustaining community life. One Ukrainian immigrant, Mary Skrypnyk, recounted her life in Timmins, Ontario, in the early years of the century, providing a similar glimpse of this kind of life:

> My parents played in the drama group. I remember one of the winter evenings when our parents bundled us up in warm clothing and took us with them to the Ukrainian Labour Temple where they were rehearsing their roles for theatrical productions. We were taken to the hall on sleds, one being drawn by my father and the other by my mother. In the Ukrainian Labour Temple, we were placed on tables in the basement where there already were other children. We slept side by side while the parents were rehearsing.

But when the day of the stage production came around, we forgot all about the tables in the basement and the rehearsals. Excited, we proudly sat in the front rows, but were unable to recognize our parents who wore make-up and were dressed in the strange costumes of the characters that they were portraying on the stage. My mother played in dramatic roles, while my father did the opposite: playing in comic roles and reciting humorous monologues.[4]

Founded in 1918, the Ukrainian Labour Temple Association (after 1925, the Ukrainian Labour Farmer Temple Association, ULFTA) was the largest and most organized of the immigrant cultural movements. By 1928 it numbered 167 branches across Canada and had organized some fifty-nine drama groups across the country.[5] Its predecessor, the Ukrainian Social Democratic Party, had started forming theatre groups as early as 1907, and records exist of nationalist performances prior to that. In his exhaustive history of the Ukrainian left cultural movement, Peter Krawchuk describes a performance that took place in the Shevchenko Reading Room in Winnipeg. The play, *The Argonauts*, concerned "young Galician seminarians in the search for brides with large dowries or property before they are ordained, so as to pay the debts incurred with Jewish and other money-lenders."[6] The troublesome tension between the Ukrainian and Jewish communities occasionally erupted into hostility. In her close study of the history of Ukrainian cultural activity in Canada, Alexandra Pritz found that when a local Ukrainian producer brought a Jewish troupe to Winnipeg from the United States to play a season of Ukrainian plays in 1913, Winnipeg Ukrainian performers and audiences boycotted the performances.[7]

The extremely active Ukrainian cultural activity did not escape the attention of the authorities, who viewed it with suspicion and diligently recorded their impressions. Pritz quotes a memorandum written in 1921 by the Commissioner of the RCMP to the Governor General's private secretary, in which he stated that the Ukrainians had "a real cultural movement, grotesquely crude as yet, but possessing the tremendous advantages of being a spontaneous expression of deeply seated racial aptitudes, and of being rooted in the common people."[8] As the xenophobia and racism against "enemy aliens" that swirled around the Winnipeg General Strike showed, Eastern European immigrants were widely regarded as a threat to morality, employment, and national security. As early as 1909 the Ukrainian Workers Drama Circle had to deal with harassment by the authorities following (in the words of the left-wing newspaper *Robochyi narod*), "malevolent denunciations by the Ukrainian nationalists who are in the service of the Conservative Party." In March 1922 city authorities in Winnipeg banned a theatrical performance on the grounds that it was performed in "a wooden building."[9]

The proliferation of dramatic societies marked serious splits within the Ukrainian community.[10] As early as 1911, drama groups began to align along competing nationalist and socialist lines, with the Drama Circle of the Ukrainian Socialist Hall occupying the left end. The group was directed by Matthew Popovich, a community organizer who represented the Ukrainian socialist movement in the founding meeting of the Communist Party of Canada in Guelph in 1921 and was later one of eight imprisoned communist leaders who became the subject of an important play, *Eight Men Speak*. Until the Russian Revolution, the lines were blurred: both nationalist and socialist troupes used the Labour Temple when it was built in 1918, but after the Canadian government banned the Ukrainian Social Democratic Party in that year, the Ukrainian Labour Temple Association became the main locus of socialist organization. It sponsored the first "Workers' Theatre," so-named. In 1925, when the association added "Farmer" to its name and passed a resolution to "establish close ties with dramatic and musical societies in Soviet Ukraine," an ideological split occurred that would sunder the Ukrainian Canadian community for the next six decades.[11]

Finnish immigrants, who provided another "language federation" pillar to the emergent communist movement, followed a similar pattern. Less numerous, but no less militant and organized, the Finnish community established an association with the Industrial Workers of the World, in the process providing the clearest link to a theatre tradition in the Wobbly movement. The Wobblies were known for their songs and public meetings, but there is no evidence of a specific IWW dramatic tradition, outside of the Finnish national and class dramas staged at the Workers' Hall in Port Arthur (where, in 1981, the Canadian Popular Theatre Alliance was born in front of old painted backdrops of birch forests, with a keynote address by the great Ukrainian-Canadian playwright, George Ryga).

With the double mission of cultural preservation and ideological polemics, performed to an urban working class in an anglo-dominated country, it comes as no surprise that the theatre produced by the Ukrainian and Finnish groups was untouched by modernism. Indeed, they were militantly anti-modernist, despite their progressive politics. One case in particular, the career of Myroslav Irchan, the Ukrainian communist playwright and director, indicates why this was so. Irchan lived in Winnipeg from 1923 to 1929 (after which he returned to the Soviet Union, only to meet his fate in the gulag in 1933). He had come to Canada in the wake of the Winnipeg General Strike, in which the contesting factions (the strike committee, the business front group that called itself the Committee of 1000, and the thousands of recently returned soldiers who supported both sides) for the most part mobilized the anglophone community. The strike leadership was entirely anglo, and even on the left xenophobia raised the spectre of socialist aliens taking jobs from patriots. Racism and government terror (especially the deportation of immigrant radicals) explain the apparent absence of theatrical intervention from the well-developed Ukrainian troupes in the strike.

When Irchan came to Canada he was already a well-established writer, with a left-wing credibility earned by combat service in the civil war in Russia and Ukraine. Of his eleven plays, he wrote seven in Winnipeg. Their frequent performances across the country by ULFTA troupes made him the most prolific and successful Canadian playwright of his day. Working as an editor, journalist, and speaker, Irchan was a literary celebrity. In 1929 *Saturday Night* called him "the most popular and influential author in the country" and asked, "Is there another writer in Canada whose appearance on the platform would be greeted with resounding, long-continued applause – whose every new play is eagerly witnessed, who can see his audience spellbound, women weeping, men grinding their teeth, and then elevated with joy when the story takes a welcome turn?"[12]

Irchan's theatre work had clear artistic aspirations, and along with the plays he wrote instructions for performance and eventually produced a training manual for the theatre school that he helped found for the ULFTA. In the preface to his version of Molière's *The Miser*, "reworked and adapted for the workers' farmers stage," he stressed the importance of theatrical discipline:

> In order for the comedy The Miser to make an appropriate impression, it is important to take it seriously. Do not show it

after rehearsing only two or three times. First reread it, study the characters that are depicted in it and give the audience a fully alive, realistic view, and not the forced tormented version filled with your own unacceptable additions – a performance that more likely deserves the name *balagan* [farcical disorder]. You must understand that comedy does not mean "Playing the fool," as many people think, but it is an important work of literature written in dramatic form that depicts laughing at human mistakes, and because of this, the audience must profit from this as much as from any other kind of drama.[13]

In his preface to the more ambitious five-act drama *Underground Galychyna*, published in 1926, he made the point:

If this play is to be staged anywhere, it is important to address a couple of words to the public before the performance begins. The audience must be taught to pay very careful attention to the action on stage. Amateur performers must put forth all their effort to portray the drama on stage. They must learn their roles and blocking. Without this, the drama will not be convincing.

For Irchan and the theatre groups he mentored, plays on stage could model an analysis of realistic conditions and were therefore an effective means of ideological schooling. The preface to *Underground Galychyna* underscores its primary lesson:

Every reader of the workers' press has heard [more than] once about the provocative work done by Polish agents in the workers' organizations. This play describes one such occurrence. Paid Polish agents intentionally plant themselves into the workers' collectives, which are forced to operate underground because of Polish persecution. This play represents truthfully how sneakily the Polish police fight the workers' movement. How it makes up various "conspiracies." And how its agents-provocateurs act.[14]

Writing two decades after the Russian playwright Chekhov gave Stanislavksy the dramatic texts that led him to perfect the idea of depth psychology as applied to actor training (resulting in what became known as "the method"), Irchan championed a pre-modern dramatic form that emphasized sensation, outward action, simple characters, and melodramatic plot. The logic of nineteenth-century romantic drama was based on an appeal to strong emotions, so that moral issues were confirmed in the audience members' feelings (of suspense, indignation, joy, and pity and fear). Irchan used the technique and structure of narrative theatre, but his model of efficacy was basically the same as that of a temperance pageant. This equation of plot sensation and moral or ideological truth was the fundamental principle that Brecht began to theorize and critique around the same time that Irchan was writing and staging his Winnipeg plays.

But if Irchan's dramaturgy was pre-modernist, his theatre practice corresponded to contemporary developments in the mainstream anglo theatre culture. For Irchan, like Massey, participation in theatrical production was a process of community development. His emphasis on educated technique parallels the concern for professionalism in the anglo art theatre movement, for the same reason. Artistic proficiency manifests cultural maturity, which is a metaphor for the nation, or the national community. Both Irchan and Massey wanted a professionalized theatre culture to enact historical principles. For Massey, the self-knowing Canadian nation was at stake; for Irchan it was the ideological orientation of the Ukrainian-Canadian nation.

Irchan was the most celebrated playwright in the Ukrainian community, but he was far from the only one. Nor was he the most prolific. Historian Iroida Wynnyckyj lists 101 plays published by Ukrainian writers before 1942. Many of them appeared in the Ukrainian-language weekly press. Wynnyckyj also provides an invaluable annotated bibliography that summarizes each of the plays she found. They included nationalist and patriotic historical dramas and comedies of immigrant life. Many of the plays, like Irchan's, advocate socialist themes, but the deep ideological fractures in the immigrant communities that had experienced Soviet rule also led to anti-communist polemical drama. In one such, performed in Hamilton in 1935, bakery workers go on strike but recognize that they have been duped by a communist agitator and resume negotiations with their employer. In another, from Winnipeg in 1931, "Idealism of the members of a Ukrainian insurgent group is contrasted with the brutality of the Soviet 'CHEKA.' "[15] The overwhelming majority of the plays are didactic and moralistic, regardless of political orientation.

For the Ukrainian communities particularly (but not exclusively), politically engaged drama performed in community-owned spaces enacted complex cultural negotiations across ideological divides that were as deep and serious as those that separated them from the anglophone mainstream. To the anglo eye of the day, and to most Canadian cultural historians since, these dramas were invisible. Over and over again engaged interventionist theatre would play to the community of engagement and only rarely leave wider traces. The Ukrainian example was unique because the degree of social mobilization left institutional traces, and cultural activism gave urgency to historical recuperation as Ukrainian Canadians assimilated into the anglophone majority. Today the same process continues in other immigrant communities; the Irchans of the present day are writing in many languages, especially Filipino, diasporic Spanish, Punjabi, and Arabic.

"Return this Indian"

If the Ukrainian theatrical performances were effectively invisible to the anglo majority, the performance cultures of the original peoples of the land, whose theatricalities had been trivialized as shamanism and banned under the Indian Act in 1885, were visible to the anglo gaze only when presented through a surrogate – and by surrogate I do not simply mean the appropriated representation of aboriginality (although that is part of it), but the transformation of cultural performance into a substitute of itself by the colonial regulation and displacement of the conditions of performance.

Virtually every history of Canadian theatre has begun with an acknowledgement of First Nations performance, usually described in terms of an atemporal present interrupted by European "contact" (or, as more commonly used today, invasion). Despite cultural and linguistic differences that were no less complex than those existing in Europe, the undifferentiated concept of aboriginality placed all pre-contact cultures on the same plane, describing their performance cultures in terms of a dehistoricized concept of pre-theatrical ritual. Recent attempts to escape the ethnographic biases of this approach have begun to acknowledge the cultural complexities and diversities of indigenous cultures in North America, but theatre historians still tend to perceive Aboriginal performances through the optic of European theatrical experience. Typically, the entry on Canada in the *World Encyclopedia of Contemporary Theatre* refers to the Pacific Northwest cultures as the "theatrically most developed" and to Nootka performances as "Mystery Cycles" in a reference to the sequential stagings of Bible stories by medieval European craft guilds.[16] In the twisted logic of imperial empiricism, nineteenth-century Aboriginal performances "anticipated" the European theatre of the medieval era.

Beyond this attempt to recognize and name (however incorrectly) the theatricality of pre-invasion cultures, theatre historians have only recognized aboriginality as a recent phenomenon because of its contemporary political affirmations and its entry into the canons of dramatic literature. They have been unable to apply the techniques of periodization to the four centuries of interim Aboriginal cultural life that continued to preserve memory and build political community through performance, negotiating complex issues of tradition, modernism, and hybridity. The absence of First Nations theatre culture in Canadian theatre historiography has arguably been a form of cultural genocide. Only in recent years has there been a concerted effort to document and theorize First Nations work in terms that have been arrived at through collaboration with Aboriginal artists, activists, and intellectuals.

Much has been written on European representations of First Nations cultures. The first European theatrical performance in what is now Canada was also the first moment of racial masquerade. *Le Théâtre de Neptune en la Nouvelle-France* was a welcome masque, or pageant, constructed around classical allusions, written and staged by Marc Lescarbot at the French habitation at Port-Royal in 1609. In the masque, King Neptune, his tritons, and four "savages" welcome the returning Sieur Jean de Poutrincourt after his summer voyage along the American coast. The four Aboriginal characters pledge their loyalty to the King of France and offer him their land as tribute. Although there is a popular tradition that local Mi'kmaq men played these roles, there is no evidence to support that assertion, and because Lescarbot devised the play to keep the Frenchmen under his command busy, it is more than likely that the "savages" who gave their land away in perfect French poetic diction were Frenchmen in "redface."[17]

The impersonation of aboriginality is a deep structure in the development of North American culture, and it was so pervasive and formative that it shaped the terms under which indigenous performers could be seen; for much of the past two centuries, First Nations performers had to "play Indian" in a system of representation built upon cultural eradication. For some, this enabled a living as "authentic" performers.

Through this system of "licensed representation" the Indian Act and its amendments progressively banned traditional performances.[18] The most famous example is the banning of the potlatch in British Columbia. The 1885 amendment to the act stipulated:

> Every Indian or other person who engages in or assists in cele-
> brating the Indian festival known as the "Potlatch" or the Indian
> dance known as the "Tamanawas" is guilty of a misdemeanor,
> and shall be liable to imprisonment for a term not more than six
> nor less than two months in a jail or other place of confinement;
> and, any Indian or other person who encourages, either directly
> or indirectly, an Indian or Indians to get up such a festival or
> dance, or to celebrate the same, or who shall assist in the cele-
> bration of same is guilty of a like offence, and shall be liable to
> the same punishment.[19]

In 1996 the *Report* of the Royal Commission on Aboriginal Affairs addressed this law with the comment:

> In 1884 official policy turned from protecting Indian lands from
> non-Indians to protecting Indians from their own cultures. That
> year amendments to the *Indian Act* prohibited the potlatch and
> the Tamanawas dance. The potlatch was a complex ceremony
> among the west coast tribes that involved giving away pos-
> sessions, feasting and dancing, all to mark important events,
> confirm social status and confer names and for other social and
> political purposes. Tamanawas dances were equally complex
> west coast ceremonies involving supernatural forces and initia-
> tion rituals of various kinds, many of which were repugnant to
> Christian missionaries. A jail term of two to six months could
> result from conviction of any Indian who engaged or assisted in
> Tamanawas dances.[20]

There have been a few points in Canadian history when performance was banned in such absolute terms. The Catholic Church banned the-atre in New France as impious after the famous "*affaire Tartuffe*" in 1693; Newfoundland banned mumming as a "public nuisance" in the nine-teenth century; and the Toronto and Winnipeg police forces banned performances of the communist play *Eight Men Speak* in 1933. But none of those instances was an attempt at cultural genocide. In those instances theatrical practices were threatening the established order; the banning of the potlatch was a response to a practice that, as Christopher Bracken demonstrates in *The Potlatch Papers*, European thought was unable to comprehend.[21] The banning of the potlatch was an attempt to uproot and eradicate not just a practice but the culture that it expressed. We know that potlatches continued. These complex ceremonies were crucial to the cultural survival of the peoples; and in that sense the very continuation of the potlatch was an expression of oppositionality and cultural resistance.

In 1914, in an attempt to further suppress traditional ceremonials, the act was amended to extend this banning of cultural practice, so that in Western Canada government permission was required to wear traditional costuming.

> Any Indian in the province of Manitoba, Saskatchewan, Alberta, British Columbia or the Territories who participates in any Indian dance outside the bounds of his own reserve, or who participates in any show, exhibition, performance, stampede or pageant in aboriginal costume without the consent of the Superintendent General of Indian Affairs, or his authorized agent, and any person who induces or employs any Indian to take part in any such dance, show, exhibition, performance, stampede, or pageant, or induces any Indian to leave his reserve or employs an Indian for such a purpose, whether the dance, show, exhibition, stampede or pageant has taken place or not, shall on summary conviction be liable to a penalty not exceeding twenty-five dollars or to imprisonment for one month.[22]

On the many occasions when Aboriginal performers appeared in rodeos, pow-wows, and pageants, did their action signify cultural surrender or defiance? Pageants are particularly problematic in this regard, because all pageants are theatricalizations of power: they are enactments or negotiations of hegemony and colonized subordination.

In the most obvious moments of a colonizing spectacle that reinforces subordination, First Nations performers "played Indian" in a narrative and cultural geography in which they became objects of spectacle for urban, white audiences. A vivid example of this occurred in the 1910

Pageant of Ontario, written by John Henderson, a British military pageant master who for many years provided scripts for the pyrotechnic spectacles of imperial glory produced by Hands Fireworks Company at the grandstand of the Canadian National Exhibition in Toronto. *The Pageant of Ontario* was written for and with Toronto's elite militia regiment, The Queen's Own Rifles. In it, Aboriginal figures, including Tecumseh and Thayendanegea (Joseph Brant), enact enthusiasm for imperial rule. Brant is listed as being played "by one of his descendants," and Tecumseh "by one his lineal descendants." The absence of names erases the material reality of contemporary aboriginality by stripping the actors of identity. The inclusion of unnamed lineal descendants is in itself an act of cultural genocide. It is quite possible that these listings are theatrical hype, although the pageant did include a group of thirty-six men from the Six Nations reserve. The regimental history indicates that these men were "very appreciative of the fact that they had been permitted to present their race according to their own interpretation."[23] They were not, however, permitted to participate in the production of the fundamental terms of representation, which cast them as the last heroes of a vanished race, people who can step onto the stage only as a cultural memory.

In the CNE grandstand, playing minor prop characters – a kind of animated set piece – to showcase the glory of white soldiers, the First Nations participants were there to perform the landscape on which empire is built, and to serve as a mythic chorus to invest old Ontario with deep meaning. This was literally the case in the first "epoch," in which Governor John Graves Simcoe takes his leave to a "chorus of Indians" who chant, "No go, our Father! No go a-way-way."[24]

But what of pageants that took place on First Nations land, or in contested public space? Numerous Hiawatha pageants occurred on Aboriginal land across Ontario and the northern states in the last decades of the nineteenth century, and well into the twentieth. Many of them were produced on and with First Nations reserves (others, of course, had nothing to do with Aboriginal land or performers). One such was *Hiawatha, The Mohawk*, performed as a tercentenary pageant on Lake Champlain in 1909 (the year following Frank Lascelles's massive Quebec tercentenary pageant). The script of *Hiawatha, the Mohawk* was published in Kahnawake in 1981 by the Kanienkehaka Raotitiohkwa Cultural Center, despite its gross inaccuracies and its contentious historical claim that Hochelaga had been a Mohawk settlement. The importance of the pageant and the reason for its republication had less to do with its actual content than with the facts of its production. As a play, it is florid and offensive to modern sensibilities. It attempts to capture the language and rhythms of Longfellow's epic poem, and to combine those elements with an elevated theatrical diction. The result is a passage like this:

> Hiawatha: Ha! Ha! I was thinking how pleasant are swift hunting and racing and archery and listening to the adventures of renowned chiefs; but more than all how the greatest joy would be war. We of the Sacred Island, Tiotake, are dishonored for want of enemies; we do not fight enough, is always peace, peace. In the spring I will give a feast to the young men, and call on them to follow me to Stadacona, and there we will form a war party. In that way I shall bring honor upon our tribe, the mother and leader of the MEN OF MEN, the Hochelagas.[25]

The pageant was written and organized by a CNR agent who had recruited Iroquois participants for the Quebec pageant the year before. According to a pre-production note cited by the editors of the 1981 text, "The Indian players are drawn from the reservations at Caughawaga, St. Francis, Oka in Quebec and from Brantford, Garden River, St. Regis in Ontario, and from Onondaga, New York."[26] The stage of the pageant, which represented a longhouse, palisades, and a beach with canoes, was constructed on a barge, which was towed to various performance spots around the lake.

The publisher's preface in 1981 commented, "It is interesting to see that the pageant players came from the very communities dealt with in the play's act." In effect, the pageant appears to have enabled a cross-community gathering in which, despite the patronizing and reductive absurdities of the text, scattered and regulated Haudenosaunee communities could maintain a sense of nation. By "playing Indian" and re-enacting their history through the colonizer's filter, were they also enacting a cultural critique that contributed to militant survival? It is possible that the performance contained dissidence that would have been invisible to the white spectators. In a similar manner, the publication of the text in 1981, at a time when issues of cultural sovereignty and colonial power were building to crisis, marked Haudenosaunee agency in historiography and documentation.

A more complex example returns us to Winnipeg, where in 1920 Philip Godsell, a British explorer and novelist who seems to have understood the Canadian West as a vast land of adventure from the pages of *Boy's Own Paper,* took his turn as an imperial pageant master for the two hundred and fiftieth anniversary of the founding of the Hudson's Bay Company. Godsell was a HBC employee who worked in various posts across the Canadian north until taking up a full-time writing career in 1936; he ended his working life as a historical researcher for the Glenbow Foundation in Calgary. He was a prolific writer of non-fiction adventure, popular ethnography, pulp fiction, and sensationalist magazine articles.

While working for the HBC, Godsell proposed that the company mark its 250th anniversary with the "Red River Pageant and Indian Reception." In a typescript memoir written three decades later, he recalled:

> I suggested the possibility of a Pageant representative of an old time fur-brigade, manned by loyal Indians gathered from the principal tribes that had laid the foundations for the company's prosperity.
>
> I immediately thought of Lower Fort Garry, the Company's stone-walled stronghold on the banks of the Red River, only eighteen miles from Winnipeg, so rich in historical associations, as an appropriate setting for the affair. Ere long, arrangements were underway. Indians commenced to come from all quarters of the land; costumes were designed; birchbark canoes rounded up, and the Sioux at Oak Lake were delegated to complete a dozen tepees, whilst I arranged with Roderick Smith at Selkirk to build a couple of York boats.[27]

The pageant was a re-enactment ceremony, in which Godsell led the Native participants by water to the old trading fort, where they were introduced to Sir Robert Kindersley, Governor of the HBC. The ceremony ended with an exchange of gifts, pledges of friendship and loyalty, and a peace pipe.[28]

The degree to which the pageant infantilized the Native participants is clear from the rhetoric of Godsell's own writings about it. His description of the participants paints them as exotic, reminiscent of Rudyard Kipling's description of the Grand Trunk Road in *Kim.* Godsell writes:

Overlooking the Red River at Fort Garry, a village of decorated tepees soon housed a hundred Indians from many different tribes. There were Swampy Cree from Hudson Bay, James' Bay, Norway House and Berens River; Saulteaux from Lake Winnipeg, Ojibways from the Nipigon country; stalwart Wood Crees from the Peace and Athabasca valleys; swarthy tribesmen from Ft. St. James and the Pacific coast, and Refugee Sioux from reserves at Portage Plains, and Oak Lake and Prince Albert.[29]

They were there because the Company, in the person of Godsell, had summoned them. Dressed in fringed deerskin and moccasins, Godsell led the flotilla down the river. "As we disembarked, I gathered my Indians around me and led them to the greensward surrounding the flagpole."[30] In his introductory speech, he orated to the Governor and his party: "I have much pleasure in assembling before you on behalf of the Company the native representatives of most of the different tribes that the Company has been so long associated with. Your Indian guests have been drawn from all parts of the North country, many of them having traveled for weeks by dog team, snowshoe, canoe and other means to meet you." At the end of his speech, in an astonishing reprise of *Le Théâtre de Neptune en la Nouvelle-France*, he re-established the colonial tie: "My Indian charges are, I perceive, anxious to shake you by the hand and express to you the feelings of loyalty they still feel towards you and the Old Company." [31]

How did the First Nations participants feel about this? In his study of this pageant researcher Peter Geller suggests they were playing along because the event gave them an expense-paid trip and rendezvous. Most of them would never have been to Winnipeg, so it may have been a bit of an adventure. But if that was the case, it was a tightly scripted and regulated experience. The participants were kept in segregated quarters and forced to carry identity cards that read: "If lost, return this Indian to Hudson's Bay Company, 96 Main St, Winnipeg."[32]

Every aspect of the performance of the Red River Pageant was licensed, and the terms of representation, as Geller notes, were produced and scripted. Was there space in this performance for dissent and ambivalent spectatorship? In a later account of the event Godsell would say that he had told the translator at the ceremony, "If any of them talked foolishly, as they are sometimes apt to do, he was to substitute words of his own more suited to the occasion." Indeed, as it turned out the translator did feel compelled to overwrite one of the speakers' statements.[33]

The ceremony ended with a peace dance, which Godsell described as a "gyrating mob of Indians."[34] But what Godsell saw as a momentary return to history ("the shadowy forms of old buffalo hunters passing the pipe once more from hand to hand"), the First Nations participants may have seen as a moment of solidarity and congress, of resistance to the laws that banned their ceremonies, festivals, and clothing. The HBC had to negotiate with the federal government for permission to involve First Nations performers in the first place, and to allow the ceremony and dress. We do not know what was said when one of the speakers was deliberately mistranslated, but in that moment of theatrical re-enactment, others may well have seen a performance of dissent.

Staging the Great (Anglo) War

A wave of patriotic fervour – the overriding response to the First World War – rolled not only across Canada as a whole, but also through the theatre world. By early 1916, for instance, shortly before shipping out to France as a lieutenant in the Canadian Army, Toronto journalist Arthur Beverly Baxter was writing about the establishment of a Canadian National Theatre in Ottawa – a short-lived venture promoted by the Ottawa Drama League and inspired by the theatrical ideals of the British actor and director (and protégé of Bernard Shaw) Harley Granville Barker. For Baxter, the idea of national theatre was a direct consequence of the war. It was a necessary correction to a Canada that was "degenerating into a nondescript republic with money as its uncrowned despot." Baxter, who later achieved distinction as a theatre critic and politician in the United Kingdom (and a member of Churchill's war cabinet), suggested that the war had stunned Canadians into a realization of who they truly were:

> A mighty shout rose from the forests of Eastern Canada, and echoing on the Ontario lakes, sped over the Western prairie with throbbing clarity.
>> By the living God, we're British!
> Canada had found herself.[35]

When Canadian theatres during the war years reflected the war, it was as an expression of this kind of imperial patriotism. Later generations would speak of the emergence of Canadian national awareness in the war, but at the time the war was felt by many to intensify the British connection and give new life to the ideals of Imperial federation. In Toronto the most conspicuous theatrical tribute to the war was the 1916 production of Thomas Hardy's epic lyrical drama of the Napoleonic wars, *The Dynasts,* under the direction of the famous pageant-master Frank Lascelles, whose credits included the immense pageant of the Quebec tercentenary and the great Indian Coronation Durbar at Delhi in 1911, with its thousands of participants. In 1916 the Battle of Waterloo was not much further in the past than Passchendaele is for us today, still within the outside reach of personal contact, and the linkage between the two wars could be comprehended generationally. *The Dynasts* mobilized the social elites of Toronto – society debutantes served as ushers, the daughters of high society danced in the ballroom scenes, principal parts were played by professors from the University of Toronto. As it turned out, the production received more notice in the society pages of the press than in the dramatic columns.

While Toronto audiences were trying to find a way to understand the war in a patriotic drama that could assuage the pain of loss, Canadian soldiers were inventing their own form of theatrical enactment. The army theatre troupes (known commonly as concert parties), such as the Maple Leafs, the PPCLI Comedy Company, and – most famous of all because of its postwar celebrity on tour – The Dumbells, offered the men of the Canadian Corps a simulation of normalcy. The concert parties had started as off-duty entertainments, but by 1917 had developed into sophisticated professional operations. By the end of the war they included a fully equipped theatre and theatre school in Mons, France. They were in effect combat vaudeville: the shows consisted of satirical sketches, song and dance routines, and, always, female impersonators. Their fundamental job was to boost morale, and they became famous for their willingness to perform at the front and for their own heroic efforts to meet the demand for their shows, performing around the clock, at times under fire. If we can picture the front not as a line in the mud but as a vast network of trenches, depots, training facilities, transportation systems, prisons, staff offices, and hospitals that overlaid an immense military city on top of the villages and roads of France, we can understand that the concert parties were the closest thing Canada had to a national theatre during those war years.

In the work of these troupes we see the first dramatic re-enactments of the war. Along with showbiz glamour and laughter, the troupes developed dramatic tropes that began to assemble the experience of war into a shared narrative. Some of the scenes that poked fun at the daily routines of military life established tropes that recur today – such as the one about a Duchess greeting Canadian troops in an English hospital. She is not very different from the aristocratic Englishwoman in John Gray's 1978 hit *Billy Bishop Goes to War*. But the recurring image is of the *estaminet*, the makeshift café in a farmyard where many young Canadians had their first experience of French wine and French women. The Dumbells' *estaminet* scene, imported from the PPCLI Comedy Company, is revealing in its self-representation of the Canadian soldier. The men are variously Canadian, Scottish, and English in origin, as evidenced by the stage dialects of the surviving scripts; their humour is sardonic, filled with trench slang and markers of authenticity – the come-on calls for crown and anchor games figure prominently. Their attitude towards authority is casual, and their primary occupations are buying alcohol and flirting with the barmaids. Like soldiers in almost all plays about the war, they break into song frequently. The humour is inclusive, in that it stresses comradeship and mateship. But at the end of the *estaminet* scene, just before the sentimental farewell, comes a curious episode. To the modern eye the scene destabilizes our understanding of comradeship:

Q.M. How the old folks would enjoy it. Say, Al, it's four years since I saw my folks. I wonder what they're doing to-night. Will you sing it again, boys? (Quartette repeats, till they are interrupted by nigger entering with dud.)

N. It's alright, boys, I think it's a dud.

1ˢᵗ S. Take that out of here; it's liable to go off at any moment.

N. It's alright, I think it's a dud.

F.S. Alles vite.

N. Alright, I'll take it out, but I think's a dud.

(Exit nigger, loud report off and nigger falls on stage.)

J. Oh, he's dying,

Q.M. Yes, he wants to say something. What is it? Speak up, speak up.

N.   If you all see my folks, tell them –

ALL.   Yes

N.   Tell them –

ALL.   Yes

N.   Tell them I don't think it was a dud.

ALL.   More beer, madame.[36]

By modern sensibilities this bit of minstrel racism in one of the most popular concert party sketches is repellent. This is the racism of exclusion, the underside of the imperial attachment, and it reminds us that we must be careful not to over-romanticize our grandfathers or simplify the sentiments that motivated them.

From the concert parties we inherit a theatrical template of singing soldiers, canteen humour, flirtation, and cheekiness towards authority. These all enter our theatre culture as signifiers of the war, but the concert parties do not as a rule offer us enactments of combat. Surrounded by death, the trench entertainments did not need to represent it, except as a comical interlude. This theatrical template reached its fullest expression after the war, when it merged with the need to call witness.

The best example of this later trend is a play called *The P.B.I., or, Mademoiselle of Bully Grenay,* produced by veterans of the war at the University of Toronto in 1921. A fundraiser for the War Memorial – Soldier's Tower – at Hart House, the play subsequently toured around Ontario. It exists in two versions, a cut-down text amounting to half the play, published serially in the *Canadian Forum* in 1921, and a typescript filed in the United States Copyright Office in Washington, where it was collected, along with several hundred other plays, by theatre historian Patrick O'Neill in the 1970s.[37] The title of the play is the familiar short form for Poor Bloody Infantry, and the play re-enacts the experience of the common soldier within the frame of a dramatic melodrama. The story has two arcs: in one, a young soldier gains promotion to sergeant for heroism and wins the heart of a beautiful French barmaid; in another a young lieutenant learns lessons in leadership and comes to understand that he must trust the experience of his men. These plotlines converge around the capture of a spy in the ranks, the surly "Swedish-American" foreigner in the platoon who is really a German agent. The scenes shift from the *estaminet,* to the company headquarters dugout, to the trench fire points and the medical station.

In his study of commemorations of the war, Jonathan Vance notes the existence of the play but dismisses it in two sentences because of what he calls its "vaudevillization of the war experience."[38] But the play is vastly more complex than that. We can get around the melodrama because we understand that in 1921 there were few available dramatic models that did not require a popular plot. Hart House Theatre was a cradle of theatrical modernism in Canada, but that condition did not yet extend to methods of theatrical documentary, which is what *The P.B.I.* actually is. The plot is simply the means by which the experiences that the play re-enacts could be uploaded into theatrical coherence. Also, just because a plot is melodramatic does not mean that it has no truth. *The P.B.I.* is a documentary re-enactment melodrama, written eight years before R.C. Sherriff's *Journey's End*, the most famous play of the genre.

The *P.B.I.* has four authors, all of whom served at the front, and their combined experiences give the play its multiocular perspective. Of these authors, two won the Military Cross, a decoration reserved for officers who showed gallantry. Of the four, three were officers, in the Artillery, the Engineers, and the PPCLI – Princess Patricia's Canadian Light Infantry; the fourth, Herbert Scudamore, who instigated the project, was a private in the Fourth Battalion. All were members of the university's Great War Veterans Association, the Varsity Veterans. Scudamore was a divinity student and later became an Anglican minister in Chilliwack, B.C. His son died in Holland as a captain in the British Columbia Regiment in the Second World War.

But the *P.B.I.* had more than four authors. It actually had closer to forty. The four nominal authors wrote the scenario and plot, but the entire cast of veterans contributed their own material in the form of dialogue, gags, slang, jargon, characters, uniforms, and memories. The play expanded to embrace the people who needed to be in it. In this very important sense, the *P.B.I.* is a collective creation that assembles the shared experience of the cast and frames it in the cohering conventions of a genre play.

Far from being a reductive trivialization, *The P.B.I.* is an important document of the war because it is an enacted memoir validated by the entire cast. The play repeatedly stresses its authenticity. In the typescript version, the character descriptions in the cast list go on for four pages. The speaking parts include not just the roles demanded by the plot, but also what seems to be a deliberate attempt to cover the variety of military types and ranks: a green lieutenant (named, of course, Lieutenant Green), an inspiring first-contingent major who has risen from the ranks, a crusty sergeant, sappers, a signaller, a surgeon, medical orderlies, staff officers, a gas corporal, an Engineer officer, a comically fatuous but efficient Brigadier General, a French officer. At times they break into song (always in dramatic context), and extended sequences seem designed only to demonstrate the accuracy of the representation. Platoon parade formations, drill commands, crown and anchor calls: all function as memoir and testimony.

The script is filled with stage directions specifying gear and equipment, which were most likely provided by the cast. Even the program for the show documents something of the grim irony of trench humour with its dedication in "loving memory" to the defeated German soldier and its production credits: "Troops by Miss Canada," "Costumes by the Army Clothing Depot." This imperative to documentary accuracy seems to have been understood by the audience, if we can judge by Charlesworth's review: "A military play devoid of heroics, in which a vast number of characters are presented with verisimilitude that convinces the auditors who know, is something of an achievement. A real grip on the psychology of the young soldier was apparent in the writing."[39]

The documentary aspects of the play are not just textual and material. Equally important are the scenographic evidence and the unprecedented attempt to re-enact the experience of combat on stage. In both versions of the text, scene descriptions are extremely detailed, from the signage in the *estaminet* to the names of the magazines on the officer's dugout table to the deposition of the platoons along the trench – and the trench itself:

CHICORY TRENCH – A section of the front-line opposite Lens. A fire-bay and part of two adjacent traverses is seen. The trench is in good repair, the bottom being provided with bath-mats and the sides rivetted with "A"-frames and corrugated-iron while the batten of the fire-step is supported by expanded-metal and two-by-four uprights. On top of the traverse at the right flank of bay is a small roughly-whittled windvane. To the military left of this, there projects over the parapet a small box-periscope which has been camouflaged with a twist of muddy sand-bag.[40]

It matters to this play that these details are exact and complete, just as it matters that the character types are documented. These descriptions are not there to help future producers – the play was never published in an actable version. They are there to solidify, validate, and enact memory. They are testimonial evidence of war, confirmed by the collective involvement of the cast and reproduced in the responses of the audiences who witness.

So too are the combat sequences. In the third act, a wiring party, including the hero and the green officer, go over the top to fix a communications line in no man's land, which is depicted as "a tangled mess of rusty barbed-wire in which numerous holes have been blown by enemy shell-fire. This wire, with the corkscrew stakes and wooden posts on which it is strung, is all that is visible above the parapet except for the blue sky." Combat is depicted from the point of view of the men who stay behind in the trench, and its immediacy is achieved – as so often today – with sound effects. Again we see the imperative to get it right: "A distant German machine-gun away off on the right flank starts a continuous rat-tat-tat hammering and it is angrily answered by the scolding, staccato splutter of an equally distant Lewis Gun firing in short jerky bursts." Against this effect the play stages the practised routine of the men who live in this soundscape: "Percy finds the box and, taking out two grenades, holds one ready in each hand. Duke gives the pan on his Lewis Gun a slight twirl to make sure that the cartridge is engaged under the feed-arm and then he clicks back the cocking-handle. Percy makes a move as though he were going to pull the pin out of his bomb."[41]

"As though he were going to pull the pin out of his bomb": I am fascinated by the implications of that direction, because the gesture can only be understood by someone who knows how to work that kind of grenade. This level of gestural knowledge, of habituated movements, poses and postures as documentary evidence that authenticates the actors as veterans.

Finally, as the party returns, missing some of its members, but with a captured German, the scenographic war intensifies in a stage description that itself stands as a powerful act of witnessing:

> The Boche lays down a hurricane barrage. The shells go hurtling
> over, the big ones rushing at the supports with an express-train
> howl, the whizbangs zipping wickedly down on the front line. No
> Man's Land is leaping with heaving geysers of ugly black earth,

shot through with swift tongues of flame. The Hun machine-guns start sweeping-around, roaring like a cataract and rattling like a flock of steam-rivetters as they pour out a torrent of hissing lead that cuts through the air like a tremendous scythe. The Vickers and Lewis Guns soon take up the chorus and start their mad and frantic chattering while a fusillade of rifle-fire ripples and crackles along the front. Fritz is now shooting up flares of innumerable varieties – white Very-lights; ruby, green, orange and golden rockets, some of which are single balls of fire while others are clusters and showers of fiery stars. After a noisy rafale of some duration, the barrage begins to grow less violent.[42]

It is unlikely that the stage of Hart House Theatre could do justice to these directions, but they testify to the need to objectify and share the experience of battle.

The P.B.I. is an act of community witnessing. But to what end? Canada is rarely mentioned in the play, and there is no tinge of patriotism. Indeed, after four years of war and the victories of Vimy Ridge and beyond, the play still hits the notes of imperial affinity. After mulling over the memory of the young officers he has seen die, the major who is the conscience of the play speaks the closest thing the work has to a moral: "Beat the Boche; that is the one idea. Play the game; win, lose or draw, but come up smiling every time. It's not the man who counts but the regiment; it's not the regiment but the job; and wherever there is work to do, the British race is the race to do it."[43]

A telling song closes the play: "Oh we've had our fun/ killing off the Hun."[44] This is the text of combat masculinism, not of nationalism or patriotism. It is not a nation that this play witnesses being forged under fire, but a particular occasion of the nation. The Canadian Expeditionary Force had for the first time in history brought men from all parts of the country – some of them unwillingly – and jostled them together to produce an elite vanguard force in the Canadian Corps. *The P.B.I.* bears witness to the birth of a national army, which would become an instrument of nation-making, giving the Canadian government leverage to sit down at the table in Versailles.

The impulse towards documentary theatre was born of the shattering of illusions in the trenches. It was the German returned soldier Erwin Piscator who first used the phrase "documentary theatre" in the

1920s to describe his vision of a non-fiction theatre, a theatre of actuality and testimony. That same impulse was the driving force behind *The P.B.I.* At the same time it is a document of an ethnic and class hegemony that had been severely disturbed by the war.

Radio Futurism: William Aberhart and the Rapture of Agitprop

In 1923 William Aberhart, a school principal and bible group study leader, took to the stage of the Palace Theatre in Calgary to preach his Dispensationalist theology. Aberhart was one of many fundamentalist Baptists who embraced the theory that human history could be charted by biblical "dispensations" leading to the immanent "Rapture" preceding the "End Times" and the millennial rule of Jesus Christ. Where Aberhart differed from most of his fellows was in his intuitive understanding of the power of mass communication. He was a gifted orator, and in 1925 the radio station CFCN began broadcasting his sermons. In the next year he became dean of the Calgary Prophetic Bible Institute, and from there he used radio broadcasts, biblical prophecy, and theatrical agitprop to preach a new populist political program called Social Credit. With his command of modern communications technology, William Aberhart became premier of Alberta in 1935 and launched a conservative political dynasty that is still a dominant force in Canadian politics, following a direct line of descent to Stephen Harper.

In his campaigns, broadcast from the stage of the Calgary Prophetic Bible Institute, Aberhart made frequent use of agitprop theatre techniques. In his most popular and effective agitprops, the "Man from Mars" skits, satiric dialogue with a bewildered alien observer elucidated the "common sense" solutions of the Social Credit platform, which advocated a social revolution against both finance capitalism and communism. Like his contemporaries, Nazi Joseph Goebbels in Germany and Father Charles E. Coughlin in Detroit, Aberhart understood that the technological futurism of radio communication could channel politics as theatrical experience. In doing so, he discovered agitprop theatre, although he never used that term.

"Agitprop" comes from the Leninist proposition (put forward by Lenin in *What Is to Be Done?*) that the work of revolutionary organization requires agitation and propaganda. The portmanteau word is typical of early Soviet instrumentalist rhetoric, with its abrupt telegraphic compression. The generally unremarked existence of right-wing agitprop reminds us of what is at stake in the study of vanguard aesthetics. Although its leftist theorists in the 1930s theorized agitprop as the performance of revolutionary Marxist dialectics, the simple caricatures, mobile form, and reiterative pedagogical structures of agitprop offered a useful means of communication for the revolutionary right. They were there to be discovered, and as Aberhart showed, they were a logical extension of the new technologies that enabled remote communication.

If agitprop theatre is the mobilization through performance of a political movement, it must be analysed not as a set of forms and structures but as a shifting practice. On the left, agitprop would take to the streets to reclaim public space, largely because that was the only venue available to insurgent theatre troupes. On the right, agitprop functioned as an ancillary of – and sometimes the occasion for – mass media, and marked the radical right's ability to negotiate its presence in the radio revolution that transformed U.S. society in the 1920s, the decade in which Aberhart took to the air from the stage of the Prophetic Bible Institute to preach his message of apocalyptic redemption, the Rapture, and, increasingly, a distributive anti-finance social gospel. Aberhart discovered early on that agitprop and electronic media are aspects of each other: agitprop is the local experience of mass communication; mass communication is the dissemination of agitprop across a field to define a movement.

In the relationship of vanguardist agitprop and populist right-wing politics, with its characteristic suspicion of aestheticism, three vectors of modernism are at play: the historical emergence of agitprop as the theatrical tool of populist unrest; the spread of religious activism released by the "call" of radio; and the nature of radio technology itself, which transmits the felt response of the live audience.

"Radio friends"

The development of the European avant-garde parallels the rapid developments in wireless technology, and can be plotted against the increase in wireless communications and radio. In the mid-nineteenth century, telegraphy opened up the commercial possibilities of remote communication: nationalism plus markets plus telegraphy equalled imperialism. Telegraphy itself, prior to the invention of the wireless, was one of the formative conditions of modernism, roughly defined as the global era in which discourses of humanity and human subjectivity came to define the principles of economic and cultural traffic. The "global" reach of modernity was in fact the reach of imperialism. At the heart of modernity was the ability of mass communications to disseminate, mobilize, and silence social phenomena. (The first truly international labour action in North America was the telegraphers' strike of 1883.)

The rapid social acceptance of radio and the exponentially increasing sales of home wireless receivers brought about a radical transformation of North American culture that can only be compared in scale to the digital revolution of the late twentieth century. The wireless revolution opened up new cultural forms, new aesthetics, new political movements, and new religions. Radio manufacturers started broadcast stations to sell radios; stations sought new sounds to broadcast to recruit listeners, and in the process discovered that radio frequencies could be owned, and that time itself is a saleable commodity. William Aberhart, along with numerous other preachers, took to the air at the invitation of a local radio station. Radio was particularly attractive to fundamentalists like Aberhart who saw it as both a medium and a manifestation of prophecy. Prophecy, said Aberhart, is history foretold; history is prophecy fufilled.[45]

Aberhart came to radio after experimenting with theatre as a method of affective preaching. His first attempt at a theatricalized sermon was a 1931 apocalyptic drama written with his protégé and successor as premier of Alberta, Ernest Manning (whose son Preston later founded the Reform Party of Canada, and mentored the Conservative prime minister Stephen Harper). *The Branding Irons of the Anti-Christ*, although written in the form of a melodrama, is an agitprop morality play with simple iconic characters and fearsome effects, with sets and costumes designed by Aberhart.[46] The play details the operations of the Rapture, as three siblings discover that their mother has simply vanished into thin air while reading her Bible. We cut to the Antichrist and Satan who conspire to rule the world in a military dictatorship, and at the end of the play the two brothers, now sworn to the Antichrist, march their sister off to her martyrdom by firing squad. The play's blending of domestic melodrama, political intrigue, and fantasy effects is similar to the eschatological pulp fiction, such as the *Left Behind* series, that makes the best-seller lists today. According to Aberhart's biographers:

> The play was performed by members of the Bible Institute Baptist Church's Young People's Society and was taken to other towns in Alberta. Those who witnessed the performance were terrified. One young lady who was a member of the church discovered that the terror stayed with her for some time. Afterwards, when visiting a Christian friend and finding no one home, although the doors were open, she feared that the Rapture had occurred and she had been left behind to face the Antichrist.[47]

The Branding Irons of the Antichrist still has public currency. According to the Edmonton *Journal* in 2009:

> The play has been circulated by Alberta beef producers angry at the provincial government's mandatory requirement for ranchers and farmers to verify the age of their calves in the wake of the mad cow crisis. "The new Alberta Livestock and Meat Strategy is an example of the government using its omnipotent power to take full control of our livestock industry by forcing primary producers to obtain permits to operate," complained one rancher circulating the play.[48]

In the year after the play was first performed, Aberhart learned of and eagerly embraced what can only be called the right-wing socialism of Social Credit, a distributive economic system developed after the First World War by a British engineer, Clifford Douglas, and popularized by the actor Maurice Colborne (the first and less well known of that name). Douglas's theories spawned political movements in the United Kingdom, Canada, Australia, and New Zealand. Arguing that the total of wages paid in a consumption economy can never match the value of goods produced, Douglas proposed that the variable difference was a social credit owed to the taxpayers. Aberhart simplified Douglas's theorems to the proposition that finance capital owed the working people a return and campaigned on the promise of reducing the power of the banks and paying a monthly dividend of $25 to all Albertans. His Social Credit platform had the appeal of populist socialism without ideology, while preserving the sanctity of private property and wealth. Not surprisingly, the Social Credit Party swept the 1935 elections in Alberta.

Unlike the populist anti-Semite Catholic evangelist Father Cough-lin in Chicago, who thundered into the radio as if preaching to a great hall, Aberhart instinctively understood that radio was a projection into the domestic life of the listener. He was a natural orator, as one witness pointed out:

> He speaks fluently … and with violent gestures, waving his arms and raising an admonitory finger when the applause has gone too far. Now and again he draws a large handkerchief from his sober black coat and mops a dome-like brow gleaming from exertions. He has his audience under perfect control, drawing laughter and cheers as from a tap. As a rabble-rouser he is in the top flight.[49]

Aberhart addressed his "radio friends" in a folksy, colloquial manner laced with humour that was often as crude as it was corny; he was fond of making dialect jokes, especially in a minstrel-derived "Negro" voice. He stressed that the radio brought his hall audience and remote listeners into one conjoined acoustic space. In a broadcast in July 1935 he made both audiences into terminals of a communication loop:

> Hello, this afternoon is becoming more and more delightful for us to feel that there is a unity, a general sense of harmony between our nine hundred or a thousand people present in our large audi-torium, and the thousands and thousands situated in the homes, in the hotels, in the restaurants, in the garages and stores all over this Western land and away south into the States.... Here we have a number of people – Social Credit – in the gallery today. We're glad to have them with us. Going to ask them to greet you people out there on the air if they will, please by saying, "Hello, Comrades." Would you like to do that? Would you mind saying, "Hello Comrades," so that the people will hear you? Go ahead. (Loud voices) That's fine. Hope you heard the folks in the gallery; they've come a long way, some of them, and just want to say hello to you. Going to ask the people in the lower floor if they can do better than that and you say "Hello Comrades"? Come on, let's hear you. (Loud voices and applause) This is the first time that 500 people spoke on the radio at one time.[50]

As he preached both gospel and politics, his disembodied voice reached communities of listeners, mostly rural, who gathered around radio sets and responded in different ways with their own songs and sermons. In a typical report from a Social Credit club: "At 9pm the radio broadcast of Mr. Aberhart and his study group was tuned in and enjoyed. Mrs. Smith and the Young People's orchestra furnished appreciated musical entertainment. Attend these meetings every Tuesday night and hear the radio broadcast from a specially equipped radio."[51] The idea of radio as the voice of prophecy seems to have informed his theory of preaching. In a handbook on *Homiletics*, Aberhart stressed the effect of the preacher on the spectator:

> A speaker with a good personality has charm, power and attractiveness. Such a personality is said to be MAGNETIC, because it consists of personal attributes which draw people to the speaker and incline them to sympathize with or rally around him. This magnetism or attractiveness resides in the speaker irrespective of what he is saying.[52]

Aberhart's emphasis on "the speaker's genuine cordiality," on "stimulating good feeling" – on magnetism and vibration – collapses technology into metaphysics, and produces power. Clifford Willmott, who sat beside Aberhart in the CFCN radio station when he performed as the Man from Mars, recalled, "I used to like to imagine that if I could get up close enough to him I could hear that faint humming that sometimes emanates from the electric meter in a home. You've often heard it: hmmmmm. He seemed to be so vibrant with that feeling that it was a joy to be near him and to do things for him."[53] For Aberhart, radio was an instrument to make futures happen.

Aberhart's Martian and jollification

Radio had brought the future into the household; in the course of a decade it developed from a hobby for boys with crystal sets to a vast industry that transformed technology into furniture and reshaped the ways people used their living spaces. Radio was the voice of futurity but it had no iconic presence in and of itself – though it did summon its icon of futurity in the image of the Martian.

Ever since the U.S. astronomer Percival Lowell thrilled the world when he claimed to have scientifically demonstrated the existence of super-intelligent Martians in 1895 by his exacting study of the "canals" of Mars,[54] radio futurism and Martians were deeply connected. Lowell was sincere in his belief that Martians must exist, but they quickly became established in popular culture as the visual signifier of futurity. H.G. Wells brought them to Earth as a critique of imperialism in 1897 in *The War of the Worlds*, in which his technologically advanced Martians did to England what England had done to India. He made concrete the trope of the hyper-intelligent but soulless Martian who mirrors human progress without human emotions.

Lowell's theories had a substantial impact on the young Hugo Gernsback, who emigrated to the United States from Luxembourg in 1905, the year before Reginald Fessenden, a Canadian engineer working in Pennsylvania, broadcast the first wireless program. Gernsback was a polymathic inventor, writer, and entrepreneur. In his numerous publications devoted to radio, science, and the new genre of popular literature he called "science fiction," he introduced Martians as the recurring Other of a united human race (and gave his name to the annual Hugo awards for science fiction). In his lifetime he published dozens of magazines, primarily devoted to radio electronics, science fiction, and sexology.

In his many stories and publications, notably his novel *Ralph 124C41+*, written and revised between its serial publication in 1911 and its book form in 1925, Gernsback insisted that science fiction was an inductive prophecy of technological progress.[55] In *Ralph 124C41+* he envisioned a world organized by remote communications and the transmission of physical capacity through Ultra-Generators, Telephots, Hypnobioscopes, Tele-theaters, and Pulsating Polarized Ether Waves – the last of which, he prophesied, would bounce off physical objects to enable remote imaging. Gernsback predicted an economic monetary system based on labour value, similar to Aberhart's Social Credit system. He also envisioned robot police to control anarchist riots. Like Aberhart, he was frequently photographed beside a radio microphone.

By the time Aberhart took to the airwaves in 1925, the two basic tropes of domestic futurism had been established: pulp magazines about Martians lay beside radio sets across the continent. For most North Americans, this was the lived experience of avant-gardism. Gernsback rehearsed those futures in fiction; Aberhart implemented them in politics. Both of them used Martians to give them iconic solidity: as a typical ad for a Social Credit meeting announced, "We are expecting the 'Man from Mars' to visit us for a few minutes and Mr. Manning says he is all rested up now and is ready with his 'What is?' series."[56]

The Man from Mars was both a stage persona and a radio voice that exposed the idiocies of human government and advocated the logical, scientific principles of Social Credit. The Man from Mars owed as much to vaudeville as he did to agitprop, although in the unruly North American radical theatre scene the boundaries between the two were often vague. Performed by Clifford Willmott, a railway conductor who "combined a cultured English voice with a slow, indefinably East Indian accent," the Man from Mars found himself puzzling over the inequities of Earthling economic systems, meeting in his way agitprop foils including Professor Orthodox Anonymous, Jerry Bluffem, and Mr. Kant B. Done. After premiering on Aberhart's radio broadcast in 1934, he became a familiar figure in the flesh, appearing, in the words of researcher Moira Day, as "a white-bearded old gentleman" in his "bare feet and ancient garments." As a Social Credit announcement promised: "The members of this group will hold a big social evening and jollification at the YMCA on Monday evening, Oct 29th at 8pm. Included in the program of musical and vocal entertainment will be contests and games for all. We want everyone to meet 'THE MAN FROM MARS,' an attraction that you cannot miss."[57]

With the personal appearances of the Man from Mars, Aberhart extracted the tactics and iconographies of agitprop from the aesthetic theatre frame in which left cultural activists such as Piscator had placed them. The Man from Mars was at once agitprop, demonstrative street theatre, and the folksy surrogate of Aberhart's political power. His popularity drew upon the range of prejudices that Aberhart animated: rural discontent against urban elites, fundamentalist anger at left-wing socialism, Albertan resentment of centralized economic power in Ontario, and working-class rage against the banking system that had brought about the Depression.

The Man from Mars was more than a projection of Aberhart propaganda into the domestic space of the living room or the social space of the community hall. His Martian provenance was a skilful demonstration of Aberhart's understanding of radio's power to generate fantasy, and it served to reinforce his own claim to authenticity and truthfulness. The science fiction futurism, broadcast over the advanced technology of the wireless, confirmed Aberhart's prophetic theology as biblical science. His local, affective agitprops transformed dialogic theatricality into aural events that activated embodied spectatorship and response in the processes of political organization. The air vibrated, and when captured by the radio receiver the work re-embodied the somatic experience of the original live performance. Aberhart had discovered that radio could transmit feeling.

Although he rejected the artistic culture of modernism, Aberhart readily embraced its technologies and vocabularies. He was in practice a fundamentalist futurist. He saw that the capacity to transmit feeling multiplied and distributed his presence to a theatricalized population – theatricalized in that the dialectic of Aberhart's self-performance and the Man from Mars transformed his listeners into both an audience and political community. For Aberhart, the Man from Mars was a rhetorical device that exploited radio's capacity as an affective propaganda technology to evoke feeling in remote spectators. But the device also had a powerful performance draw, bringing the spectator into the spatiality of radio, a space of vibration, of being grounded and distributed. In that sense, the Man from Mars, and by extension perhaps all agitprop, was not a revolutionary artistic form but an avatar of mass communication technology. This principle the revolutionary left would earnestly refute – for them, agitprop was the proof of an internationalist proletarian modernism.

4

Six Comrades and a Suitcase

From Agitprop to "Eight Men Speak"

The only visual record of the only performance of *Eight Men Speak*.
L.W. Conolly Theatre Archives, McLaughlin Library, University of Guelph

Comrades, I hope the situation is clear to you. The question
is not: Agitprop theatre or stationary theatre. Our task is to
develop both types. For: we need both types as weapons in
the class struggle, the flashlight effect of the mobile up-to-
date agit-prop theatre as well as the impetus of the slower
but broad attack of the more complicated stationary theatre.
  – *John E. Bonn, director, Prolet-Buehne*

The business of the Russian Revolution was too brisk for
unnecessary syllables. Early Soviet industrial rhetoric exported around
the revolutionary left a telegraphic apparatus-speak: "Politburo" for
"Political Bureau" and "Comintern" are well-known examples, but my
favourite is the "Dram Buro" of the New York Workers' Laboratory
Theatre, which sponsored "Dram Contests." Dram Buro did not exactly
catch on, but another Soviet export, "Agitprop," has become so prevalent
today that its meaning has been distended. Following Lenin's linkage of
agitation and propaganda in *What Is to Be Done?* the original upper-case
term was introduced in the years following the Revolution as the name
of a Soviet agency set up to encourage the dissemination of propaganda
through art, especially books, films, and plays – art for political ends,
in other words. While contemporary agitprop carries a connotation of
radical anti-authoritarian dissent, the term originally expressed a highly
centralized, authoritative understanding of radical culture, and the very
collapsing of the two constituent terms – agitation and propaganda –
into "Agit-Prop" expresses that centralization.

    As *agitprop*, though, the concept has become the cultural noise that
it once attacked. If Agitprop was coined as a projection of power, its
lower-case cognate slips into the realm of what can only be called chaos
aesthetics, characterized by mobility, migration, and the dissolution of
formal aesthetics.[1]

The occasion of a visit to Edmonton in October 1933 by Prime Minister R.B. Bennett illustrates this point – demonstrating the undisciplined and icon-based performance that later came to be associated with 1960s counterculture "guerrilla theatre." The Unemployed Married Men's Association mounted a response to Bennett's arrival in town, and a series of photographs from their demonstration show a man, in tailcoat and top hat, holding a huge key (the key to the city, presumably) on what appears to be a railroad truck. The man is surrounded by other men wearing flour sacks advertising a mass meeting. The truck is covered in signs:

OUR BOYS CAN GET BETTER TRAINING
AT HOME THAN IN A CAMP

WE WANT WORK WITH PAY – NOT CHARITY

HERO'S 1914
BUMS 1933.[2]

The overt theatricalization of the Bennett impersonator and the costumed demonstrators signals a deliberate invocation of player and spectatorship, but the dissolution of dramatic pretence and causality – that is, dramaturgy – appears to undermine the coherence of performance. We can put a name to the performer because the RCMP was there and later filed a security bulletin: "J. 'Sambo' Bespalsko impersonated Premier Bennett from a so-called 'Bennett Buggy,' decorated with unemployed slogans, and men with flour sacks answered the address and afterwards the buggy was wheeled in front of the MacDonald Hotel."[3]

From the beginning, agitprop contained two tendencies, derived from the same point of origin, manifesting again the dialectic of order and disorder, the aesthetic and the unruly. That origin point was the automobile, which introduced the possibility of a new kind of performer-controlled mobility. Cars and trucks draped with icons, flags, and posters had become the basic structure of the parade float by the time of the First World War, and the realization that a performer-protester could now be mobile spiralled into a host of new practices, on the right as well as the left. In Alberta Social Credit took to the streets with motorized parades, and the Man from Mars was able to show up at picnic rallies because he could drive to them.

For theorists of the left, theatrical mobility provided much-needed evidence of a transnational proletarian art. In Germany, Piscator had envisioned a theatre that would be "technically as perfectly functional as a typewriter," a theatre-machine for the industrial age.[4] Left cultural theorists, like John Bonn and his collaborator Al Saxe, took this a step further to propose that the theatrical form of agitprop was a performance-machine specific to workers' culture. This was the plank on which the proposal of an international workers' theatre movement was built.

Weapon-Grade Theatre: The Theory and Practices of Agitprop

In Canada the workers' theatre movement occupies an important canonical position not only as one of the first theatrical projects to challenge the nation-building cultural analysis of the liberal elite, but also as one of the principal avenues of theatrical modernism. There is another sense in which the movement (both internationally and in Canada) was less a movement as such than an organizational rhetoric, but its influence is no less real.

In Britain, as Raphael Samuel points out, the reach of the Workers' Theatre Movement "was closely associated with the 'Left' turn in the Communist International (1928–1934), and its translation into terms of 'class against class.'"[5] In 1929 the changing political climate in Europe, particularly in Germany, the crisis of the Wall Street crash, and power struggles in the USSR resulted in the Comintern's declaration of what is commonly known as the Third Period militancy, after Stalin's phrase describing the final crisis in capitalist development and "a new frontal attack on the capitalist class of the world." To a large extent the Third Period policy was one of the instruments that Stalin used to consolidate his power in the Communist Party of the Soviet Union. But as reproduced through the Comintern, Third Period politics was an instruction to member parties to intensify political opposition and exploit "growing ferment among the masses."[6] In the Western industrial nations, the chief task of the Communist parties lay in the sphere of unionism, but in the first three years of the 1930s a prolific increase occurred in the number of party-regulated cultural activities, including theatre.

By 1929 the various practices of the militant theatres of the left had already clarified into two tendencies expressed in artistic methods and structural organizations. The first tendency, and the most evocative to modern minds, was the mobile agitprop founded on the model of the German Red Rockets and exemplified by the Prolet-Buehne and the Shock Troupe of the Workers' Laboratory Theatre in New York, Workers' Experimental Theatre in Toronto, and, in the United Kingdom, Red Megaphone and the self-named Workers' Theatre Movement. The second tendency was the "stationary" drama of companies such as the Yiddish-language Artef (Arbeter Teater Farband, or Workers' Theatrical Alliance) and later the Theatre Union and Group Theatre in New York, Theatre of Action in Toronto, Unity Theatre in the United Kingdom, and New Theatre in Australia. A number of companies had been constituted in the mid-1920s, but by the end of that decade the movement was running out of steam. The major exception was Prolet-Buehne, which announced in 1928 that it would henceforth focus exclusively on political action performances. In the renewed militancy of the class war, the mobilization of Communist agitprop troupes became an integral and often leading part of the wider social mobilization caused by the intensified unrest that followed the Wall Street crash in 1929.

In the years 1930–33, for instance, the Workers' Laboratory Theatre revived and formed its Shock Troupe; the first crudely typed, hand-lettered, and mimeographed issues of *Workers' Theatre* began to map the ideological ground of the movement; the Group Theatre formed out of the Theatre Guild; the various troupes in New York formed the League of Workers' Theatre and associated with the Workers International Relief (a sponsored organ of the Comintern); the newly formed League hosted a national "Spartakiade" in New York; Artef formed an agitprop troupe and publicly acknowledged the "splendid cooperation and guidance of the Jewish Bureau of the Communist Party."[7] In 1933, while she was studying theatre in New York, the young Toby Gordon saw Prolet-Buehne perform, and she subsequently returned to Toronto with a desire to do similar work; meeting a Young Communist organizer with the revolutionary pseudonym Oscar Ryan made it possible.[8] In 1933, too, the International Olympiad of Revolutionary Theatres in Moscow was exerting a direct influence on the development of agitprop troupes around the world by revising the terms of critical authority.

This was the period of Stalinist consolidation in the Comintern, when member parties around the world were purged of "right deviationists" (an echo of Stalin's victory over Bukharin), and Stalinist cadres, many of them trained at the Lenin School in Moscow, captured local party leadership. In most cases the Communist Party was only involved with theatre troupes at a distance, as a source of inspiration and ideological authority, and as the organizing body of performance events. The major exceptions in the United States were the Prolet-Buehne and Workers' Laboratory Theatre of New York, both of them closely connected to the organizational structures of the Comintern, and which together produced the *Workers' Theatre* publication. The other clear exception was Toronto's Workers' Experimental Theatre, where the close affinity of party authority and theatre can be explained by the relatively small size of the Communist Party of Canada and the personal involvement of senior party members and their families in the troupe. Despite the pretence of distance, Toronto's Workers' Theatre, with its 1933 presentation of *Eight Men Speak*, would represent an explicit staging of party authority.

In the United States, the CP–USA encouraged a wide diversity of troupes with complex differentiations. In the New York area, on the margins of a heavily capitalized theatrical culture, various workers' theatres claimed doctrinal authority but were distanced from the actual organizational centre of the party. The core ideological site of authority was the Prolet-Buehne and Workers' Laboratory Theatre, and the journal they jointly produced. These were the instruments employed by John Bonn, a German emigré who became director of Prolet-Buehne in New York, editor of *Workers' Theatre*, and later head of the New Theatre School. Bonn used them to begin a process of rationalizing and centralizing the New York troupes, deploying the language of political organization to legitimize and map political territory. As Herbert Kline, who assumed editorial leadership when *Workers' Theatre* became *New Theatre*, told the American Writers' Congress in 1934, the magazine was "not just a cultural organ, but a reporter, an ideological guide and an organizer as well."[9] The movement was defined by its exclusions, and terminology marked territory: in its second issue, *Workers' Theatre* published an open letter by the Workers' Laboratory Theatre to a "self-named Workers' Theatre," accusing it of appropriating the label for political opportunism.[10] The troupe's signature resonates with the industrial modernism of Comintern rhetoric: "Workers' Laboratory Theatre / of the W.I.R. /

Org.Comm." Reproducing the Communist Party's claim for control over the discursive terrain of the revolutionary left, the core groups of the workers' theatre movement claimed authority over the licence to invoke both ideological site (the working class) and political instrumentality (the "Movement").

But party regulation was never simple or uncontradictory; changes in hegemonic systems take place through negotiations for power between factions, sites, and practices. In its Third Period phase, the workers' theatre movement was marked by a struggle expressed in aesthetic debates that were codified in binary oppositions reflecting international factional struggles in the Comintern. In the recurring debates over form that fill the pages of *Workers' Theatre*, the major binary was that of the mobile and the stationary stages, and the issue at stake was their relation to bourgeois traditions.

Bonn was the most prominent advocate of the view that the mobile agitprop was a new, revolutionary, and sophisticated form that found its most developed practice in the troupe he directed. Its template was the highly disciplined mass drill of the German-style troupes, which migrated to North America with Prolet-Buehne, which Bonn immodestly (he had, after all, founded the troupe and was still its director) called "the most disciplined, and politically and artistically most advanced Workers' theatre in the U.S.A." The aesthetic of the mobile agitprop achieved its clearest articulation in Bonn's stagings and in the writings of Alfred Saxe, one of the principals of the Workers' Laboratory Theatre (he later came to Canada to run acting courses for the Theatre of Action and in the 1950s established one of the first method acting studios in Toronto). But their project of theorizing the theatricalist modernity of the widely circulated U.S. template agitprop, *Newsboy*, came under attack.[11] In his review of the Spartakiade, Nathaniel Buchwald, a member of Artef and a reviewer for *The Daily Worker*, criticized Bonn and the Prolet-Buehne, arguing that its "ringing, galvanic forcefulness" and "perfect rhythm" were "devoid of effective theatrical form" and "dramaturgical shaping."[12]

The international retreat from agitprop (indicative of the pressures leading up to the Popular Front) was foreshadowed in December 1932 at the Second Plenary of the International Union of Revolutionary Theatres (IURT) in Moscow, which "set out tasks" to correct "mistakes and failures." These all focused on the militant sectarianism that agitprop enacted. They criticized the "Serious underestimation of the bourgeois theatre" and "the inability of most of the IURT sections to create a 'united front' of the workers with social democrats and other theatre-organizations." The Plenary concluded that the "vigour and militancy of the agitprop troupes had caused the mistaken view to arise, that such troupes were the only form a revolutionary theater could take. This was left sectarianism which despised other theatrical forms." Finally, the Plenary announced, "Artistic weakness must be overcome.... The Olympiad could hope to overcome these weaknesses."[13]

The 1933 Moscow Olympiad of Revolutionary Theatre, projected as the climactic moment of the workers' theatre movement, was to be the stage for its ideological and formal retooling. The Olympiad was also to be the stage that firmly grounded the international workers' theatre in the ascendant politics of Stalinism. A ceremonial letter to Stalin written by (and likely for) the international delegates (which included U.S. observers although there were no U.S. or Canadian entries in competition) offered, "And we say to you Comrade Stalin: All our strength, all the power of our art we will devote to the cause of transforming the whole world into a Union of Soviet Republics."[14] This strategy failed; in North America Stalin's name was conspicuously absent from discussions of the workers' theatre movement, and in Britain the clumsy attempt to impose the cult of personality on the movement backfired when the dismal appraisal of the British entry in the Olympiad produced a backlash that exacerbated factional tensions.

The debates over form were closed in 1934 by the endorsement of socialist realism in the Soviet Union. There had been a hidden crisis in those debates. The opposition of transnational class practices, of international proletarianism versus international bourgeois aestheticism, masked a more complex debate about the discourse of nation. Agitprop had been put forth as a transnational form, a class practice, that modelled the historical process of revolutionary change in industrial society; the Olympiad used score sheets to rate entries from around the world on quality of performance, political analysis, and stage movement. But the Olympiad in its very structure embodied a critique of agitprop as a circumstantial form subject to what Nathaniel Buchwald called "infantile diseases." The Soviet entries in the Olympiad ostensibly demonstrated a post-revolutionary proletarian aesthetic that, having moved through the pre-revolutionary agitprop phase, could revisit questions of dramatic technique and artistry. Their presence demonstrated that agitprop would henceforth be considered a transitional form that preceded the artistic recuperation of national traditions. Buchwald, perhaps typical of the Western delegates, noted, "That [the Soviet entries] displayed superior artistic form and skill goes without saying."[15] For the visiting companies, and particularly the British movement, the experience of this turn of affairs was traumatic.

The renunciation of agitprop as a sectarian political practice called for a new rigour of craft and artistry, and was thus received as a release from the constraints of a form now understood to be inherently flawed. Michael Blankfort and Buchwald provided a typical text for this reformation at the American Writers Congress. They stated: "The agit-prop theater, as it was called, made a virtue of its crudity and started off on the wrong foot by proclaiming its independence not only from the content of the bourgeois theatre but also from its forms and techniques.... Gradually the agit-prop theater grew out of its infancy and began to show a decent respect for competent acting, staging, writing, etc."[16]

Reporting on the Moscow Olympiad, and the lessons learned there, Bonn capitulated in a statement that prepared the ground for the critical reception of the new socialist realism:

> Our attitude to the bourgeois theatre was up to now incorrect. I in particular had taken a wrong leftist standpoint in my report to the Workers' Cultural Conference on June 14, 1931, when I stated that there is no relation between bourgeois theatre and workers' theatre, as the bourgeois theatre approaches the rich while the workers' theatre approaches the workers. This attitude led to a dangerous neglect of the bourgeois theatre. But after a closer study and wider experience I now fully agree with my critics who urged a more active attitude towards the bourgeois theatre. The bourgeois theatre, as an instrument of our class enemy, must be fought by exposing its class character to the workers, by replacing it by a qualified workers' theatre art.[17]

This reassessment of artistry entailed a reconsideration of national tradition and popular form that would resituate agitprop in a history of popular "folk" art. Revisionism of this sort exposed agitprop as something more local than the Prolet-Buehne model; it could be seen as a chaotic anthology of local forms. In the United States these forms included vaudeville, Coney Island sideshows, "red puppets," and revolutionary circus. But at the same time that these localisms appeared to express national "people's" traditions, they also reinforced an organic notion of artistic form as something that evolves through stages of immaturity, maturity, and, ultimately, decadence (usually figured as "formalism"). In this process of revision, agitprop was not art, but the precondition of art.

Performing (for) the Party

In Canada agitprop developed as the primary effort of what has become known, largely without question, as the workers' theatre movement. It emerges in an ideologically conditioned history that has been retro-inscribed in the discourse of national popular art and placed in an ideological genealogy of oppositional culture. The existence of the movement has been accepted as a matter of record by theatre historians, based on a small number of recuperative historical surveys, interviews, archival documents, newspaper coverage, and a few memoirs (by Toby Gordon Ryan, Dorothy Livesay, and Peter Hunter) and biographies (of Joe Zuken and Tim Buck).[18] Clearly there was in the 1930s a productive field of engaged radical theatre culture that intervened in the public sphere, most famously in December 1933 with the production of *Eight Men Speak* by the Workers' Theatre of the Toronto Progressive Arts Club. But was it a "movement"?

The canonized history of the workers' theatre movement maintains that it was independent from but allied with the Communist Party, that it "evolved" or "matured" into the professionalized aesthetic regime of the Popular Front "Theatres of Action" and "New Theatres," and that it was a genuine movement within a movement. So why did a movement that was described in its moment as popular and widespread collapse (or "evolve") into a very small group of professionalized theatres?[19] And if it was not a movement but a simulation – an organizational tactic to give the appearance of a movement – why has it been remembered and recorded, by its participants and historians, as the real thing?

The term "workers' theatre movement" surfaces in Canadian usage in 1933, and appears to have become current in the months after the performance and subsequent banning of *Eight Men Speak*, a play that developed out of the complex of interrelated mass organizations actualized by the illegal Communist Party. The Canadian Labour Defense

League had authorized the activation of drama groups as part of its campaign to organize "Youth Defenders" in 1931 and had planned presentations of *Eight Men Speak* "through Canada." In the end, there was only the one performance (a subsequent production was banned in Winnipeg before it reached the stage).[20] Prior to *Eight Men Speak*, the Workers' Theatre in Toronto had been staging a series of agitprops and mass recitations at factories, picket lines, party rallies, and May Day celebrations for over a year. It was one of many drama groups on the Communist left, but unique in that it was closely affiliated with the centre of the party leadership through the agency of Oscar Ryan, who at one time or another (and often at the same time) appeared as a founding member of the Progressive Arts Club, a founding editor of its cultural journal *Masses*, publicity director of the Canadian Labour Defense League, a member of the Political Bureau of the party, and organizer of the Young Communist League. Ryan initiated *Eight Men Speak*, was one of its authors, directed it, and was a principal actor in it. He was also the husband of Toby Gordon (they had been living together as a couple since 1934, and would marry legally in 1949; she retained Gordon as her stage name). In his work Ryan embodied the complex of roles and positions through which the underground party activated itself as an alliance of mass organizations. This is the complex that Earle Birney satirized in his novel *Down the Long Table*, when his Trotskyite hero sets off to "reconnoître the Stalinite cover organizations" located "over a store on upper Granville Street" in Vancouver:

> Arrived in this dusty warren, Gordon first located the Left Library, from which Hansen had recently been expelled, and the Workers' Sports Association and the Friends of the Soviet Union, whose cards were clustered on one dark doorway; across the hall he saw the stenciled signs of the Vancouver Committee of Unemployed Councils and the Workers' Unity League. Walking past these down an empty dirty corridor whose walls were splattered with posters, including an elaborate, colored chart of the Second Five Year Plan, Gordon entered an open door marked Workers' International Relief, Workers' Holiday School and Canadian Labor Defense League.[21]

Outside of the frame of party organization, the Workers' Theatre was understood to comprise dozens of local drama clubs across the country. It was a party propagandist, Ed Cecil-Smith, who initially suggested (in *Canadian Forum*) that the workers' theatres represented a popular movement of progressive groups that had "sprung up" across the country, and who suggested that there were "more than sixty" such groups shaping "the probable growth of the movement." Like Oscar Ryan, Cecil-Smith was a journalist on party newspapers, a writer of agitprops, co-author of *Eight Men Speak*, and an actor in the play; later he commanded the Mackenzie-Papineau Battalion in Spain. Writing in the party newspaper *The Worker*, Cecil-Smith amplified his claim about the sweep of the movement with the statement that the Progressive Arts Club "has contacted nearly a hundred other groups."[22] But even Toby Ryan admitted decades later:

> I think the catalyst for the spread of these kinds of organizations was when our publication, *Masses*, carried reports, opinions and informational matter. It's hard to separate – the chicken or the egg – because we had to have somewhere to sell the magazine to. But I think the magazine stimulated the proliferation of these organizations. Plus little towns that would write to Workers' Experimental Theatre and say that they would like to start a theatre like ours. "What should we do?" they would ask. "Send us some scripts. What kinds of things are you doing?" We gradually grew as word got around.[23]

The problem for the incipient movement was that most of these new groups were organs of the ethnic "language mass organizations," which, although they surrendered their status as founding "federations" in the party by orders of the Comintern in the Stalinist reorganization in 1929, stubbornly and jubilantly performed their cultural autonomy. The largest of these was the Ukrainian Labour Farmer Temple Association, which in 1935 sponsored eighty-three drama groups across the country.[24] After having formed the first radical theatre troupes in Canada in 1907, by the 1930s, when its members were discovered to be part of a working-class movement, the Ukrainian left had built a vast repertoire of radical plays inflected with the shifting crises of Ukrainian left nationalism and its unsteady alliance with Stalinism. A 1926 RCMP report on an event in Drumheller, Alberta, observed: "This play was very interesting from the Bolshevik's point of view; it represented the most miserable life of the working class under the capitalists' system in Russia, and after this a change took place in that country [and] the workers possessed all the wealth, and used the same for their own benefit. There were about 150 present, composed of Ukrainians and a few Russians and Jews."[25]

Workers made theatre, and some of the theatre they made was workers' theatre as the term was cohering into a definition regulated by the International League of Workers' Theatres. But this was far from a *movement* of workers' theatres, and the further it was removed from the doctrinal centre, the more varied were the forms of its performances, as Peter Hunter discovered when working with ethnic federations – which "constituted the base" for the Communist Party – in Toronto as Secretary of the Youth League Against War and Fascism, attached to a "closed YCL [Young Communist League] unit":

> The Ukrainians stressed folk dancing, mandolin orchestras, and plays which always seemed to revolve around a buxom peasant girl whose poor parents and her chastity were threatened by the local landowner. The Russians' plays were in a more historical vein and usually based on the 1905 Revolution. The disciplined, hardy Finns insisted on physical culture, co-ops, and steam baths. The Polish Workers' clubs' plays dealt mostly with high society and provided an opportunity for the cast to wear dress suits; Polish national pride always showed through.[26]

Poet Dorothy Livesay worked with the Montreal Progressive Arts Club in 1934 and later recorded a similar reaction:

> One of the tasks I was given at the time was to help create an ethnic festival of working class plays and songs. This meant contacting Ukrainian, Russian, Latvian, Swedish, Finnish and French labour organizations and getting them to send their singers, dancers and actors in competition to the festival. I wish I had kept the programmes! I was entranced with Swedish and Finnish singing, and rather horrified by a Polish play which depicted capitalism as a serpent with a long tail, thrashing about dragging the Workers down. This was a bit too much agit-prop for me![27]

Such diversity dazzled activists who were more familiar with the contained, barely expressed theatricalities of an anglophone Canadian culture that had not yet learned to accommodate an emergent multiculturalism. Anglophone Canadian culture has few discernible antecedents of a workers' theatre; rather, it shows a certain resistance to it, as the communist chairman of the Halifax Trades and Labour Council discovered in 1926 when he proposed that the TLC sponsor a workers' theatre; as the RCMP reported (its agents were everywhere), "The Trades and Labour Council, however rejected the idea and it is unlikely that the scheme will prove effective."[28] When theatre culture does appear in the anglophone centre of the party, it is couched in terms of cozy paternalism, not mass action. So it is that Oscar Ryan, in his folksy biography of Tim Buck, evokes the picture of "A summer Saturday afternoon, Toronto, 1927. Half a dozen young communists rehearse a one-act play, something about the underworld, a barge, the River Styx. It will have a single performance as part of a youth evening. Draped in a sheet as the mythological boatman is Tim Buck, intoning his tongue-in-cheek lines with very obvious relish."[29] Years later Toby Gordon Ryan insisted that the Workers' Theatre received no support from the Communist Party, and in the material sense – in the sense that the party expected its organs to raise their own funds – this was obviously the case. More than that, the party was mainly concerned with the theatre only insofar as it provided one more field of mass action. For the most part, the Workers' Theatre in Toronto served as an evangelical propaganda service. It performed at May Day rallies, party picnics, and summer excursions, and even in this it encountered the blunt antitheatricalism of anglophone Canada. One of the historic ironies about the Workers' Theatre is that it was directly subsidized by its one refugee from bourgeois wealth, Jim (Jean) Watts, who figures prominently and ambivalently in the memoirs of both Toby Gordon Ryan and Dorothy Livesay.

The crisis for the activist planners of the workers' theatre movement was that the groups that were most active, that actually produced and attended theatre productions, were the ethnic constituencies for whom theatre marked autonomy and difference (and for that reason they generally performed in their languages of origin). The normative culture sphere – that of the "Canadian people" – had shown little interest in theatre. The governing scripts of the Workers' Theatre – its vocabularies, staging conventions, theoretical statements, and many of its play scripts – were largely adapted from U.S. and British sources. In the United States and Great Britain the workers' theatre movement functioned as a radical counter-discourse on the edge of an informing metropolitan theatre culture; in Canada it defined itself against the absences of an imagined theatre.

In consequence, the workers' theatre movement was marked by conditionality and desire, as something that was always coming into being, and so it remained until the cultural activism within the party revised its terms and discourses to embrace the "people's" culture of the Popular Front period. The historical moment of the workers' theatre movement (understood as an aspiration rather than an achievement) occurred, then, in the period between 1933 and 1935. In spring 1934 *Masses* and the Progressive Arts Club took part for the first time in the annual international Ten Day Campaign for Workers' Theatre, but the focus in Canada was less on theatre culture than on the circulation of the magazine, which offered a centralized regulatory practice for the hypothesized movement. After admonishing activists that the campaign should focus on the magazine, *Masses* made an explicit point:

> Remember, this is an International Theatre Night and this must necessarily be reflected in the programme, which should be as varied as possible. Only one short one-act sketch is needed on the programme. The rest of the time will be taken up with musical selections, choirs, bands, chalk talks and so-forth. The aim should be that every organization in your district must be represented on the programme of this theatre night.[30]

Theatre work didn't matter, because the work of making theatre mattered more. The descriptions of the workers' theatres in *Masses* invariably focused on the number of new groups that "may" come into being, or "are interested" in or "in touch with" the magazine. This provisionality was the essence of the movement, which was manifest not through theatre work but rather through the organizational efforts to define the network of emergence. This is in the end why the workers' theatre movement disappeared (or "evolved") with the formation of Popular Front troupes: the movement had never been more than a regulatory practice.

The workers' theatre movement is remembered as a text that supersedes its historical practice, but it has been dismembered through complex intersections of historical trauma and political necessity (if not expediency). The major work of record on the movement is Toby Gordon Ryan's memoir, *Stage Left: Canadian Theatre in the Thirties*, in which she narrates the Workers' Experimental Theatre as a youthful, naive prehistory of the professionalized Theatre of Action (with its U.S. director from New York), which she helped found in 1936. Nowhere in the book is there. a mention of the Communist Party, nor does the party make an appearance in the several interviews that she and Oscar gave in later years.

When I first met the Ryans in the mid-1980s, they were deeply troubled by any linkage between the Workers' Theatre and the Communist Party.[31] I found this evasion difficult to understand until I began to appreciate the imperatives of the mantle of secrecy inherited from the days of the underground party, pressured by the internal trauma of Khrushchev's Twentieth Congress revelations and the external force of vicious anti-communism. This was a culture of defiance and secrecy, of concentric circles of knowledge. It had its origins in the activist work of the underground party, which stressed the importance of secrecy, but it was fossilized by the very real persecutions of the 1950s (and beyond). Even in 1933, when the party was underground, Cecil-Smith spoke of the Workers' Theatre as playing to a meeting that included delegates from "Labour Parties, Socialist Parties, C.C.F. clubs, Labour Defence League branches and Mass and Cultural Organizations of Workers."[32] In the 1950s no one spoke of the party at all, and when Toby Gordon Ryan reorganized a left-wing drama group after the war, she gave it the innocuous, heavily masked name of "Play Actors."

At the same time this denial was also a renunciation of the political aesthetics that the workers' theatre movement was proposed to articulate, and which was overturned by the move to the Popular Front. In this, mindful of Raphael Samuel's observation that history is made by a thousand hands, the problem takes on different characteristics in Canada than it does in the United States and Great Britain.[33] British cultural historians such as Samuel tend to agree that the workers' theatre movement (and in the United Kingdom there was indeed such a movement, so named) was terminated by the right turn to the Popular Front; they see the workers' theatre movement as a highly theorized moment of radical working-class culture. In the United States the dissident left position is represented by Michael Denning, who argues in his exhaustive study *The Cultural Front* that the workers' theatre movement was a stage in a vast historical bloc of radical culture in which the Communist Party was one of many players.[34] British historians recuperate the radical left in a vision of a working-class culture absorbed into the soft centre; U.S.

historians recuperate a progressive working-class culture that may still retain a capacity to resist dissolution in right-wing conservatism. In both cases the question of the workers' theatre and the shift in the era of the Popular Front raises issues of contemporary cultural genealogy.

But what of Canada, where the workers' theatre movement was both a movement without theatres, and theatres without a movement? Historians on the left have been divided, not because of ideological pressures but because of shifting loyalties. The knowledge of a workers' theatre has been a personal gift, transferred under conditions of loyalty, so that dissent has had an ethical price. Communist Party loyalists and friends have reiterated the thesis that there were no discontinuities, that the workers' theatres evolved and matured into the theatres of action, and in this they have also reiterated the governing tropes of Canadian cultural federalism as articulated by Massey: we were young, we were naive, but we matured into a professional culture. Communist Party doctrine always mirrored statism in its structures, and this tendency carried over into the cultural field.

Against this, dissident left historians have been more comfortable with the image of ruthless Stalinist commissars liquidating the workers' theatre and erecting monumental bastions of socialist realism in the name of the people. This was the subtext of the minor controversy that followed the 1976 publication of an anthology of workers' theatre plays, *Eight Men Speak and Other Plays from the Canadian Workers' Theatre.* Produced by an independent socialist publishing collective, New Hogtown Press, the book carried two introductions, a preface by the publishers, and a longer historical introduction by Robin Endres. The publishers distanced themselves from party orthodoxy and made the point that the workers' theatre movement "was not allowed to die a natural death" but had been "cut off by the Communist Party's move toward the Popular Front."[35] This statement directly contradicted the thesis of the editors, Endres and Richard Wright, who argued for evolutionary continuity and, following party practice, avoided a direct linkage of the Workers' Theatre to the Communist Party. (You can imagine the phone calls. This is why most copies of the book came with an insert in which the editors in turn publicly distanced themselves from the statements of their publishers.)

Both of these positions are equally right, and both are equally reductive, because in Canada the indeterminacy of the movement meant that it could follow equally indeterminate paths to its futures. It was and was not a movement; it was and was not terminated by the Popular Front;

it did and did not evolve into the humanist social action theatres of the later 1930s; it did and did not initiate a continuous tradition of interventionist collective creation that lives on in Canadian theatre culture.

As the workers' theatre movement occupied its ambivalent historical space, confirming and contesting ideologically conditioned narratives, memorialized as the one productive legacy of the Communist Party that it elides, it also erased the wider field of performativity that generated it. In this sense the very proposition of the workers' theatre movement is an act of disguise and dismemberment that collapses a vast,· plural historical experience into a narrow canonical record. In this event the tactical naming of the movement has been historically successful: theatre history has faithfully followed the script.

What has been lost is the historical complexity that generated that script. Even in its inception the workers' theatre movement was recognized as an organizational tactic sustained by a wider field of performance than it could contain. In the summer of 1932, shortly after the Workers' Experimental Theatre staged its first performance (an agitprop called *Deported*), a writer in *Masses* made the point that "street parades and demonstrations are all part of the Workers' theatre."[36] The proposal of a workers' theatre movement effectively sectioned the organized stage from this wider field of performance, but in fact the two fields were tightly integrated, and most of the model performances of the Workers' Experimental Theatre took place in larger social contexts, at party and Canadian Labour Defense League festivities and rallies (in June 1934, for example, the troupe performed on a cruise boat taking party members from Toronto to a jamboree in Port Dalhousie).

The rousing performances that gave the ephemeral practices of living the party a larger sense of social structure and a feeling of shared emotional experience took place in a broad horizontal field of performativity that included not only such festive gatherings but sports associations, celebrations of "ethnic" culture, summer camps, parades, demonstrations, and "red funerals." Some of these were overt attempts to enact a calendar of ceremonial observance, such as memorial rallies to commemorate the Paris Commune and the Polish-born German revolutionary Rosa Luxemburg. Closely related to these events were the semi-private rituals of the party and the solemn parades and oratories of party funerals. Most public were the staged displays of power at the high points of the revolutionary calendar; of these the most important was the May Day parade.

May Day was not a Communist event, but the party claimed it as its own and dominated organization of the parades and events that took place across the country; the size of the May Day parades directly reflected the party's popular standing. Political performances and Communist theatrical organizations merged in these events: they were demonstrations of the party's claim to ideological control of the left and displays of political will. In Edmonton in 1936 (the RCMP tells us), the parade numbered "about 1,700" participants:

> An old wagon drawn by five members of the Communist Party and loaded with sacks of sawdust representing capital headed the parade. On the sacks of sawdust sat three participants representing Capitalism, Fascism and War; the latter being represented by a fellow dressed as a soldier with an imitation machine gun. Behind the wagon marched four men carrying a black coffin bearing on its side the word "Capitalism," also the inscription "Here Lies the Body of War and Fascism." After this came four grave diggers carrying shovels beside a banner with the inscription "People's Unity," the "Grave Digger of Capitalism."[37]

In that same year Toronto's May Day featured three parades numbering some twenty thousand (including a thousand Young Pioneers in uniform). The parades converged on Queen's Park and passed in review before Buck and visiting Communist and trade union dignitaries. A large meeting that evening featured "mass singing, gymnastics, dancing and speech making."[38]

A particular moment in the party's history proved to be its grandest moment of performance and marked the high tide of the organization's fortune. In 1934 the Bennett government gave in to the public pressure so successfully orchestrated by the Canadian Labour Defense League and released Buck and his comrades from jail. The party rally staged at Maple Leaf Gardens to welcome him home in December 1934 was a mass spectacle of power and solidarity – a combination of festival, political rally, and simulation of a mass movement – clearly marked by signifiers of Soviet power. The Toronto *Daily Star*'s report captured the sense of mass elation and spectatorship that filled the Gardens to its capacity of seventeen thousand (with another eight thousand people standing outside):

> Youngsters wore red caps and the young pioneers from Fair-
> bank looked like a small army of red riding hoods with berets
> crushed down on their heads and big red scarves around their
> necks. Some wore complete red costumes tinted with silver....
> On the platform were baskets of red carnations and red roses
> and a wreath with long red taffeta streamers.... Thirty-four
> men in white trousers and gym shorts from the Workers' Sport-
> ing Association carried Tim Buck shoulder high to the platform
> amid a storm of cheers. Behind came 14 young women in wine-
> colored knitted suits walking with military precision.[39]

The RCMP report confirms these details (except that it dresses the
women in "black skirts with knitted, maroon sweaters") and adds the
presence of a "monstrous picture of Lenin and Stalin almost 40 feet long
and 30 feet high. It was a contribution from the Progressive Arts Club."
In its editorial comment the next day, the *Star* downplayed the obviously
impressive effect of this spectacle by commenting, "It must have seemed
to Tim Buck that all his meetings that the police had ever dispersed had
come together in one place."[40]

   On this occasion, generating an embodied, physiological rapture
though spectacle, the party performed itself as a simulacrum of the revolution. The performance *was* the party, not just iconically but materially. In
this wider field of performance the Workers' Theatre was relatively incon-
sequential even though, decades later, the workers' theatre movement
continues to occupy canonical space. In part this is a sign of the failed
cause: tactically detached from its party origins, the narrative of the workers' theatre movement survived the erosion and collapse of the Communist Party. At the same time the inner discipline of the party confirmed its
power as a historical condition of memory. It is because of this discipline
that the radical diversity of revolutionary agitprop vanishes from memory
and the workers' theatre movement appears as an overwritten narrative.

Motoring to the Masses

In her memoir, *Stage Left: Canadian Theatre in the Thirties*, Toby Gordon Ryan describes how as a young woman in a working-class Jewish
family in Toronto she defied her parents and made her way to New York

to study acting. Her two years in New York at Artef introduced her to the theories and techniques of Konstantin Stanislavsky (still considered experimental and tinged with Soviet modernism). When parading in the Artef contingent on May Day in 1931 she was exposed as well to the agit-prop performance of Prolet-Buehne. For the young Toby Gordon, this was a transformative moment – or so she recalls (it is difficult to believe that it took her more than a year at Artef to discover Prolet-Buehne): "Their theatre was completely mobile. They wore a basic neutral costume adding props and bits of clothing for each characterization. Their mass recitations were beautiful and well expressed their feelings."[41]

Returning to Toronto, Gordon soon fell in with a group of young cultural radicals who were coalescing around the newly formed Progressive Arts Club. Through Avrom Yanovsky, then beginning a distinguished artistic career and making a name for himself with his caricatures and chalk talks (inspired by his reading of Bengough), she met Oscar Ryan (born Weinstein; Ryan was an adaptation of his mother's surname, Rein). As collaborators, partners, and spouses, the two would remain together until Oscar's death in 1988. Oscar Ryan was at this time publicity director for the Canadian Labour Defense League. In 1929, as a delegate to the party convention from the Young Communist League, he had been an early supporter of Buck and the hard left turn. A novelist and a biographer of Buck, Ryan was dedicated to a revolutionary life. In later years, as theatre critic for more than three decades for the *Canadian Tribune*, he wrote under the name "Martin Stone."[42] In *Masses*, the cultural magazine that he co-founded and for which he wrote the inaugural editorial, he sometimes took the pen name "Maurice Granite." Insiders would recognize the minerality of these proper names as a gesture to Stalin's "Steel." In *Down the Long Table*, Earle Birney includes a dramatic sketch of a meeting of the "Social Problems Club" in which his young protagonist is demolished during a presentation by a dogmatic and authoritarian proletarian intellectual, who may well have been modelled on Ryan.[43]

The founding of the Progressive Arts Club and its theatre troupe, originally called Workers' Experimental Theatre and soon truncated to Workers' Theatre, was Ryan's initiative – possibly after meeting Gordon and hearing about Prolet-Buehne – but it flourished because of the remarkable community of writers and artists it attracted. Among them were Dorothy Livesay, Stanley Ryerson, Yanovsky, and a young electrician, Frank Love, who was one of the Club's few actual proletarian workers. Love came to the group with no experience but soon found himself writing plays, including major sections of *Eight Men Speak*.

A mobile agitprop troupe could not be possible without a means of mobility, and for a troupe of students and unemployed workers in the middle of the Depression, that was a far reach. The solution was provided by the troupe's one wealthy member and its de facto patron, who not only provided transportation but also paid the rent for the office and often fed the troupe. Jim Watts was a sometime medical student at the University of Toronto, and the rebel daughter of a wealthy business family. Described by researcher Larry Hannant as a "female gender maverick," she was a catalytic figure whose charisma and energy dazzled many who worked with her.[44] Her mixture of androgyny, zeal, and creativity made a profound impression on both Toby Gordon and Dorothy Livesay; for both, Watts appears to have modelled a new kind of feminist sexuality and social autonomy. Her wealth and class background gave her access and cultural power, but she also had a forceful character. It was after a heated debate with her that Earle Birney ended his brief flirtation with the Communist Party and turned to Trotskyism. Later he caricatured her savagely as Kay, the sexual predator Stalinist in *Down the Long Table*. Watts became one of the few Canadian women to serve in the Spanish Civil War, first as a correspondent for the Communist paper *The Daily Clarion* and then as a member of the International Brigade, joining a British medical unit.

Watts's leadership role in the emergent Workers' Theatre appears to have been gradually suppressed as the activities of the group neared the inner circle of the party, particularly around *Eight Men Speak*, but she rebounded to play a major leadership role when the troupe was reconstituted as Theatre of Action in 1936. Her career exemplifies the stratum of women's cultural and political work that made the radical left movement possible in the 1930s.[45]

Gordon and Watts were the creative and organizational team that made the Workers' Theatre a success. For them it was a full-time activity, but it was the two men employed by Party organizations – Oscar Ryan and Ed Cecil-Smith – who were the public voices of the troupe and controlled its repertoire. As Defense League publicity director, Ryan encouraged the troupe and facilitated its touring schedule; as a journalist (although he preferred the term "newspaperman" as more working-class) with *The Daily Clarion*, Cecil-Smith was the troupe's propagandist and public defender. Both Ryan and Cecil-Smith wrote for the troupe;

neither Gordon nor Watts did (or if they did, the work never reached the stage). The Workers' Theatre in that sense operated with two pairs of directors: the artistic women and the apparatus men.

The Workers' Theatre became the model for a small network of similar troupes that weathered the shift from agitprop to Popular Front mainstream social realism. The other troupes that left discernible traces and active cultural memory were located in Montreal, Winnipeg, and Vancouver. In each case a connection was made to the organized Communist left, but only in Toronto was the troupe deeply tied into the party's leadership structure. This is an important point in light of the Ryans' later repeated denials that the group had any involvement with the party. On one level, they were literally truthful, in that the party as such did not exist legally in 1933; on another level their avoidance of even the word "communism" leads to historical elisions only flimsily covered by such phrases as "a small group of interested people."[46]

When Gordon saw Prolet-Buehne in New York she was impressed first of all by its mobility. But Prolet-Buehne's drilled, mechanistic performances enacted a vision of proletarian modernism that proved difficult to replicate. The two-year history of the Workers' (Experimental) Theatre was a constant process of emergence, of coming into being and negotiating a critical attitude towards modernist aesthetics and experimentation. The elimination of "Experimental" from the troupe's name may have been more than editorial economy. Perhaps it was the product of an ideological struggle within the Progressive Arts Club over the correct line of artistic theory. The high point of proletarian modernism and radical cultural theory was also the period in which the ground of theory was shifting to adjust to the move towards cultural alliances and classical aesthetics that helped prepare the ground for the Popular Front. In this shift, experimentation came to be associated with counter-revolutionary formalism. Proletarian vanguardism was giving way to a wider concept of "people's art."

By training and experience, the founders of the Workers' Theatre were for the most part conservative in their artistic interests. The exception was Toby Gordon. Her theatrical tastes had been formed when she was growing up and watching the classics of the Yiddish theatre, including Shakespeare in Yiddish, at the Standard Theatre in Toronto; but they expanded in high school when she studied under Herman Voaden, the pre-eminent theatre modernist in Canada. Voaden's theatrical vision of imagistic "symphonic expressionism" required a highly technical theatre plant with flexible staging and sophisticated lighting to produce the scenographic complexity of the new theatre movements.[47] The Workers' Theatre could not hope to aspire to that kind of *mise en scène*, although traces of the techniques would emerge in *Eight Men Speak*. Gordon's early formation in traditional dramatic theatre was reinforced by her studies at Artef, one of the earliest promoters of Stanislavsky in New York.

Most people today who recognize Stanislavsky's name associate him with the concept of "method acting." The method, however, is one particular adaption of his ideas, brought about when members of the Group Theatre, the mainstream successor of the Workers' Laboratory Theatre in New York, began complementing Stanislavsky's analytical techniques with psychoanalysis. By the 1930s Stanislavsky had become a venerated icon of Soviet theatre, where his once revolutionary ideas had become institutionalized doctrine. For Stanislavsky, acting a part in a play entailed creating a coherent character discovered through minute analysis of dramatic action. Character is action, revealed in the subtext, the through-line of actions and reactions that propel the character through the crises of the plot. Having developed a role through a demanding process of analysis, the actor then must enter a physical and mental state that allows creative spontaneity. Performance is thus always new, and always discovered in the moment; analysis ensures that the actor's discoveries in performance will be consistent to the needs of the text. For Stanislavsky, acting was as technical, and as metaphysical, as performing a concerto.

For a theatre artist like Gordon, Stanislavsky provided a systemization of effort that accorded with Marxism and rewarded a disposition to discipline and artistry in cultural practice. The approach also reinforced a dramatic model based on character action expressed in plot and narrative. As the pressure towards the Popular Front grew, cultural theory from Moscow increasingly emphasized "realism" as a primary value. Critical realism plus dialectical materialism produced the concept of socialist realism – realist analysis and representation predicated on the scientific inevitability of the proletarian dictatorship – which was adapted as the official artistic stance by the Soviet Writers' Congress in 1934 and immediately uploaded by satellite parties around the world. In Canada Cecil-Smith began writing about it in *Masses* in that same year. The key word in socialist realist textual analysis was the same as in the new discourse of the Popular Front: *unity*.

Cecil-Smith, like Ryan, demonstrated no particular interest in theatrical modernism, but both were effective agitprop pragmatists. Older and more politically engaged (and accountable) than the other members of the Progressive Arts Club, they stayed away from the youthful debates about form and aesthetic value. They saw the utility of agitprop but did not advocate it as a cultural practice. For them, theatre was a weapon indeed, and the calibre changed according to the fight. Their contributions to *Eight Men Speak* were the most theatrically conservative.

The other members of the Workers' Theatre, particularly the students who wrote for *Masses*, tended more towards agitprop as a productive artistic form. The two signal names here are Dorothy Livesay and Stanley Ryerson, the Progressive Arts Club's artistic intellectuals, both at the beginning of their distinguished careers (Livesay as a leading Canadian poet; Ryerson as the pre-eminent Marxist historian of Canada). Livesay in particular wrote the most effective and innovative agitprops for the troupes, although her most popular one, a mass recitation entitled *Eviction* (also known as *Zynchuck*), perhaps the most widely performed Canadian agitprop, appears not to have survived. Another student writer was Mildred Goldberg, who wrote *Eight Men Speak*'s mass recitation section, which was published in *Masses* and sporadically if illegally staged at various rallies after the play was banned. Goldberg left the Workers' Theatre after that climactic moment. Livesay and Goldberg in particular appear to have constituted the modernist wing of the Theatre, a stance expressed in one of the first issues of *Masses*, in which an article on "Red Theatre" articulated the proletarian culture position that linked modernism to revolutionary action:

> Street parades and demonstrations are all part of the Workers' Theatre. But for the more intensive representation of ideas all that is required is a platform, players, ideas and audience. Scenery and properties, beyond the most elementary suggestion of atmosphere, are only necessary for a bourgeois audience which is too mentally enervated by the stupid wasteful routine of its daily life to think or have ideas of its own.

Like the "propertyless theatre for a propertyless class" argument advanced in Britain, this stance refused the tradition of the dramatic playhouse theatre and began to build a counter-tradition based on the collective, the carnivalesque, and the processional.[48] This tradition – with its outline and legacy developed most fully by Ewan MacColl and Joan Littlewood – would in time become the dominant mode of theatre focused on political intervention, achieving position in Toronto in the late 1950s with George Luscombe's Toronto Workshop Productions.

As the Workers' Theatre developed over the two years preceding *Eight Men Speak*, the tension between mobile agitprop innovation and stationary theatrical drama was never clearly resolved. It persisted into the script of *Eight Men Speak* and was the reason for both the blunt criticism of the play in the U.S. magazine *New Theatre*, and for the position of Oscar Ryan and Toby Gordon Ryan, which they maintained all their lives, that the play was flawed and "lacking unity." Or as Toby Gordon once said, "It was a bad play."[49]

With enough room in the "Jesus Chrysler" for "six comrades and a suitcase," the Workers' Experimental Theatre began operations in June 1932, two months after the first issue of *Masses* came off the press. They took their first play, *Deported*, from a U.S. worker's magazine. According to *Masses*, it was "a realistic play depicting a family of foreign-born workers, celebrating the betrothal of their eldest son when they are served notice they are to be deported as charges of the State."[50] That brief outline makes it seem very much like the plays the Ukrainian Labour Farmer Temple Association had been doing for the better part of a decade.

Their next major effort was another imported script, *Solidarity, Not Charity*, performed at a benefit concert for the Workers International Relief. It was a satire on red tape and "boss charity," in which a family is caught up in bureaucracy (the *Masses* reviewer helpfully suggested that it would have been improved had they literally tied the actors in red ribbons). The second scene of the play was a mass recitation (a form also known as a mass chant) in which the workers denounce the charity system. The review suggests that the troupe had not yet found the technical mastery that had so impressed Toby Gordon in New York: "Here, where a mass scene was to be depicted, we found a great lack of collective enunciation. Instead of recitation of lines in a chorus, a motley, rather jagged effect was produced.... The players, furthermore, did not move in rhythm. The gestures, the swaying of bodies in unison, the striking of symbolic poses, are as important as the lines, with which close unity is essential."[51]

Similar criticism followed their next major performance at the Progressive Arts Club social in November, when the repertoire included their adaptation of a British mass recitation, *Theatre – Our Weapon*. This short chant (less than ten minutes long) was in effect a commercial for the Workers' Theatre:

> 1st: Down with the theatre where the bourgeois comes to digest his heavy meal!
> 2nd: Down with the theatre where the idle parasites come to amuse themselves!
> 3rd: Down with the theatre where drunken debauchery dopes the minds of the masters and their obedient slaves!
> 4th: Down with the theatre which lulls the indignation of the hungry slaves of capitalism!
> Chorus: DOWN WITH IT!
> 1st: Long live the theatre of revolutionary anger![52]

The mass recitation was perhaps the most innovative agitprop form, and the one that most clearly modelled the aesthetics of revolutionary modernism. It was one of those rare forms discovered in praxis. It combines the cadence and oratory of nineteenth-century recitations with the staccato rhythms, segues, and transitions of radio. It is telegraphic in its terseness, and semaphoric in its use of gestural bodies. At its most efficient – and this was a level that the Workers' Theatre never quite attained – it was drilled and choreographic. As a polyphonic chorus, the mass recitation could achieve a percussive musicality that is familiar today in hip hop, and it may be that the first New York performances of this type were influenced by African-American oral poetry, as, for example, in Prolet-Buehne's *15-Minute Red Revue*:

> 1: Comrades, workers, listen-stop—
> Prolet Buehne Agit-Prop.
> 2: Agit-Prop – against hunger and destitution—
> Agit-Prop – theatre of revolution—
> 3: Agit-Prop – wakes the masses to fight—
> Agit-Prop is the workers' fight.[53]

The mass rap was an enactment of revolutionary dynamism (or, as Prolet-Buehne put it, "Tempo – action – Fights reaction") and offered practical performance advantages. It was adaptable, able to adjust easily to changes in location, audience, and cast, and it suited the sightlines and acoustics of outdoor performance in found space. Short phrases, heavy cadence, and repetition allow a performance to project through noisy and unruly audiences. For mobile street performance, the critical performance problem is the beginning and end. A show must have an entrance and an exit of some kind, and the more theatrical and intentional they are, the more effective. For a costumed agitprop drama, this issue calls for some form of introductory moment to capture the audience's attention, or to turn a crowd into an audience. For the mass recitation, apparent formlessness snaps into form much as a group of soldiers can snap into a parade.

As the Workers' Theatre discovered, a successful mass recitation is harder than it might seem. For young activists committed to making their theatre a revolutionary work effort, this was doubly frustrating. Feedback from audiences and reviewers in the party press often noted that the technique needed improvement, and that performances were uneven. Some of these comments may have been generated by adherence to the party principle of blunt criticism, but for the members of the Workers' Theatre the critique risked losing position in the overall agitprop effort. If they were always seen as amateurish and untrained, their attempt to win legitimacy for theatre as a form of agitprop within the larger party struggle would be futile. The Workers' Theatre members were all serious in their intent, but the party did not take them particularly seriously. In 1933 the Canadian Labour Defense League's national convention did not even list theatre as a possible means of propaganda, despite Oscar Ryan's presence.[54] The Workers' Theatre itself showed two diverging directions of interest: Toby Gordon and Jim Watts wanted recognition for theatre as a form of activist art; and Oscar Ryan and Ed Cecil-Smith were primarily interested in theatre for immediate political ends.

Things changed rapidly in 1933, when the Workers' Theatre moved outside of the Toronto party circle and took to the road in three tours. By this time the group had seventeen members in two units, one comprising more experienced members and one with those in training.[55] The season began on May Day, with a high-profile presentation of Oscar Ryan's *Unity* at Hygeia Hall on Elm Street (the same hall where Emma Goldman frequently gave public lectures). Toby Gordon Ryan describes how on the day of the performance the Toronto Police Red Squad arrested two of the actors (who were released in time for the show through the intervention of the Defense League). That performance was followed later in the month with a program of three plays that were once more criticized for "lack of preparation."[56]

The first tour, in June, showed the Workers' Theatre that plays could be more than propaganda, that they could be a form of intervention. As another generation of Canadian performers would discover forty years later, an unexpected power and sense of elation could arise in taking theatre to audience-defined spaces. According to *Masses*, "In some of these places not even the barest of aids were provided for the actors. In Niagara Falls, for instance, there were neither curtains, lights, wings, nor anything else. Just a speaker's platform raised a few inches from the floor. On the other hand in Welland they had the use of a very good stage."[57]

As the tour took them around the Niagara Peninsula, the members of the troupe discovered the political relationship of performance and community. In Niagara Falls they presented Livesay's *Zynchuck* agitprop at a Free Tim Buck rally. This, after a year of work, was their first outdoor performance. But the high point was in St. Catharines, where for the first time the Workers' Theatre intervened in a labour dispute, performing for striking cannery workers (most of them immigrant women) in a concert and on the picket line. They were hauled to the police station and ordered out of town. The second tour, later that same month, took the troupe to the London and Windsor areas. The primary objective on this tour seems to have been the seeding of new troupes. In London two members stayed behind for a time to help train a troupe there, and in East Windsor, according to a report in *Masses*, a new troupe began performances that summer.[58] These projects were not destined to flourish, however, because the ideological shift away from class-war agitprop was already beginning.

The third and last tour was a series of performances on the road to Ottawa, featuring a short dramatic agitprop called *Looking Forward*, written by Frank Love. The piece, which advocated for unemployment insurance, had a family on welfare arguing out their political positions. Toby Gordon Ryan includes Love's brief recollection of the play in her memoir.[59] In it Love explains that he had no dramatic experience and could not understand why the play was reportedly so popular on tour until he saw it himself in Gananoque; he then discovered that it was unexpectedly comical in performance. Based on the success of *Looking Forward*, Ryan and Cecil-Smith invited Love to participate in the writing of *Eight Men Speak* that fall.

The Workers' Theatre found its greatest moment of solidarity (until *Eight Men Speak*) in the late summer at the Stratford Furniture strike. One of the great successes of the militant communist labour movement, the strike resulted in a victory for the workers. The group members performed before the largest audience in its entire history, with 3,500 workers watching them in the old Brooks Steam Motor plant.

By the end of 1933 the Workers' Theatre had undergone a process of change: developing skills, expanding its repertoire, and moving out of the containment field of the party into the wider public sphere. Ryan and Cecil-Smith were promoting the troupe as the model centrepiece of a movement. But just as they were mastering the skills and uses of a mobile agitprop troupe, their direction was shifted by the needs of the struggle. In their work, if not in their understanding of the work and their theorization, they were discovering that the critical question in revolutionary theatre did not concern mobile or stationary staging; as they found, that was merely a matter of technique. Rather, the key issue was the choice between traditional textual narrative or a radically new kind of theatrical delivery. Ideologically, narrative won out with the gradual ascendency of narrative realist drama, but theatrically the genius and the legacy of the Workers' Theatre would be a new method of collectively created *mise en scène*, in which radicalism came to be expressed in the creative process and the moment of performance as much as in the textual content. This process created *Eight Men Speak*, and it would become a key moment in the "other history" of Canadian theatre.

Eight Men Silenced

In November 1933 brief notices, like this one from the Toronto *Daily Star* on the 25th, began appearing in the press:

> With settings designed by the artists group, Progressive Arts Club, the six act play, Eight Men Speak, now in its sixth week of rehearsal, promises to be an unusual dramatic production, the first of its kind written and produced in Canada.
>
> The play, a dramatization of life in Kingston penitentiary, is replete with rapid action, keen humor and powerful dramatic climaxes. Opening in the garden of the warden, the audience

is taken into Tim Buck's cell, several courtroom scenes, a newspaper office, a streetcar, a cabaret, a home, a whipping scene
and others. The play will be staged on Monday, December 4, at
the Standard, Dundas and Spadina.

The fifteen hundred people who turned out for the one and only
performance of *Eight Men Speak* at the Standard Theatre – the same venue
where the young Toby Gordon saw Shakespeare in Yiddish – were not
for the most part there out of a love for theatre, or for the whipping
scene. The show was one more event in a very busy public campaign
launched the month before by the Canadian Labour Defense League
to agitate for the release of Tim Buck and the seven other prominent
Communists and to repeal the draconian Section 98 of the Criminal
Code under which they had been convicted for "unlawful association."
During a notorious riot in Kingston Penitentiary in October 1932, shots
had been fired into Buck's cell in what appeared to be an assassination
attempt. In the escalating public debate, the CLDL staged meetings and
congresses across the country in a massive campaign against Section 98.
Rev. A.E. Smith, the general secretary of the League, had already been
turfed out of R.B. Bennett's office while trying to deliver a petition. The
cause started a chain of events that led not only to the production of *Eight
Men Speak* but also to Smith's own sedition trial for remarks made while
denouncing the police censorship of the play, a mass campaign that generated over four hundred thousand signatures, and the eventual release
of the eight men. What drew the audience to the Standard Theatre was
that the play was in effect a co-production by the Progressive Arts Club
and the Defense League leadership, including senior Communist Party
members. It was a party rally in theatrical disguise. Oscar Ryan remembered the audience as "tense and exceptionally responsive."[60]

 Eight Men Speak would turn out to be an important moment of Canadian modernism in the history of Canadian radical theatre, but for the
Progressive Arts Club and the Workers' Theatre the play was the cul-
mination of their agitprop work. It produced a new theatrical form that
they could barely discern, and from which they quickly withdrew. In the
larger history of the radical left movement in Canada, *Eight Men Speak*
represented a critical point in a series of events that marked the high point
of Communist prestige. It brought onto the stage an avatar of the imprisoned leader and framed him in a scenario that reversed the polarity of

the trial that had convicted him. Although no more than fifteen hundred people saw the play, because they did see it the ensuing judicial actions, and the activism produced by those official actions, culminated a year later in the mass rally that brought the real Tim Buck onto the stage of Maple Leaf Gardens before a crowd of seventeen thousand. From this perspective, *Eight Men Speak* was the first act in a year-long perform- ance that multiplied popular support for the outlawed Communist Party. Never before or since has a theatrical production played so instrumental a role in a Canadian political crisis.

During Buck's 1931 trial Oscar Ryan had sat in the press seats as a reporter for the party newspaper *The Worker* and as publicity director of the Canadian Labour Defense League (which undertook the defence of the eight accused). He was involved in the League's "Workers' Jury," which watched the trial and issued a verdict of not guilty in a widely dis- tributed pamphlet. In the social uproar that followed the riot in Kingston Penitentiary and the shots fired into Buck's cell, Ryan proposed another take on the Workers' Jury. This time, with the help of the Workers' The- atre, they would put the unknown guard who fired the shots on trial on the stage of a theatre.

From this decision it is easy enough to trace the development of the play into its innovative anthology form that was critiqued as flawed in the leftist press, and which Oscar Ryan and Toby Gordon Ryan them- selves later renounced, but which has attracted the admiration of sub- sequent generations of critics and theatre activists. As with the Workers' Theatre agitprops, Ryan's purpose was utilitarian rather than cultural, but he seems to have been open to theatrical experimentation. *Eight Men Speak* began as a collaborative exercise, in which the four authors (Ryan's colleague Ed Cecil-Smith and, from the Workers' Theatre, Mildred Gold- berg and Frank Love) each undertook to write a section of the play. This creative process may seem to account for how the play switches styles and tone drastically between the sections, but in fact it does not. Ryan and Cecil-Smith exercised tight control over the writing, and if the play was "a confusion of styles" leading to "uneven development of the dra- matic idea, confusion of conflicts, and lack of political clarity" (as judged by the U.S. magazine *New Theatre*), it was because Ryan had agreed to that result.[61] From Ryan's point of view, as he told me in an interview, the play was artless and lacking in unity because the authors were young, inexperienced, and working on a tight deadline. But from a modern perspective the play is artful and theatrically clever, and it is not a reach to assume that the authors and the audience of the day thought so as well.

Ryan may have approved of the play's unusual structure because his utilitarian purpose was to mount a workers' rebuttal of the justice system, and to that end the issue of dramaturgical form was simply not important. It is possible that the authors did not at first see the play as a coherent unified drama at all. The initial idea was to stage a workers' court, with a prosecution and a defence. The Workers' Theatre had been developing its ability to perform mass recitations, and it would have made good theatrical sense to begin the performance that way. But to make the show into a good night out, it needed to be more than a few short scenes. Perhaps it grew incrementally until it was fleshed out enough to stand as an evening's entertainment. What began as a paratheatrical mock trial became an agitprop frame that grew a dramatic skin. *Eight Men Speak* is a play that recapitulates the history of left theatre and takes the audience in stages through parody, agitprop, expressionism, melodrama, and documentary. It is also an archive of performance methods, and that element of theatrical technique provided the "unity" in the performance.

Cecil-Smith notes in his preface to the play that it was developed in the space of two months (which itself establishes an interesting precedent for the normal practice of collective creation in Canada). Love, who had already showed some promise as a playwright with *Looking Forward* in 1932, later said that he "plotted the play, and it was a simple enough plot. We just put the government on trial."[62] His memory was that he wrote the content for the prosecution and Cecil-Smith wrote for the defence. Mildred Goldberg wrote the mass chant; at least it was published under her name in *Masses*. The authorship of the satiric first act is unclear, but it was probably penned by Oscar Ryan. In the writing process Ryan was the one who looked for places in the script to build the theatrical effects. As he later wrote, "We felt it needed intensity, color, conflict, theatricality. We added blackouts and mass recitations and some light humorous elements."[63] Love also noted that Ryan and Cecil-Smith worked together closely.

Originally Jim Watts was to be the director, but in the program her name is excluded from the four listed as directors (Ryan, Toby Gordon, Cecil-Smith, and Cecil Greenwold, who played the attorney general). As Oscar Ryan recalled in 1976, "Jim Watts directed the early rehearsals and, when the load became too big, turned over the job to me but continued as assistant."[64] This is a conveniently simple gloss, which may be true but incomplete. Ryan does not actually define what he means by too big a load, nor does he explain why he was the one to whom Watts turned. In the end Watts was answerable to Ryan, who was, after all, not only the representative of the Defense League, a senior party official to whom some ideological deference would have been expected, but also a co-author of the play, a witness to the original trial, and friend to Buck. The play needed more actors than the Workers' Theatre could provide, and recruited more from the Unemployed Council. Perhaps in the meeting of two social worlds – of unemployed working-class men and politically engaged students – Watts found it difficult to sustain directorial authority. The history of Canadian theatre reveals many examples of male actors refusing the authority of female directors; this may have been an early case.

With its innovative structure, narrative use of overtly theatrical lighting, and quick, dynamic blackout scenes, *Eight Men Speak* is one of the first Canadian examples of the modernist theatre in which the director functions as the author or conductor of the performance text. Its theatrical genealogy can be traced back through the revolutionary anti-illusionist avant-garde in New York to early Soviet staging, especially as developed by Vsevolod Meyerhold. In some of its features, such as the tribunal in the workers' court, the play resembles Brecht's experimentation with agitprop form in his *Lehrstücke* (learning plays) in Berlin several years earlier. As a general principle, the play follows a montage structure, in which scenes are presented through rhythmic and staging contradictions. Transitions tend to be abrupt and contradictory rather than smooth elisions. The play makes liberal use of blackouts, tightly focused and moving spotlights, comical stage effects (such as pop-up masks in the jury box), abrupt sound effects (such as the banging of a gavel), and tableaux. The choreographic arrangement shown in a photograph of the final moment (see p.96) indicates a stylized physicality reminiscent of Soviet formalist performance.

Eight Men Speak is billed as a play in six acts, but the acts are fairly short. Neither the script nor the program makes any mention of an intermission. The play begins satirically, with the corrupt representatives of the governing classes (the prison warden, a reverend, a torch singer) in a garden party as they receive the news of the riot.[65] Caught in the converging gazes of the audience and the party, the satire initiates the argument of the play by disallowing the moral and political legitimacy of the state. From this initial point of satire – which also serves to warm up the house – the play moves through an emotional register that concludes in triumphant anger. As an orchestration of emotional responses, the play ranges from self-congratulation (in the Red Scare parody of Act Two) to melodramatic sentimentality (when Buck reads a letter from his daughter in his cell) to passionate anger in the careful rhythms of the monologues and mass chants of the imprisoned eight. The polyphonic effect is carefully timed, and fully exploits contemporary notions of experimental performance – as in the mass chant in the dark that begins the second act, and the use of lighting to isolate, move, and then unify the dramatic fugue that takes place later in that act. The audience sees a series of blackout scenes, which are then reprised in shorter segments until they are all brought together in an intensified choral climax.

During this scene the spot from the projection room weaves up and down across the entire stage, revealing from right stage to left: Newspaper office, Street Car, Cabaret and the Old Man's Room. The voices are shrill and follow quickly.

EDITOR: Tim Buck riot leader!

MAN IN CABARET: Buck said kill the screws.

WOMAN IN CABARET: Those Russians.

YOUNG MAN IN STREET CAR: Com-yunists!

RADIO: Buck's complicity.

The next set of voices follows immediately. They are louder and faster than the first set, almost overlapping each other.

MAN IN CABARET: Buck said kill the screws!

EDITOR: Tim Buck riot leader!

YOUNG MAN IN STREET CAR: Com-yunists!

WOMAN IN CABARET: Those Russians.

RADIO: Buck's complicity.

The next set of voices are shouted simultaneously and are much louder. Each line is repeated three times and the chorus ends with "Buck's complicity."

EDITOR: Tim Buck riot leader!

MAN IN CABARET: Buck said kill the screws!

WOMAN IN CABARET: Those Russians!

YOUNG MAN IN STREET CAR: Com-yunists!

RADIO: Buck's complicity.

As the last "Buck's complicity" dies away, the Old Man's voice
can be heard.
OLD MAN (very hysterically): Quick Elizabeth![66]

At this point the curtain drops, and when it reopens the scene has shifted
to Buck's trial. Here documentary extracts from the trial record are
framed in grotesque parody and what seems to be the first use of puppetry in Canadian political interventionist theatre:

> Immediately the Mountie lifts the lid of the Jury Box, up pop SIX
> JURORS. These six Jurors are all clad in black and are visible
> only from the waist up. Each Juror wears an identical mask –
> that of a stodgy, vacant looking face. Each waves white gloves.
> When the lid is lifted, the six heads pop up with hands lifted.[67]

With scenes like this, *Eight Men Speak* is remarkably similar to the kinds
of solutions that radical theatre-makers would invent in the collective
creations of the counterculture a generation later. The play demonstrates
a clever scenographic imagination, yet the production had no trained
designers and a one-night stand on the stage of the Standard Theatre
could permit only quickly built and easily changed set pieces.

Unfortunately, only one visual image of the production remains, but
that one image allows us to see how the directors created a visual design
using rudimentary platforms, backdrops, and actors' bodies. The photograph captures the final tableau in which the members of the Workers'
Court point accusing fingers at the cringing guard and the cowering figure
of Capitalism (the defence attorney for the accused guard), played by
Cecil-Smith. The tableau is organized around the presiding authority of
the three worker judges, on a raised platform in the background. The primary judge, standing in the centre and commanding the stage, is Oscar
Ryan, whose upraised fist, clenched in revolutionary salute, provides a
dynamic contrast to the diagonally pointing fingers of the other actors.
Ryan is the iconic authority of the party at the centre of play.

Standing before and beneath him are the eight, dressed in striped
clothing, whose testimonies and mass chant give the play much of its
structural movement. Amongst their number is an actor representing
Tim Buck; near him stands the young Toby Gordon Ryan, as the
Defense League prosecutor. The Communist Party is thus configured as

an authority both within and outside the terms of representation, with party officials assuming roles and rank-and-file actors representing party officials. The play, a pageant of party leadership, combined the mimetic product of analysis and the power that authorizes the work. This authority is signified by the iconic use of colour: the three judges are dressed in the Workers' Theatre uniform of black shirt and trousers with red neckerchief, and their bench, according to the *Star* report, is draped in red cloth. Behind them a painted panel shows a mass scene, including a red flag and a sea of faces.

From that backdrop a representation of the working class gazes out over the action to the audience. The meeting of these two gazes enables and validates the representation on stage, which is performed by workers who enact workers between the material (the audience) and the ideological (the backdrop). The result is an embodied revolutionary analysis that claims authority for the Workers' Court. The *mise en scène* exemplifies the play's principle that the revolutionary will of the people, configured as the Communist Party, exposes the government as an instrument of class war. The Workers' Court, like the Workers' Jury during the trial, contests the constitutional claim to governing authority by the ruling classes. It was this challenge to authority that incited the Province of Ontario to ban the play after its only full performance. As the Toronto *Daily Star* reported the next day:

> According to this report: "The Internationale" was given preference over "God Save the King" by an audience which crowded the Standard theatre last night to applaud "Eight Men Speak," a dramatic protest against the imprisonment of Tim Buck and his seven comrades in Kingston penitentiary.
>
> When the curtain fell at the close of this six-act play the orchestra rose and played the National Anthem. Boos and cat-calls rang out from the gallery. The musicians struck up the Internationale. With one accord the hundreds joined with the actors to fill the little theatre on Spadina Ave. with their enthusiastic voices.
>
> The ovation climaxed the players' finale in which Guard X (Max Bloom), a penitentiary "screw," stood on trial before the workers' court accused of the attempted murder of Tim Buck during the prison riots last October 12. Charged with firing five shots

at the Communist leader, the guard faced a tribunal of three, dressed in black and red on a bench draped with a red banner. At the close of the trial the judgment was left to the audience and in a thunderous voice they returned the verdict – guilty.[68]

The success of the performance led to the announcement, on December 30, of a second show to be held on January 15, 1934. But that other performance never happened. The *Star* reporter was not the only person taking notes during the show. So too was Detective Sergeant William Nursey of the Toronto Police Special Branch, known as the Red Squad. He had been sent to take notes after the Police Commission met on December 1 to hear a report from the Chief Constable about the upcoming play, and ordered him "to take steps to have notes made of the performance and also to have the play censored."[69] Nursey's notes were the basis of a special meeting of the Commission on December 7, and then again three days later, when the decision was made to send the report on to the Crown Attorney. From there it went to the provincial government, which tried to conceal the police initiative by having the Inspector of Theatres (whose job it normally was to inspect film projectors) to threaten to revoke the Standard's licence if the show went ahead. The theatre owner cancelled the play, and the University of Toronto student paper, *The Varsity*, which had ties to the Progressive Arts Club, scooped the big dailies with the news that the show was off.

Over the course of the next week tempers were inflamed, first at a mass meeting at the Labour Temple, which passed a "resolution on the freedom of the stage in Canada,"[70] then in an impromptu demonstration outside of the Standard Theatre on the night of the scheduled performance, and finally on January 17 at Hygeia Hall, where selections from the play were performed and A.E. Smith made his famous declaration that the government had tried to murder Tim Buck. In that moment, Smith compressed the banning of the play, the imprisonment, and the attack on Buck into one issue. In effect, the banning of the play was one more stage in a continuing government conspiracy to silence Buck. The government took the bait, and on January 31 the press reported that Smith had been indicted for sedition. So began the most public sedition trial in Canadian history. The press covered it closely, with a general sympathy for Smith and the cause of free speech. By the time Smith was acquitted in early March, public opinion had turned to support Smith and the

Defense League. The turning point was Buck's own appearance in court, where he was able to say clearly, "I was shot at." Public pressure intensified until the Eight were released.

Having precipitated the sequence of events that led to Buck's triumphant return to Toronto, *Eight Men Speak* was the most effective and consequential production of the workers' theatres in Canada. Indeed, it was no less consequential when it *was not* produced. In Winnipeg another police action prevented a planned production on May 2 at the Walker Theatre by the local Progressive Arts Club. The play, to be directed by Joe Zuken, then a young law student, was cancelled the day before the performance when the police, acting on instructions from the Manitoba Attorney General, temporarily revoked the Walker Theatre's licence. Winnipeg had seen a great deal of left-wing and communist theatre, but rarely in English, and the government had clearly moved to thwart the performance of the play, with pressure from Ottawa, because of its perceived slander of the federal Attorney General.[71] The pre-emptive ban in Winnipeg is not as well known as the Toronto censorship, but it is more characteristic of the methods of police repression of dissident arts. Censorship of produced work, whether in a theatre or a gallery or a concert hall, invariably results in public controversy, but pre-emptive censorship provides less of an occasion for outcry.

The stated reason for the cancellation was that the producer had reneged on a promise to let the police read the script of the play. Zuken denied any such promise, and as *The Worker* commented, the police demand to see the script was "correctly refused, on the grounds that plays are only censored after their first appearance." The chill persisted after the ban when the Progressive Arts Club was denied the use of "seven or eight" theatres to hold a protest meeting.[72]

The production of *Eight Men Speak* in Winnipeg was denied, but the issue energized the radical theatre movement in the city. Zuken later recalled that the ban provoked mass public outdoor meetings, and "segments of the play" were performed at various halls around the city.[73] In effect, the ban decomposed the play and redistributed it as agitprop; as in Toronto, the ban was a multiplier that increased the reach and effect of the play. It also energized the Workers' Theatre in Winnipeg, and as the Progressive Arts Club morphed into the New Theatre, it commenced a history of left performance that continued, through the efforts of theatre activists like Zuken and Roland Penner, well into the 1950s.

Eight Men Speak was both the high point of communist agitprop in Canada and the point at which left theatre shifted its orientation towards the embrace of theatre disciplinarity and canonical tradition. In that sense it marked the end of the workers' theatre movement and the beginning of the theatrical Popular Front. *Eight Men Speak* became an outlaw text – literally so when the Canadian government placed it on the list of prohibited publications for the Post Office later in 1934. Because it disturbs the boundaries of categorization by exposing the social phobia that disallows any positive representation of communism, it remains an outlaw text to this day. As a work of propaganda it sits outside the critical boundaries of Canadian modernism. Writing in *Canadian Forum* in 1991, literary critic Morris Wolfe called it "goddawful propaganda."[74] For the same reason, it sits outside the active repertoire of the professionalized theatre. It may be the only Canadian play that is so transgressive that it can never be staged at a major theatre.

Yet *Eight Men Speak* still has a theatrical life on the fringes, including various student productions, staged readings by politically engaged actors, and one fully mounted public production, in 1982, by a radical artists' collective, Popular Projects Society, in Halifax. Oscar Ryan led a post-show discussion from the stage after that first Halifax performance, and his presence (as well as Toby's) lifted the play from historical footnote and brought it into active cultural memory for the audience. The Popular Projects Society deliberately sought to "re-create" the play as a vehicle of social analysis and to link the historical production with the re-creation as moments in an ongoing struggle. According to Rose Adams, a visual artist who participated in the remounting, the play "acts as a metaphor for corporate and granting suppression as well as for the lack of funding for popular theatre." By "popular," she explained, she meant a theatre that "is not classified as amateur or professional but is popular in the sense that it reflects actual conditions and is performed by those who are part of the milieu to whom the play is presented."[75]

In the Halifax performance the Popular Projects Society resituated *Eight Men Speak* by reframing the cultural historical space that it occupies. *Eight Men Speak* may have been the climactic moment and the last play of the workers' theatre movement, but at the same time it was an initializing moment and a first play of the popular theatre movement that continues to this day.

5

Crafting Theatre Work
Mid-Century Radicalism

Theatre of Action in rehearsal, as sketched by Avrom.
L.W. Conolly Theatre Archives, McLaughlin Library, University of Guelph

In January 1935 a play written as an intervention in a taxi strike premiered in a small Greenwich Village theatre. That opening-night performance famously brought the audience to its feet, stamping and yelling with the cast, "Strike! Strike! Strike!"

Waiting for Lefty was the brainchild of Clifford Odets, then a young actor in (and a co-founder of) New York City's Group Theatre; and his one-act play would go on to achieve an almost mythic stature in American theatre history. With some changes, including the writer's own self-censorship of the more overt communist references, the play quickly moved uptown, where it became a smash hit on Broadway and launched Odets's literary and screenwriting career.

Waiting for Lefty begins with a meeting of striking taxi workers demanding action while the corrupt union boss and his goons try to stop them. In a series of vignettes the audience sees the background stories that led each of the workers to the decision to strike. The theatrical success of the play was in large part due to Odets's skilful use of dialogue in these moments. Each scene is a powerful miniature play, and as the pieces progress a feeling of rage builds up to the point of explosion. The Group Theatre was one of the earliest Stanislavsky studios in New York, and Odets created a form that combined the theatricality and immediacy of agitprop with the depth characterization of realist drama.

The wide popularity of *Waiting for Lefty* was instrumental in the move of the radical theatre groups into the social-democratic centre of the budding Popular Front culture. In Canada after *Eight Men Speak*, the Workers' Theatre had drifted to a halt, but the move towards the Popular Front led to a revitalization of theatre as Toby Gordon and other activists laboured to create a socially engaged and professionalized theatre culture. The left theatre troupes that comprised the New Theatre Group (Theatre of Action in Toronto and Vancouver; New Theatre in Montreal and Winnipeg) were remarkably successful at building audiences and critical opinion, although legitimacy came with a price. As the left theatres made their way into the theatre mainstream, they found themselves increasingly detached from their audience base and radical origins.

That mainstream, such as it was, was still largely amateur, with aspirations to professionalism in a society that lacked cultural policies or arts funding for theatres. The mainstream was essentially the busy world of community-based "little theatres" (or what Robin Whittaker, in his work on the history of amateur theatre in Canada, calls "non-professionalized" theatre),[1] drawn into community by the annual local, regional, and national competitions of the Dominion Drama Festival. Many of these groups responded to the issues of the day with dramas of social conscience, and some of these efforts were well received at the festivals. In her examination of the Vancouver Progressive Arts Club's production of *Waiting for Lefty*, Bonita Bray tells the fascinating story of a communist play with a cast of unemployed workers who found themselves socializing with the Governor General at the Drama Festival finals in Ottawa in 1935.[2]

Waiting for Lefty was the Toronto Theatre of Action's inaugural production in 1936. Years later Toby Gordon Ryan was still enthusiastic about the play, although neither she nor Oscar Ryan remembered the famous scene in which a Broadway producer's secretary offers an unemployed actor a copy of the *Communist Manifesto* with the invitation to "Come out in the light, Comrade."[3] This failure to recollect the scene was not completely surprising because the Toronto production had omitted it, as had many U.S. productions. Odets and the Group Theatre had dropped the scene from the play at some point in the seven-month period between its opening at a benefit variety performance for the New Theatre League in January 1935 and its Broadway restaging in July at the Belasco Theatre. After the first magazine and book editions in 1935 the scene would appear only in occasional anthology editions. Its excision coincides with, but was not necessarily consequential to, Odets's repudiation of the Communist Party.

More surprisingly, though, when I spoke to the Ryans, Toby Gordon Ryan vehemently denied that such a scene could even have been in the play. Why was the most overtly communist scene in *Waiting for Lefty* – and not just the scene, but the memory of the scene – removed from history even though the play had entered the international canon as an artistic triumph of the workers' theatre movement? Gordon Ryan's own copy of the original 1935 edition of the play (published shortly after its premiere in *New Theatre* magazine) contains pencilled marginalia, indicating that she had thoroughly read the original version at some point. She had, apparently, forgotten this particular scene.[4]

Playing the Popular Front

As a playtext and an event, *Waiting for Lefty* enacted the shift of the movement to the Popular Front. Across the English-speaking world in 1935–36, theatres with names that recurred across national boundaries – Theatre of Action, New Theatre, Unity Theatre – used *Waiting for Lefty* to both enable and obscure their transition from agitprop beginnings to professional "people's theatres." The Left Book Club's Theatre Guild in London supplied an explicit model of the play's function as enactment of the Popular Front in its pamphlet *Notes on Forming "Left" Theatre Groups*:

> We believe that the fight against war and Fascism can best be conducted on the basis of a popular front, and we are convinced that the theatre gives as good, if not a better basis for such activity than the Left Book Club itself. This applies equally to actors and audiences. An example of this is the Unity Theatre Club's production of "Waiting for Lefty." The twenty or so actors who form the cast of this play number among them members of the Liberal, Labour, and Communist parties, members of Co-Operative Societies, Trade Unionists, and so on.[5]

Because Odets initially released the play without calling for royalties, dozens of productions were mounted across the United States. In Canada the play was produced in Montreal, Toronto, and Vancouver as a charter play for new theatre groups. In Australia *Waiting for Lefty* was a foundational play for troupes in Brisbane, Melbourne, Newcastle, and Sydney; in New Zealand it enabled the founding of the People's Theatre in Auckland. It had equal currency in the United Kingdom, in Bristol, Glasgow, and Manchester, and in London it became the site and occasion of a rupture in the Rebel Players, which led to the dismantling of the Workers' Theatre Movement and the founding of Unity Theatre. Outside of North America the productions tended to include the Communist Manifesto scene because they were based on the original magazine

publication and, as Colin Chambers shows in the case of the Rebel Players, were produced without licence from Odets's agent.[6] The scene also
appeared in Joseph Losey's production mounted in the centre of world
revolution by the "Moscow Red Players, Anglo-American Section of the
Foreign Workers' Club," who sent Odets a copy of the program with a
fan note:

> To Clifford Odets,
> With revolutionary greetings from the Red Capital where the
> premiere of "Waiting For Lefty" (May 1935) was a great success.
> A swell play! We're waiting for more "Lefty's."[7]

Waiting for Lefty had, then, quickly moved from its apocryphal
beginnings to serve international notice of the Popular Front as a non-
sectarian alliance. In its use to enable new formations of Popular Front
troupes in Australia, Canada, New Zealand, and the United Kingdom it
circulated as a confirmation of non-partisan humanist values suitable for
export. The inaugural mounting of the play around the world marked
the coming dominance of American popular culture on the left. It would
be a colonizing system in which the cultural work of the New York
Popular Front theatres circulated as normative values of artistry. The
Toronto Theatre of Action reinforced this tendency in practice. Shortly
after it turned to *Lefty* as an enabling text, it also imported a director
from New York to give the company the gloss of professionalism in its
formative years.

Outside of New York, the most important result of the advent of
the Popular Front was the overwriting of past practice. In this process
Waiting for Lefty, with its accelerating celebrity, functioned as both site
and marker. The best-known example of this function came in London,
where the play was the means of a transition from Rebel Players to Unity
Theatre. Although that transition was contentious, that it centred on a
celebrated foreign script may have somewhat safely displaced the struggle away from local texts that could have been more deeply invested
with personal histories and class allegiances. At the same time it has
become identified as the birth moment of radical theatre to the point that
it obscures previous, unclaimed histories of Third Period agitprop.

In Canada the play allowed for the occurrence of a different shift,
one somewhat implied in Australia, Britain, and New Zealand. Less than

twelve hours by train from New York, Toronto was the cultural centre of the closest satellite in the emerging U.S. imperial sphere, and the demographic, social, and linguistic affinities between anglophone Canada and the United States made cultural exchange sufficiently easy that the border often disappeared in the popular imagination. In this context *Waiting for Lefty* domesticated national difference even as it reconciled class practices. In Toronto in 1936 the Theatre of Action not only distanced itself from its previous life as the Workers' Theatre, but totally erased the history of that past. In its publicity pamphlet the new Theatre of Action invoked the romantic genealogy of a popular people's theatre, making the explicit point that it was announcing a "new and quite unknown group" – which technically it was – and that it "did not seek to make the theatre a political platform."[8] Its inaugural production of *Waiting for Lefty*, which, again, did not include the sectarianism of the Communist Manifesto scene, was not the localized, naturalized agitprop that Odets had originally created for the Group Theatre, but a text that had circulated beyond those origins to become an internationalized talisman of U.S. cultural leadership. A subtext to this was the voice of the brash American proletarian, an inherently dissident choice for a Canadian theatre in a cultural milieu still demanding British accents and tastes on the stage. The adjudicators at the Dominion Drama Festivals were still drawn in the main from England, and when the bourgeois amateur Montreal Repertory Theatre jumped on the bandwagon and staged *Waiting for Lefty*, members of the radical New Theatre, who had done the play first, were shocked to see the character of Edna, the feisty tenement wife who challenges her husband to go out on strike, costumed in a silk blouse and tweed skirt, with the strike leader in clean shirt and ascot.[9]

In Toby Gordon's memoir – cautious as it is to the point of evasion about politics except in the most general sense – what comes through clearly is that all of the troupes were "social" in the widest sense. They attracted members from a spectrum of leftist and progressive positions. In Toronto and Winnipeg in particular the organization of the troupes maintained connections with the Communist Party, although in this case the party did not directly involve itself.

As the groups came into formation, Toby Gordon Ryan was the energizing force. In 1934–35 she and Oscar Ryan had been in Winnipeg, where they had encouraged the creation of a local troupe. She knew the Montreal community well, going there often with Oscar to visit his family. She returned to Toronto around the same time that Jim Watts came back from studying theatre in New York, and the Theatre of Action was initially their invention. It was Watts who secured the troupe's office space and directed *Waiting for Lefty* in February 1936. But Watts soon left the troupe. Gordon Ryan does not explain why, but in summer 1936 David Pressman arrived to teach at the Theatre of Action's summer school and stayed on for the next two years as the group's director. Clearly, Watts's departure and Pressman's arrival were related. Possibly Watts's uncompromising radicalism did not adapt well to the new spirit of ideological compromise. A program for an evening of five one-act plays that took place before Watts left provides some evidence of this issue. The evening was presented under the auspices of "The New Theatre League Committee."[10] Although they were called "one-act plays," the works were agitprops (including the only Toronto production of *Newsboy*). Watts directed three of them. They were the last of the communist agitprops staged in Toronto. A year later Watts was in Spain and Theatre of Action was striving for mainstream attention.

The most significant features of the new theatre movement were the nature of the repertory, the organization of the companies, and the reach towards professional disciplinarity. All of these features revolve around the difficult transition from a class-based cultural analysis to a popular nationalist analysis. In the end the Toronto Theatre of Action could not reconcile this conflict. In Winnipeg and Montreal the somewhat less institutionalized theatre troupes were able to survive through the war years, in the main by clinging more stubbornly to their radical origins. Regardless of their political stance, they remained the object of harassment and surveillance. The Montreal New Theatre was routinely targeted by the provincial police. On one occasion it was locked out of the theatre under the notorious Padlock Law passed in 1937 by the Quebec government led by Maurice Duplessis.

One of the Theatre of Action's stated goals was to develop a professional theatre culture and a Canadian dramatic repertoire. As a people's theatre, it aspired to a Canadian dramatic literature. The Workers' Theatre had written most of its own work, but in the five-year history of the Theatre of Action the entire repertoire was foreign in origin. In her memoir Toby Gordon Ryan seems a little uncomfortable about explaining the absence of Canadian plays in the group's program. Lacking "an indigenous professional theatre," she wrote, the country did not have many playwrights who took up homegrown subjects. "The few who were producing scripts did not write about the issues of the time which were so important to the majority of people in this country. Thus, for a theatre such as ours, committed and socially aware and looking for scripts to dramatize the themes of our day, virtually no one was writing."[11] The absence of scripts had not deterred the Workers' Theatre, which produced its own work to address particular issues. But under the Theatre of Action's redefinition of drama, most of the Workers' Theatre projects would not be considered dramatic art. Cabaret scripts, mass recitations, agitprop, and "living newspapers" – an early form of non-fiction documentary drama presented as stage journalism – were the weapons of combat theatre, but they did not count as drama within the new terms of cultural theory.

After its second season in 1937, Theatre of Action joined with the New Theatres in Winnipeg and Montreal (as the New Theatre Group) to hold a national one-act play contest. One prize was awarded out of sixty-six entries. Gordon Ryan recorded the judges' comments:

> Playwrights need to be further schooled in the limitations and requirements of the one-act play form. Too many attempted to make the one-act a full play in miniature. Others adopted such moving picture techniques as the flashback and something approximating close-ups. One person tried to give the one-acter the scope of a novel. All these things had disastrous effects upon the unity or the clarity of the work.[12]

In effect, the groups were reaching for the kind of play that would score well with critics and the theatrically conservative adjudicators of the drama festivals, at which legitimacy would be tested and won. The new theatre movement's insistence on correct form entered the theatre of the left in a trajectory that would take it to the dead end of socialist realism in the 1950s. Popular Front cultural theory argued that the arts were the expression of the nation; that they had arrived at their formal aesthetic principles through the work and craft of the people but were then taken over by bourgeois elites. What had been critiqued in the Third Period as bourgeois form was now understood to be popular form. It followed that the artistic forms of working people would resonate with the values of craft, artistry, and discipline. This in itself was not an unproductive position. In the United Kingdom Joan Littlewood and Ewan MacColl were following a similar logic to a different end, and that approach would return to revitalize left theatre in Toronto with George Luscombe in 1957. Their craftwork, however, was focused not on the making of a play script but on the making of a performance. For them the theatrical craft worker was the creative actor, not the playwright.

The New Theatre Group's conservative dramaturgy was a bid for position in the elite cultural sphere and the professional theatre culture that was beginning to come into form in Canada. As the New Theatre of Montreal stated in its first program, "We believe that the play – in other words, the idea which is being projected from the stage – is the basic art motif of the theatre. That acting, stagecraft, etc., represent the secondary art."[13] The new theatres were moving towards a production system of play delivery that did not adapt well to the creation of original work, or to collective creation, both of which entail long creative processes. As part of that movement, the new theatres launched themselves into professionalism by hiring directors from the United States or Britain, and systematizing their training regimes. Theatre of Action's most enduring legacy is in the careers that began in its summer school, including notables such as Lorne Green, Johnny Wayne, and Frank Shuster.

The repertoire of Theatre of Action showcased both the non-partisan progressive politics of the "cultural front" and theatrical sophistication. Most of the plays performed were contemporary U.S. hits. Of the thirteen major productions between 1936 and 1940 (some of them on double bills), eight were major U.S. plays (*Waiting for Lefty, Private Hicks, Bury the Dead, Class of '29, Steel, It Can't Happen Here, Life and Death of an American, Of Mice and Men*); and three were Russian (*Roar China, The Marriage Proposal, The Inspector-General*). Only one – the winner of the one-act play contest – was Canadian. The dominant theatrical style was the new realism, which was more theatrically adventurous than picture-frame naturalism but grounded on psychologically "real" character action. What is striking about this programming is that if we replace *Waiting for Lefty* with Shakespeare, it could be swapped into the season of any large regional theatre of the 1960s.

In her list of Theatre of Action productions, Gordon Ryan appends a tantalizing note: "This list does not include plays done for the mobile section of the theatre, nor studio productions of one-act plays, Living Newspaper, readings or cabaret performance."[14] In her memoir she excises most of these presentations, although she does include some of the cabaret songs and her archive contains traces of these less formal performances. Indeed, it is this less formal sector of work, done for local audiences rather than drama festivals, that reveals the continuing operation of a more politically engaged theatre.

Signing up: meet the military

Although the left theatre had taken an integrationist turn, it remained on the whole a theatre of dissent and social criticism. The beginning of the war in 1939 plunged the movement into another crisis because of the conflicted allegiances experienced by many members. Theatre of Action had always been a coalition organization. Run by an elected Production Council, its meetings, as evidenced by the surviving minutes, showed a functioning collective democracy that maintained a general left consensus.[15]

That consensus began to fray with the war given the demands of patriotism (which was the position of the Popular Front) versus the anti-war sentiments of those who, at a time when the German invasion of Russia was a year away, saw the war as an imperial conflict. Gordon Ryan makes this point when she writes: "If there was one major reason for the disintegration of Theatre of Action in 1940 it was that the leadership of the group simply could not agree on our role during the war." She devotes space in her memoir to the dissolution of Theatre of Action, which had begun to stagnate, but again avoids detail about the ideological struggles. She merely states: "I was one of those who felt we could continue, on a much reduced scale, to provide programs for a touring theatre which could get bookings from organizations and trade unions.... Unfortunately not too many members of the group agreed with me. At that point I withdrew from Theatre of Action."[16]

Especially after the German invasion of the Soviet Union in June 1941, left cultural activists joined in to promote the war effort as a people's war. One striking example was a living newspaper in support of the yes vote in the conscription referendum that Bob Orchard mentions in passing in his memoirs.[17] Others activists did not have a chance to make a choice because they found themselves spending the war in internment camps. Peter Krawchuk was one of them, and in his account of the experience he offers a glimpse into how a different kind of dissent theatre functioned in the camp:

> We tried to make our stay in the camp as easy as possible so
> that it would not be monotonous and boring. Thus we often got
> together and had our little concerts or friendly group dinners,
> particularly on the occasion of holidays – May Day, November 7
> and the New Year. We celebrated jubilee birthdays of individual
> comrades – thirtieth, fortieth, fiftieth and so on. At such parties
> we could not do without anecdotes, jokes and friendly jest, cre-
> ated already in the camp. Particularly popular were burlesques
> of the hearings before the commission and impersonations of
> behaviour, mannerisms and so on.[18]

Performances like these are part of the mechanism of group cohesion
and survival in isolated societies, and for men forced to live for years
without the company of women, they create a safe homosocial play-
space. The burlesques that Krawchuk recalls could be found in just about
every work camp across the country. In Newfoundland men in logging
camps entertained themselves with mock trials; in prisoner of war camps
inmates could produce relatively ornate theatrical productions. In each
case the work of performance established a social concord that enabled
men to let off steam, sustain solidarity, and channel dissent.

Conventional wisdom posits that the war years brought a paradigm
break in Canadian theatre history, but what they did was simply reallo-
cate theatre work to the war effort. As the war progressed many people
signed up for the cause (including Watts, who became a lieutenant in
the Canadian Women's Army Corps). A number of the performers and
songwriters from the New Theatre cabarets reappeared in uniform in the
new military showbiz spectacles.

Unlike the concert parties of the First World War, the new military spectacles were not devised as entertainment for fighting troops,
but instead as public relations in the war economy, to raise morale and
war bonds. They were lavish revues involving chorus "girls," skits, short
comic plays, song and dance, and full orchestras that toured across the
country and to New York and London. Entertainments were designed
specifically for the troops, including local unit concert parties, but they
were, to use Laurel Halladay's term, renegade. Halladay relates the suppression of the local concert parties with a wider anxiety verging on panic
over female impersonation and changing social roles of women in the
war economy. She argues that the four Canadian concert party troupes

formed by soldiers in England were shut down in part because of their use of drag performance. With changing gender roles in society and in the military, performances in drag were no longer contained by the masculinism of the soldier-actor and the absence of women, which had been the case in the First World War. What had been female impersonation had now become something more unstable in military culture. It had become drag. "By the summer of 1942," Halladay points out, "the Canadian Army, Navy and Air Force established more formal entertainment plans and the renegade Concert Parties were reined in and subjected to orders from the highest levels of the Department of National Defense, a change in administration that coincided with the beginning of the end for female impersonation in the Canadian forces."[19]

If the concert parties and military garrison theatricals had the capacity to express social and, as Halladay suggests, sexual dissidence, the overproduced service revues were organized in military command formations. *Meet the Navy,* with a cast of eighty (comedians, actors, dancers, singers) and more than fifty support personnel, had an organizational structure like any other naval establishment. *The Army Show*'s program listed all performers by rank, and in a rare congruence of military and theatrical organization, the stage manager was a sergeant major. The two shows filled a similar purpose but followed different trajectories. *Meet the Navy* grew larger and more ornate, and wound up in Germany after tours in Britain and France; *The Army Show* was split into five smaller units that were attached to the Canadian Auxiliary Services Entertainment Unit. By 1947 *The Army Show* had included over twenty contributing troupes.[20]

The military shows reflect a continuity of practice for socially engaged theatre that bridges the Popular Front and the Cold War era. They were not political except in the sense that they were ideological spectacles deployed for recruitment, fundraising, and propaganda purposes, but they were a form of interventionist theatre. In one sense they were the most lavish and costly agitprops ever produced. As the war progressed and the shows grew larger and more complex, they relied on corporate sponsorship. Pepsi-Cola sponsored the programs for the national tour of *The Army Show,* with its producer "loaned" out by Famous Players Corporation. *Meet the Navy* had support from Player's cigarettes (with its "Navy Cut" brand), Max Factor and House of Hollywood, T. Eaton Company, and Robert Simpson Company. The shows also served as a training ground for the next generation of performers; many of the cast members from the shows went on to celebrity in their later careers.

These shows revealed that just maybe government and business could work together to make art happen. If a nation could win a war by incurring massive national debt and intervening in the economy, perhaps it could build a culture that way too. For some there was no distinction between protecting a nation and nurturing a culture. By the end of the war senior government officials, including Massey and Brooke Claxton, the minister of defence, were advocating a cultural policy that included state intervention (a concept disguised under the term "patronage"). As Massey wrote, "Our military defences must be made secure; but our cultural defences equally demand national attention; the two cannot be separated."[21] The war was over and the communists were coming.

Performing a People's Canada

When the Stratford Shakespearean Festival opened in the summer of 1953, it was welcomed as a milestone event in Canadian cultural development – and the radical left joined in the applause. The *Canadian Tribune*, the newspaper of the communist Labour Progressive Party, saw Stratford as the first step in leading Canadian theatre to "really break loose from its derivative fetters, and begin to assume the mature and healthy features of a truly national theatre, reflecting our people's life and consciousness."[22] It added, "The rapt attention and enthusiasm with which the audience views and receives the plays is comparable only to what you witness in the theatres of the People's Democracies."

The Stratford Festival was backed by Canada's political and cultural elite, and this embrace of a canonical theatre enterprise by a Stalinist Communist Party seems far removed from the oppositional aesthetics and militant rejection of establishment culture by that same party (and party leadership) in the years before the Second World War. But a crucial shift in the cultural radicalism of the left had occurred – as exemplified by another theatrical beginning in the very same year of the Stratford Festival anointing. The juxtaposition of these two events sheds light on one of the unexamined problems in the history of Canadian political theatre. What happened to radical theatre culture in the period between the militancy of the workers' theatre movement and the emergence of a radical countercultural aesthetics in the 1960s?

The other beginning took place in April 1953, when a group of amateurs calling themselves the Play-Actors took the stage of Hart House Theatre in Toronto with the North American premiere of *Thirty Pieces of Silver* by Howard Fast, the popular but blacklisted author of the self-published *Spartacus* and a literary giant of U.S. communism.[23] A domestic melodrama about an American civil servant coerced into "naming names," and his wife who slams the door and exits with the newly militant African-American housekeeper, the play's equation of anti-communism, racism, and anti-Semitism was a radical public statement at the height of the inquisition-happy Cold War panic. The Play-Actors were the direct successor of the pre-war Theatre of Action and, like the previous incarnation, were seated close to the centre of the party. In its three-year history the group, under the leadership of Toby Gordon Ryan, produced a series of plays that shared common features of left-wing political analysis and theatrical realism. Without ever using the phrase, the Play-Actors introduced socialist realism to Toronto audiences.

In its program to advance a people's theatre, the radical theatre movement strove not only to occupy and claim the disciplinary centre of theatre practice but also to meet the standards of professional mastery exemplified in the founding of the Stratford Festival. While that combination may seem to indicate that its radicalism dissipated in a fundamentally conservative aesthetics and theatre practice, the actual political shifts were more complex. The adopted conventions of theatrical realism both represented and concealed a bitter political struggle over the contested terrain of theatrical "truth."

The disappeared radical theatre

For historians of Canadian theatre, the 1950s have always posed a problem as a decade of false starts, of cultural unrest and unfulfilled aspirations, of postcolonial autonomy deferred by a scarcity of resources. The historical consensus is that it was the decade of origins, foundings, and transformations. It began with a sense of cultural poverty and ended with an emergent professional canon-building theatre culture. Even at the beginning of the decade this perception was engraved in policy when the Massey Commission earnestly depopulated theatre culture with its observations: "Except in the few largest centres, the professional theatre is moribund in Canada, and amateur companies are grievously handicapped, through lack of suitable or of any playhouses," and "There are other professional or semi-professional companies, notably in Toronto, which appear from time to time, and there are, of course, many hundreds of amateur groups, some of them of genuine distinction."[24]

These kinds of thoughts would form the myth of the 1950s in Canadian theatre. They became the precondition of a school of analysis that saw theatrical development in the shape of a professional theatre institution organized around the production of a national canon. To establish such an institution and the cultural economy it manifests, the ground had to be cleared. Hence, when launching *Canadian Theatre Review* in 1974 Don Rubin wrote that after the Massey Report and the founding of the Stratford Festival in 1953, "Suddenly Canada had a theatre. Suddenly major cities across the country were producing the classic plays from world dramatic literature with professional companies."[25]

The key concept was the notion of "professional" in its economic and disciplinary meanings. Historians and memoirists have written much about the emergent professional and semi-professional theatres of the 1950s. In Toronto the list includes Jupiter Theatre, Theatre Toronto, Crest Theatre, New Play Society, and Canadian Players, amongst others. For Rubin and the critics and historians who followed him as the discipline of Canadian theatre studies consolidated in the 1970s, the theatre culture of the 1950s had begun to establish a theatre economy. But it could not yet be considered a national theatre culture because it had not yet developed a reliance on, or an audience for, Canadian playwrights.

The actual theatre culture of the 1950s, though, was not anything like that well-established myth. It was, instead, marked by diversity, plurality, activism, and fierce cultural nationalism. There was nothing sudden about the emergence of a sustaining theatre culture: it had always been there. The failure of theatre historiography in Canada is that it has tended to chart the historical progress of theatres as companies and structures rather than as practices. When historical genealogies record aborted attempts and false starts, they assume that the movement of structures is evidence of what actually happened. But theatre companies are strategic ventures and not just structures; they work their way through practices, through continuities and linkages, creating a phenomenon that disrupts conventional historiography.

For their part, leftist historians have tended to accept the verdict that the radical theatre of the 1930s and the Popular Front ended with the outbreak of war in 1939. In 1976, in her critical introduction to *Eight Men Speak and Other Plays from the Canadian Workers' Theatre*, Robin Endres endorsed Frank Watts's statement that "the proletarian drama of the thirties appears naturally to have disappeared with little trace. The tradition in Canadian dramatic writing has never been continuous, and it may well be that the years of the thirties represent a serious break." To this Endres added, "While we might agree that Canadian dramatic writing has been discontinuous (World War II certainly diverted people's attention from theatre) the 'traces' of agitprop are very much in evidence."[26]

Both writers are incorrect: Watts because his focus on published texts deflects attention away from performance and thereby misses continuities of practice; Endres because she seeks continuity in the forms and methods of textual production and thereby misses the continuity of practitioners. Seeking continuities of work, she overlooked the continuities of workers. Their statements of discontinuity are endorsed by historians of Canadian theatre, notably Eugene Benson and Leonard Conolly. For them the Workers' Theatre "disappeared with the outbreak of the Second World War," although "its vision and technique later resurfaced in the political style of George Luscombe's Toronto Theatre Workshop."[27]

In accepting the notion of discontinuity, left-wing theatre historians have been complicit in the erasure of the 1950s as a period of active theatre practice, social unrest, and dissident aesthetics. The myth of the empty pre-national 1950s enabled a narrative of self-discovery in the 1960s and 1970s, when the counterculture "rediscovered" the principles of activism, radical aesthetics, collectivity, and theatrical mobility. Like the narrative of nation-building, and professional canonicity that it shadowed, this narrative required any theatre-building to take place on a depopulated, empty ground.

The conventional narrative, then, grounds the discipline of theatre studies in Canada in a periodization myth of a radical thirties, a war-torn forties, a postcolonial sixties, and, in between, an empty, provisional, pre-national, and ideologically hostile fifties. This narrative reflects many problems, but the most important issue is that the radical theatre artists of the 1930s did not "disappear." They were still there, making radical activist theatre, and they never really stopped.

The real breakage was in the Communist Party itself. It was officially banned in 1941. But even that breakage was illusory because immediately in its place rose the Labour Progressive Party, under the same leadership and guided by the same principles. Before it reverted to the Communist Party of Canada in 1959 the LPP made remarkable progress in the Canadian political sphere – until it suffered an irreversible decline after the twin blows of the Soviet suppression in Hungary in 1956 and Khrushchev's speech to the 20th Congress of the CP-USSR in 1957.

"The people's culture flourishes"

Under the banner of the Labour Progressive Party, Canadian communists struggled to maintain public legitimacy in the viciously anti-communist panic and repression of the McCarthy era. The LPP and its youth wing, the National Federation of Labor Youth (formerly the Young Communist League) continued the Popular Front policy of solidarity with other progressive movements. Consequently its cultural programs attracted participants from a broad political spectrum. Over the course of the first half of the 1950s, the party's advocacy of a flourishing "people's culture" entailed a concerted move to broaden its cultural activities and audiences beyond the immediate embrace of the party and its community of affinity.[28] As in the 1930s, the major allied associations continued to be the Association of United Ukrainian Canadians (the new incarnation of the Ukrainian Labour Farmer Temple Association) and the United Jewish People's Order, formed in 1945 with the merger of the Labour League and the Canadian Workmen's Circle. The UJPO would play a central role in the development of a progressive culture that extended far beyond its Jewish constituency, principally in the emerging folk-song movement and the pageants, songs, and dances that originated at Camp Naivelt in Brampton, Ontario. (Its enduring legacy may be the Traveller's Canadianized version of "This Land Is Your Land," still heard around campfires at summer camps in Canada.)

Both of these associations had numerous branches across the country and actively encouraged the performing arts. The performances of the AUUC alone dismantle the proposal of discontinuity, because most of the troupes that had comprised the workers' theatre movement had been Ukrainian-language troupes of the Ukrainian Labour Farmer Temple Association. The ULFTA had been banned in 1940 and its Labour

Temples confiscated under the War Measures Act, but with the German invasion of the USSR it reformed as Ukrainian Society for Aid to the Fatherland and resumed its cultural programs, changing to the AUUC in 1942.

By the end of the war the fundamental structures that had provided the context and ideological support for the radical theatre of the pre-war years remained intact: a vanguard leadership party operating in industrial organizations, a cadre of cultural activists and intellectuals, and affiliate organizations with busy cultural programs. Much of this work went unnoticed by the mass media but was dutifully recorded by the Labour Progressive Party's newspaper, *Canadian Tribune*, and by *Champion*, the paper published by the National Federation of Labor Youth.

The LPP was, as James Doyle says, "anxious to get involved" in the cultural initiatives that attended the formation of the Massey Commission, and it paid close attention to the hearings.[29] As a party that sought electoral victory the LPP needed to develop a coherent cultural policy as part of the platform of the "new national policy" that Tim Buck outlined in his 1949 book *Canada: The Communist Viewpoint.* Positioning itself as a party fully prepared for electoral victory and governance, the LPP developed a cultural policy that emphasized nationalism and democratic access. Its cultural nationalism continued the theory of people's culture that had superseded ultra-left theories of proletarian culture in the 1930s, and brought it into line with the party's pro-Soviet, anti-American foreign policy in the era of the Korean War and the escalating nuclear arms race. In its annual cultural conferences, the LPP argued that Canadian culture was under "assault" by U.S. cultural imperialism and, perhaps for the first time in Canadian cultural criticism, introduced the concept of cultural "resistance." Charles Sims, chairman of the party's cultural commission (and occasional drama critic for the *Canadian Tribune*) made the express point, "There has been a new surge of democratic Canadian cultural expression: festivals, concerts, ballet, theatre. In many respects the cultural expressions of democratic Canadianism are sharper than the expressions of Canadian resistance to U.S. domination on the fronts of economics and politics."[30]

With this ideological investment in the arts, the LPP followed the developments of the Massey Commission closely. In its review of the commission's final report, the LPP criticized Massey's statement that culture must be considered a form of national defence: "Throughout the entire 517-page 200,000 word report there is not a word to suggest that an independent Canadian people's culture can only be built in peace."[31] On the practical level, the party criticized the report's failure to address key issues. The party wanted to see a ban on U.S. comic books (which it denounced as a corrupting and war-mongering influence); it wanted to see specific mention of the "national culture of French Canada"; it wanted to see a recommendation for a national theatre. The most significant failure of the commission, however, was its fundamental aversion to cultural pluralism: "Of all the millions of words written into hundreds of 'briefs' submitted to the Massey Commission on Arts and Sciences," the *Tribune* opined, "pitifully few touch upon the rights of Canadians to cultural expression and participation regardless of race, creed, color or religion."[32]

The LPP cultural policy, with its emphasis on democracy, nationalism, and human rights, was summarized as a major plank in the 1953 election platform:

> Develop and enrich our Canadian culture. Encourage the talents of our people and provide opportunities for musicians, singers, painters, writers and actors to practice their arts in Canada.
> Stop the pollution of our national life by preventing the importation of U.S. "gangster culture." Ban crime and horror comics.
> Federal grants of $100 million annually to stimulate the arts in English-speaking and French Canada, making possible the cultural expression of our growing democratic consciousness.
> Maintain federal control of TV and provide subsidies to give high quality Canadian programs. Guarantee freedom of expression on the CBC.
> Cultural exchanges with all countries.[33]

Within this policy framework, and the implicit policy that turned to the USSR for authority in aesthetics and cultural theory, two domains of cultural activity overlapped: cultural work and performance within the party and its affiliates; and work that addressed a wider public and invited wider participation. In both areas the LPP's bid for political legitimacy, its emphasis on patriotism, and its promotion of a national culture exerted a pronounced conservative influence on artistic practice, to the point that political and artistic radicalisms were increasingly opposed. The pages of the *Tribune* carried lively, informed, and heated debates about artistic practices, formalism, and cultural innovation, and, as Doyle explains in detail, these debates drew upon a rich canon of progressive literature and theory. But in the theatre critical issues remained untheorized and for the most part uncontested.

In general the left theatre in the 1950s in Toronto expressed the content-driven, cultural interventionist work of engagement – work that sought "to bring vital social theatre to the people, to their trade unions, churches, organizations and centres anywhere and everywhere"[34] – but that also functioned primarily as an organizational and community-building tool. It also went in the direction of the nation-building project of a professional, canonical theatre, as exemplified in the history of the Play-Actors, the direct successor to the Theatre of Action.

"The Paul Bunyan ideal"

The field of interventionist theatre in Toronto was framed by the work of the AUUC's Temple Theatre, the United Jewish People's Order's Theatre Workshop, and the National Federation of Labor Youth. These projects intersected with related groups in other fields, notably the AUUC's New Dance Theatre and the Labor Chorus, and with sporadic theatre ventures, such as the Toronto Labor Theatre, the direct antecedent of the Play-Actors. On occasion these groups conjoined, as they did in October 1951 in the production of *No Time to Cry*, "a folk play with music and dance about the life of needle trade workers," which had been "tested" at Camp Naivelt the previous summer. As described in a press release reprinted in the *Canadian Tribune*:

> The theme of the play is the struggle of the needle trades workers against layoffs, which inevitably must become a struggle against the war program. It is built around the life of Al Zippin and his wife Julia who have just succeeded in making the down payment on their new home.
>
> The scenes shift from early morning Spadina Avenue coming to life, into the interior of a cloak shop, to the office of the union bureaucracy, the beer parlor and the home of Al and Julia.[35]

With its combination of cultural specificity, theatricality, and community-building, and its collective authorship (by Reuben Blazer, Sam

Walsh, John Holmes, and Emil Gartner), *No Time to Cry* offers a bridge between *Eight Men Speak* and the collective documentaries of the popular theatre movement of the 1980s. Like *Eight Men Speak*, it was a pageant that offered an iconography of social positions in dramatic form and mobilized the power of cultural production seated close to the centre of the party. Like the later popular theatre documentaries, it foregrounded issue advocacy, multiculturalism, cultural location, and the testimonial presence of the actor.

No Time to Cry was a showcase event that enabled the *Canadian Trib-une* to announce that "the establishment of a people's theatre" was now "much closer to fruition."[36] In a phrase echoing the combat aesthetics of the 1930s, the *Tribune* concluded, "We are now on the road to having a vital theatre force." Performed at the UJPO's theatre on Christie Street and the Labour Temple Theatre on Bathurst, *No Time to Cry* was contained within the field of reception defined by the party and its affiliates.

Perhaps the most successful push into the wider public conscious-ness was the campaign to promote Paul Bunyan as a national heroic symbol. "The Mightiest Canadian," as *Champion* described him, "aris-ing out of the struggle for the people's rights, symbolizes in a very real sense the vigor, courage, inventiveness and determination of the Can-adian tradition." *Champion* in particular adopted Paul Bunyan as its own icon, and held annual "Paul Bunyan" subscription drives. Young "lumberjacks" could win Paul Bunyan pins – the first of which was cere-moniously awarded to LPP leader Tim Buck. For the party, the legend of Paul Bunyan offered more than a model "doer of mighty deeds."[37] In a version of the legend prepared by Tom McEwan in 1952, Bunyan personified Canadian demographic history. He was born in Quebec, the son of "Ivan Bunyan" and "an Ojibway Indian lass named Saraphina." The "Paul Bunyan ideal" was also an act of cultural resistance to the United States, where Bunyan held currency as a popular American folk hero. McEwan's fanciful reconstruction of the legend begins with a verse from a song by John Weir that emphasized the reciprocal complex of heroic Canadianism, anti-capitalism, and anti-Americanism: "Paul Bun-yan didn't do it for the wealthy or the banks, Paul Bunyan didn't do it for the money-grabbing Yanks, Paul Bunyan didn't do it for the grafter or the drone; Paul Bunyan is the people – and we rise to claim our own!"[38] As the embodiment of the Canadian people, Paul Bunyan appeared at various party rallies and events through the early 1950s, semiotically coded with a bushy black beard, lumberjack shirt, and massive axe. In 1955 he made his dramatic appearance on stage in *Little Paul Bunyan,* a musical produced by the National Federation of Labor Youth.

Written by *Champion's* business manager, Rube Bromstein, with Mary Holmes and John Holmes (leader of the NFLY Drama Group and co-author of *No Time to Cry*), *Little Paul Bunyan* featured lyrics by John Weir and music by Sam Golberg, Gene Mitchell, George Brand, and prominent LPP activist Mitch Sago. In dramaturgical form, plot, and content, *Little Paul Bunyan* fulfils the expectations placed on an internal party community-building performance. The hero, a meek worker in a factory faced with an impossible deadline to produce immense generators for the new St. Lawrence Seaway project, suffers the sneers and harassment of his foreman without complaint. He lacks the courage to express his love for Laura, the perky union steward. The opening scenes of the play take care to authenticate Paul as a worker, a sweeper who dreams of being a lineman. But the world of profit-driven industry gives him no opportunity to follow his ambition. The workers shiver in their unheated plant . One of them complains:

> When I started this job they told me the work was interesting – I'd learn a profession – I'd make good pay – I'd go places – I'd be somebody – and – – – What do I do? I get up at six – I go to work – I eat my lunch – I work till five – and then I go home. And then the whole darn thing starts all over again.[39]

This is the cue for the first song in the play ("Trouble, trouble, worry, worry/ Everything is hurry, hurry, hurry, hurry") in which the cast of workers sings and dances on a set dominated by an immense electric generator. (The setting of the play is itself an indirect citation to the party's campaign to have the St. Lawrence Seaway built entirely in Canadian waters, under Canadian control.)

Having been on holiday to St. Eustache, the legendary birthplace of his namesake and the site of the Patriotes rising in 1837, Paul receives in the mail his souvenir purchase, a very large axe:

> Paul: I know it sounds silly, but the storekeeper told me that this axe once belonged to a man so strong that he could, well, maybe even finish the generator himself in ten days.[40]

The axe is the token that summons the real Paul Bunyan, who is visible only to Little Paul and the audience. He discovers that the work deadline is a ruse, that the company has turned off the heat in the plant to slow production so the factory will lose the government contract. A pair of U.S. efficiency experts, sent ostensibly to advise on production, are exposed as corporate spies colluding with the company to turn the factory into a warehouse for U.S. imports. "Oh, American experts are we/ We've come from the great U.S.A./The land of the blue, white and free/ We've abandoned the red on the way."[41]

Big Paul teaches Little Paul to stand up in defiance. As he begins to defy the petty orders of the foreman, the truth comes out and the workers are fired on the spot. Prompted by Big Paul's voice, Little Paul offers a solution:

> LITTLE PAUL: That's right, the problem's right here, and we're the only people who can solve it. Why walk out? Let's see this thing through to a finish. Yeah, that's it, let's see this thing through and finish the job. Let's finish the generator.
> RHODA: Finish it?? How can we? We don't work here any more, remember?
> BIG PAUL: The biggest job we've got is to fight for our jobs.
> LITTLE PAUL: Yeah, we've got to fight for our jobs. If we don't finish this generator, I'll never get to be a lineman.
> BIG PAUL: The only time to finish this job—
> LITTLE PAUL (*Taking it away from Big Paul*): The only time to finish this job is now. The government ordered the generators now. The Seaway needs the generators now. And we need the jobs now.[42]

Hefting the axe, Little Paul offers the play's concluding message: "Paul Bunyan used this axe to build this country. And when it comes to building this country, we've all got a big axe to grind." When Laura asks how he became so strong when the going got tough, he answers, "It's just an old Canadian tradition."[43]

Like the Camp Naivelt pageants, *Little Paul Bunyan* was an exercise in community-building and morale. Its slapstick humour, sentimental songs, and affirmative dramaturgy – the positive representation of position – are common to spectacular forms that address a complicit audience. The innovative feature of *Little Paul Bunyan* is the ironic strike that climaxes the play, in which the dissenting workers claim the right to keep working for the sake of the nation. As one character announces, "I've heard about walk-out strikes, I've heard about slow down strikes, and I've heard about sit down strikes. But I've never heard of a stand-up-and-work strike." *Little Paul Bunyan*, then, offers a representation of heroic labour and selfless patriotism. The *Canadian Tribune* considered it a "triumph."[44] Despite noting minor flaws – the American villains were "too easily routed to be characteristic" and the cast more spirited than experienced – the reviewer concluded, "The important thing is that Little Paul Bunyan has a good plot, and lots of imagination, humor and song behind its Canada-first message. It is a major step forward."

No Time to Cry was "on the road" to a people's theatre; *Little Paul Bunyan* was a "step forward." The building of a progressive theatre was a necessary corollary of the establishment of a people's Canada, and as such had to remain a subjunctive, deferred aspiration. These shows demonstrated an archive of national progressive themes and a roster of creative artists. What they could not demonstrate was a public audience and a cultural legitimacy in the wider national sphere.

Disciplinarity and National Culture: The Play-Actors

Mrs. F.G. Sterndale Bennett and Mrs Louise Wolfenden will preside at the coffee table this evening at the on-stage party following the One-Act Play Festival at Hart House Theatre. The three groups competing are the Canadian Group Theatre, Play Actors and Pedagogy Players.
  – The Globe and Mail, *May 3, 1956*

In the 1930s the New Theatres had crashed the gates of the Dominion Drama Festival and carried off regional and national prizes with carefully rehearsed, socially progressive plays. Drawing upon experience and expertise in new forms of staging and production management, and having as an advantage the tradition of discipline that operated in left politics, these groups made a strong impression with their artistic standards. They also introduced new plays and dramatic techniques into the Dominion Drama Festivals, which had from their inception expressed the theatrical tastes of the cultural gentry. In her book Toby Gordon Ryan recounted the feelings of hostility encountered in the Festivals in the 1930s: "We were made to feel that we were intruders."[45] This response on the part of the Festivals only intensified in the 1950s, when communist affinities were widely held to be treason.

And yet the period of Red-baiting persecution and war panic saw increased political theatre coming from the left, especially before the internal crisis arose in the Labour Progressive Party in 1956. Continuing the strategies of the Popular Front, the party-affiliated theatre troupes reached out to a wider progressive membership and audience to address global issues of shared concern. For Gordon Ryan and other alumni of the Theatre of Action, this enterprise entailed a return to the Dominion Drama Festival, which had expanded and changed in character in the postwar years. As the emergent cultural economy enabled more career possibilities in the arts, the boundaries between professional and amateur became more blurred, establishing the domain of production that the Massey Report called "semi-professional." Like the Fringe Festivals of today, the Dominion Drama Festival became a showcase event in which aspiring professionals might earn distinction and possibilities of further work. Amateur companies advanced through local, regional, and provincial competitions, and the field of competition was fierce. Someone in the Play-Actors in this period typed up a contact list of forty-three amateur and would-be professional theatres in Ontario; it included such groups as Welsh Players, Avro Rapier Players, Canadian General Electric Players, and the Erin Junior Farmers Theatre Group.[46]

When Toby Gordon Ryan founded the Play-Actors in 1953, she had in mind a theatre that would specialize in finding new Canadian scripts, produce them at a professional standard, and win legitimacy in the system of competitive festivals that defined the field of amateur and semi-professional theatre. Previous efforts to establish a public theatre, including the theatre troupes of the United Jewish People's Order, Association of United Ukrainian Canadians, and the Toronto Labor Theatre (which had appeared in 1948, and again in 1951) had kept a progressive repertoire in the public eye but attracted little attention – although the UJPO's Belmont Theatre had won first prize in the 1950 Central Ontario Drama League competition with its staging of Odets's *Awake and Sing!*

More typical was an evening of performances in May 1952 that saw two one-act plays directed by Rose Kashtan for the Labor Theatre on a bill with the Finnish-Canadian Drama Group's production of *Waiting for Lefty* at a gala celebration for the *Canadian Tribune*. The Labor Theatre appears to have been the earliest incarnation of the Play-Actors; the *Tribune's* review noted that the group's next project would be *Thirty Pieces of Silver*.[47]

The Play-Actors drew upon the corps of actors and production crew that had developed around the Labor Theatre and UJPO and AUUC troupes. Walter Balay, John Holmes, Oscar Orenstein, and Louise Sandler were involved in most of the Play-Actors' productions. The Play-Actors in this sense emerged as the meeting of these groups, and as their joint effort to launch a non-sectarian troupe in the wider theatre community. The earlier pageants had shown that in its internal operations the LPP was the product of cross-cultural co-operation. In like manner the Play-Actors, although not a party operation, drew upon cross-cultural co-operation to present what might be considered a model theatre for a People's Canada: playing a progressive repertoire to a wide public, winning distinction for artistic mastery, operating as a democratic collective, training students. It was also one of the first theatres to enact a policy of colour-blind, cross-cultural casting and a commitment to cultural pluralism.

In 1954, when the troupe produced George Tabori's *The Emperor's Clothes*, it drew attention to its own diversity – possibly to dispel misapprehension about its cultural identity with this second Hungarian play in two years. Recirculating a press release, *The Globe and Mail* dutifully reported under the headline "The Play Actors, Ethnic Alliance":

> The Play-Actors represent a wide variety of ethnic groups but in their next production, The Emperor's Clothes, there are no Hungarians to fit its Hungarian setting. Walter Balay, its hero, is a Canadian of Ukrainian parentage, while Bella, his wife, is played by a well known Negro actress, Kathleen Livingstone. Their son Ferike is played by 12-year-old Johnny Wilcox, who is of Scottish, Irish and English heritage. Sig Illamachi is of Finnish stock; Aubrey Forbes is a Canadian Negro and others are of English, Jewish, Scottish and Irish descent in the company.[48]

In its three years of operation the Play-Actors tried to produce two shows a year, following the system developed by Theatre of Action. The work began in April 1953 with *Thirty Pieces of Silver* and was followed in December of that year with Ferenc Molnar's *Arthur*. In its second year of operation the group presented staged readings of Charles Mair's verse drama *Tecumseh* and Aristophanes' *Lysistrata*, and the full production of Tabori's *The Emperor's Clothes*. In its final year the Play-Actors staged a double bill of one-act plays: *Trifles*, by Susan Glaspell, and *Anniversary*, by Roland Penner, who had been active in the Winnipeg New Theatre and was a frequent contributor to *Champion*. The two one-acts shared the bill with a children's ballet, *The Magic Touch*, from the Walter Balay Canadian School of Dance. Choreographed by Balay with a libretto by Mitch Sago, the dance depicted a playground statue of Paul Bunyan coming to life to reconcile the disputes of children who had been led to violence by comic books. The group's final production, in March 1956, was Herman Heijerman's *The Good Hope*.

Along with this program, the Play-Actors also offered annual satirical cabarets and both evening and summer courses. In 1955 the summer courses were taught by Al Saxe, the New York Workers Laboratory Theatre member whose 1934 essay "*Newsboy*: From Script to Performance" was an articulate statement of the modernist æsthetics of agitprop.

The Play-Actors' choice of scripts related to the group's need to balance two fundamental objectives: to bring progressive themes, issues, and methods into the wider theatre culture, and to show supporters on the left that they could do so without sacrificing political integrity. But the very pressure of those goals may have led to difficulties in producing new Canadian plays.

Before the opening of *Thirty Pieces of Silver*, Gordon Ryan told the *Tribune*, "And most exciting of all is the possibility of producing plays about Canadian life by Canadian authors." In a 1954 publicity letter, she wrote that the Play-Actors "were vitally concerned with the growth and encouragement of Canadian Dramatic Literature."[49] Yet in three years of operation the group staged only one Canadian play. Of the others, *Thirty Pieces of Silver* was a dissident U.S. play about the McCarthyite culture of persecution and informants, premiered by the New Theatre in Melbourne and widely produced in Eastern Europe; *Arthur*, a minor comedy, was a satire of Americans in Europe by a Hungarian playwright; and *The Emperor's Clothes*, by a noted Hungarian resident in the United Kingdom, was a study of a man called upon to inform in a political witch hunt.

At this early stage the troupe's community on the left was indeed most concerned with ideological legitimacy. The *Tribune's* review of *Thirty Pieces of Silver* pointed out that although the play was not Canadian, with "sundry witchhunts loose in the land, its content was far from foreign." The unsigned review (most likely by Oscar Ryan) found minor faults with the script, but pronounced the play as being "timely." It ended with the hope that the Play-Actors might develop into "a living Canadian theatre group in this city dedicated to portraying Canadian reality and thus a part of the struggle for the broadening and deepening of Canadian consciousness and independence."[50]

That attitude explains the aborted production of *Tecumseh* that was announced to follow the staged reading in February 1954. Mair's *Tecumseh* was a problematic choice for the group. Written in 1887 in blank verse, this five-act tragedy is not so much about the Shawnee chief Tecumseh as it is about his alliance with the real hero of the play, Isaac Brock, the British general who repelled the U.S. invasion of Upper Canada in 1812. *Tecumseh* is an early expression of Canadian nationalism, written explicitly as a model national epic, and its U.S. characters are homicidal buffoons. The Play-Actors' pre-show publicity stated: "Charles Mair, who was prominent in the Canada First movement after Confederation, wrote *Tecumseh* as a contribution to the idea of Canadian nationhood. The Play-Actors are presenting this Canadian classic in the belief that it will contribute to the growing interest and pride in Canadian culture. We plan a stage production in the fall."[51]

But *Tecumseh*, as written by Mair, expresses an extremely conservative, pro-monarchist, anti-French nationalism. It is a literary monument to the nineteenth-century Tory dream of Imperial federation, and it is difficult to envision a room full of progressive leftists reading it without irony or anger. Some twenty years later, when Toronto's Factory Theatre Lab took on *Tecumseh*, the disruptive aesthetics of the counterculture enabled the cast to plunder and rewrite the play, fashioning it into their own postcolonial text. For the Play-Actors, that was not an option. The group was drawn to the play as evidence of an anti-American dramatic canon; to revise the play would in effect dismantle the canon they were trying to build.

The real anomaly in the Play-Actors' programming was their final production. *The Good Hope* was a classic Dutch socialist play, written in 1900, about living and working conditions in a fishing community.

Although Gordon Ryan mentions the play briefly in her memoir, she merely notes that it brought her group into contact with the Dutch community in Toronto.[52] She does not discuss their reasons for doing the show, but *Champion*'s pre-show article on the play provides a few clues. After a short explication of the play, the article switches to focus on Play-Actors' grounding in Stanislavskian principles and "group acting." *Champion* noted that the Play-Actors had twenty-seven members, "most of whom are under 25."[53] This noted youthfulness, combined with the inexperienced casts who had performed one-act play entries in the festival competition in the previous year, suggests that the major effort behind *The Good Hope* was pedagogical. The play was chosen in part because, as a social realist classic requiring an ensemble cast, it was ideal for training young actors in deep character work.

In the 1930s, Theatre of Action had made its reputation with innovative productions that drew on new staging techniques. Compared to those plays, the Play-Actors' choices were theatrically conservative. All of them were written in a high realist mode. They conformed to the expectation of socialist realism in the party. For an artist like Toby Gordon Ryan, this representational realism placed more weight on acting and directing as processes of revealing "truth" on stage, which meant that the real creativity in the theatre had to be the actor's construction of subtextual character. At this high tide of doctrinaire socialist realism on the left, Stanislavsky's focus on "truth" was interpreted to mean literal representation. *Champion*'s five-paragraph digest of Stanislavsky, offered as an explication of *The Good Hope*, stated flatly: "Acting should be real, live and human – not dead, conventional, or theatrical.... Actors must avoid falseness, that is they must avoid everything which is directed against nature, logic, and common sense."[54]

Nevertheless, Gordon Ryan's commitment to the aim of producing new Canadian plays was solid. "We will not have a national theatre until we have a found a national voice – and that adds up to scripts," she wrote to Herbert Whittaker, whose warm review of *The Good Hope* in *The Globe and Mail* proved to be the only notice that the Play-Actors received in the mainstream press.[55] The scripts she needed were of a particular kind: realist dramaturgy, progressive themes, and "truthful representation," which in effect meant a Canadian socialist realism.

The troupe's one effort to stage a Canadian play, Roland Penner's *Anniversary*, was a disaster. Penner, an army veteran and young lawyer, was a prominent activist in the Labour Progressive Party and National Federation of Labor Youth in Winnipeg. His family had a long history of cultural and political activism. He had acted in the New Theatre, which Oscar Ryan and Toby Gordon Ryan had helped found in the mid-1930s. In the mid-1950s Penner was also an aspiring impressario who brought Pete Seeger, Odetta, and Paul Robeson to Winnipeg. He went on to a distinguished career as a lawyer, law professor, and attorney general of Manitoba. Penner would recall, "My one and only play was so tendentious that even the 'lefties' in the audience hated it. I destroyed all copies."[56] But a carbon typescript did survive in Gordon Ryan's papers. Written in a detailed social realist style, the play depicts a couple celebrating their tenth wedding anniversary, haunted by the memory of the child they lost in the Blitz. As they babysit their neighbour's child, the sirens and rehearsed bomb effects of a civil defence air-raid drill evoke memories of the war and terrify the child. By the end of the play the couple determine to resist the war-scare tactics and have another child and work for peace. An unsigned reviewer in the *Canadian Tribune* judged the play "disappointing" – "It set out to create in the audience a horror of atomic war and at best generated only mild interest laced with embarrassment."[57]

In a lengthy and candid letter to Penner after the production, Gordon Ryan offered useful dramaturgical and directorial advice and encouraged him to write another play for the group. She suggested that the play was too short to allow for the necessary character development, but that "the play has an impact and the thing you did achieve was to create warm human beings and good human relationships on stage that are valid and easy to watch." She was disappointed in the adjudicator, Robert Gill, then director of Hart House Theatre, who dismissed the play as propaganda. "Mr. Gill is a very superficial adjudicator from whom inexperienced writers, actors and directors can learn very little." But her major disappointment was with the audience, and in particular "our own people," some of whom were "very critical of the play and referred to it as a 'dramatized leaflet' or [said] 'if I want to read pamphlet I'll read it.' These are just a couple of remarks – from what I understand there were even more violent reactions from some of our people." She concluded, "There is terrible negativism in our movement when dealing with matters cultural.... The lip service some people pay to the promotion of Canadian culture is not borne out by their actual attitude when they see or hear anything.... My own opinion is that we have not yet developed a criticism yet which is commensurate with the developments on the cultural field in this country." [58]

Negativism in the movement there may have been, but like Theatre of Action before, the Play-Actors needed the movement to provide its community of response even as it reached out to a wider public. Gordon Ryan complained bitterly that their work met with hostility, and even though she had won an award (given to a "new" director, despite her twenty years of theatre work) for *The Emperor's Clothes* at the Central Ontario Drama Festival, the Play-Actors troupe was for the most part ignored by the mainstream media. Like Theatre of Action, the Play-Actors group was sensitive to major changes in its "movement."

The Good Hope was in its last weeks of rehearsal when the Soviet leadership released to the world its revelations of the crimes of the Stalin era. The effect on the Labour Progressive Party was catastrophic, and the impact was compounded later in the year when the party supported the brutal Soviet suppression of the Hungarian uprising. These two events led to a massive wave of resignations, leaving the party in the hands of its most determined loyalists. With this trauma, which effectively reduced a community to its party organization, the Play-Actors ceased operations. In her memoir Toby Gordon Ryan merely says that the group disbanded because "the load of running this theatre was just too heavy for the few of us involved."[59]

And so it ended. But once again an ending was not the end. If 1953 was a year of beginnings that enables us to plot the continuities of radical theatre, in its way 1956 was equally momentous. At the same time that Gordon Ryan decided to shut down the last best attempt by the cultural left to claim space in the emergent professional theatre domain, the young George Luscombe, inspired by five years of work in Britain with Joan Littlewood, and steeped in the disciplinarity of Stanislavsky and Rudolf Laban, came home to Toronto. He had a burning ambition to build a theatre there that would be radical in voice and method. Once again, radical theatre would "begin" in Toronto.

Radical Futures

Of course I'm a tyrant, but then, so is the theatre.
  – George Luscombe

By the mid-1950s, Toby Gordon Ryan had spent twenty years working as a director. By any measure she must be considered one of the major theatrical figures of the first half of the twentieth century in Canada. But she has always been relegated to a footnote, as the memoirist of one historical moment. She was aware of that herself, as evidenced by her wry amusement that after those two decades of work she had finally won an award for a "new" artist. She was consigned to the left margins not because of her communist affinities but because she never did turn her theatre practice into a producing theatre facility. Today she would be understood as a successful indie theatre artist. In her day she was just one more failed semi-professional because she did not conform to the template that developed in the 1950s by which a company becomes "real" when it acquires a theatre plant, an audience base, an Actors' Equity agreement, and a not-for-profit charter.

A gendered text is clearly at work in this case. In some instances companies did come into formation through the efforts of strong-willed and powerful women (Dora Mavor Moore at the New Play Society in Toronto, Martha Allan at the Montreal Repertory Theatre), but by the mid-1960s the professional theatres that had formed around charity incorporations and public boards were almost all directed and managed by men. The women who built the Canadian theatre movement in the 1940s and 1950s were by and large shoved aside. In most cases when the developmental template worked, the driving leadership came from men who knew how to work the system and could present themselves as authoritative, masculine, and dynamic. Meet George Luscombe.

Perhaps no person did more to bring a radical vision into the professional culture in Canadian theatre, but to the end of his days Luscombe insisted that he was a humanist whose main allegiance was to a living theatre that emerged from and performed to its community. He was a lifelong socialist and scrapper, and in the thirty-odd years in which he directed Toronto Workshop Productions, his greatest projects were those in which his vision of a rigorously trained ensemble found poetry, theatrical joy, and physical excitement in plays that brought life to social and historical struggle. For Luscombe theatre had to be engaging both socially and politically. He believed in a theatre of ideas, but he also believed in passion and in theatre as a primal form of human communication. Towards the end of his life, when he was awarded an honorary doctorate from the University of Guelph, he rose from his wheelchair, leaned over the podium, and began, "In the beginning was the word." A dramatic pause for effect, and then he roared, "BULLSHIT!"

His legacy is mixed. While he trained, provoked, and sometimes bullied the emergent generation of theatre artists who took Toronto theatre into the counterculture sixties, he was repaid with the rebellion that he nurtured. That rebellion was only partly a response to his reputed "autocratic" nature. It was also a rejection of the deep system of craft discipline and work regime that he saw as the core principle of a truly professional theatre.[60] In his work at Toronto Workshop Productions Luscombe achieved what Theatre of Action and Play-Actors had sought, but the nature of theatrical radicalism was changing in a direction he could not follow. Luscombe and TWP thus came to occupy a space in which shifting cultural ideologies, generational dissent, and a changing field of reception obscure the theatrical genius of his work. Luscombe began his career in a theatre culture that craved the disciplinarity he brought to it; in the middle of his career he awed audiences, critics, and the profession with the mature work that he could produce with that discipline (most famously, his production of *Ten Lost Years* in 1974); by the end of his career he was criticized as a dinosaur, as out of touch, as fixated on one particular theatrical method. In response he would say, at least he *had* a method.

When Luscombe began his Workshop Productions in 1959 he had more than fifteen years' experience as a working actor. He had started performing as a teenager with a Co-operative Commonwealth Federation troupe in East York during the war. He was a talented performer. Surviving photographs show him playing the piano, and later he was known for his dancing ability. He began his training in 1946 in the theatre school affiliated with the CCF, and after a short stint as a graphic artist he became a full-time actor, working for room, board, and a meagre box-office share with the touring People's Repertory Theatre (which, despite its name, was not a socialist project). That was as far as a stage career could take him at the end of the 1940s. Determined to get more training, he went to England in 1950, where he spent six formative years in pantomimes and melodramas, becoming, after his first year in the United Kingdom, a core member of Joan Littlewood's Theatre Workshop ensemble. After returning to a somewhat more enlivened theatre scene in Canada he ground out a living as a journeyman actor, taking whatever roles he could get on Toronto stages and performing in CBC television dramas (acting alongside Mavor Moore, Larry Solway, John Drainie, and Powys Thomas). For one memorable summer in 1958 he acted at the Garden Centre Theatre, a summer stock company in Vineland, Ontario. In Kenneth Robert's wildly popular and nostalgic war play *Mr. Roberts* he played Ensign Pulver, the role made famous on film by Jack Lemmon.

Luscombe was building a resumé and a network of connections that might well have taken him further as an actor. He was perfectly positioned to move into the early company of the Stratford Festival, along with contemporaries such as William Shatner and Christopher Plummer. He had experience playing the classics with Littlewood at London's Theatre Royal Stratford East, and had performed with her company on tours to Paris and Warsaw. By the early 1950s, Littlewood's populist style and commitment to popular audiences were percolating through the professional theatre world, and if anything the connection gave Luscombe added credibility. (One of the ironies of Canadian theatre in the 1960s is that many of the British directors who ran the regional theatres, and who were criticized as colonists by the cultural nationalists of the new alternative theatre, identified themselves with the left working-class movement in Britain.)

But Luscombe was consumed by another vision. At a time when the theatrical futures in Toronto were up for grabs, he was determined to build the kind of theatre that Littlewood had built in London. She and Ewan MacColl had revolutionized British theatre in the 1940s by taking the idea of ensemble "group theatre" and applying it to a form of play development that began with the creative actor and improvisation. They were both largely self-taught (although Littlewood had been to drama school). Their early agitprops established a firm link between the workers' theatre movement and contemporary radical theatre.

Looking back in his autobiography to his early attempts at agitprop in Salford, MacColl wrote, "The agitprop sketches in our repertoire made no demands on us as actors and this was the real cause of our dissatisfaction. We were clumsy, didn't know how to move properly, and knew nothing about developing our voices." In her own memoir, Littlewood has MacColl (then known as Jimmy Miller) saying to her when they met, "Only the best is good enough for the workers. Agitprop is crude in the age of [Adolphe] Appia. Don't discount beauty."[61]

For MacColl and Littlewood, the hierarchical distinctions of creative control were to be resisted and reformulated. Their anti-authoritarianism chafed at the regimentation of agitprop but thrilled at its theatrical power.

They sought a craft discipline that could train actors as creative artists rather than scenographic elements, that would honour their own cultural traditions of artisanship and work and could be used in the widest possible spread of theatrical styles and texts. Littlewood and MacColl sought discipline and regime, but they also sought out a personal sense of aesthetics that would fuse craftwork and art, with disciplinarity imposed by the artistic task, and regime developed by the creative self. They found their solution in a conjunction of Stanislavsky and Rudolf Laban.

From Stanislavsky, they took – and taught themselves – techniques of rigorous dramaturgical analysis that gave actors agency as creative analysts and led to clear procedures for improvisational scene-building. This was a new understanding of Stanislavsky. They saw him not as an architect of depth psychology in the performance of dramatic character, but as the originator of disciplined procedures for entering and controlling creative states and for analysing and embodying subtext.

The circulation of Stanislavskian techniques in left theatre culture had always operated as an ideological barometer. In the radical agitprop phase of the militant Third Period of class struggle, the emphasis was on the actor's creative imagination, the physical exercises devised to control that creativity, and the microanalysis of text in terms of action objectives. In the Popular Front years, Stanislavsky's work became a regulating script that proved the necessity of unity as a thematic and aesthetic condition, and as such became one of the critical means of justifying the theory of socialist realism. For Littlewood and MacColl, socialist realism was an anti-theatrical retreat to bourgeois aesthetics. Having been expelled from the Communist Party (in part over this very issue) and thereby released from doctrinal authority – and rebellious by nature – they found a Stanislavsky that favoured the actor as investigator of process rather than student of the text.

And they danced. In modern dance, fascination with mechanics as social text and method had led to an appreciation of the performer's muscular effort as a creative process that expanded the endurance and reach of the body. In their early work Littlewood and MacColl integrated classes in ballet and mime into their training sessions. Howard Goorney, a member of Littlewood's troupe, offers a fascinating anecdote that suggests one source for this early integration of dance: Ernst Toller's production of his play *Draw the Fires* at Manchester Repertory Theatre in 1935. As Goorney explains it, Toller needed actors to play stokers, stripped to the waist, shovelling coal into boilers. The actors in the company were totally unconvincing. Toller was in despair, and Littlewood suggested that he use MacColl and his friends, who were quite used to handling a shovel and making themselves heard over the noise of machinery.[62] MacColl's performance was an early expression of what would become a signature element of Theatre Workshop: the working body of the working-class actor, the body that works to demonstrate its own ability to work, that transforms muscularity into performance. Littlewood referred to the new form as "dance theatre." The new form of documentary exemplified by *Johnny Noble* and *Uranium 235* – plays that established a template for the collectively created documentary agitprops that typified the radical counterculture in both the 1960s and 1980s – was built out of movement and mime sequences. Luscombe would continue in these methods at TWP. Like Littlewood, he believed that every actor must be a dancer.

Littlewood and MacColl had been using Laban's technique well before they actually met the man and trained with him in person. The encounter offered a secularization of modern dance that relocated the aesthetics of dance in the muscular effort of the actor-worker. Laban speaks of "the human body engine," and his "efforts" became well known only after they were directed towards educational and instructional ends.[63] Like Vsevolod Meyerhold, Laban studied the body as a machine, but rather than looking at the mechanics of body movement and articulation – the body as instrument – he studied the "human engine" in terms of the work it produced. The result of his workshops with Littlewood's ensemble was a team of actors trained to exercise creative exploration – but people who could work in unison and whose muscular work on stage served to authenticate the material they performed.

Equipped with this discipline, Littlewood created a revolution in British theatre. MacColl left Theatre Workshop when it moved to London, pursuing his own historic career as a songwriter, musician, and radio producer. Littlewood then embarked on the directing career that would culminate in her 1963 production *Oh What a Lovely War*. But by then the original Theatre Workshop ensemble had broken up. Personal politics and changes in artistic and political philosophy had led to a major split in 1955.[64]

A major consequence of that split was George Luscombe's return to Canada in 1956 and his commitment to continuing the ensemble workshop method in Toronto. Indeed, later in his life he maintained that Littlewood herself had acknowledged that he was the only director who continued her work. In his three decades of directing in Toronto, Luscombe, like Littlewood, returned to touchstone productions over the years to remake them. His theatre specialized in the performance of non-dramatic materials, all using the same workshop method. But unlike Littlewood, Luscombe showed little interest in the classics or the new dramatic literature springing from the theatrical revolution of the sixties and seventies. He kept his black-box theatre small and simple (it was famous for its uncomfortable bench seating). He demanded rigorous ensemble training even when it ran into opposition from an emergent anti-authoritarian theatre culture.

Like Littlewood, Luscombe developed a theatre that blurred the boundaries of documentary and invention in the larger project of actor-centred non-dramatic performances. The "document" might be a transcription of oral history, but it might just as well be speech from Shakespeare or text from a book by Dickens. In one of his most celebrated plays, *Chicago '70*, the ensemble improvised scenes from phoned-in reports from the notorious Chicago conspiracy trial, performing them in a parodic frame drawn from *Alice in Wonderland*. For Luscombe, the real work of documentary theatre was the working actor bringing a disciplined craft to bear on political issues. Actuality and fiction were equally real in the working body of the actor.

Luscombe, then, was not particularly interested in playwriting as drama. He saw plays as raw material for performances, and playwrights who were possessive of their scripts did not last long with him. Nor did he see plays as ever finished; each production was simply a stage of development. As a result few of his productions were ever published. Authorship was always a stressful issue with Toronto Workshop Productions. Luscombe treated writers the way Hollywood directors treat screenwriters, but as the Canadian theatre profession developed in the 1960s it was rapidly moving towards a playwright-centred system. For Luscombe, a writer might provide words, but he as director was the author of the *mise en scène* and the actors were the authors of their performances. But copyright law as it developed during this period, and as patrolled by ACTRA and other professional associations, made no provision for the director as an author. *Ten Lost Years* was published in *Canadian Theatre Review* and later anthologized, but it became mired in copyright disputes.

On this ground of text and ownership two radical theatre futures came into contact in TWP's second season. In 1964 Luscombe received an unsolicited script that he found "very powerful," but he was put off by its narrative realist style and its theme of homosexuality and prison rape.[65] The playwright was John Herbert, a drag performer, dancer, and director who was in the process of starting his own theatre. The play was an early version of *Fortune and Men's Eyes* – which would eventually open in New York three years later. In his study of the history of queer theatre in Toronto, Paul Halferty considers the question of why "the city's most ideologically-aligned theatre, whose stated commitments were to staging politically conscious plays, would neither support nor produce *Fortune.*" He suggests that "whether or not the reason for Luscombe's rejection was aesthetic or his own homophobia," the avoidance was a factor of the Toronto theatre community's own homophobia and, moreover, that "homosexuality was *not* considered an important political issue. Indeed, it seems that *Fortune*'s inclusion of homosexuality as a political issue prevented its staging, and its broad critique of Canadian society at TWP."[66]

Luscombe did invite Herbert to work on a planned adaptation of Georg Buchner's proto-expressionist play *Woyzeck.* Herbert delivered an adaptation but conflict arose in rehearsal when Luscombe sought to add improvised material to the script. In the end, Luscombe fired Herbert, who threatened a law suit. Herbert later produced his own version at his Garret Theatre in 1969.

This moment of conflict and disconnect is one of the most telling examples of how dissident theatre became chaotically and unsystematically institutionalized in Canada. Luscombe and Herbert were both radicals and outsiders; both refused accommodation with the dominant system of theatre production; both despised the affectations of the profession; both were committed to oppositional and angry theatre. But their political worlds took them in different directions. Luscombe was still a working-class radical for whom collectivity (but not collectives) was a first principle; Herbert was a radical queer man who had the courage to live a drag life in a profoundly puritan and homophobic social climate. He was the model and inspiration for the next generation of queer theatre activists – one of whom, Sky Gilbert, would found the most famous queer theatre in North America and eventually move it into the theatre that Luscombe built on Alexander Street. What was once Toronto Workshop Productions became Buddies in Bad Times (founded

1979), and over the following decades, on the same floor that Luscombe and Herbert had drawn an irreconcilable line, a new generation of dissident artists would drive one of the most creative theatre plants in Canadian history.

In the end Luscombe's place in the narratives of Canadian theatre history would remain contested. To the historians who understood Canadian theatre in terms of the construction of a capacity to produce a repertoire of plays written by Canadians, Toronto Workshop Productions was part of neither the colonized past nor the alternative present. In 1972 Don Rubin, later the founder and editor of *Canadian Theatre Review*, attempted to pull together an outline of Canadian theatre history inflected by the then-popular discourse of cultural nationalism. He was clearly disturbed by how TWP did not fit into a narrative scheme that identified alternative theatre with a commitment to the Canadian playwright. He found that TWP deserved "positive mention" because of its "original productions at a time when original productions were not considered chic." Still, he went on, "Most of TWP's original work did consist of adaptations of foreign literature, particularly American works and American concerns, and as such, its contribution, while interesting, has not really been all that significant." Others agreed. Denis Johnston, in his history of Toronto alternative theatres, glances briefly at Luscombe to explain why he is not part of the story. He notes that when the young radical directors who launched what we know of today as the Toronto theatre scene formed into a "New Directors Group" in 1970, they did not invite Luscombe, nor was he invited to participate in the epochal Festival of Underground Theatre in that same year. Johnston calls Luscombe "a separate force in Toronto theatre, a maverick."[67]

Gordon Vogt, who until his untimely death in 1985 was one of the best theatre critics in Canada, and a fierce advocate of TWP, had a different point of view on Luscombe. He wrote:

> Luscombe has not given us artifacts by way of scripts to be reworked by future generations. What he has done is to put his talent and his heart and soul into moment after moment of stage time. I regret that his work will someday be available only indirectly through inspiration or memory. Yet to say that his particular ongoing achievement is not as important as those who carve on stone is to value the artifact over art.[68]

In his signature play *Hey Rube!* Luscombe crafted the story of a rag-tag group of circus folk stuck on the edge of nowheresville, besieged by rubes bent on driving them out of town. First staged in 1961, *Hey Rube!* was TWP's first hit, and Luscombe restaged it again in 1966 and again in 1984. At times the rubes really did try to drive him out of town. In 1976 the theatre was gutted by a fire on the night before the opening of *You Can't Get Here from There*, a play created with longtime collaborator Jack Winter about Canada's refusal to admit refugees from Pinochet's fascist Chile. The cause of the fire was never determined, but it was widely perceived to have been politically motivated arson. In 1989 the rubes struck again – and won when they used their majority on the TWP board to fire Luscombe. Soon thereafter they voted to dissolve the company.

Toronto Workshop Productions was Luscombe's circus. He trained numerous actors, designers, and writers in a rigorous process of hard performance work. The names that passed across its stage add up to a virtual history of the left wing of the theatre profession, which alone secures his place in Canadian theatre history and in the history of radical cultural activism. He degentrified theatre in Toronto. He was instrumental in infusing a radical spirit in Canadian theatre.

Luscombe and the Ryans knew one another; Oscar Ryan reviewed his plays, and Toby Gordon was a supporter of his work. Indeed, I first met the Ryans in the foyer of the TWP theatre. These artists never worked together, but they pursued similar goals. Luscombe and Toby Gordon Ryan both valued topical content over cultural nationalism. Both were deeply invested in the idea of theatre as work. Both found in Stanislavsky the analytic tool to transform work into creativity, and both had tried to develop a theatrical relationship with the organized labour movement, although neither of them got much further than the stage of encouraging interest. Both of them, in their own terms, achieved their ambitions, but both became narrated as historical dead ends. Still, in the continuity of their practices they were connected by a living, performing thread of engaged theatre work that continued on after their work ended. Their successors were the activist theatres of the popular theatre movement. This new breed would find their own way to working in and with social justice communities and rethinking the fundamental principles of theatre discipline.

6

Generation Agitprop, with Puppets

STRIKE!

THE PLAY!

The faculty of the University of Guelph are in a legal position to strike on March 14. A strike would shut down classes, and the students of the university would be among those most affected -- but <u>no</u> <u>one</u> <u>is</u> <u>telling</u> <u>us</u> <u>anything</u>!

Find out what's really going on, how we got here, and how it could affect you; in an all-new play, written and performed by Guelph students.

There will be a discussion/Q&A about the issues and the play, following the show.

**Thursday, March 6, 2008
5:45 PM
MacKinnon Room 117**

TONIGHT!

In the theatrical sixties the social rules of performance, spectatorship, and critical reception changed astonishingly quickly.[1] In this event the theatre as a domain of practice was actually somewhat behind the pace of cultural change in general. While self-identified theatre radicals were challenging the theatre estate with ideas of democratization and underground and alternative culture (and the arts councils had to brace themselves for the sudden appearance of hundreds of new theatre troupes that were popping up, seemingly out of nowhere), a new kind of bootstrap chaos performance had already become well established in North American culture. Its sources were not in the canonical theatre but in rock'n'roll, television, street theatre, and all the media hype of a cultural revolution. Chemical enhancement was part of it too. The performative was normative; Howdy Doody's kids were acting up.

There are countless examples of how popular culture performance interrupted and challenged politics, because dissent in the 1960s was heavily represented in the media and well aware of audience. Photographic records and film archives reveal the defining icons – not just of folk singers but of giant puppets, parades, and hippies levitating the Pentagon – but these were merely the peak moments of a performative dissent that was seemingly everywhere.[2]

In 1971 – to take just one example – a group of high-school students in Toronto invaded a school board meeting. An article in the *Toronto Telegram* described the event:

> York Borough trustees were "treated" to a little guerrilla theatre last night, but they didn't appear entertained and certainly weren't amused.
>
> The act, replete with a girl in a bikini, one in a strait jacket, a boy with a capgun and another in clown mask, was staged as a reply to the board's deferral of a request for political clubs in York Memorial Collegiate.[3]

These high-school kids were picking up and playing back images that were circulating in popular culture, in a reciprocal flow of influence from the stage to the street. They were making themselves part of the show. Although they had probably never heard of the Situationist International or Fluxus, they were replaying the dadaist refusal of aesthetics at the same time as they were claiming the right to use their bodies as instruments of dissent in corporate space. They were also consumers of cultural industries that targeted their dissent as business. The seepage of radicalism and profit makes for unstable historical boundaries.

In Toronto in 1970 audiences could see George Luscombe's rock-inflected carnivalesque documentary on the Chicago conspiracy trials, *Chicago '70*, Richard Schechner's theatre encounter *Dionysus in '69* as reinterpreted by Studio Lab Theatre, *Hair*, which seemed to be running forever at the Royal Alex, and the emergent local alternative theatre at the Festival of Underground Theatre in, around, and under the new St. Lawrence Centre. All of these shows presented themselves as being radical in some ways, but the public performance of the radical self was by then losing credibility as an effective political position. The high-school students in their agitprop invasion of the school board meeting were apprehending something else: that radicalism is not just in performance, but also in spectatorship; that is, in applied performance in tactical situations for targeted audiences.

From 1965 to the late 1970s agitprop evolved through clearly defined stages, each of them generating numerous vectors of adaptation. The prevailing practices had a wide social distribution, as revealed by a number of examples: the carnivalesque street theatre of the counter-culture in Vancouver; the tactical use of advocacy agitprop by a professional theatre group in Ottawa in the mid-1970s; and the reinvention of interventionist agitprop for the labour movement at the end of the 1970s. Then too, as a more recent example from a university campus shows, agitprop continues to offer a useful means of mobile, quick, and low-tech political response for student activists.

Deregulating Agitprop

Interested in theatre? making plays happen – outdoors, indoors, guerilla-style. Also do mind-expanded

improvisations. This will be a very different style
of theatre than anything done here in the past
(yesterday). Box 148 Georgia Straight.
   – Georgia Straight, *want ad*, Sept. 8, 1967

From the early years of the decade U.S. theatre troupes like Bread and
Puppet Theater and the San Francisco Mime Troupe had explored new
performance forms that became part of the cultural vocabulary of the
anti-war movement. The Bread and Puppet Theater played with giant
puppets and processional parades in a spirit of pacifist anarchism. It
gave the period its defining and persistent visual image in the puppet
figure of Uncle Fatso. The troupe's founder, Peter Schumann, famously
baked and shared bread after every performance (and continued to do
so for another half-century from the troupe's farm in Vermont). The SF
Mime Troupe, through its various incarnations and political stances –
from an almost Stalinist revolutionary dogmatism to community-based
activism – developed a cartoon sit-com agitprop style that proved to be
easily imitated and highly effective in outdoor performance spaces. At
the same time theatre critics and scholars were excavating the archive
of popular performance forms (including 1930s agitprop), and journals
such as *The Drama Review* (familiarly known as *TDR*) in the United States
and *Theatre Quarterly* in Britain circulated manifestos, scripts, and performance documentations. These became performance templates for
radical students who advanced the idea of "guerrilla theatre."
   That very term – "guerrilla theatre" – would become so overworked that its original equation of performance with masculinist violence was lost somewhere along the way. The term plays with the notion
of performance as combat. In his essay "Notes in Defense of Combative
Theater," published in Henry Lesnick's highly influential 1973 anthology, *Guerilla Street Theater*, Charles Brover made the point that "even
theater has a role to play in history, and the role of combative theatre is
to expose, challenge, and tell the truth necessary for purposive work."[4]
Indeed, for most of the twentieth century political theatre was at least
partly a property claimed by mass revolutionary socialist parties in their
historical course from the Second International to the Cold War. The
military discipline of Leninism and the regimentation of Maoism provided a model for the relationship of the political centre to performance,
with political theatre understood as an expression of the suppressed

popular state that would be restored by the revolution. Political theatre was thus understood as both tactical (an arm of the revolutionary party) and popular (the theatre of the people). In the breakdown of centralizing mass movements in the Cold War, the practices of radical theatre began to detach from its location as the theatre estate of the revolution, and the years after 1968 experienced a remarkable growth in a cultural world that now came to understand oppression in terms of hegemonies rather than ideological scripts. Rarely today in the industrial world do we hear people speak of "theatre for the people." The humanist proposition of "the people" lost purchase.

Yet the image of the guerrilla artist persists as an icon of political theatre. This figure, which originated in images of guerrilla fighters in national liberation movements, began to circulate in the insurrectionary theatre practices of the 1960s. Chief amongst these images was the ubiquitous portrait of Che (recently recirculated in the anti-globalization movement), but perhaps more influential was the image of the Viet Cong guerrilla fighter. One of the best-selling titles of the period was Vo Nguyen Giap's "insurrection manual," *People's War, People's Army*, in which the victor of Dien Bien Phu (and later strategist of the Vietnamese victory over the Americans) summarized guerrilla tactics as a particular "way of fighting the revolutionary war." The method, he stated:

> relies on the heroic spirit to triumph over modern weapons, avoiding the enemy when he is the stronger and attacking him when he is the weaker, now scattering, now regrouping one's forces, now wearing out, now exterminating the enemy, determined to fight him everywhere, so that wherever the enemy goes he would be submerged in a sea of armed people who hit back at him, thus undermining his spirit and exhausting his forces.[5]

Young radical Americans resisted the war and the military draft. Theirs were the postures of combative masculinism, and possibly the rhetoric of the guerrilla may have had more to do with testosterone and the military complicities of theatre culture than it did with actual cultural strategy. Certainly no one could argue that guerrilla artists arose from a sea of (culturally) armed people. The guise of the guerrilla was as loaded with masculinist heroism as was the "theatre is our weapon" rhetoric of the 1930s. The language of guerrilla theatre began to diminish at the end of the 1970s, primarily because as agitprop became more directed towards social justice and ecological issues it experienced a significant regendering that smoothed its combative edge.

U.S. troupes and practitioners crossed the border into Canada frequently. The San Francisco Mime Troupe began performing in Vancouver in 1964, and Bread and Puppet made an appearance at the Toronto Festival of Underground Theatre in 1970. (In Robert Kramer's 1969 underground revolutionary film *Ice*, Bread and Puppet's main contribution to the new American revolution is in smuggling guns across the border in their puppets.) These groups were part of a theatrical traffic that made the new radical theatre movement truly international. Abandoning the attempt at organizational and ideological regulation that had been the case with the workers' theatre movement, they represented an undisciplined migration of forms, bodies, and practices. Affluent young Canadians coming out of universities with artistic aspirations travelled the world – especially to France and Britain – and came back with new ideas, and troupes like Bread and Puppet brought the ideas to Canadian audiences. Often they stayed. The impact of U.S. war resisters was arguably more profound in the theatre than in any other cultural domain.

Politically, "the taste of the sixties" may have soured and the movement burned out by 1969, as historian Bryan Palmer suggests, but culturally it was just taking off by then.[6] By the end of the sixties agitprop was everywhere, in the giant puppets of anti-war demonstrations, in parks, in the staged media events of the Yippies, in courtrooms, on university campuses, and at schools. Much of it was a form of busking, but for a period of about three years many pickup troupes received funding through the Secretary of State's Opportunities for Youth program, which provided a minimal wage and overhead for community projects. At first glance the street theatre and agitprop performances of the sixties seem like a steady reiteration of overly familiar forms. We see a recurrence of traditional theatre motifs, especially *Punch & Judy, commedia dell'arte*, and medicine show citations – and these were "citations" rather than polished performances because often the events were a case of young, barely trained actors presenting their own versions of complex performance practices. The effort was often a deliberate political tactic that, at least in Canada (and Australia and Scotland, where very similar citations occurred), represented a postcolonial moment, with young actors from auxiliary imperial cultures playing their own theatrical roughness – their local accents, their lack of highly trained performance polish – as a critique of a professionalism that was identified with cultural imperialism.

One such moment revealing the cultural mechanism of citation and postcolonialism came early in the history of the Mummers Troupe in Newfoundland, while the troupe was working on its first show, a panoramic comic book history play variously known as *Newfoundland Night, Regular Weekly Entertainment, Cards 50¢*, or *The Mummers History of Nfld, or Cod on a Stick*. Early in the collective process, as actors were plundering the social archive of traditional forms, Mummers founder Chris Brookes envisioned "a bit w. merchant & fisherman as Legree and Sambo."[7] That bit never made it into the show, although the underlying trope of racial impersonation certainly did. Some three years later the piece warped into the structural principle of a play called *What's That Got to Do with the Price of Fish?*, another panoramic agitprop that examined the history of the fishery as a colonized Third World economy. The show opens with fishery workers singing:

Newfoundlanders sing and dance
Do da, do da,
Inshore fishery got no chance
Oh da do da day.[8]

This may not be a technically accurate performance of a minstrel routine, but it is a citation of the Mummers' *idea* of minstrelsy as recovered from the theatre of memory. That Brookes was deliberately citing the minstrel show as a metaphor of Newfoundland's colonial history is clear from a rehearsal diary note, in which he wrote (in words that I expect would cause him great embarrassment today, but which clearly show their textual origins): "what makes a stage nigger à la minstrel show? what makes a caricature? how do we ... make Nfld stage niggers?"[9] The minstrel show, Brookes wrote, was "Obsequious yet subversive." He overlooked the minstrel show's origins in Jim Crow racism, preferring to see it as a subversive replay of stereotyped images. And so *Price of Fish* entertained audiences across Canada by legitimating its claim of oppression with a citation of white images of black America.

The cartoon history play was one of the most common and productive developments arising from agitprop in the early 1970s. It was a popular form not just in anglo Canada but also in Quebec, Australia,

Scotland, and England, though only one of several distinct vectors of growth and change. Agitprop is a spatial practice, and the spaces and contexts in which it happens open different fields of reception. In the domain of visual art, the proliferation of performance art (or, more commonly now, "Performance") that began with the Happenings of the early sixties produced a self-referential, often parodistic agitprop that frequently crossed into theatrical domains. In their encyclopedic calendar, *Performance in Canada: 1970 to 1990*, Alain-Martin Richard and Clive Robertson document close to a thousand art-centric performances. At the same festival that brought Bread and Puppet to Toronto, the art collective General Idea staged the 1970 Miss General Idea Pageant: "Performance scored as a rigged, televised beauty pageant in which a begowned Miss Honey ... is chosen by a panel of judges as the winner over six other contestants dressed in bear costumes. For the talent competition the bears sing and dance, while Miss General Idea demonstrates her skills at the telex machine."[10]

Some of these art interventions, like Mr. Peanut's campaign for mayor in Vancouver in 1974, attracted wide public notice. Many others never passed beyond the immediate context of a small gallery. Frequently the only difference between Performance and theatrical agitprop was the receptive domain of the audience and the discursive frame of the critical discussion – in other words: who was watching, and what they were saying about it. In the context of the theatre culture and the art gallery world, vanguardist agitprops marked the radical perimeter of visual art; in activist spheres, especially in the social justice movements, the women's movement, and post-Stonewall queer action, they marked social mobilization for the public gaze – which frequently meant television cameras.

Agitprop's proliferation does not mean that it was always effective, or even done well. Participants often learned to do it by trying it out, and the effect could easily backfire. Unlike the agitprops of the 1930s, which usually had a predetermined audience, the new forms were often surprise public interventions They had to be fast and precise (Bread and Puppet still speaks of "precision attacks on war and capitalist megalomania").[11] In practical terms this approach involved learning how to gather and start a performance quickly and sharply, how to keep it terse enough to maintain the attention of passers-by, and how to end it cleanly. Street agitprops might refuse the disciplinarity of theatre, but they still need theatrical discipline. When a performance failed, the result could be catastrophic. In 1971 the *Georgia Straight* reported on one of those apparent failures at a women's conference in Vancouver:

> At one point, when a Canadian woman was speaking about her experiences as a Canadian at the Conference, five women came in (ta da, ta da) with signs and props evidently to do guerrilla theatre, setting up a sign announcing they were C.U.R.S.E. (Canadian Union of Rabid Senseless Extremists). Immediately a woman stood up grabbing away the sign. She demanded that the C.U.R.S.E. women leave. Other women then came forward shoving and pushing, trying to get the guerrilla theatre women out of the meeting. The C.U.R.S.E. women linked arms and refused to leave. At this point, a couple of women began beating on one woman in the theatre group, the other woman in the skit shouted, "Don't hit her she's pregnant." But the American woman kept on slugging her, shouting "She shouldn't be here then." The five C.U.R.S.E. women formed a circle so as to protect their pregnant sister.
>
> Somewhere amidst the confusion one of the C.U.R.S.E. women grabbed the mike and explained that they were a guerrilla theatre group, the skit would only take a few minutes, and that it was relevant to a criticism of the conference. A woman from the audience asked for a vote. The theatre was voted down, and a woman jumped up from the audience shouting, "Down with the tyranny of the majority." More confusion.
>
> The theatre group, shocked and hurt at the behaviour of their so-called sisters, burst out with "Pigs! You beat us up just like the pigs in uniform. How can you call yourselves our sisters?" By this time the theatre group was in tears, along with half the audience. Some women from the audience rushed up to stop the attackers and calmed them down enough for the group to do its skit.[12]

This kind of fundamental miscalculation was often played out across North America. Clive Barker, the British historian of radical theatre and editor of *Theatre Quarterly*, saw such episodes in Britain as well, where there were "too many examples of groups of students explaining to car-workers how the car-workers were exploited, a subject on which the car-workers were experts and the students were not."[13] In Newfoundland Chris Brookes (after returning to his home province with a U.S. graduate degree in theatre followed by a hippie stint at Rochdale College in Toronto) launched what would become the Mummers Troupe with a puppet performance in support of a local projectionists' strike. The surviving handwritten notes for the show suggest that *The Coronation of Cecil B. DeMille* was an adaptation of the *Punch & Judy* show, with a traditional booth (in this case, a curtain held up by actors) combined with filmic motifs, including subtitles on sticks, which Punch and Judy eventually use as clubs. Judging from the outline, the play was ultimately pointless. Rather than intervening in the projectionists' strike action with agitprop information about the struggle, the play tried to point out the amount of power wielded by the film industry. But the puppet show never does fully articulate even that thesis, and in the end the routine does not move beyond its simple metaphoric equation of puppeteer and Hollywood mogul. The outline consists of six pages of handwritten notes and dialogue, suggesting a performance of ten to fifteen minutes. In part it went:

> (*drum*) This is the story of the Coronation of Cecil B. DeMille (*boom*)
>
> Once when Cecil was a little boy, he saw a film. (*Cecil appears as actor with cigar and rattle*)
>
> (*Scene from Gone with the Wind or something*) P&J appear, do passionate love scene. Finally, Judy says "wait darling. I must go get something before we go any farther."
>
> P - "hooboy this chick is hip."
>
> Little Cecil thought to himself, this is a X film.
>
> J - *returns with stick clobbers P w/ some jabber, much chasing & off. J gives V sign, down.*
>
> Little Cecil felt something was wrong. He felt he could make bigger, better films.
>
> So (*boom*) when Little Cecil grew up, he was called Big Cecil (*Fatso appears*) now, he became a director.
>
> *Big Cecil swaggers, is decorated w/ a sign that says "Director"* and he made bigger & better films.

The scenario ends with an oblique reference to the strike, but in the end deflects the issues back to the audience without explaining them:

> Until someone got tired of being in CB's movie ... And the
> films stopped.
> (*The Curtain turns around & on it is written, or P & J hold up banner*) Whose movie are you in?
> (*Play Star Spangled Banner, as over the banner rise signs saying "only 58 shopping days till Xmas," "support the air cadets," etc*).[14]

Afterwards Brookes realized that his agitprop assumption was based on a fundamental misunderstanding of his audience: "We intended it as a strike support piece but it was a failure: sloppy, preachy and pretentious. Passers-by thought we were just another bunch of hippies doing silly street theatre. They were right."[15]

Still, for the persistent theatre artists who kept at it, these early agitprops led to discoveries that would recalibrate the relationship of performance and spectator.

The Legacy of the Vancouver Street Theatre

I don't do popular theatre. I do unpopular
theatre. In public space.
    – David Anderson, of *Clay and Paper Theatre*, 2008

For some, the countercultural theatre scene offered more than a chance to stage revolution; it offered a means to remake lives outside of the dominant cultural economy. Some of the members of the Vancouver Street Theatre were still at it forty years later. The VST may not have been the first agitprop troupe of the counterculture in Canada – there were many, and most were unrecorded and unremarked – but it occupies a position of significance because its legacy can be traced over four decades. It shows one of the trajectories of the sixties agitprop into street performance and radical life.

The Vancouver Street Theatre began in 1967 as a casual coming together of like-minded friends, only one of whom had any theatre experience. Leonard Angel had done some playwriting as an undergrad at McGill University in the early 1960s and by 1967 was in the middle of an MA program in playwriting at the University of British Columbia. The other participants were students and activists, people who overlapped with the same community of activists who founded the *Georgia Straight*. Their first productions were small protest agitprops: a photo in the *Georgia Straight* in May 1969 shows them at a Vietnam demonstration holding placard-sized masks on sticks.[16] Their signature show was an hour-long comedy called *The Bribe*, which was first performed in city parks that summer. Influenced by the San Francisco Mime Troupe, Leonard Angel wrote the script, with input from the others, in the style of the *commedia dell'arte*, or, rather, in a citation of *commedia*. The theatrical tradition of the Italian comedy – the comedy of Arlequino, Pantalone, and Truffaldino – developed in the sixteenth century from rustic origins to peak professional disciplinarity, demanding a rigorous lifelong training in acrobatics, mime, juggling, and the immense repertoire of comic bits (*lazzi*) that actors might need to summon without warning. The tradition of the *commedia* was one of improvised scenes around a framework scenario featuring stock characters who have become part of our language. Arlequino became known to the English world as Harlequin; Pulcinella survives today as the puppet Mr. Punch. Both were numbered among the clown characters known as the *zanni*, from which we derive the word "zany." In the Italian tradition an actor would specialize in one particular role (which may have hundreds of local variants) and spend years studying complex routines that were passed generationally from master to apprentice. The art of making character half-masks was equally arcane.

Commedia dell'arte continues to exercise a fascination for theatre artists because of its capacity for anarchistic comedy, its raucous (and often coarse) gags, and its extreme physicality. But most *commedia* that North American audiences see is a citation without the deep training that gives the form its life. In plays like *The Bribe*, the *commedia* style is a performance mask that enables cheerful buffoonery, improvised comedy, and audience exchange. In effect it is vaudeville with a *commedia* skin.

The Bribe was joyously vulgar and in-your-face, as much Marx Brothers as *commedia*. The plot is simple: Arlequino falls in love with Lucinda, the daughter of the capitalist Pantalone. Both are suicidal: he is despondent from being hassled; she is tired of revolutionary sexist men who only want her body ("I held the hands of the male heavies when they couldn't stand their theories any longer"). Pantalone breaks their relationship by bribing the policeman Spavento (a localization of the *commedia*'s braggart captain) to have Arlequino thrown in jail, but

Lucinda bribes Spavento again to have her lover released. On this simple frame, typical of a *commedia* scenario, in which young lovers triumph over corrupt elders, the cast play out extended comic antics made up of dope jokes, bad puns, pratfalls, and farts. In the end Arlequino and Lucinda are left with the bribe money:

> Arlequino: (*in a flash*) That's it! That's it! That's it? Wahoooo!
> That's it! We can take the money and give it to the
> people who need it. (*Arelquino indicates everyone.*)
>
> Pantalone: Me! Me! I need it! I really need it!
>
> Arlequino: Hmm ... Claims of need won't work.
>
> Pantalone: No?
>
> Arlequino Everybody will say "I need it." Manufactured needs
> are the biggest plot of businesses. Businesses
> manufacture the needs. Then the needs-manufac-
> turers control everything. They control the women,
> the men, the students, Spavento!
>
> Pantalone: Someone manufactured a need in me!
> *Pantalone grabs Spavento from the rear, and starts*
> *bumfucking Spavento.*
>
> Arlequino: (*to Spavento*) Look what Pantalone's doing to you!
>
> *Spavento turns around, sees Pantalone continuing the fucking*
> *motions in the air, with his eyes closed. Spavento is*
> *disgusted.*
>
> Arlequino: We need to control the basics, our own lives, our
> speech, our desires, we need to control the real
> wealth of the country.
>
> Pantalone: Real wealth? No. No. Not bad. That's ... commun-
> ism! ... Socialism ... anarchism. And that's ...
> revolution!
>
> A,L,S: Oh!
> *They all come to the front in a line and bow.*[17]

In one important respect *The Bribe* was true to the *commedia* tradition. This kind of rude knock-about farce in a public space is how *commedia dell'arte* began, and it is what most theatre has been throughout history. Shows like this were being staged in parks all across the country. It is important precisely because it was so typical.

In one of *The Bribe's* central episodes, Spavento busts Arlequino for operating an illegal street theatre puppet show. Although the Vancouver Street Theatre had city permits to perform in parks, the right to perform became one of its core political issues. One day in the *Vancouver Free Press* two photographs caught a police officer inspecting their performance permit before an audience of young kids; he was unknowingly writing himself into the performance. There was always some measure of public defiance in street theatre performance, and the alternative press had a field date when the police took the bait.[18] "Park Players Jailed by Pigs" screamed the *Georgia Straight* when Leonard Angel and Bob Mercer (as Arlequino and Spavento) were arrested for disturbing the peace after supposedly "shouting" at mounted police officers during a performance in Stanley Park. Following the performance the police demanded to see the troupe's permit, and in the exchange of insults that followed, Mercer joked, "It's a real barnyard display we have here ... Pigs on horses." Describing the incident years later, Angel commented, "Now, the main substantive issue of the trial was, 'Was this innocent kidding? Or was it a disturbance of the peace?' So the whole thing revolved on the quality of the repartee. The trial was, in effect, a literary investigation."[19] They were convicted and banned from Stanley Park for two years. A second trial led to an acquittal.

Over the next few months the Vancouver Street Theatre migrated to Toronto, with performances in Calgary and Winnipeg along the way. In Toronto the group retained its Vancouver name, found a rehearsal space, and eventually petered out. As Angel recalled, "In Toronto we were trying to philosophically figure out what our ideology was. And then it sort of didn't go anywhere. So we were trying to do things and we didn't have a real successful second project, and we didn't really have a second project."[20] Whereas in Vancouver the troupe had an iconic presence and public profile (aided by their overlap with the founding collective of the *Georgia Straight*), Toronto was a very different cultural scene. Vancouver counterculture politics had organized around civic politics, police repression of street culture, and the use of public space; in Toronto the theatrical left was dispersed across many different causes. In 1969–70 there may have been more street theatre in the apartments and parking garage of Rochdale College than in all of Vancouver (and of course the VST performed *The Bribe* at Rochdale).

As the various members made their way back to Vancouver, the troupe continued its work, although the members used the original name loosely. David Anderson, a graduate student in philosophy who joined the troupe during the original Vancouver run of *The Bribe*, remembered, "We didn't take that name very seriously so it wasn't an entity, it was just a tag so people would understand what we did."[21] In 1970, when Sarah Barker joined the troupe, the Vancouver Street Theatre had a core of eight members and landed an Opportunities for Youth grant. For some troupes, employment program grants like OFY were the first step to bootstrap professionalism. Having developed producing capacity in an organizational structure, members began knocking on the arts councils' doors when the original grant programs expired. Although VST was offered a large Opportunities for Youth grant, in the end the group saw the money as a form of co-option that would draw them into a process of institutionalization. The members turned down the grant. Sarah Barker remembered the group as being "very idealistic" but "politically naive":

> We were responding to world and local events like crazy, one after another without deep thought or time to develop our pieces. Not only were we politically simplistic, but often our shows were not very sharp. The scripting and the performances left a lot to be desired. I don't think they were as forceful and well-structured by any means as *The Bribe* was. It was also politically simplistic but stronger as theatre. We continued to use *commedia dell'arte* techniques a lot of the time. We went in for simple images, visual theatre. The problems we had with structure were particularly evident in our longer pieces but there was only one that really didn't work. The others were enthusiastically received and vigorously performed and had lots of entertainment value in that way.
>
> Our shorter pieces and events, those based on one or two strong images, such as Happenings, were rather clever, and they were well presented. With time we began to make a distinction between pieces that we'd put on for the people in front of us, and those that we'd put on for the media. The media wanted something that they could get into that little TV.[22]

In this agitprop phase, the VST joined in some of the most visible protest actions, including the fight to save Jericho Beach from an expressway construction and the cartoon cross-border "invasion" of Blaine,

Washington, in May 1970, when a carnivalesque group of anti-war demonstrators pushed past immigration control. They also enacted situationist interventions. Barker described one at Christmas:

> We had rewritten some Christmas carols, "Jingle Bells," etc. A whole lot of us went downstairs in one of the big department stores in Vancouver.... And [we] sang these songs. The management had to smile. Even though we were a ragged bunch, hippie-looking, we were after all singing what sounded like Christmas carols. Of course our "Jingle Bells," for instance, had verses like this:
>
> > Dashing through the store,
> >
> > With an open shopping bag,
> >
> > Taking what we need,
> >
> > Poverty's a drag.
>
> At the same time we had a guy, a big guy, dressed up in a very good Santa Claus costume, who went up into the toy department and started giving away the toys to people. Saying "Ho, ho, ho, I'm Santa Claus, no take it, you don't have to pay for it, take it. I'm Santa Claus." But even more cleverly we had another person dressed in the only suit that we all collectively could put together, and who had relatively short hair, playing the part of a store detective. As he saw the real store detectives get antsy and start moving in, he moved in, grabbed our Santa Claus by the arm, and looking at the others, said, "I have this under control." He took him down the escalators, out, and into a waiting car, and they got away before Santa was arrested.[23]

In the summer of 1971 Anderson and Barker met two puppeteers, Bill Dalrymple and Antoinette Martens, who were performing a *Punch & Judy* show in Stanley Park. Dalrymple had performed with Bread and Puppet Theater, and the four soon came together as Breadbakers Puppet Theatre. The focus shifted more to the art and craft of puppet performance, drawing on Bread and Puppet's repertoire, focusing on puppet shows and "crankies" – hand-spooled strip drawings accompanied by a storyteller narrator. As the troupe moved past insurgent agitprop to theatrical fables, their work became, like Bread and Puppet's, more affirmative, mythic, and ritualistic, but always retaining a clear social critique.

By 1973 Breadbakers had become not just a theatrical endeavour but theatrical life. Anderson and Barker and their daughter lived in and worked out of an old school bus. (In that same year the Mummers were making their way across Newfoundland in another old school bus.) They lived by passing the hat and taking odd jobs. It was both hard work and a radicalization of an ancient form of theatre work.

> We were always there, in the park at the same spot, rain or shine. Our school bus was also the vehicle that pulled the trailer full of puppets and props on weekends into the park, and it was our green room as well. So we would just take our home to Stanley Park and we had the right to pull it up in front of Lumberman's Arch. We would sit in there if it rained. And the minute the rain stopped, up went the banners, up went the show, and people would start coming out of the woods. It was as if they were waiting under the trees. I don't know what they were doing nor how they got into the park so quickly, unless they just happened to be hanging out in the rain. Anyway, even before the grass was dry it would be covered with people, on that slope, waiting for the shows, and also playing games with each other. It looked like a scene from a Brueghel print. I remember sitting there, exhausted, nursing Rosa, between shows and watching people with their picnics. They were spread out almost like a tapestry up the hill. And then when we banged the drum, and announced the show, they'd all come close. We'd have four, five, maybe six different shows; we'd do maybe eight performances in a day. We lived by passing the hat. It was essential, that's how we lived. But it was also a way of interacting with our audience. What this loyalty on our part did was to create a loyal audience. People came back, week after week, day after day.[24]

What had started as insurgent antics had now become a trade, and it was developing into artisanship. In time, after the troupe had been shaken by Dalrymple's accidental death in Europe while touring with Bread and Puppet, the family moved to Toronto. In Toronto they reconstituted themselves as Whole Loaf Theatre and moved towards a kind of self-professionalism. David Anderson became a familiar performer on Toronto streets and in subways, where he could be seen singing and storytelling as a one-man band with a string of puppets dancing from his knee. Often his daughter, who grew up as a trouper, would accompany him. They became a familiar presence in parks and at folk festivals. Their repertoire continued to expand – including Barker's *Judy Show* (a puppet without Punch: "no punch lines").[25] As Whole Loaf, and after Anderson and Barker went separate ways in 1995, forming Clay & Paper Theatre and CounterClockwise Theatre respectively, they continued working in the same idiom.

Today this kind of theatre work has a marginal (economically at least) niche in the professional discipline, as "Community Arts," and artists like Anderson and Barker have mentored a significant revival of puppetry in Canadian theatre culture. Their work has intersected with other processional troupes, like Shadowland on Toronto Island, an artists' collective inspired by the Trinidadian Carnival master Peter Minshall, and the various small puppet troupes that eke out a living doing highly innovative work for school audiences. Their work may be eligible now for arts council grants, but it still operates at the bottom of the theatre economy. No one in Canada gets rich or famous doing street theatre and operating giant puppets. In the world of Canadian theatre, puppetry is living off the grid, in a place where reclaiming ancient traditions enables radical living.

The Cultural Nationalist Moment: The GCTC Agitprops

... to fix this human image firmly in the eyes of the audience.
– *Larry Macdonald, "Production Notes for the Big Nickel"*

When a small group of left nationalist English professors and grad students at Carleton University in Ottawa decided to found an all-Canadian theatre company in 1975, they gave it an ironic name that would flag its nationalist platform: the Great Canadian Theatre Company. Today GCTC is the regional English-language theatre in Ottawa, with a structure and repertoire not unlike that of other theatres in its bracket across the country. But for the first decade of its existence it was radical in voice and stance, if not in programming, and for a brief period of time in the late 1970s it initiated a visible series of outdoor agitprop interventions on labour, peace, and prison reform issues. In contrast to the sixties street agitprops, these were micropolitical interventions.

When GCTC was founded Ottawa had very little professional theatre outside of the National Arts Centre, which tended to program for its national profile rather than the local community. The mid-1970s saw several theatres start up, in English and French. Of the English companies, only GCTC survived; its nearest rival, Penguin Theatre, folded at the end the decade. For the first four years of its existence, GCTC attempted to steer a path that embraced cultural nationalism, a left political orientation, and emergent professionalism. Its impetus came from Robin Mathews, a professor of English at Carleton. Mathews had achieved academic celebrity for his deeply researched and passionate attacks on the Americanization of Canadian universities. In his published work, which included essays, literary criticism, poetry, and drama, he argued tirelessly for a Canadian tradition of anti-colonial struggle. He was (and would remain over the following decades) a polemicist, quick to rise to the bait and always ready to leap into public controversy.

Although he was a powerful personality in the group that founded GCTC, Mathews was also committed to democratic process. The founders strove to create an organization that would enable any interested person to join and have a say in its direction. They wanted at the same time to establish a stability of purpose and structure that would survive the original charter group. That was not as easy as it might seem. Because theatre companies are often built on the core vision of founding artists, their organizational stability is often tied closely to that artistic vision, with the result that when the artistic vision leaves, institutional crisis follows. Ottawa's Penguin Theatre collapsed in just that way when its artistic director, Don Bouzek, was ousted in a dispute with his board. After Bouzek left, the company survived several more seasons but never again had the artistic purpose that it had been founded to enact. The same principle of leadership held true, on a larger scale with more devastating consequences, when the Toronto Workshop Productions board fired George Luscombe and then committed institutional suicide.

The first meeting of the Great Canadian Theatre Company determined that the new entity would "a) use Canadian citizens b) do Canadian plays and should be very clear about that policy." It skirted around the issue of political commitment: "Theatre of engagement wouldn't be done if it was bad, but good theatre of that kind would be produced." A follow-up meeting established a structure that would supersede personality: "There would be a Board of Management. That board would choose the directors to do the plays of the theatre."[26] The intention to create democratic governance was sincere, as evidenced by the detailed and formal minutes of the board meetings, even at this early stage.

The structure that emerged was flexible and resilient. Any person could join the company (and receive a membership card). The only qualification was that membership and employment were restricted to Canadian citizens. The membership voted for the board, which operated as a steering committee and oversaw the work of the artistic director and technical staff. At first these functions were distributed amongst the membership, but by the end of the 1970s the company was on arts council funding tracks and preparing to move into its own theatre facility. Arts council accountability, artists' contracts, and technical operations required a professional staff. In time this need would place stress on the charter vision of a managing board, and in 1979 Mathews resigned from the board in anger, accusing the staff of operating as a "Company within the Company" and arguing that "the purposes for which the Company was created are being subverted."[27]

The citizenship clause gave GCTC instant notoriety, particularly because it came less than a year after the Stratford Festival had excited a national controversy when it bypassed Canadian applicants and imported a young, unknown British artistic director in the person of Robin Philips. In that same year Don Rubin, himself a recent immigrant, founded *Canadian Theatre Review* with a defiantly nationalist editorial slant. The nationalist insurgency in the theatre was as much a generational conflict as it was one of principle. The many young, localist, and often collectivist companies that championed the primacy of Canadian playwriting were engaged in a war of resources with the large institutionalized "regional" theatres, many of them indifferent to or actively hostile to demands to produce Canadian plays. Pressure had been building since July 1971, when the Canada Council had convened a meeting of invited playwright and administrators to discuss the conditions of production for Canadian playwrights. The result of the meeting was the institutionally ineffectual but rhetorically powerful Gaspé Manifesto. The group reported that it had "examined the working conditions of the playwright, looked at his economic prospects, discussed practical ways to enhance his professional status and improve his economic lot, and sought ways to enable him to take his proper place in the theatre and in the cultural life of Canada."[28] The gender bias of the language coincided with the deeper, more problematic issue that when Canadian plays were produced they were usually written by men. The marginalization of Canadian playwrights went hand in hand with a marginalization of women and minority cultures, but the group's analysis and proposed solution were at this point asymmetric.

The manifesto demanded that all theatres receiving public subsidy be required to fill 50 per cent of their programming with Canadian plays (but made no quota demand on gender or cultural location). It went on to argue "that among the first criteria for subsidy is the question of the content of the theater's repertoire, which is to say, what percentage of the season is Canadian work."[29] Beyond the concern for the livelihood and status of "the" (male, white) Canadian playwright was a set of assumptions that would begin to erode in the 1980s and 1990s: that the content of the play is what the play "is"; that plays by virtue of their appearance on a stage express meaningful cultural truths about national experience; that the kinds of plays that work best on professional theatre stages are the exemplary models of dramatic artistry. The radical impulse of the cultural nationalist demand for Canadian content not only reduced "Canadian" to reproducible content, but also rested upon a set of conservative assumptions about theatre practice. Those assumptions were not very different from the principles articulated by Vincent Massey a half-century earlier.

GCTC's Canadian clause ramped up the rhetoric into praxis, and by extending the qualification to employment practice as well as repertoire further radicalized the debate. As Mathews wrote in a letter to the editor of *Canadian Theatre Review* in 1979, taking exception to an article on theatre in Ottawa:

> I regret that an insistence upon doing Canadian theatre was, and to some extent, is radical. But it is. As we observed again and again: when companies in Ottawa didn't do anything Canadian for three, four, or five years no critic or commentator turned a hair. But when we decided to do only Canadian theatre, we were described as that "narrowly nationalistic," that "chauvinistic," that "militantly nationalistic" company.[30]

In a *Members' Handbook* prepared for the company in 1979, the issue was still active.

> Members occasionally wonder how we justify a constitution that insists we do only Canadian plays, using only Canadian talent ("Canadian" being defined as citizenship – which is available after three years). Is that not excessively narrow? Does it not smack of censorship? We think not. The vast majority of plays performed in this country is not Canadian. The *status quo* in this country amounts to a de *facto* censorship of Canadian plays and prejudice against Canadian talent.[31]

As it worked towards professional status, GCTC offered a repertoire that was roughly similar to the "alternative" Toronto theatres of the day. If anything it was more politically focused and less adventurous artistically. The opening production was a rare staging of Vancouver writer Herschel Hardin's *Esker Mike and His Wife, Agiluk*, about the devastating impact of white encroachment and government policy on Inuit life in the Mackenzie Delta. Part comedy and part Brechtian parable, *Esker Mike* had been published in 1966 in *The Drama Review* and became a favourite of Canadian drama scholars, but received few productions. Its episodic, distanced style, cynical vision, and political edge proved to be too much for most Canadian theatres, although Factory Theatre Lab had taken it on a successful tour of Britain in 1973.

That first season also included a new play about the history of the Ottawa Valley (*Yonder Lies the Valley*, by Bernie Bedore) and James Reaney's *Names and Nicknames*. The season established a pattern that would hold for the better part of a decade, with a leaning towards historical subjects (including Mathews's own *Selkirk* in season two), revivals of innovative socially engaged plays from other parts of the country (season two also featured the only revival production of the Mummers Troupe's community documentary *Company Town*), plays on local history for school tours, and occasional collective creations (the most celebrated of which, *Sandinista!*, about the Nicaraguan revolution, had a national tour in 1982). In the early seasons volunteer actors made it possible to produce shows with large casts. In time, as with other theatres converging on the funding track that enabled professional status, plays with smaller casts became the norm.

GCTC was negotiating a tricky balance of topicality, audience development, and political engagement. Its success was in large part due to its location. The Ottawa South and Glebe neighbourhoods where the company began were undergoing a major gentrification in the 1970s, and GCTC rode the curve of upward mobility. The move into a permanent theatre facility in a converted truck garage on Gladstone Avenue in 1982 was made possible by significant public support. GCTC was becoming in its way the national theatre of the liberal anglophone sector of the federal civil service and a marker of cultural urban development in Ottawa.

This path tended to tame the company's engagement with politics, or at least its identification with partisan causes. Although Mathews believed that radical theatre "deals with the people as subject, with work-ing-class battles against big interests, with subjects that take Canadians into their own history and identity, and with present contests between labour and capital," that was not the public image that the company marketed.[32] The 1979 *Members' Handbook* sidestepped the issue:

> Theatre and Politics
>
> Periodically, the company finds itself agonizing over the relation-ship between theatre and politics. This is because some of the founding members saw the abject failure of theatre in Canada to deal with the important issues of our history and society as itself a "political" fact. Hence the terms of reference according to which we founded state that we shall be *sympathetic* to plays that deal in a thoughtful, stimulating, critical and entertaining way with the social realities and histories of our culture. None-theless our primary commitment is to good theatre.[33]

Within this liberal humanist envelope, the charter group of the company retained a core orientation to more politically engaged work. In the late 1970s GCTC mounted a series of agitprops outside of its regular season programming. These agitprops are a significant feature of the company's history, but are not included in the production history included on GCTC's website. The first project was in support of the strik-ing women at Fleck Manufacturing in Centralia, which became a land-mark strike in the development of the feminist movement in Ontario. In 1978, when the employees of Fleck had unionized with the United Auto Workers, the company tried to use its political connections with the Conservative government to break the strike (Fleck was 50 per cent owned by a minister in the Ontario government). At the height of the six-month strike, the Ontario Provincial Police deployed nine hundred officers, including assault teams, in an attempt to control the situation. GCTC performed a half-hour of material from the Mummers' *Company Town*, a documentary on the history of union activism and culture in the mining town of Buchans, Newfoundland. The Fleck strike was a flash-point for labour solidarity and women's union activism. There were only 130 workers at Fleck, but GCTC played to crowds of 2,000.

In December of that year the company performed its second agit-prop at an Ottawa benefit for miners in the Inco strike at Sudbury. That was followed in March by a show in support of the Canadian Union of Postal Workers at a defence rally (which also featured singer-song-writer Rita MacNeil and the folk group Stringband, then at the height of its popularity), and in August by an agitprop on Parliament Hill for National Prisoners Justice Day. Subsequent agitprops over the next two years dealt with multinational corporations and nuclear weapons, and the struggle to award war veteran status to survivors of the Mac-Paps, the volunteers of the Mackenzie-Papineau Battalion of the International Brigade, which fought for the Spanish Republic against Franco in the Spanish Civil War.

The GCTC agitprops were one-offs (as most agitprops have always been) and never published, but archival scripts survive. They show important parallels and divergences from the agitprops of the 1930s and 1960s. Familiar agitprop tropes are repeated – exaggerated character, easily telegraphed political tags, quick set-up, and strike – but the differ-ences suggest that fundamental changes had taken place in the under-standing of audiences and the politics of spectatorship.

The Big Nickel, performed at the benefit for striking miners and writ-ten and directed by Larry Macdonald, begins with the president of Inco (played by Mathews) addressing the annual general meeting of the com-pany. The speech is done straight, that is, without irony or satire. The president welcomes those in the room and speaks about the development of the company in congratulatory terms. His remarks are juxta-posed with short documentary testimonials and theatrical commentary:

Pres.:   Guatemala and Indonesia. We have new mines com-
           ing in on schedule in Guatemala and Indonesia. I'd

	like to say a few words about the situation in those countries.
Siti:	My name is Siti Suratih. I am one of more than 55,000 prisoners of conscience in my country. I have been in jail for ten years. What am I charged with?
General:	There are no specific charges.
Pres.:	Their governments agree that political stability is the guarantee of progress.

The first half of the fifteen-minute play continues this rhetorical structure of countering the executive's corporate-speak with evidence of repression. The second half pits the president against Inco workers who challenge him with evidence of health and safety violations and unsafe conditions. The play ends with each of the four actors correcting the president's final statement that "INCO is a global corporation taking free enterprise development around the world":

Arthur:	INCO is a company involved in the murder and exploitation of people in Indonesia and Guatemala.
Merle:	INCO is a company that is trying to bust our union.
John:	INCO is a company that puts profits ahead of the health and safety of its workers.
Phil:	INCO is a company that will be all right – the day we take it over and make it ours.[34]

Theatrically this scene is as stripped-down and minimalist as agitprop can get. It does not have the semiotic playfulness of the thirties or the cartoon foolery of the sixties. Yet it is no less effective than its predecessors. *The Big Nickel* derives its techniques from the new forms of documentary theatre as developed by groups like the Mummers, Theatre Passe Muraille (in *The Farm Show* in particular), and the Globe Theatre in Regina, which combined inventive theatricality with testimonial authenticity. It is this sense of performance authenticity, of *witnessing*, that enables an actor to use the phrase "our union." The actors are positioning themselves not as outsiders coming in to comment or entertain, but as partners in the struggle. Their authority – their right to speak and to be believed – stems from their alliance and acceptance of the union's leadership, rather than from outside expertise or ideological affinity. Don Bouzek, who would take his Ground Zero Production in a similar direction, working in partnership with unions on union-defined terms, later called this kind of work "industrials for the social services."[35]

Larry Macdonald's notes, written for groups in Sudbury and Winnipeg that had expressed interest in the script, show how by de-theatricalizing the performance the troupe generated theatrical power:

> The sketch was conceived of as a kind of agit-prop from the beginning. I think it works best if people don't know too much about it in advance. It should not be a piece of "theatre." It should be part of the event at which it is presented. We set up four flats quickly and unobtrusively just before we went on. Then the M.C. announced a special surprise. A special honour. The president of Inco himself has flown in to speak to the crowd. Up comes a spotlight ... on a podium and in strides the president in this three piece suit. He addresses the audience as if they were shareholders at the annual general meeting – they booed, hissed and heckled and laughed at his speech. It is an event, and the crowd is part of it.
>
> I think the sketch could be done without lights and without flats. It does not present as theatre, but as a presentation of reality that both informs and moves emotionally an audience which is eager for precisely this kind of experience. I mention what we did with lights just to give you a feel for how we thought we were building the thing. The flats, by the way, were a quickly sketched, impressionistic imitation of Picasso's "Guernica" (miners and picks in silhouette, etc.).
>
> We used 5 actors: four men, one woman. We used bits and pieces of costumes on occasion – for example we put together an outrageous costume for the "General." Other times, we used nothing more than a shawl, sports coat, hard hat, etc. We had no furniture. We happened to find 4 two-foot square boxes covered with [a] bright rug on the day of the performance. We just moved them around to build prison cells, chairs, machines.

The technical notes to the script indicate that lights were used to define space and political relationships. After one sequence of grim testimonials, including one by an actor representing a disabled Guatemalan lawyer:

> We staged this scene so that the actors formed a tight static por-
> trait, grouped around the paraplegic. We had a tight red spot
> on them throughout the scene. At this point we snapped off the
> white light and they were left in this blood-red glow that slowly
> faded into darkness. The aim, in any event, is to fix this human
> image firmly in the eyes of the audience.[36]

The relationship here between the expressive power of sculpted light
and the body of the actor is not very different from that at work in *Eight
Men Speak*. Both plays were written for an indoor performance where
the gaze of the audience could be directed towards the *mise en scène*, no
matter how rudimentary it might be. Although written forty years later
than *Eight Men Speak*, the GCTC agitprops confirm that the techniques
discovered by the Workers' Theatre in 1933 were dramaturgical and staging solutions to recurring problems in activist-targeted agitprop.

That approach was even clearer in GCTC's next agitprop, *Mail
Blox*, which bears an even greater resemblance to *Eight Men Speak*. It is a
longer play, written in nine scenes that range through social satire, dramatic character dialogue, and excerpts from parliamentary and union
speeches to mimed workplace scenes. Like *Eight Men Speak* it is at once
an accusatory polemic and a celebratory affirmation of solidarity.

These similarities point to a continuity of practices in Canadian
agitprop, as successive generations of activist artists rediscover the same
techniques and methods of building a performance. Although it is tempting to suggest that this rediscovery represents a continuity in radical
culture with sources in the specifics of Canadian activism, as it turns
out the techniques recur for the same reason that most cars have four
wheels: they are the obvious, most efficient and workable solution to the
problems posed. If there is a cultural continuity at work, it may be that
Canadian artists have tended to value the utilitarianism of the workable
solution over aesthetic ornamentation or literary invention.[37]

The main distinction between the 1930s agitprops and GCTC's
reinvention of the form is that the performance had migrated out of the
theatre into an audience-defined space. That space is ideological and
discursive as much as it is physical. The recognition of this approach
was the tipping point that gave birth to the popular theatre method in
Canada, as developed in the late 1970s by theatres as far apart as the

Mummers in St. John's, Catalyst in Edmonton, and Headlines in Vancouver. The GCTC agitprops may have looked at first to be a reprise of the Workers' Theatre agitprops, but they were pointing to a more participatory understanding of theatrical engagement with struggle.

Agitprop, Picket Lines, and Ooze

The GCTC agitprops marked one instance of a return to disciplinarity – of work produced by playwrights, directors, actors, designers, and technicians who brought professional skill and experience to them. In one sense they were a projection of disciplinary theatre beyond theatrical representation into activism – not plays *about* but plays *with* allies. They were a solution that enabled radical artists to reconcile the often conflicting demands of artistry and activism.

As in the 1930s and the 1960s, agitprop begins here as undisciplined, or not-yet disciplined, and acquires rigour, form, and principle as artists infuse it with craft knowledge. At the same time, groups in struggle are always rediscovering agitprop as a solution in struggle.

In 1985 – to take only one example of this rediscovery, but one typical of countless similar endeavours, most of which are known only to the participants and their target audiences – the Canadian Farmworkers' Union and the Punjabi-language theatre collective Vancouver Sath collaborated on a short (twenty-five-minute) play called *Picket Line*. The CFU was active in organizing underpaid Sikh farmworkers who were subjected to racism and sexism and intolerable working conditions. As David Jackson, a CFU activist, wrote at the time:

> If CFU cannot plug directly into the networks of the mainstream Punjabi community, then in asking farmworkers to give up (or fight) their dependence on those networks, it must provide powerful alternatives. Socially, this means that you must promote social relations and activities which break down rather than reinforce the feudal hole which growers and contractors exert through the temple At the same time it must respect and uphold the positive aspects of existing social structures and traditions.... Cultural work is an important way of doing this.[38]

In May 1984 eleven female workers at Hoss Mushroom Farm unionized; in retaliation the owner – himself a member of the Sikh community – fired five of them. When the union set up a picket line the next day, he fired the remaining six. Soon two members of Vancouver Sath joined the women on the line. The strike spread, with the help of supporters from the labour movement and churches, to the Fraser Valley Mushroom Growers' Cooperative. The strike came at a critical time in B.C. labour relations, when the Social Credit government was attacking workers' rights and outlawing secondary strikes. The Labour Board ordered a stop to the picketing; in the end public pressure forced the owner to hire back some – but not all – of the fired workers.

The two members of Vancouver Sath, Sukhwant Hundar and Sadhu Binning, who had joined the strikers on the line used their experience to gather material for a play. They wrote it in four short scenes, with each scene defining a particular step in labour consciousness. In the first scene the women discuss their problems after a shift and decide to form a union; in the second, a woman defies her husband to help the union organizer sign up members; in the third, the growers fight back by hiring scabs; and the fourth scene takes place on the picket line, when the last holdouts join the strike. The play was addressed to the whole community. According to Hundar, "In the Indo Canadian community if we just educate the farmworkers, we are not going to get anywhere. We have to educate their families, even if they're not working on farms, because they have the decision-making power."[39]

That community had little in the way of theatrical tradition in Canada, which led to a simple, utilitarian theatrical form designed to convey information efficiently. In that respect, it was not unlike the early plays of the Ukrainian Labour Farmer Temple Association. Theatre was a cheap, mobile way of communication in an immigrant community. Binning's analysis of the efficacy of theatre echoes Macdonald's comment about fixing an image in the minds of the audience: "The function of art, for political people, is to get political ideas into people's lives. Art makes it easier, although it's a fake, and it doesn't have the same effect as a political speech or political article would. But through a play people are being entertained, ridiculed at times, and it stays with them, becomes part of their unconscious."[40]

For Vancouver Sath, agitprop was a solution to a communication problem – which goes back to the notion that agitprop has always functioned as a derivative of mass communication. This tendency was clearly the case in another, much later, example of the same phenomenon; and this time I have to put myself in the frame, as one of the subjects, rather than the spectating object, of the agitprop. In winter 2007 the University of Guelph Faculty Association was deep in first-contract negotiations with the university, and things were not going well. With some amount of effort, the union had been able to get a strong strike vote to power its negotiations, which in time stalled and went into mediation. Everyone on the union side knew that the issue had to be resolved before the end of the semester; after that point, the union's strike leverage would dissolve. As the semester came to a close, a strike seemed more and more likely.

During this period I was one of the organizers of the strike committee, and I was also in rehearsal, directing our departmental mainstage show. The dress rehearsal was scheduled for the same day as the strike deadline. I knew either the strike or the show would be a go, but not both. At the eleventh hour, to my immense relief, both sides reached an agreement. The strike was averted and the show went on.

As the tension increased on campus, a small group of theatre students produced an agitprop documentary on the negotiations. The play did not take sides; rather, it articulated student discontent and critiqued both the university and union for using students as pawns. The playwright and initiator of the project, Gabe Pollock, had dug through media releases and interviewed key players. The play expressed anger and disbelief at the slow pace of labour negotiations and ridiculed how it had taken eighteen months and fifty-two negotiation sessions to *not* come to an agreement. During the mediator-imposed media blackout, many students were unaware of and confused about the reasons for the impending strike. The final line of the play demanded:

> And, in the end, why is it that the students of the University of Guelph need to dig through archives, harass members of the faculty and administration, and ultimately come to a student-produced play in order to find out what's going on under our very noses? This is our education, our future, and we are being left in the dark.[41]

The forty-five-minute play, entitled *STRIKE! The Play*, took the form of a satiric living newspaper that was updated daily as events developed.[42] It had no set, and only rudimentary props (such as a professor's mortarboard). It satirized everyone involved, including student organizations and media. The only campus group treated sympathetically and not subjected to ridicule was the part-time sessional instructors, who were not part of the Faculty Association and who had, as the students saw, the most to lose in the event of a faculty strike.

In its tone and method the play may be one of the first documentary efforts to personify new social media and critique its efficacy as an information source:

A new, confident, powerful, ACTOR has appeared.
MYSTERIOUS NEW ACTOR: Come with me. I lead the way for students on the campus, with the most up-to-date information. Communicate directly with representatives from the CSA [Central Student Association], UGFA [University of Guelph Faculty Association], and the Administration. Express how you feel about the strike, and get in touch with people across campus who feel the same way as you.
Everyone else is in awe.
NARRATORS: Who … who are you, mysterious stranger?
MYSTERIOUS NEW ACTOR: *(majestically)* I … am Facebook.
The NARRATORS are sceptical.
NARRATOR 1: Facebook?
FACEBOOK: Yes. I am the Facebook group "University of Guelph Strike! Beware!"
NARRATOR 2 *(looking at the rest)*: This is the best we've got?
FACEBOOK: I provide a free exchange of ideas, opinions, facts, and stories, among over 2500 members, representing a wide cross-section of the university population.
NARRATOR 1: So… what are people on Facebook saying?
All actors, except the NARRATORS, remove their costumes, and disperse around the room, and alternate lines of text.

- a strike would be sick
- hey guys!! I was hoping that maybe we could come up with some ideas on how to stop this strike?! I really want to graduate on time!
- if strike happens = riot, TAKE EVERYTHING
- Emailing Alastair [Summerlee, the university president]

won't do anything – it's the profs who need to be emailed, they're the ones who want the strike, not him.

- I heard that they might actually go on strike next Tuesday (Feb 12th) ... so it might be a lot sooner than anyone expected.
- I better not get fucked over.... I have one course to graduate and it's only offered in the Winter semester
- Oh dear god let there be a strike....
- According to Magic 106.1's reporting team, the university faculty did indeed vote "Yes" by about 85% which puts them in a legal position to strike on March 13th, assuming all the proper procedures are followed and an agreement is not reached between the university and faculty. I find it sad that I'm relying on a radio station to tell me what's going on at school :(
- Only at university would you find a play about an upcoming strike. Can we get the CSA to send out a clear, concise and to the point release regarding exactly what's going on and exactly what is in store for the students? No, we get obscure emails about how they want a "fair resolution" instead of taking a friggin' stand for students. But, can we have a pretty little play put on to describe the possible strike in fanciful artistic terms? Hell ya. What do my tuition dollars that get given to the CSA et al. actually go to?
- So we rioting or what?

The NARRATORS stand in shocked silence.

NARRATOR 2: This is it? This is the best resource to keep students updated on the future of their education?

NARRATOR 1: Does anyone know what's actually been going on?[43]

STRIKE! The Play was as casual, mobile, and theatrically reduced as agitprop can be. Performances took place in various venues around the campus: in classrooms, bars, and the indoor courtyard of the University Centre as tour groups of prospective students passed by. I saw it in a lecture hall with an audience of forty, made up of students, faculty, and staff. The performance was understated, almost without affect, and barely rehearsed; the actors held scripts in their hands and interacted informally with people in the audience. This sense of theatrical minimalism and disregard for theatre discipline was particularly noteworthy because most of the students involved were theatre majors. Whereas in studio classes they are taught to move with purpose, energy, and form, here they shuffled. Their focus was on communicating the script, not on "performing."

The resulting performance was compelling and urgent. Like Vancouver Sath's *Picket Line* twenty-five years before, *STRIKE! The Play* upset the protocols of theatre aesthetics and demonstrated that agitprop works effectively and with power when it steps out of the referential frame of the theatre. What others might have seen as chaotic and under-rehearsed performance, I saw as a courageous step, as theatre students took the risk to rebel against the theatre discipline we teach them. They had rediscovered what agitprop could do, and how it could come to define public perception of an event. As Gabe Pollock wrote at the time, "You know in schlocky monster movies, when something gets covered in radioactive ooze, it grows incomprehensibly huge (see Mothra, Teenage Mutant Ninja Turtles, etc.). If this were a schlocky monster movie, I would swear someone had given *STRIKE! The Play* a good long soak in radioactive ooze."[44]

7

A Case of
Cultural Sabotage
The Mummers Troupe

The Mummers Troupe, 1973: Paul Sametz, Christopher Knight, and
Mr. Punch replay Newfoundland's colonial history in *Newfoundland Night*.
Chris Brookes

The history of engaged theatre in Canada is the story of a small and closely connected (but not always harmonious) community. I first met up with the Mummers Troupe of St. John's in the summer of 1974 when they were creating a labour documentary play in Buchans, Newfoundland, and I stayed with the troupe for the following year as a dramaturge and occasional actor. After that I kept in close touch with the troupe through our parallel engagement in the popular theatre movement. As it turned out, my long connection with the Mummers provided a front-row seat in an interventionist theatre that broke new ground. But I also got more than a glimpse of the unhappy backstage preoccupations that can all too often beset a radical theatre troupe.

The Mummers Troupe occupies an almost mythic status in Canadian theatre history. It was a politically motivated theatre group that moved from radical agitprop to community animation. It was also in design a mobile form of theatre, moving from community to community in the province. It not only launched independent theatre in its province, but also pioneered the principles of social justice partnership that came to define the popular theatre movement. Reviving the traditional Christmas mummers play in Newfoundland, it opened an artist-run performance space that remains a driving force many years later in the local community. The troupe also imploded in one of the most public and acrimonious episodes in Canadian theatre.

Yet in its near-decade of work, from 1973 to 1982, the Mummers Troupe may have been the least representative of Canadian theatres because it refused to play by the rules – any rules. The historical significance of the troupe derives not only from its development of a working methodology that came to typify the work of popular theatre for social action, but also from its contentious relationship to funding bodies. While initiating a methodology that required a new form of theatrical organization, the Mummers Troupe exposed a crisis in the model of production and administration enforced by arts council policies. Indeed, the Mummers would prove to be a test case for the arts councils at a critical point of development. It was highly personalized, because the history of the Mummers and the arts councils is one of volatile and powerful personalities in conflict. But what entered history as a series of personal conflicts and rivalries was really a battle over the rights of artists to create their own forms of cultural organization and over the constraints of radical intervention theatre in a cultural economy. In the end the story of the Mummers illustrates, even establishes, the principle that radical intervention theatre is a theatre of refusal.

The theatrical sixties had produced the conditions for a major reconfiguration of Canadian theatre, in practice and in organizational structures. The countless new groups that had come into being around the turn of the decade coalesced into what was at the time called the "alternate" theatre movement, or in Quebec, "*jeune théâtre.*" The participants were invariably avant-gardist, nationalist, and young. Their commitment to local culture and writing brought a demand for new plays. This, combined with a generational surge and the pedagogies of new university and college theatre programs across the country, shifted the creative centre of the theatre away from the large, heavily invested, and very similar regional theatres to the new, smaller troupes popping up around them in garages and warehouses converted to "black-box" theatre spaces. These theatres continue even now to dominate the institutionalized theatre profession and provide at least meagre incomes for Canadian playwrights.

Many of those theatres – like the Great Canadian Theatre Company – began with radical principles or aspirations, and many still produce socially and politically provocative work. Buddies in Bad Times, for example, balances institutionalization with a commitment to edgy performance. In Vancouver, Headlines Theatre functions as a politically engaged theatre with a sustainable organizational model and a high degree of cultural legitimacy in the community. In Victoriaville, Théâtre Parminou has been operating for more than thirty-five years as a playhouse company (that is, one that functions out of its own theatre facility) producing social and political awareness theatre "*en demande*" while operating as a co-operative that provides secure employment and benefits to its members. Ground Zero Productions, founded in Toronto in 1984 and based in Edmonton since 1997, has created work for unions and social justice partners by *not* operating a theatre facility.

In each of these cases radical purpose accommodates the demands of institutional and corporate survival. But historically most radical theatre workers who sought to take the road that the Vancouver Street Theatre rejected – to formalize as theatre companies that would enable working careers – could not achieve such an accommodation. The reasons for failure were many and often specific to the personalities involved, but radical troupes showed a recurrent tendency to crash and burn because of irreconcilable conflicts between ideological principles and the institutional demands of an increasingly corporatized cultural delivery system.

In the early 1970s the Theatre Section of the Canada Council was not at all prepared for the dozens of new theatre companies that had begun their work based on grants provided by short-term federal make-work programs, especially Opportunities for Youth and Local Initiatives Project (LIP) funding. Once established, these new groups sought to acquire ongoing operations funding after meeting the Council's criteria for eligibility, and as a result the number of theatre companies backed by the Canada Council more than doubled between 1972 and 1977 (from 49 to 125).[1] Faced with the dozens of applications from prospective new theatre companies in the early 1970s, the Canada Council insisted that funds go to an incorporated body that could prove public accountability (usually in the form of a not-for-profit corporation with an elected board of directors) and evidence of administrative and artistic stability. The Council assessed theatres groups according to two fundamental criteria: administrative (season planning and financial management) and artistic, for which it usually depended on outside assessors.

Most of the new companies, like the Mummers, had been started with limited funds managed by young artists with little administrative experience – beyond the crisis management in the micro-economy of the small theatre sector – and many of these people were ideologically suspicious of the very concept of administrative structure. The small companies that proved to be creative managers on the micro level would manage to survive from one project to another, and eventually, by doing so consistently, they could make a claim for Council subsidy. For the theatres that survived this process, the shift from crisis to rationalized management usually came first with the acquisition of real estate and a permanent basis of operations, followed by a contract with the Canadian Actors' Equity Association (the Canadian Theatre Agreement, negotiated between Actors' Equity and Professional Association of Canadian Theatres, or PACT), which normalized employment policies.

In the Mummers' case these conditions were not attainable in the early 1970s. As a mobile intervention collective, the troupe at first saw the establishment of a permanent base as strategically unnecessary. The decision to acquire a space in St. John's in 1975 would be a major factor in the company's eventual collapse. Founder Chris Brookes's early attempts to enter into an agreement with Actors' Equity were rebuffed. The institutional context of theatre in Newfoundland – in which the Mummers functioned as an "alternative" theatre, but without a large "regional" company to define the terms of that entity – did not conform to the structural patterns that Equity was equipped to respond to – with its paradigm being the urban metropolis with large regional companies and satellite "alternatives."[2]

In 1972 the Province of Newfoundland and Labrador was one of the few jurisdictions in Canada without a cultural policy and provisions for funding the arts. The province had no arts council, and when one was formed in 1974 by a group of artists, it had no budget. Such cultural funding as existed was under the discretion of the province's Cultural Affairs Division and its director, an appointed civil servant whose responsibilities included the programming of the four Arts and Culture Centres across the province. Brookes's dealings with the province's cultural branch were therefore dependent on the good will of a bureaucrat whom Brookes saw as an ideological antagonist – and who, indeed, proved to be that – as well as a competitor for audience support. For the duration of its history, the Mummers Troupe was one of the few funded theatres in Canada to receive no sustaining funding from its provincial arts agency.

As for the Canada Council, in making assessments of merit its officers, themselves drawn from the theatre, could not deny their own aesthetic judgments, although they seem to have taken care to err on the side of liberality. Brookes consistently argued that this liberal humanist model was not universally applicable, and that it was incapable of responding to the realities of a company that aimed at developing unique administrative and planning procedures to fulfil a mandate of political advocacy.

For the most part, Council officers were satisfied with the Mummers' artistic work; although they had serious reservations, any doubts were generally assuaged by evidence of community support. In the realm of administration, though, Brookes was under constant pressure from the Council to clarify the company's standing as a corporation and employer. The more Brookes tried to meet Council procedures, the more the internal composition of the group was disrupted by conflicting analyses of what the company should be. The pressures of crisis management intensified personal conflicts.[3] These were the very dangers that the members of the Vancouver Street Theatre had foreseen when they declined their OFY grant.

For the first three years of operation, until the Mummers Troupe was able to receive operations funding from the Canada Council in 1975–76, Brookes hired actors, including myself, on a project-by-project basis. Many of the actors came from outside Newfoundland, but as he began drawing more exclusively on local talent the need to resolve questions of internal relations and contracts became more pressing. By the mid-1970s Brookes was relying on a corps of performers who quite understandably came to believe in the ownership of the material they were creating, and some of them challenged his creative authority and control of the company. Although he was the director of a company that hired employees on a job-to-job basis, Brookes could not relinquish the idea of a company of comrades whose work together was cemented by bonds of friendship and political affinity. He preferred to establish close rapport with his actors, with the idea that each of them would feel a special bond. These intimacies inevitably conflicted.

Brookes dispensed information as required by the moment, giving news in confidence to some, withholding it from others. He created a complex entanglement of loyalties. Disputes over policy inevitably became complications in personal relationships and resulted in frequent accusations of manipulation. In 1976 a schism led to four members leaving the company to set up a rival theatre, which would become Rising Tide, now the largest theatre company in Newfoundland. The experience left deep feelings of personal betrayal on all sides, exacerbated by the financial sacrifices the actors had made. During the Mummers' first season wages averaged $80 a week (ranging from $40 to $125 depending on the funds available), out of which actors were expected to pay all of their own personal expenses; over the following decade, wages rarely exceeded $150 per week for the life of a particular project. For his part, Brookes insisted on receiving the same wage as his actors. In the early years he frequently subsidized company budgets with income that he received himself from occasional outside employment.

Brookes was an avowed socialist, as were many of his co-workers, but he was never able to establish a structure that reconciled his socialist principles with the imperative to conform to Council expectations. His socialism was expressed in his artistic practice and in his outspoken attitude of cultural resistance, and it was inevitable that his actors would replicate this attitude.

"Agit-Prop Political Warfare"

When Brookes returned to his native Newfoundland in spring 1972 he was completing a journey that began with a degree as a professional engineer and an apprenticeship at the Neptune Theatre in Halifax. After doing graduate studies in the United States (at Yale and Michigan) he performed briefly with John Juliani's avant-garde ensemble Savage God at Simon Fraser University in British Columbia before moving on to Toronto. It was while hanging out in Toronto's Rochdale College and developing a repertoire of radical puppet shows that he began making plans to return to St. John's to start a theatre. With his partner Lynn Lunde, he travelled to Newfoundland, performing *Punch & Judy* shows en route. At that point he was already aware of the need to develop a structure in which his theatre ambitions, shaped by street theatre and puppetry, could develop. In the winter of 1971–72, while living in Toronto, he wrote a letter to Jeanne Sabourin at Theatre Canada, an association of amateur theatres formed out of the ashes of the Dominion Drama Festival (it held national drama festivals of amateur theatres until 1973). He asked Sabourin for a $1,500 grant "to create a theatre resource in Nfld that will be a small travelling theatre-resource, able to function as a well-trained theatre ensemble when appropriate, and also able to function as 'catalysts for expression' – to be able to enter a community and show them/work with them to find tools for their own expression, forge mirrors for their own existence."

In the letter Brookes proposed that this company would consist of a "core group of about six," but beyond that he did not seem to have as yet defined whether it would operate as a collective or a company of employees. He recognized the need for a corporate parent. "I think it may be a help to set up as a non-profit charitable corporation and I intend to begin those arrangements soon if it is possible."

He was, however, clear as to the political function of this company. In a paper attached to his file copy of the letter to Sabourin, and titled "Disjointed Notes," he proposed that he would "Work with what is there – create with people the tools they need to forge a mirror for their own existence NOW. Tools that are as accessible as the tom-cod off the wharf, that don't cost $50,000 or a mainland income." The group would, he said, "Work with something that is as close and deep as mummering, not the imported bullshit upperclass theatrical titillations that grace the polished boards of the Arts and Culture Centres."[4]

Brookes and Lunde incorporated their company when it was still in its early planning stages, calling it Resource Foundation for the Arts. The articles of incorporation, dated November 21, 1973, were standard for not-for-profit organizations, which require an elected board of directors. But the criteria for membership were left deliberately vague: "Any person engaged in furthering the aims of the Foundation shall be eligible for membership and may be added to the membership by the Board of Directors. The Board of Directors may decline to accept any applicant as a member of the Foundation without assigning or being required to assign any reason for refusal."[5] This was boilerplate, and not very different than the structure that the Great Canadian Theatre Company had enacted three years later. The difference was that the GCTC saw the board as an instrument of governance and collective control, while for Brookes it was a legal fiction to enable him to apply for grants.

In April 1973 the federal Department of National Revenue approved the Resource Foundation for the Arts request for charity status. This step secured the company's existence more solidly than Brookes may have expected at the time, and would have severe repercussions six years later. The three founding members of the board of directors (Brookes, Lunde, and actor and filmmaker John Doyle) were also the only legal members of the Foundation, a situation that remained unchanged for several years. It was not until 1976 that the Resource Foundation held its first real annual general meeting. Brookes seems to have intended the Foundation to be a legal fiction that would enable the operation of the theatre company, but for his co-workers this legal entity was their obscure employer.

As Brookes recalls in his memoir, the name "Mummers Troupe" was introduced in the summer of 1973, months after he had mounted his first Christmas mummers play in St. John's.[6] By reviving the old

Newfoundland tradition of the wandering home–invasion play of Father Christmas, St. George, and the Turkish Knight, Brookes invested the troupe with a social legitimacy that would help him develop strategic alliances. It also gave him a name. Although Brookes writes that he came up with the name for the summer 1973 tour of *Newfoundland Night,* the posters for that play announced the name as "The Travelling Mummers." It was not until the end of the tour that the name was stabilized. Unlike Resource Foundation for the Arts, the name "Mummers Troupe" evoked a concrete image with a strong resonance of local tradition. Although the difference between these two names would later prove critical, it seems that at first the Mummers Troupe was intended as a catchy label for the public face of the Resource Foundation for the Arts.

The cartoon agitprop history play *Newfoundland Night* determined the course of the troupe's future political work. In August 1973 the company arrived in the outport of Sally's Cove and stayed to create an agitprop documentary play (*Gros Mourn*) to assist in the community's struggle against a planned relocation of the village, which was inside the newly formed Gros Morne National Park.[7] The *Gros Mourn* experience was a pioneering example of theatre as a political tool in a community struggle, establishing the principle of collaborative intervention that would later define the popular theatre movement. But if it was a breakthrough for political theatre, it was perceived as something else altogether by the provincial government and Canada Council. As Brookes later recalled, he sent a copy of the transcribed text, which contained satiric lampoons of federal and provincial politicians, to Timothy Porteus, then theatre officer at the Canada Council: "He was appalled at what an awful piece of shit the show was." In his memoir Brookes writes that Porteus told him, "As soon as you use real names your theatre becomes political rather than creative."[8] Faced with this attitude, Brookes began clarifying the principles that would qualify the Mummers for Council funding as a professional and artistic company. In October 1973, in an application to the Council's Explorations program, which was administered by a separate Council branch, he argued that the unique conditions of artistic development in Newfoundland required unique funding solutions: "We feel that Council funding concepts should be tailored to fit theatre structures as they exist in Canada, not vice-versa." He argued that the group's projects, "for the most part, don't have a clear beginning and end," which meant, "in part, that we prefer not to predict, eight or nine months in advance, where we will be in this process and exactly what we will need to do."[9] The need for flexibility was a constant refrain in Brookes's subsequent applications, even after the onset of operations funding in 1975. As the company grew, the debate became more bitter, reaching a climax of barely restrained hostility in 1978–79 when Walter Learning, a Newfoundlander and former director of Theatre New Brunswick, took over as theatre officer. Learning's refusal to accept the principle of flexibility and last-minute changes in programming created an ultimately irresolvable conflict for the Mummers.

During the fall and winter of 1973–74 Brookes mounted another Mummers play in St. John's and prepared for a spring tour of *Gros Mourn* and a summer project that would take the troupe to the mining town of Buchans. They had toured *Newfoundland Night* there the previous summer, at a time when the Steelworkers local was engaged in a long and bitter strike with the U.S.-based mining multinational ASARCO. Conversations with the local union led to the proposal to return to create a community documentary play based on the town's labour history. Busy with fundraising and grant applications, Brookes was supported in February 1974 by a community artist-in-residence grant from Memorial University's Arts Extension service. It was during this period that he began discussions with other local theatre artists to "hammer out some reasonable scheme for Council's support for theatre in the province."[10]

In January 1974 Brookes met with Michael Cook, whose reputation as a playwright was on the rise across Canada, and Dudley Cox, who had formed the Newfoundland Travelling Theatre to take Shakespeare to the outports. In the summer of 1974 Cox would be touring a pageant of Newfoundland history to commemorate the controversial twenty-fifth anniversary of Confederation in the province. Cox and Cook presented the draft proposal of a scheme they had developed, with the endorsement of the Director of Cultural Affairs for the province, to unite Brookes's group and their own efforts in a new company under the name of Theatre Newfoundland. Brookes was opposed to the scheme unless the Mummers could continue to operate as an autonomous unit with a fixed portion of the budget. According to Cox's minutes, Cook stressed that "Agit-Prop political warfare type productions" (a phrase that delighted Brookes) had no place in the proposed company. For his part, Cox disagreed with Brookes's belief that a populist theatre should be available to all possible audiences even if it had to be offered without charge. Cox argued that the theatre "must sell tickets" and that "every ticket sold is a public endorsement." He said, "With the provincial government's multi-million dollar investment in a chain of public Arts and Culture centres across the province, and its most recent school auditorium improvement programme, it is *not* sensible to suppose they will finance a theatre company, only half of which is designed to avail itself of these above mentioned facilities while the other half is given over to an anarchist."[11]

For Brookes this was a clear indication that the Mummers would never receive a sympathetic hearing from the provincial Cultural Affairs Division. To find a solution to this impasse, the Canada Council commissioned Keith Turnbull, who had the year before spellbound Toronto audiences with his production of James Reaney's *Sticks and Stones*, to visit Newfoundland and make recommendations for Council policy. Turnbull's report, submitted in May 1974, recommended that a Newfoundland professional theatre should be "small, highly mobile, organizationally committed to audience development and artistically committed to the realities of working in a theatrically unsophisticated context." This description might seem to fit the Mummers, but Turnbull was aware that his proposal would require the support of the province. He therefore recommended a company of "5 to 8 members" that would produce "one or two adult touring shows, one school tour and one full mainstage production to be presented in the arts and culture centres." He further suggested that the Director of Cultural Affairs should be an ex officio member of the company's board.

Turnbull's comments on the Mummers form the conclusion of his report. Clearly sympathetic to Brookes's position, he recommended that the Mummers "should be allowed to develop in individual and idiosyncratic directions which would not be possible as part of a provincial company." Turnbull's recommendations did not clarify the situation for the Canada Council; if anything, they muddied the waters even more by recommending a group that seemed to combine the antithetical positions of a company that was wedded to the Cultural Affairs office yet "highly mobile."[12]

By fall 1974, when applications for funding were due to the Canada Council's Theatre Section, the Council's theatre officer David Peacock was faced with yet another complication in the form of Codco, which had been formed the previous year in Toronto by a group of

Newfoundland actors and had since relocated to St. John's. In an attempt to impose a resolution, Peacock asked the three potential client companies, the Mummers, Codco, and the Newfoundland Travelling Theatre, to submit a joint application under the name of Newfoundland Theatre Ltd., a company established for that purpose. The idea of the tripartite company did not survive the funding year, and in 1975 it was as the Resource Foundation for the Arts that the Mummers group submitted its next application.

The Turnbull report and Peacock's response at the very least signalled the Council's desire to treat the Mummers seriously and to find a workable formula. By this point, Brookes had built a solid body of work with very little funding support, and his Buchans project seemed, especially at a distance, to be a Newfie version of *The Farm Show*. It was much more political than the Ontario model of community documentaries, although that was not yet readily evident. The Mummers' gains in institutional credibility, however, were shaken by the first collective expressions of discontent from within the company.

With the cast in Buchans made up mostly of people from the mainland, issues of labour relations were confined by and large to working conditions. Although the cast felt some proprietary interest in the show that they created, and for the most part valued their affiliation with the Mummers, they did not look to it as an ongoing source of work. They therefore did not claim the right of ownership that would later be expressed by members of the cast who lived in the province.

Nevertheless, the cast of the Buchans project identified enough areas of discontent to issue a "Mummers Manifesto" to Brookes in the fall of 1974, after completion of the arduous tour of *Buchans: A Mining Town*. As was the case with the *Newfoundland Night* cast, the Buchans Mummers worked long hours for low wages, a condition they cheerfully accepted as necessary. But in the manifesto they advised Brookes that the administrative structure of the company needed to be clarified.[13] The company lacked a full-time administrator, and the actors strongly believed that the director should not occupy both functions. The Buchans project precipitated Brookes's first major labour dispute in the winter of 1975, when he negotiated a remount of the play (retitled *Company Town*) for a Toronto run, to be followed by a tour of mining towns in Ontario and Manitoba. The negotiations with the actors, most of whom had by then returned to the mainland, raised recurring questions of airfare subsidies and salaries.

Brookes had to settle these demands in the face of an unstable budget; because the tour itself was still in the planning stages, budget projections were incomplete. In April, a week before they were scheduled to arrive in St. John's for rehearsals, the actors were notified that the tour was being cut back severely because the United Steelworkers of America, which had initially agreed to support the tour and book a performance for its upcoming convention, had withdrawn its sponsorship (of the first play ever developed with and for a USWA local) on the grounds that the Mummers Troupe did not operate under the jurisdiction of Actors' Equity. Lunde had pulled the plug in Toronto, and Brookes was stranded by blizzards in Labrador, where he had gone to research the possibilities of doing a show.

The administration of the company was in shambles, even though Brookes was poised for an ambitious year, with the *Company Town* tour concurrent with rehearsals and performance for *East End Story*, the first show to be presented in the LSPU (Longshoremen's Protective Union) Hall in St. John's (which the Resource Foundation would purchase in the following year). To follow *East End Story* Brookes had planned *Dying Hard* (based on an oral history of miners dying from silicosis) and *I.W.A.* (about the violent 1950 loggers' strike, with Rick Salutin as writer) to take the company through to the end of the calendar year. These plans called for a twelve-month season of research, rehearsal, and perform-ance, and yet the administrative support for the season was unstable and tensions with actors were explosive. Cast members were further alienated from the administration because the only company office and telephone were in Brookes's house in Petty Harbour, eighteen kilo-metres from St. John's.

To the Canada Council, the Mummers' future appeared stable. The joint application in fall 1974 had brought a $35,000 grant from the Theatre Section, and a letter from Timothy Porteus that commented, "Increased funding brings with it increased responsibility in the con-trol of budget and in your accounting procedures."[14] But the promise of funding intensified Brookes's problems with the actors because it raised once again the question of ownership and responsibility: Brookes was still not accountable to anyone but the Resource Foundation, which was under his control and still occupied the phantom space that it had taken up when it was formed as a tactical necessity. He instituted regular meet-ings in January 1975, which until the implementation of a "core group" policy later in the year were attended by whoever was involved in a show at the time. The result was a changing roster of Mummers who found themselves articulating recurring complaints. In the meetings, usually held in bars – at least as recorded in the minutes (handwritten in several different hands and informal) – Brookes was apparently willing to discuss problems and ask advice for resolving issues, but tended to appease rather than commit to specific solutions.

In May, with Lunde still in Toronto, the *Company Town* cast in St. John's for rehearsals, and the *East End Story* project about to begin, the tenor of the meetings changed. Demanding contracts and transparency, the actors were pushing the Mummers Troupe towards a more conventional model of theatrical organization. This might have suited Brookes's purposes, but even so he hesitated to empower the Resource Foundation's board of directors, which had neither met formally nor changed its composition since 1972. In the conventional model of a public theatre, the artistic director is accountable to an independent board as a contracted employee, but Brookes, it seems, was reluctant to surrender his control over board decisions. The issue remained unresolved until June, when Brookes accepted the proposal of a "core group" policy. The "core group," which initially comprised Brookes, Lunde (who had returned from Toronto), Donna Butt, and Rhonda Payne, functioned as an executive committee. It was accepted that members of the group would have ongoing status in the operations of the company and could depend on it for steady employment.

The core group policy realigned the company once again to a collective model. Although the company was now on a funding track with the Canada Council, it still operated on a level of administrative improvisation that would have alarmed the Council officers had they realized its extent. The Council imperative of careful pre-planning simply could not be reconciled with the exigencies of collective decision-making. Moreover, because Council policy maintained that no company should be fully subsidized by Council funds, the Mummers had to seek other funding to compensate for the lack of a provincial subsidy. Brookes was an effective fundraiser, managing to secure commissions for projects from public interest organizations such as the Community Planning Council of Canada, Newfoundland Division (for *East End Story*) and Oxfam-Canada (for *Price of Fish*). While such commissions brought funds into the budget, their granting and reporting procedures rarely coincided with those of the Canada Council, and funds frequently had to be moved from one project budget to another to make ends meet. These decisions contravened the basic tenets of Canada Council procedures, but they were unavoidable. Many of the planned projects required long negotiations with sponsoring agencies and host communities, and decisions were often forced to wait until the last minute, with Brookes juggling alternatives until funding for a particular project might lock in. Again, this pattern complicated his dealings with actors, who were often kept on edge waiting for confirmation of project dates.

For the Mummers, even amidst these conflicts, the prospects for 1976 seemed relatively secure. The Mummers had already enjoyed favourable exposure on the mainland with the Toronto run of *Company Town*, and a run of *I.W.A.* was booked into Centaur Theatre in Montreal. With the Labrador project on the back burner and the Oxfam show scheduled for work in the spring (with a projected national tour), Brookes looked to round the season off with a community show on the South Coast. Although the minutes do not record the decision, Brookes states in his memoir that Butt was scheduled to direct the play. To the Canada Council, which granted the company $45,000 in 1976 "in recognition of the substantial strides Mummers have made in this past year both artistically and administratively," it may well have seemed as if the Newfoundland question was happily resolved.[15]

"A Capitalist Structure ..."

For the Mummers in 1976 two principal events would lead to a crisis from which the company never fully recovered: the Foundation purchased the LSPU Hall, placing a new burden on the administrative structure of the company; and the Oxfam show project contributed to extremely complex and antagonistic working relationships within the group. The move into the hall gave the company a tangible material reality – no longer was it just a constantly renegotiated matrix of working relationships – but now that the company had material assets, a performance space, and an office, its newly acquired public face promised a permanence that made the questions of ownership even more critical.

Brookes had rented the downtown hall for *East End Story* from the Longshoremen's Protective Union, which was in decline and willing to sell the building. In 1976 the Resource Foundation managed to put together a funding package (including a $57,000 grant from Secretary of State) that enabled the company to buy the hall outright for $50,000.[16]

The operation of the hall demanded a clarification of the relationship between the Mummers and Resource Foundation, which could no longer continue as a legal fiction. Brookes was heavily involved in the preparations for the performance season, and Lunde managed the financial arrangements for the purchase. Brookes felt increasingly alienated from the decision-making process, and his personal relationship with Lunde had deteriorated. The two of them barely spoke to one another.

As Brookes details at length in his memoir, tempers were at a pitch during the rehearsal process for *Price of Fish* in February and March. The issues were the familiar ones of collectivity and authority, compounded by hostile personal relationships. In February the problem had intensified. Rehearsals stopped for five days so that the company could consider "collective processes; aims and objectives of company." The sketchy minutes from the meetings record the circularity of the arguments and the emotional stakes at play.[17]

In July, after the cast had returned from the performances of *Price of Fish* on the mainland, matters came to head when four of the six cast members publicly announced their disassociation from the Mummers and issued a manifesto demanding that the Resource Foundation allow the name Mummers Troupe to "die an honorable death."

> We, as workers, feel cheated and betrayed. Each of us has contributed significantly to the growth and the reputation of the Mummers' troupe but we worked under a false premise, the premise that we all owned the company, which we do morally, but unfortunately legally it lies in the hands of Resource Foundation for the Arts....
>
> It should have been stated clearly in the beginning that this company, through that legal corporation, in fact belonged to Chris and Lynn, and that we were employees – then we could have decided if we chose to work under such an arrangement. But instead we were strung along, for the management knew we would likely turn down such a set up....
>
> We cannot condemn the evils of capitalism and find ourselves working under a capitalist structure.[18]

The turmoil in the company had reached the ears of the Canada Council, whose relations with the Mummers began to disintegrate. The company was now reporting to a new theatre officer, Anna Stratton, whose responses to the Mummers' work was less than enthusiastic to begin with. In March 1976, after Stratton saw *I.W.A.* at Centaur Theatre in Montreal, she added her jotted impressions to the Mummers' file at Canada Council:

> 27 Mar 1976
> overall impressions – good
> – Performers certainly capable of this kind of theatre
> – need for specific voice and movement training is apparent
> – Show itself did have dramatic interest and some depth – probably due to Salutin's writing –
> but it was
> – essentially a sketch of situation.
> not enough background information given ... – very one-sided view – fine – but not enough information given to support it....
> show suffered from lack of depth and subtlety that most collectives do.[19]

Such judgments reinforce Brookes's position that the Canada Council was assessing the Mummers' work according to inappropriate criteria. As the controversy surrounding the Council's attempts to establish a policy on collectives in 1978 suggest, Council officers tended to confuse collective creation (which they saw as relatively inartistic) with the operating structures of the companies that created them.

In November Stratton contacted the Resource Foundation and asked for details on its structure. When Lunde sent her a copy of the articles of incorporation, Stratton responded by suggesting that Resource and the Mummers separate:

> re Resource. –
> I advised they should
> – establish themselves as community org. w/ representatives of several artists and make hall Resource's
> – Mummers should be separately incorporated as a theatre co.
> – suggested Resource – could be a centre for info, organization, etc.
> – start w/ summer festival and establish a committee.[20]

After four years of struggle and negotiation Brookes was left with few choices. The collective model had collapsed. The only functional alternative was to accept the terms of organization that he had always opposed from Council, but he was not yet prepared to do this. Stratton's informal advice was a perceptive foreshadowing of the eventual solution, and had Brookes and Lunde been prepared to accept this advice they might have averted a painful struggle. But the Mummers Troupe had barely survived the schism evident in the July manifesto, and Brookes was clearly in a state of emotional and creative exhaustion that made a major reorganization of the company unlikely. Internal conditions necessitated crisis management, and his control over the Resource Foundation apparatus was still Brookes's principal tool of creative survival.

The Canada Council's interest in the Mummers organization did encourage Brookes to reform the Foundation. By the end of the year it had an active membership of eight, of whom only half had worked with the Mummers. In December the Resource Foundation held its first actual annual meeting, in which it re-elected the long-standing board of Brookes, Lunde, and Doyle, and discussed, inconclusively, the problem of the Mummers' status: "General discussion re incorporating the Mummers Troupe separately under Resource Foundation. Fears were expressed at creating a complicated legal and bureaucratic structure that would be to the detriment of Resource Foundation and the Mummers Troupe."[21]

With the company now devoting more of its time and administrative energies to the development of the hall, Brookes scaled down his plans for the Mummers Troupe. From 1974 to 1975 he had produced five shows a year – a rate of production comparable to most Canadian theatres in the Mummers' budget range – but because his plays were collective creations the process of mounting them involved more research and development than usual for such companies. In 1977 he produced only three shows: *Weather Permitting* (the Labrador show), *The Bard of Prescott Street*, and the annual Christmas Mummers play. The Canada Council appears to have been satisfied with this apparent stability following the crises of 1976; although it encouraged the Mummers to develop its in-house programming in the hall, the expected grant increases did not materialize. In May 1977 David Peacock's notification of a $50,000 operations grant (as opposed to the requested $78,000) advised, "Now that the company has a permanent home, the possibilities of raising

revenue through the box office, fund raising, rentals and special projects (e.g. benefits, auctions, concerts, flea markets, etc.) should now
be increased."[22]

Although the operations grant promised secure funding, it remained
at the same level for the next year. In a 1978 position paper, Brookes
estimated that inflation had decreased the value of the Canada Council
grant by 30 per cent since 1976, against an increase in salaries of 40 per
cent since 1975.[23] Total annual revenues for the company at this time
amounted to $140,000; a third of this was raised in box-office sales, and
about another third from the Canada Council. The Mummers record for
private-sector fundraising (chiefly through commissions) was comparable
to the national average, but the company's major handicap was the continuing absence of provincial support. Moreover, while Canada Council
funding to the first generation of alternative theatres across Canada had
increased substantially during the 1970s as the Council sought to regular-
ize a select few (such as Tarragon Theatre and Factory Theatre Lab in
Toronto), the Mummers Troupe had been effectively frozen since 1975,
thus finding itself relegated to a permanent third-rate funding status in an
already marginal arts funding ghetto.

This state of affairs was in part a reaction to its history of erratic
administration, but Brookes perceived a deeper reason in the Council's
mistrust of collective theatre. Council officers are technically neutral parties in the granting process; their function is to monitor the theatre's ability to fulfil the terms of its grants, to solicit advice from outside appraisers,
and to facilitate juries of peer assessors. But the officers choose their
sources and jurors. In November, for example, the Council asked Walter Learning, then artistic director of Theatre New Brunswick, to assess
The Bard of Prescott Street. Learning's response, which in accordance with
Council policy was kept in confidence from the company, is of particular
significance because he would himself take over as theatre officer in the
following year.

> The Mummers' finished work always seems, to me, to have a
> "work-in-progress" quality about it. My usual reaction is – "now
> there's the basis for a really fine and exciting production."
>
> They always seem to lack really tight script editing and dir-
> ection. This, of course, is in part the result of their work method
> and perhaps this would be adversely affected if another element

were introduced into the process. Maybe they need a chance to work with some really experienced directors from the collective creation area.[24]

But few directors were as experienced in collective creation as Brookes was (and there were none who had as much reason to understand the political pitfalls of the form). The particular values that Learning addressed (script editing, direction) rested on aesthetic assumptions that were not necessarily appropriate to the kind of work that Brookes was doing. As the 1980s drew nearer, Brookes began to analyse his relationship with the Canada Council as an ideological condition that had less to do with the internal history of his company than with the Council's inability to understand the fundamental principles of politically engaged theatre.[25]

The "Mysterious East"

In the 1977–79 period the Mummers were embroiled in an increasingly complex series of financial crises from which the company never recovered. In an ironic pattern that was becoming familiar, these crises followed the company's moment of national celebrity with the highly publicized mainland tour of *They Club Seals, Don't They?*, the Mummers' pro-sealing intervention in the media circus of the anti-seal hunt campaign.[26]

Although the sealing show brought the company new credibility with the provincial government (which supplied 20 per cent of production expenses through the Department of Rural Development), no promise of operating support was forthcoming. The province, it seemed, was willing to provide funds only when the Mummers' political agenda accorded with its own. The one-time grant for the sealing show seemed to confirm the official view that the Mummers group was no more than a renegade propaganda troupe. When the Cultural Affairs Division finally began handing out arts grants in late 1978, the Mummers Troupe was not on the list, but Rising Tide Theatre (newly formed by Donna Butt and David Ross) was.[27]

In March 1978 Brookes applied for a $65,000 operations grant from the Canada Council, and received $50,000. His original submission proposed a continuation of the sealing show, a tour of *The Bard of Prescott*

Street, a new tour of the sealing show, *The Post-Card Show,* and an as yet unplanned community show. The shortfall in the grant required a revision of the plans, for which Brookes was reprimanded in the following year by Canada Council. In March 1979, Learning, informing Brookes of a $45,000 grant, wrote:

> There is a serious concern about the ability of the company to consolidate and build upon its success, assuring a firm basis for future development. Ad hoc and re-active programming seems to indicate some problem in realizing the mandate the company has set for itself.... Some vestige of your pre-planning must remain, otherwise the real viability of the organization is brought into question.[28]

Consequently, the notification stipulated, the grant would be paid as a series of project instalments conditional on "receipt of budget and production details of new work." In short, Learning was placing Brookes on a very short leash. Brookes responded in fury, answering each of Learning's charges in detail. He was particularly enraged that Learning had brought his commitment to the Mummers' mandate into question: "My company's ability to deliver on its mandate is measured by the response to the society of its region, by the production of shows which are relevant to the issues confronting that society. This means that our production plans may have to change as rapidly as the social issues they express."[29]

Learning's pro forma statement of Council's concerns about Brookes's ability to deliver on his mandate was evasive; he had formulated those concerns himself in his annual grant recommendation to the Council. The underlying cause was the founding of Rising Tide Theatre in September 1978. Citing "serious doubts" that the Mummers "can deliver what they promise," Learning reported to Council: "Newfoundland is our very own mysterious East and the Mummers Troupe one of its more inscrutable institutions." He spoke of how Newfoundland's "theatre scene" had "no real leadership at any level" and was being dominated by "three primary characteristics a) schizophrenia, b) paranoia and c) diffusion." From Learning's point of view, "the emergence of Rising Tide Theatre, which is doing a similar type of collective creation," was clouding the issue. Rising Tide had already "presented one very successful show" and received an Explorations grant for a second production. The new company would soon be eligible to get grants from the Theatre Section, which had already met with the group. The Theatre Section was "impressed with a) the quality of their work, b) the thoroughness of their artistic planning and c) the effectiveness of their administration."[30]

In normal circumstances the founding of a new theatre should have no effect on subsidies to existing companies, but Learning, aware of Butt's history of conflict with Brookes, perceived Rising Tide's claim to the Mummers' history as an indication of the fundamental instability of collective theatre. In December 1978 Learning had announced a reorganization of Council granting procedures; henceforth operations grants would be awarded for three-year terms to companies receiving more than $25,000; companies under that "floor" would compete annually for project funding. In May 1979 he announced that "for a trial period of one year collective companies would not be eligible to receive base operating grants" regardless of their funding level.[31] This move affected over a dozen companies across the country, and many of them agreed with Brookes that it was a repercussion of the Rising Tide/ Mummers situation. Although Learning stated to the board of directors of Kam Theatre Lab in Thunder Bay (the company that would host the Bread and Circuses Festival a year later) that the policy was never intended to deal with the Mummers, Kam Lab's co-director, Michael Sobota, reported to Brookes that a Council officer had told them that the policy was designed to "assure a situation like the one in St. John's would never happen again."[32]

Just what that situation was, none of the documents state explicitly, and details are obscure. Whether Rising Tide had lobbied Learning for the Mummers' operations grant on the grounds that they were the real Mummers is difficult to ascertain, but there were widely reported ripples through the theatre community that this was the case, and it would explain Learning's perception of unstable collectives. The new collectives policy did not remain in effect long; Learning tempered it after a meeting in Toronto in January 1980 in which representatives of more than twenty variously defined collectives argued that they were as stable as any other company model, and that Council was confusing working methods with administrative structure. But the policy did succeed in resolving the Newfoundland anomaly: by displacing the Mummers from the new three-year funding formula, it further destabilized the troupe, which was already reeling from the aftershock of the battle for the LSPU Hall.

The struggle over access and control of the hall was the final chapter of the debate about the relationship of the Mummers Troupe and the Resource Foundation. Brookes gives the episode only a short space in his memoirs, referring to it as a "byzantine political dogfight" precipitated by the Mummers' desire to find another group to assume responsibility for the hall.[33] As Fran Locke, a local community organizer and cultural activist, notes, the hall had become an important community resource: "From September, 1977 to September 1978, over 27,000 people came to the Hall. During that year there occurred 20 musical concerts, 75 performances of 13 different plays, 76 meetings, 50 weeks of rehearsal, 4 workshops over 7 weeks and 4 visual arts/crafts exhibitions. The users of the Hall included 45 different arts/community groups."[34]

The struggle for control of the LSPU Hall was more than byzantine; it was extraordinarily bitter. It concentrated all the recurring grievances held against the Mummers, and added new ones. The first documented stage of the controversy was a letter from Lunde to the St. John's arts community on April 2, 1979, in response to a petition calling for open membership to the Resource Foundation. In the letter Lunde invited signers of the petition to an open meeting on April 6 and advised, "Resource Foundation is exercising the proffered option in the petition to suggest a viable alternative to an open membership for Resource Foundation for the Arts."[35] An undated, unsigned handwritten document records a motion presented from the floor:

> That the people present at a public meeting held at the L.S.P.U.
> Hall, April 6, 1979
> a) elect a council of people to set up a charitable organization
> with public membership to investigate assuming responsibilities for the L.S.P.U. Hall & its contents
> b) That the people present at this public meeting call upon the
> Resource Foundation to negotiate transfer of the L.S.P.U. hall &
> its contents to this charitable organization and that this council and the RFA find a mutually agreeable mediator to oversee
> this transfer.[36]

Brookes and Lunde resisted this proposal for a public takeover. On April 13 John Doyle, the other long-standing board member, resigned from the board, and Brookes and Lunde incorporated the Mummers

Troupe as a privately owned limited share company. Ironically, because the articles of incorporation were taken from standard forms, Brookes found himself to be, on paper at least, the capitalist that his actors had once accused him of being; one of the legal objectives of the Mummers Troupe Ltd. was "to establish, transact, and carry on the business of an investment company in all its branches and to carry on and undertake any business commonly carried out or undertaken by financiers, discount houses, capitalists."[37]

Public meetings continued to mount pressure, and on April 23 the Resource Foundation received another petition for open membership. Tempers rose. Mike Riggio, a well-known local artist, sent an open letter to "All Prospective Members of Resource Foundation for the Arts" that argued against any proposal that would acknowledge Brookes's right to retain control over the Mummers Troupe and artistic residency in the hall. His letter reopened the old sores of collectivity: "I believe that evidence can be brought forward which will show that 'The Mummers' is not an artistic direction under Chris Brooks (as presently constituted). It is my opinion that 'The Mummers' is a *collective*, a collective from which some of its founding members have been 'locked out.' "[38]

By the end of the summer, the Resource Foundation for the Arts was facing a boycott. Participants at yet another public meeting, on August 14, debated three motions: a) to establish a boycott and set up a new board to be bound immediately by an arbitration committee; b) to set up a board of trustees immediately; or c) to establish a boycott committee. On the following day Andy Jones, a principal member of Codco, wrote to Brookes and Lunde, "At the public meeting held last night the proposal of an arbitration body was unanimously accepted with the proviso that the public be admitted as members immediately."[39]

Brookes and Lunde accepted the proposal for both a separation and an arbitration committee. Considering the temper of the controversy, the arbitration report, issued in September 1979, is a model of restraint. The report determined that since government capital investment was being given to performing arts companies, not buildings, the Mummers Troupe had a valid claim to residency in the hall. It awarded the troupe a guaranteed minimum of 25 per cent of the hall's rehearsal and performance time, but recommended that the arrangement be reviewed after three years. In December the first annual report of the new Resource Foundation celebrated the victory in the form of a thirteen-verse ballad in the style of Johnny Burke (the subject of the Mummers' *Bard of Prescott Street*), written by chairman Gordon Inglis, complete with a dig at the Mummers' trademark hobby horse:

> Now the R.F.A. and the Mummers Troupe were one thing and the same,
> The difference between them being only in the name,
> And both of them were managed from but one single source –
> Chris Brookes and Lynn Lunde—and perhaps the Mummers' horse,
> They resisted all the arguments – and not surprisingly
> For their interests were threatened. If the art community
> Were to take the whole thing over, who could tell what they might do?
> Might they take, not just the Hall, but the Mummers' old horse too?[40]

In the space of a year, the Mummers Troupe had lost both its guarantee of continued funding from Canada Council and its base of operations. Lunde returned to the mainland, and when the smoke cleared Brookes was left with what he had started with years before: the name of a company, possible Council funding, a van and the old Mummers bus, a few lighting instruments, and some office supplies. He would do only one more show, a rock-based revue on the false hopes of offshore oil, *Some Slick*, before handing over what was left of the company to long-time associate Rhonda Payne. Unable to secure ongoing funding, Payne managed to produce six shows before deciding to cancel the 1982 season. On October 26, 1982, she and Brookes sent out a press release announcing the death of the Mummers Troupe.[41]

The Mummers Troupe's ten years of struggle and controversy saw their fair share of successes in the creation of radical performances. But they also reflect a history located in a constant drift of crises – of ideology, of personality, of structural management – with these conflicts questioning the conceptual vocabularies and larger narratives that shape the discourse of Canadian theatre. Brookes's repeated insistence that the Canada Council failed to understand the cultural specificity of oppositional political theatre was a fundamental repudiation of the humanist construction of national culture embodied in the very concept of the

Council, which delineates binary models of alternative and mainstream, centre and region. The Council's funding policies reiterated these binaries in a model of competing establishment and marginal theatres, each with its aesthetic sphere, each with its appropriate economic profile.

As seen through the eyes of the Canada Council, the troupe merited funding because support of politicized art – the tolerance of dissent – is commonly offered as a proof of the validity of liberal humanism. By the same token, the liberal humanist position defines political art as the oppositional voice of a minority, which means in effect that it must accept minority funding. But the Mummers Troupe was also an expression of regional culture, which could not be relegated simply to minority status. The arrival of Rising Tide, which soon renounced its original political agenda in favour of a more institutional notion of regionalism, resolved this paradox for the Council. It could now respond to the Mummers purely as a political theatre collective.

The Mummers Troupe was an index of overlapping postcolonial contradictions: of Newfoundland vs. Canadian culture and nation; of collective vs. hierarchical models of production; of artistic authority vs. collective responsibility; of generational attitudes; and of class. These contradictions defined the material conditions in which the company could work, and their replication within the company led to its collapse. Although these conflicts led the Council to conclude that the company was an unstable anomaly, the same conditions exist, with various degrees of containment, in most Canadian theatres.

In a way the experience of the Mummers turned out to be an inverse mirror of the experience of Toronto Workshop Productions. Believing firmly that radical theatre needed professional mastery, Luscombe sought to produce engaged and activist art within the established boundaries of the theatre as a disciplinary economy. He negotiated the contradictions of that position for close to thirty years. but in the end was defeated by the professional institutionalism that he had helped to build. Brookes attempted to carve out a space in the cultural economy and funding system for a theatre that refused the idea of professionalism as understood in the theatre community. He attempted to construct a theatre that was responsive, disruptive, and honest about its class analysis. Brookes and Luscombe suffered the same fate, ousted by the boards they had created. Clearly, the public-sector board model was not workable if a theatre wanted to move outside of the theatre domain into radical engagement.

Others saw this same phenomenon at work too, and tried to build alternative structures that would maximize capacity, maintain stability, and enable uncompromised activism. They frequently came to the same solution: that radical activist theatre cannot happen in the framework of a box-office financial structure. It cannot be actively interventionist if it is a machine for putting bums in seats. But if theatre does not sell tickets and ensure its own existence, how can it find and maintain an audience? The answer would appear in what came to be known as the popular theatre model – a model based not on selling tickets but on providing a service.

8

Powering Structures and Popular Theatre

Thandie Mpumlwana as a health-care worker fighting a puppet germ in *Where's the Care?* – Ground Zero's 1991 agitprop intervention around the issue of health-care funding in Ontario.
Ground Zero Productions

We share a common belief that theatre is a means and not
an end. We are theatres which work to effect social change.
— *Canadian Popular Theatre Alliance, Statement of
Principles, Thunder Bay, Ont., 1981*

The popular theatre movement, as it came to be known in
the 1980s, was an attempt to formalize and share theatrical methods
of engagement with community activism and to create a radical space
in the theatre profession for the increasingly diverse cultural practices
entailed in this work. It was on one level a national movement, and in
another an attempt to harness a tendency into a productive network.
When we speak of popular theatre as a movement, we gesture both to a
cohesive formation that came into being and the vast domain of activist
theatre work that the people involved helped to define and reveal. All
of the work was engaged; some of it was radical, and much of it was not.

In Canada new groups are always in formation because for the most
part theatre here is a young person's profession, and every year hundreds
of students graduate with the awareness that they have to produce their
own work. Over the course of the 1970s and 1980s the emergent, small,
project-based theatres became institutionalized as the "R&D" sector of
the theatre industry; and as small theatres clustered around the unfunded
fringe they developed new creative vocabularies. Often these new
approaches flowed out of an engagement with minority cultural politics
and seeped into the mainstream. But the economics of the theatre world in
Canada creates a series of stepped barriers to the basic rewards of theatre
work (prestige and a decent living). Even at the best of times, theatre is an
underpaid profession; for people labouring at the bottom of the creative
pyramid – people generating new work, new ideas, and new audiences – it
often offers no pay at all. Indeed, the well-known concept of the Fringe
Festival is in essence a showcase in which artists pay for the right to work
for free in hopes that they will recoup enough to cover their costs.

One result of this trend was a growing community of theatre work-ers who had developed multiple skills and professional flexibility. An actor might eke out a living by supplementing theatre engagements with commercials and TV work, but an actor who could write a play or a solo show would increase the possibilities of work exponentially. An actor-writer who can direct, compose, or produce leverages even more possibilities of work. In an ironic way, the relative lack of professional institutions in Canadian theatre produced an extremely skilled creative workforce – and one in which broad leftist sympathies became common. The hardships of a freelance theatre life, with minimal income and no benefits, tended to produce a widespread sense of radicalism and dissent throughout the most creative sector of the theatre. This tendency did not always find expression in activism, but it helped to create a cultural climate in which theatre work and activism could meet.

By the mid-1970s activists were picking up on the use of theatre in popular and participatory education. A major figure in this regard was Ross Kidd, a Canadian who worked in popular education campaigns in Botswana in the 1970s and began to connect with other Africa-based educators who were exploring the application of theatre techniques in community development. Kidd would go on to spend many years in Africa, building and training "theatre for development" projects and, more recently, from his home in Botswana, AIDS and water supply education programs. For a period of time in the early 1980s he returned to Canada to complete a Ph.D. in participatory education at the Ontario Institute for Studies in Education in Toronto.

Kidd, like others in this tradition of work, understands theatre as a collaborative process in which communities draw on their own cul-tural performance traditions to create a social dialogue aimed at raising critical awareness and capacity for change. A typical example – one of many hundreds – of how this form of popular theatre worked in the Can-adian context was Enviromaniacs, a troupe formed out of the Waterloo Public Interest Research Group at the University of Waterloo in the early 1990s. Drawing on works by Kidd and other popular educators, the WPIRG student activists taught themselves popular theatre techniques and wrote a manual based on their experiences. One of the authors, Jennifer Anderson, explained, "It seems to me that somewhere around Grade 5, we forget how to play. We begin to think that only 'profession-als' can act and sing and dance and create art. I say, NOT TRUE!"[1] The

manual takes readers through the steps of planning and group formation, showing how to run meetings and set goals, and introduces some
of the participatory games that are crucial in group formation in any
popular theatre process. It then outlines methods of group analysis and
assessment. Only three of its eighty-eight pages actually look at ways of
creating a "play." The advice is sensible and useful, and defines aesthetic
choices as instrumental decisions:

> When putting on a skit: it may be appropriate to have a narrator
> telling a story, or voicing some details. Determining the inten-
> tion of the play (change attitudes, to empower, or to make people
> aware), will give the group more direction. Choose a method for
> performance. Will the audience participate? If so, how will the
> audience participate? What types of activities, role-plays and
> exercises will be built into the process to allow this direction to
> happen? Which characters will explain the steps and when will
> these activities happen? Will props be used? Costumes? Will
> there be lots of dialogue, or no talking at all?[2]

The manual offers a succinct definition of street theatre, stressing that
it is most effective when "less than three minutes" long. It also includes
a new twist on guerrilla theatre as "civil disobedience": "An example of
guerilla theatre would be people donning gas masks and lying on the street
and on cars to protest the amount of inner-city pollution and to encourage
people to ride bikes, walk, carpool or use public transport."[3] For WPIRG,
as with many activist groups using performance techniques, popular theatre is a process of group conscientization and cohesion. The performance
is only important as one phase of public presentation of the issue.

Even then, what matters is clarity of the issue rather than the
aesthetic pleasure of the performance. The WPIRG activists came to
understand popular theatre as defined by Tim Prentki and Jan Selman:
as "a *process* of theatre which deeply involves specific communities in
identifying issues of concern, analyzing current conditions and causes
of a situation, identifying points of change, and analyzing how change
could happen and/ or contributing to the actions implied."[4]

In keeping with the suggestion that interventionist theatre practices
follow changes in mass communication technology, this de-aestheticized
use of theatre as a form of applied communication development in a

group has its sources (in Canada, at least) in the reorientation of mass media technology to local communication. One significant moment that had repercussions in both popular education and interventionist theatre was the National Film Board's Fogo Process, which used film as a technique of community animation in remote Newfoundland fishing outports. Produced as part of the NFB "Challenge for Change" series in 1967–68 by Colin Low and the Memorial University of Newfoundland's Extension Department, the process consisted of filmed interviews with fishery workers in each of the island communities. As each community responded on film, the results were screened back in what was called a "communication loop."[5] The process of participatory research on film was by its nature a form of community development. The project drew considerable attention not only because of its innovative process but also because its political result – the establishment of a fishing co-op – demonstrated how cultural action could lead to material change. The Fogo Process had another effect in Newfoundland, when it inspired Chris Brookes to take the Mummers Troupe in the direction of community engagement.

For activists, the Fogo Process was an early application of Freirean pedagogy. In his work, beginning with the foundational *Pedagogy of the Oppressed*, Paulo Freire offered a critique of traditional systems of knowledge and education that reinforced structures of social oppression. He argued that when people "lack a critical understanding of their reality, apprehending it in fragments which they do not perceive as interacting constituent elements of the whole, they cannot truly know their reality."[6] For Freire adult education was a process of working with communities to codify and decode representations of reality in order to identify points of possible change. His theories of activist community education, with their emphasis on participatory democracy and local knowledge, circulated through Canada via development educators and literacy workers. The approach provided theatre artists with a vocabulary that enabled them to theorize and reconceptualize their largely self-taught work in community animation.

In the popular theatre movement Freire would become a guru figure who entered the discourse from two different directions: the popular education sector, as in Fogo and the theatre practices and theories promoted by Kidd; and the theatre sector of the early 1980s, through the work of Freire's friend and compatriot, Augusto Boal. By the time Boal's Theatre of the Oppressed techniques began to remake Canadian popular theatre practices in the mid-1980s, Freirean methods had already been well established in a number of theatres. The most notable of these was Catalyst Theatre in Edmonton, which during that decade established itself as a funded agency of the Alberta Alcohol and Drug Abuse Commission, using Freirean principles to develop interactive role-play methods with target audiences.[7]

These two sectors came together in 1978 when Ross Kidd and Chris Brookes convened a meeting in Newfoundland of left-wing and collective theatres from across the country. The main results of that meeting were a sense of solidarity combined with an offer by Michael Sobota on behalf of the small collective Kam Theatre Lab in Thunder Bay to host a festival, plus the beginnings of a consensus around the term "popular theatre." In claiming this term, Canadian practitioners found a rhetorical instrument that identified their work as instrumental and populist.

The rhetoric became a structure two years later at the Thunder Bay festival. Kidd organized an international "community animation" workshop in 1981 in Thunder Bay as part of Kam Theatre's Bread and Circuses Festival of small, vaguely left-wing theatres (which became, retroactively, the first Canadian Popular Theatre Alliance festival). With financial support from CUSO, Kidd's week-long workshop brought a dozen Canadians together to exchange skills with popular theatre workers from seven African and Caribbean nations. By introducing the term popular theatre, Kidd gave the workshop participants an instrument that enabled them to define their commonality clearly and relocated the defining criteria for political theatre to active collaboration with a community in the process of struggle. The Canadian contingent in this workshop drew up the original proposal of a popular theatre alliance for ratification by the companies at the festival.

The original intention of the workshop was to bring theatre workers from Canada, Africa, and the Caribbean together to create a piece of theatre on the international food economy. That plan fell apart quite quickly as the realities of the situation changed the script. The visitors were shocked and disconcerted by their exposure to poverty in Thunder Bay. The experience disturbed their preconceptions of North American society, and the Canadians had a hard time finding a political consensus. In the end the workshop broke into three teams that spent several days sharing skills and developing short performances on aspects of food production and consumption.

I was present as a participant/observer, and teamed up with a Canadian director, a white Nigerian theatre educator, and cultural activists from Grenada and Dominica. Together we created what we thought was a dialectical agitprop, writing the outline in Magic Marker on a twenty-foot roll of newsprint. After two long days of improvisations, analysis, and cross-cultural talk we came up with this scenario:

> "Empty Plates"
> 1. Gary and Joe cut sugar. Gary leaves to play cricket. Joe's wages are cut because he misses his quota.
> 2. Gary is accepted to college and cricket team, but his scholarship is insufficient. Joe must forgo his electricity course to take a second job.
> 3. Gary becomes a star and team captain. He makes TV commercials for a giant sugar company.
> 4. The workers in the fields have their wages cut as sugar prices fall. Angered, Joe's friend Man-Man strikes the paymaster and flees to the city. Joe stays behind to organize the workers.
> 5. Gary is given a position in the Canadian head office of the sugar company. He is forced to approve the decision to close down a West Indian plant rather than let it face a long and expensive strike.
> 6. Joe is chairing a meeting of workers who have occupied a closed-down sugar plant. In this scene, the audience is asked to assume the roles of delegates to the meeting; the actors are the delegation leaders. Joe argues that the occupation must be extended into a general strike, because the workers, having "inherited sabotage," cannot get the plant in production, and cannot stand alone. But he doesn't believe in violence. Man-Man returns from the city with news of militant action. He tells the delegation that the only recourse is armed struggle.[8]

In my notes for the workshop I recorded:

> The play only works if the audience accepts the characters' justifications at the end of every scene and is prepared to seriously discuss the issues presented in the final scene. Twice in the final scene an audience discussion takes place as the

several delegations argue amongst themselves and votes are
called. When Joe asks whether the strike should be extended;
and again when the issue of armed struggle is raised. But the
real argument is in the form of the play itself. The dramatic story
is the particularization of that argument.[9]

In effect we had rearticulated the fundamental principle of Brechtian
agitprop: that the play really only works as an exercise in critical thinking. Each step of the play produces a moment of decision in which the
audience is made complicit (by logic, emotion, or theatrical power);
these eventually and dialectically bring the audience to a point of contradiction that cannot be resolved within the world of the play. This was
the method that Brecht had pioneered in his *Lehrstücke* like *The Measures
Taken*, and developed dramaturgically in plays like *The Good Person of
Szechwan*. Brecht was, however, a better dialectician than we proved to
be. After we performed it at the festival, a colleague from the Great Canadian Theatre Company made the (very accurate) comment: "Not much
more information was presented, in a not much more powerful way, than
a half-decent speaker could have presented to a half-sympathetic audience." The point of the exercise, as it turned out, was not the play but our
experience of learning to work together, of learning how to negotiate the
balance of argument, information, and theatricality. It was in this way
a very ordinary popular theatre process, made somewhat complicated
because it called for the trained theatre professionals to unlearn much of
what we took for granted.

If the popular theatre movement really was a movement, it was
because the techniques and methods it produced were developed over
time to be tested and improved in thousands of such workshops across
the country. The Thunder Bay workshop was by no means the first, but
it was the key moment that marked the convergence of professional
theatre workers and popular theatre educators. It was also significant
because of the subtexts of power, gender, and race that filled the room.
Jan Selman, then the artistic director of Catalyst Theatre and one of
the formative figures in legitimizing popular theatre as theatre work in
Canada, later wrote:

To my middle-class, white, female, northern eyes this international crowd was very male (entirely), very patriarchal, was

dominated by the white men in their group and was very convinced that they had the answers. It was tempting to dismiss
much. However, what remains dominant for me almost two decades later, is that the experience was perhaps the most deeply
challenging national experience of my life.... For me, theatre
was redefined: as a political *process* within community, as
opposed to, to be simplistic again, a well-intentioned expression of the community's social issues.[10]

From the standpoint of the twenty-first century it seems inconceivable that a workshop on social action theatre would be predominantly
male and that the Canadians would be all white. But in inviting participants, Kidd had looked to representatives of the theatre companies that
he identified as principal agents of interventionist theatre (including the
Mummers, GCTC, and Catalyst), and in the early 1980s, even in leftist
theatres, residual masculinism was only just beginning to pay attention
to feminist critiques of male power. At the time issues of oppression and
colonialism were framed almost entirely as issues of class, and gender
inequity was understood by most of the men involved as a superstruc-
tural consequence. No one questioned the absolute whiteness of the Canadian contingent, although that – the unquestioned whiteness – would
soon change.

The Canadian Popular Theatre Alliance

The plenary sessions of the Bread and Circuses Festival of Canadian
Theatre accepted the proposition brought by the members of the workshop to establish a national organization to be known as the Canadian
Popular Theatre Alliance. It was originally proposed as an association
of professional activist theatre companies, however loosely that term
might be applied (in general, "professional" was a code word meaning
recognition by the Canada Council). A separate category for individual
memberships was accepted, but with resistance from those who saw the
organization as a left-wing alternative to the entrenched theatre estate.
For that same reason "amateur" companies were to be excluded from
company membership but could apply for individual membership. This
provision failed to anticipate the later realization that in popular theatre

the distinctions of professional and amateur were always problematic, and both of these conditions very quickly evaporated.

The original principles of the CPTA articulated a vision of popular theatre that owed much to the collective tradition of the alternative theatre. When the idea for an alliance of organizations was proposed at the festival's plenary, the political definition of popular theatre was a subject of considerable debate. The term had been introduced in the workshop that preceded the festival to convey political engagement, but was accepted by the companies attending the festival as a description of their shared populism. The statement of principles is perhaps the first articulation of theatrical refusal – of critical standards, of the theatre economy, and of dominant aesthetics – to emerge out of the theatre profession:

> a) Notwithstanding our various methods and structures, we share a common belief that theatre is a means and not an end. We are theatres which work to effect social change.
>
> b) We see our task as an ongoing process in which art is actively involved in the changing nature of the communities in which we live and work.
>
> c) We particularly attempt to seek out, develop and serve audiences whose social reality is not normally reflected on the Canadian stage.
>
> d) Therefore our artistic practice grows out of a social rather than private definition of the individual.
>
> e) Therefore there is a fundamental difference of purpose, priorities and aesthetics which separates us from the dominant theatre ideology in Canada today.[11]

One of the expressed objectives of the association was the "development of aesthetics, theory and criticism related to the nature of our theatres."[12] Mindful of what happened to the Mummers, the companies present recognized the danger of their particular work being marginalized and downgraded by arts council peer review juries. They saw the need to legitimize popular theatre as a distinct sector of theatre work in cultural policy. The formation of an alliance provided them with a structural tool that provided proof of legitimacy to the arts councils and could also provide a letterhead for fundraising. The small groups of volunteers who sustained the sequence of biennial festivals through the next decade looked to the arts councils for major funding but saw international development agencies as being no less important.

By formally constituting itself as a movement, the CPTA was a textual fiction given materiality by the signs of institution: an executive, a newsletter, and a mailing list. By 1983, when Catalyst Theatre (which by that time had emerged as perhaps the most innovative popular theatre in North America) sponsored the Bread and Roses festival in Edmonton, the movement was less of a counter-professional structure than an instrument to lever funding for festivals.

Bread and Roses established a biennial tradition that was followed in Winnipeg in 1985 with Bread and Dreams; two years later the festival located to Sydney, Nova Scotia, as Standin' the Gaff. By the time of that 1987 festival, popular theatre had clearly consolidated into a movement very different from that envisioned by the founders of CPTA only six years previously. Now instead of an alliance of professional companies, the CPTA had evolved to include as well a broader network of community-based groups and individuals, many of whom were not theatre professionals but popular theatre facilitators and development educators. This evolution turned out in effect to be the gradual penetration of the movement by the very sector its founders sought to exclude.

If the structural terms of a movement defined by radical work in theatre culture, bidding for legitimacy in the theatre estate, had clearly shifted, the movement was still largely a narrative that kept alive a text of common purpose and enterprise. As the definition of popular theatre moved away from the past emphasis on companies and structures, the statement of principles expressed by the emergent CPTA began to more clearly reflect an emphasis on process. Over the course of the following decade local groups of volunteers staged five more festivals at two-year intervals in Edmonton, Winnipeg, Sydney, Guelph, and again in Edmonton. The evolving content of these biennial festivals indicates the expansion of popular theatre as a discipline in itself, as a movement negotiating a shift of focus away from subsidized professional theatres to the wider domain of community-specific troupes and popular educators – while at the same exposing the fault lines and conflicts in the community of theatre workers who were trying to make livelihoods doing popular theatre.

The companies that performed at Bread and Circuses in 1981 represented the populist and collective theatres that had surfaced in the 1970s.

They were in essence the political left wing of the professional theatre: Catalyst Theatre; Theatre Energy, a feminist collective based in the B.C. interior; Resource Centre of the Arts, the successor to the Mummers Troupe; Mulgrave Road Co-op; Théâtre Sans Fils (a puppet theatre); and the Great Canadian Theatre Company of Ottawa. The theatres involved were all small – GCTC and Catalyst were the most established – and the performances dealt in the main with local community issues or history. The only show that could truly be called popular theatre in the developing sense of the term was GCTC's *Red Tape, Running Shoes and Razzamatazz,* a show on public housing produced in collaboration with the Ottawa Tenants' Council.

In contrast, few of the troupes that participated in the Bread and Butter/ du Pain sur la Planche festival held eight years later (June 1989, in Guelph) would have met the Canada Council's criteria of professionalism. That festival's performances came from a variety of companies: Puente Theatre, a group of Hispanic refugee women from Victoria; Siyakha Cultural Productions, an émigré South African troupe based in Toronto; Second Look Community Arts Resource, an inner-city Toronto forum theatre collective; Le Groupe Montréal Serai, a Southeast Asian community theatre; Tunooniq, an Inuit theatre from Pond Inlet (Mittimatalik); and a collaborative project involving Headlines Theatre of Vancouver, Sheatre, a rural women's collective from Southern Ontario, and a Guelph public housing advocacy group. Among the troupes, three presented shows dealing with safe sex and AIDS prevention. Along with the performances the festival included a full program of workshops ranging from introductory skills to advanced sessions on methodology. It also included an academic panel on the history and theory of popular theatre. Funding from the arts councils, employment programs, and non-governmental organizations enabled the festival to bring performances from Zimbabwe and South Africa.

As the relationship of the popular theatre movement and the NGOs suggests, popular theatre structures (and by corollary, the work methods and artistic principles they produce) adapt to meet the economic conditions of funding, as activist theatre workers seek the means and opportunities to continue working. The grant-conditioned climate in which popular theatre work developed in Canada was in reality a benign form of state sponsorship that lasted so long as it served the interests (inarticulate, negotiated, and ad hoc as they might be) of state and quasi-state policy. In those terms, popular theatre work was part of the larger hegemonic workings of the liberal social contract. A popular theatre festival such as Bread and Butter typically received funding from five or six different government agencies. Federal and provincial arts councils, touring offices, multicultural programs, women's directorates, job creation programs, the Canadian International Development Agency: all of these bureaus contributed their bit, on their own terms, in a funding web that drew on social service funding, community development, and cultural programs. Each of these offices saw the festival as a line item fulfilling program requirements in an annual report. The CPTA festivals exposed the extent to which popular theatre work in the 1980s depended on a workshop-based culture funded by NGOs. Many such projects existed, and each of them generated a report as a condition of the received grant. In a very real sense the movement emerged from a vast pile of unpublished, and generally unread, bureaucratic documents.

The river of funding from NGOs was never deep and fast-flowing, but it was constant: through the 1980s, major agencies such as CIDA and CUSO funded numerous projects that brought theatre workers from the so-called underdeveloped world to share skills with Canadians. A productive series of exchanges followed, including the Food Chain workshop organized by Catalyst in 1988, which brought a small group of core theatre activists to Alberta to work with First Nations and Jamaican popular theatre workers. CIDA and CUSO funding was crucial to the CPTA festivals and brought to Canada groups such as Teocoyani from Nicaragua, Jagran from India, the Philippines Educational Theatre Association (more commonly known as PETA), and Sistren from Jamaica. More than anything else, this funding sustained popular theatre as a movement.

These contacts began to dwindle as successive federal governments pulled the plug on international aid programs. In retrospect, the turning point was the defeat of apartheid in South Africa, after which the Canadian government backed away from its widely recognized stance of moral and economic eminence in the field of international aid and exposed more clearly its deeper commitment to transnational finance. With no more political capital to be won by sponsoring dissidents, Canadian government policy began to replace sponsoring dollars with pepper spray.

Rehearsing Revolution, with Augusto Boal

Theatre is dangerous. You are adults. You came here of your own free will. You may leave whenever you wish. People cry.
– *Augusto Boal*

After Thunder Bay the defining condition of popular theatre had been the process of making theatre with communities in struggle, in partnership with activist organizations. Few companies were able to secure ongoing funding in those terms, and those that did invented new models of partnership that moved away from the dominant frameworks embedded in the theatre economy. Catalyst survived through the 1980s as a funded agency of the Alberta Alcohol and Drug Abuse Commission; Ground Zero developed a model of entrepreneurial commissions within the labour movement; in Vancouver, Headlines developed as a Boal-authorized Centre for Theatre of the Oppressed. As these kind of companies became entrenched in their particular niches in the theatre economy, a series of increasingly fraught workshops exposed growing conflicts over access to funding and legitimization.

In general the popular movement expanded to become a common meeting ground for theatre activists from increasingly diverse cultural and ethnic communities, with the result that it became too pluralized to be represented metonymically by an organizational structure, no matter how democratic. By the end of the 1980 the CPTA was losing cohesion and funding opportunities were declining. The slow death of the CPTA was not the end of a movement but a withering away of the need for an organizational structure. In a sense the CPTA and its affiliates – such as the Ontario Popular Theatre Alliance and International Popular Theatre Alliance – that had been summoned into being to create boards of directors for funding and letterhead purposes were the residual traces of the statist institutionalizing strategies of the 1930s in the cultural sector. The degrading of international development programs and the massive cutbacks to cultural funding in the 1990s further contributed to the collapse of this system. Companies that survived during this period managed to find ways of developing new initiatives and expanding their work possibilities, often by adapting to the market-driven culture. The ground-up, collectivist approach of the grant-driven popular theatre movement was in effect replaced by a business template in which corporatized political theatres sell their services to left-wing allies. The recapitalization of popular theatres in the 1990s would be part of an identifiable North American social trend towards the corporatization of structures of dissent.

In response to the trends, in July 1992 Ground Zero, then a small production company working out of Toronto and Peterborough, sponsored a retreat of popular theatre workers from across Ontario. Most significantly, those gathered at the retreat, held in Peterborough – about thirty people – chose not to once again form themselves into a centralizing organization, but as an expression of solidarity they issued a statement of principles that revised the original CPTA statement substantially to acknowledge the politics of cultural diversity.

> 1. We do theatre for, with and by specific communities who have not been given access to resources in our society.
> 2. Our audiences are our judges.
> 3. We believe in taking theatre to the people, rather than making them come to us.
> 4. We see our work as engaged in a process of Popular Education.
> 5. We believe our work does not begin and end with the performance of a play.
> 6. We believe our work must speak the language of the people.
> 7. We agree to treat our fellow popular theatre workers with respect.
> 8. We acknowledge that the conditions of our work must change with the needs of our communities, and we must respond flexibly.[13]

A later draft of that statement of principles emphasized that the interaction with communities would be participatory, including "development and collection of stories from individuals affected by an issue." The theatre groups would be accountable "to the participating individuals and their communities for further use of the stories in other contexts," and make "appropriate acknowledgment of direct sources and contribution." They emphasized respect for other people's cultures and would do shared evaluations of the work undertaken together. Assessments of the "impact" of this work would be "a long term process."[14]

A defining trait of this new popular theatre estate would be the institutionalization of Augusto Boal's Theatre of the Oppressed as the currency of legitimization. In the thirty years since his Theatre of the Oppressed (TO) techniques were introduced to anglophone Canada, Boal has become the world's pre-eminent theoretician and trainer of political theatre. He has spawned a minor industry of publishing, pedagogy, and critical analysis. His books have been published in numerous languages, and his authorized Centres for the Theatre of the Oppressed around the world have achieved a kind of networking that theatre radicals of the 1930s envisioned but could not realize. Boal's popularity derives not just from the proven efficacy of his interactive forms of politicized psychodrama, but also from the release of his protocols for free use by anyone who wants to use those techniques. Until his death in 2009 he continued to develop his methods and to seek new venues for their application.

Boal was born in 1931 in Brazil, where he began his work before running into political difficulties in 1971 with the military dictatorship – he was arrested and tortured – and then going into exile. He lived in Argentina for five years before travelling to Peru and Ecuador and finally ending up in Paris, where he established his Centre for the Theatre of the Oppressed, which attracted the attention of a number of Canadians. In Paris Boal perfected the procedures for Forum Theatre, which remains his most widely practised technique. In a theatre forum, the performers act out a series of scenes that delineate the experience and model the dynamics of an oppressive situation familiar to the audience. They are facilitated by what Boal calls the "joker," who explains to the audience that the performance is a game and encourages the interventions. Once the show has been played through once, the joker restarts the play, and invites the audience to stop it whenever they think the oppressed character can act differently. The audience member who does so is then invited to step into the performance and replace the character to see if a different action can change the outcome of a situation.

The rules are simple, but they rest on a set of carefully worked out procedures. Boal reiterated in all of his work that theatre is a human language shared by all, and his goal in TO was to eliminate the distinction between actor and spectator. As the "Declaration of Principles" of the International Theatre of the Oppressed Organization states:

> The Theatre of the Oppressed offers everyone the aesthetic
> means to analyze their past, in the context of their present, and
> subsequently to invent their future, without waiting for it. The
> Theatre of the Oppressed helps human beings to recover a lan-
> guage they already possess – we learn how to live in society by
> playing theatre. We learn how to feel by feeling; how to think
> by thinking; how to act by acting. Theatre of the Oppressed is
> *rehearsal for reality*.[15]

This statement is a reformulation of Boal's original point: "Perhaps the
theatre is not revolutionary in itself; but have no doubts, it is a rehearsal
of revolution."[16]

Forum Theatre proved to be an effective and engaging practice that
could be adapted to any context of theatre work, from local workshops
with actors drawn from the community of activist engagement with an
issue, to a professional theatre delivering a sophisticated script with built-
in trigger moments for interventions. In each case the forum empow-
ers the audience to play with and transform the represented reality in a
shared space. Practitioners new to theatre forums are often astonished
at the amount of laughter and playfulness they generate, even when the
topics being dealt with are grim.

As Boal's work spread, his approach inevitably entered Canada.
In the francophone theatre world, Théâtre Sans Détour, already established as a TO company in Quebec, performed a forum play at the
Bread and Roses festival in 1983. At the same time the 1979 translation
of Boal's 1968 book *Theatre of the Oppressed* introduced his ideas outside of the theatre community. In Sudbury a group of women who had
been performing feminist satire joined with women from Le Théâtre de
Nouvel Ontario to form what would become a collective called Sticks
and Stones. They began to explore TO techniques while researching for
a show on domestic violence. Group member Laurie-Ann McGauley
described how her "group of working-class women, most of us born and
raised in Sudbury, and all of us familiar with domestic violence," experienced the power of a theatre forum:

> After weeks of research, interviewing police and social workers,
> after exchanging stories of our own experiences, after raging
> and crying and listening, we finally ended up with two short

forum skits. The first performances were clumsy and insecure: asking the audience to participate in a tense scene of potential violence and to try to change the outcome can be a pretty challenging situation for everyone involved. When an audience member shouted stop she removed the passive mask of observer in order to stop the action on stage and replace the oppressed character herself. She was willing to make herself vulnerable in their opposition to this oppression and in her attempt to find a solution and she could do this because she found strength in everyone's support for her, for her courage.[17]

In McGauley's account of that forum, one particular intervention moment clearly demonstrated the dynamics of the game. If a scene is formulated correctly – if it correctly and clearly models the audience's experience of the situation – it does not need to be overly dramatized. The scene she relates is as simple as a scene can possibly be, yet it is dense with knowledge of the oppression.

> *A family is sitting at the supper table. Strained silence and tangible tension.*
> **Father/** What's the matter with you? You want to die or something?
> **Daughter/** I'm not hungry.
> **Father/** (*slams fist on the table, yelling*) I told you to eat your supper.
> **Audience Member/** Stop![18]

For Boal, the actual style or genre of the play is of no concern because those are elements that are specific to the audience community. For professionally trained performers, the hardest aspect of the method was letting go of habituated expectations of dramatic structure in performance. For actors trained to understand their roles as a flow of actions from the beginning to the climactic end of a play, it was not always easy to accept that a forum theatre might never go past – or need to go past – the first scene. In forum theatre, the audience is the director. Nor does it matter if they do not uncover "correct" solutions to moments. Heavily programmatic forums might bury political solutions for audiences to discover ("let's form a union!"), but others – such as the play *Baby Buggy Blues* on the subject of parental stress, performed by the Outaouais Popular

Theatre at the Bread and Butter festival – do not necessarily encode simple political fixes.

As a corps of Boal-trained facilitators grew in the 1980s, their skill functioned as a means of professional legitimization. This invariably produced competition. The free circulation of Theatre of the Oppressed techniques decreased as Boal became more popular, and the stakes accordingly grew higher. In 1987 Boal led an intensive five-day workshop at the Standin' the Gaff festival in Cape Breton – and the result was to effectively distribute his model across Canada as the new operating system of popular theatre. Some five years later another workshop, this time on Manitoulin Island in Ontario, erupted in crisis over cultural, racial, institutional, and regional conflicts in the popular theatre community. The deeper conflict in the workshop was one of ownership. Boal's practice of authorizing "centres" empowered to teach his models in his name effectively disenfranchised the caucus of freelance popular theatre workers and gave the weight of legitimacy to two companies, Headlines Theatre in Vancouver and Mixed Company in Toronto. In one sense, nothing had changed since 1981. Although the typifying popular theatre worker was as likely to be a woman of colour, the structures of the popular movement were still dominated by white men.

The crisis of legitimacy may have been accelerated in part by increasing discursive control over anglophone Boalian pedagogy by U.S. centres. Boal's work entered the United States via Latin American, Canadian, and European vectors, but became naturalized as a U.S. discovery. The gravitational locus of Boal legitimacy in the United States, though, became Nebraska, where the Centre for the Theatre of the Oppressed – Omaha, Inc. has been remarkably energetic at sponsoring conferences, workshops, and training courses. Its presence again raised the stakes of power and ownership by furthering the transformation of a freely distributed system into a disciplinary regime. That systemization would be offset by two major and openly democratic international organizations: the U.S.-based Pedagogy of the Theatre of the Oppressed (PTO), which continued the development of TO by a network of popular educators and community activists with biennial conferences; and the International Theatre of the Oppressed Organization, an open network that lists ten Canadian theatre companies and five individual facilitators (now often calling themselves "consultants") in its membership. Over time, Theatre of the Oppressed emerged into its own professional disciplinarity, the more so because Boal's later refinements integrated aspects of psychotherapy aimed at enabling "spect-actors" to identify the boundaries of individuated and communal psychological consequences of social oppressions.

Popular Theatre Dramaturgy: "Straight Stitching"

As they became prevalent the Theatre of the Oppressed techniques effectively divided popular theatre into two broadly overlapping sectors. One sector is the continued use of theatre as a form of community mobilization, political dissent, and radical challenge in movements for social justice. The other is what has become known as "applied theatre," which works within institutional frameworks (schools, prisons, health care, and development agencies) to produce collaborative knowledge and analysis. Often these applied theatre applications work in concert with government programs.

Out of the hundreds, if not thousands, of existing examples of the applied theatre sector of work, a paradigmatic case in point is *Are We There Yet?* This theatrical program on sexual health for young teenagers has been in operation since 1998. The script, written by Jane Heather, an Edmonton playwright, actor, and director with a long history in popular theatre and labour arts, uses documentary, comedy, and interactive play to create a dialogue among teens about sexual health, choices, and alternatives. It includes sections in which the actors enlist the teen audience to coach them through the stages of a relationship, from asking for a date to negotiating contraception and sex acts. The play's producer, Concrete Theatre, works with Options (formerly Planned Parenthood) to deliver the performances to schools across Alberta, and it has worked with organizations in other provinces to produce adapted versions for specific communities and cultural groups. A five-year national research project based at the University of Alberta determined that the play and its follow-up workshop succeeds in helping youth participants articulate and negotiate sexual boundaries and practices.[19]

In a project like that one, the theatre negotiates the empowering, audience-centred ideology of popular theatre with the often restrictive conditions set in place by an institutional sponsor. Still, the approach does not eradicate the possibility of a critical or even radical intervention. In the case of *Are We There Yet?* the play is one way in which teachers, social workers, and sexual educators can deliver information that is not included in the curriculum.

The two sectors of institutional partnership and radical dissent do have one area of overlap, and that is in the labour movement.[20] In the late 1980s, when the arts councils were more amenable to Artists in the Workplace programs, labour arts became publicly visible, and since then the labour arts movement has continued to grow through both the network of Mayworks festivals scattered across the country and active cultural programs in unions. In broad terms, labour arts in the theatre is the meeting point of activist theatre workers and the educational programs of district labour councils and large unions. Of these, the Steelworkers, Auto Workers, Canadian Union of Public Employees, and the Communications, Energy and Paperworkers have been major participants.

The relationships have had a reciprocal benefit. The advantages to unionists are obvious, because labour arts projects advance a social justice agenda and can be used in mobilization drives. For the artists the projects did more than bring work opportunities: they instilled a sense of artists as workers, with workers' rights. Above all else, popular theatres working with labour groups did so under the jurisdiction of Actors' Equity, which had the additional effect of further legitimizing popular theatres with arts councils as "real" theatres.

Many labour-theatre projects tend to follow the popular theatre model, developing shows with and for workers and performing them in workplace environments. Sometimes, though, unions have underwritten larger public performances. One of the most far-reaching events was the United Steelworkers' 1995 support for an original production by a small Nova Scotian company, Two Planks and a Passion, which mounted a play about the human effects of the 1992 Westray mining disaster. According to Chris O'Neill and Ken Schwartz, who created *Westray: The Long Way Home*, "The Steelworkers sent a cheque for the entire sponsorship before they had seen a word. They made it clear that they would respect our artistic freedom throughout."[21] The Steelworkers also helped to fund a national tour of the play.

For the most part theatre and labour projects were more instrumental, with activist theatre and unionist collaborations made possible by project funding, often through union education campaigns. A recurring issue in this work – and one that still excites debate among theatre activists – is the accessibility and appropriateness of modernist and avant-garde theatrical styles in the context of working-class or marginalized audiences. This question invariably raises the problem of narrative form and realist storytelling, a problem that arose in the earliest stages of popular theatre and featured in the debates over experimental modernism and critical realism in the 1930s. Looking back at the Thunder Bay workshop, Jan Selman related her own rediscovery of story-centred narrative:

> This powerful form, the use of story, the creation of narrative which enacts and reveals contradiction, remains central to much Canadian popular theatre work. It remains the skill most needed and perhaps least understood in creating truly provocative work; its lack is a source of much mediocre work, both presentational and participatory; its application moves much well-intentioned work out of the realms of naturalism and soap opera and into the realm of realism which exposes disabling social dynamics and asks hard questions about where communities might move.[22]

Narrative realism and theatrical realism are not quite the same thing, although they do trigger common principles of performance and spectatorship. The dominant model adopted in the 1980s had its theatrical roots in the presentational theatrical documentaries of the 1970s, in which actors combined oral history monologues, songs, dialogue scenes, and playful ensemble pieces. What gave this form power was the direct, eye-contact address of actor to spectator. The content was realist in that it derived from a combination of documentary research and analysis. The performance was real in the phenomenological sense of actual and perceivable, but it was far from the theatrical "realism" of the removed fourth wall and detailed scenic depiction. This distance was also a product of material conditions: like the agitprops of previous decades, most popular theatre was mobile, designed to be played in a variety of spaces, and produced on a minimal budget. By and large this theatre was scenographically simple. In modernist dramaturgy, scenography becomes part of the narrative toolkit that can produce meaning in spectacle and imagistic sequences as well as spoken word. Most popular theatre has had to compress narrative power in the bodies and voices of the actors.

This combination of ensemble theatricality and actor-centred narration produced a dramatic form that became widespread because it was efficient to develop, adaptive to any subject, and effective with audiences. The 1987 production of *Straight Stitching* by playwright Shirley Barrie and director Lib Spry, sponsored by the International Ladies' Garment Workers' Union in Toronto, offers an example of how defining material conditions become dramaturgical choices. It also shows how theatrical methods have changed in the thirty-five years since the Labor Theatre produced the needle-trade play *No Time to Cry* in Toronto. In 1951, in the prevailing mode of social realism on the left, that play had developed its depiction of oppressive working conditions as a plot-centred story. Writer Lib Spry had been central in bringing TO techniques from Quebec to anglophone Canada, and *Straight Stitching* began its life in a series of workshops and interviews that generated the material out of which the show would be built. Originally the project intended to focus on the garment industry strike of 1987, but as Barrie and Spry worked with the women issues of workplace accommodation and supervision came to the fore. The play that came out of that process two months later – with songs and music by Arlene Mantle – was meant to show that despite their various linguistic and cultural backgrounds, women in garment factories (represented in the play by immigrants from Hong Kong, Portugal, Jamaica, and the Philippines) can overcome their differences and come together to unite and unionize. In choosing to depict the workplace accurately as racially diversified, the project turned itself into a diversified theatre workplace, creating professional acting jobs for marginalized women.

The working process for the play reflected what has become a conventional method of workplace dramaturgy. Barrie's description of how it came about effectively explains why the constant rediscovery of a participatory process leads to story-based dramatic realism. Barrie and Spry began by meeting once a week with the needle workers in the Union Hall.

> As the women told Lib and I both hilarious and tragic stories of their lives and work, certain themes began to emerge. Most of the women were immigrants – many of whom couldn't speak English when they arrived in Canada. What this means and how it affects their lives was the subtext to many of the stories.

The treatment of the newcomer, both by the Supervisors and by other workers revealed a complex situation in which fear, control and the necessity to be tough all played a part.

I developed an outline – the story of a fictional character, Mei Lee, a recent immigrant from Hong Kong, who comes to work in a garment factory. The women were wonderfully helpful in exploring what would and would not happen to this character, and in setting the limits on just how far and in what way workers in their situation can make a stand. Several of the workers decided to join with the actors who were brought in, and perform in the reading of the play.[23]

In the play's plot narrative each of the characters wants to achieve a goal and has an obstacle to overcome, all situated in the familiar micropolitics of a workplace framed by oppressions of race, language, and gender. The outcome is small, incremental victories: one woman decides to take a union training course over her husband's objections; another finds the courage to demand accountability from her supervisor.

The opening moments of the play establish its theatrical rules. The actors enter through the audience, each speaking in her own language of the dreams that have brought her to Canada. After an opening song, the women mime an immigration line at an airport. As they go along the line they introduce themselves in short monologues. Following this prologue the stage becomes a garment factory, with the stage divided between the factory floor, where the work procedures are mimed, and a lunch area. The action covers more than three months of narrative time, but instead of dividing that time into separate scenes, the script stipulates that it is played as one continuous action. The character of Mei Lee functions as a narrator who shifts the modes of representation. She moves between a confident narrative voice and less proficient English for in-scene actions. She encounters her supervisor, who speaks in a gibberish she cannot understand. The play thus has a fluid shifting of positions and points of view.

MEI LEE: (*Narrator*) Everything is different here. It's so big! And right away there was a job for me. My auntie talked to a friend, who had a daughter who knew somebody who used to work ... well anyway ... I was going to work! I couldn't speak very much English. Just a few words. (*In hesitant English*) Hello. Goodbye. (*Back to narrative voice*) You know. But my auntie said that didn't matter. If you can run a sewing machine, she said, you don't need to talk.

(*She enters the factory. Immediately the noise from a variety of machines hits her. The workers all turn to look at her. They stare but hardly miss a beat in their work.*)

MEI LEE: Is something wrong with me? Is my sweater dirty? I must've come to the wrong place. (*She starts to leave.*)

THERESA: (*Enters*) Ahhhh. Mei Lee.

MEI LEE: (*Relief*) Ahh. (*She smiles broadly and begins to introduce herself in Chinese.*)

THERESA: (*Ignores this. She begins to talk in gobbledegook. The essence of it is that Mei Lee is late. She points to her watch etc. Punctuality is important if you want to keep this job etc. etc. Still jabbering she begins to walk away.*)

MEI LEE: She's talking English so fast I don't understand a word.[24]

With the shifting points of view, overlapping time periods, and a clearly delineated narrative plot, *Straight Stitching* found a language that retained the storytelling power of a realist play but was flexible and direct enough to speak to audiences that might have English as a second language.

Straight Stitching replayed women's work experiences and challenged the deeply resilient structures of racial and gender privilege that had continued to shape the field of possibilities in Canadian theatre. After an enthusiastic response for the play at the first readings and the 1987 Mayworks festival, Barrie, Spry, and Mantle formed Straight Stitching Productions and remounted the play – reworked for a smaller cast because of the cost of Equity actors – to present it in the main to school audiences. Barrie soon discovered another institutional pressure working covertly on popular theatre. Because Actors' Equity required theatres to contract actors for full-time employment for a specified period, a producer like Barrie had to set up a tour to sell the show to sponsors. According to Barrie, "It would have been easier to work part-time over a long period, but Equity has no provision for this, or for one-off performances, which meant that we were unable to perform at several community and conference occasions which were tied to specific dates."[25]

Although popular theatres like Straight Stitching Productions were signing Equity contracts out of ethical and political commitment to unionism, Actors' Equity was slow to modify its contract language to help make their work possible.

Theatrical Access:
The Working People's Picture Show

In *Straight Stitching* the playwright, director, and cast sought to ensure accessibility of the play for diverse audiences – and thus make sure that it would be usable by those audiences. The question of accessible form was understood as an issue of communication, not of cultural experience or audience expectation, which in turn was a shift from earlier positions, such as the operating assumption in the Thunder Bay workshop that popular theatre must default to a narrative realist mode as being more accessible and understandable to theatrically inexperienced audiences. This position was another residual prejudice from the 1930s, as expressed in John Bonn's comments that "worker players are not able to express, and worker audiences are not able to understand, complicated structures of ideas and refined intellectual language." The notion that popular audiences must be addressed in their "own" cultural language is one that is continually rediscovered on the left. It was instrumental in the theatre criticisms that launched the Cultural Revolution in China; it had wide currency in the community-based theatre movements in Canada and Australia in the 1980s; it was inherent in John McGrath's valorization of "good night out" working-class culture in the United Kingdom; it was evident in the work of the San Francisco Mime Troupe; and it establishes a critical substructure in Boal's typification of the "bourgeois artist-high priest." My own favourite expression of this attitude came from Canadian left-wing playwright George Ryga. In his keynote speech at the Bread and Circuses festival Ryga denounced the work of the Polish avant-garde director Jerzy Grotowski as "mystical quasi-medieval fascism."[26]

The prejudice against "formalism" began to dissolve when theatre workers came to understand that "the people" cannot be reduced to any one set of cultural assumptions or practices. They recognized, for instance, that audiences that grow up watching musical videos are sophisticated visual spectators. A major point of change in this regard was the 1984 production by Nightwood Theatre of the Anna Project's *This Is for You, Anna,* a theatrically innovative, image-centred play about violence against women. Both advocacy theatre and avant-garde performance, the piece was widely received as one of the peak moments of Canadian theatre in the 1980s.

Nightwood Theatre had been founded in 1979 by a collective of women brought together by Cynthia Grant with the express purpose of exploring the boundaries of feminism, avant-garde performance, and social issues. As part of an alliance of experimental, socially engaged companies that shared space and resources (the others were Buddies in Bad Times, Necessary Angel, and Theatre Autumn Leaf) they constituted the second wave of alternative theatre in Toronto, pushing the discourse away from theatrical citizenship and the primacy of Canadian playwrights to new performance methods, scenographic dramaturgy, actor-centred textualities, and hitherto marginalized communities. Still a major force in Canadian theatre today, Nightwood has been at the forefront of pushing for change in the professional theatre culture, committed to developing new work by women and to racial and cultural equity. But by the mid-1980s a growing number of theatre workers associated with the company were moving in divergent directions. As Nightwood came to exercise more influence in the dominant theatre culture, ideological differences began to fracture its consensus base. In 1986 Cynthia Grant, along with Aida Jordão, Lina Chartrand, and Amanda Hale, left to form a more politically activist troupe, which they named Company of Sirens. Grant has described the split as a "breakaway" sparked by the "homophobic undertones" of Nightwood's rejection of a proposed lesbian performance by Hale and Chartrand.[27] As Nightwood went on to become a central locus of reforming cultural identity politics in the theatre, Sirens adhered to a socialist analysis of class and gender.

The creative basis for Sirens was a project that had developed in the preceding year, when members of Nightwood were commissioned by Organized Working Women, a caucus group within the Ontario Federation of Labour, to produce short skits on women and work for a conference. According to Amanda Hale, the first fifteen-minute performance grew into a four-year project, during which time the show developed into a working archive of sketches and topics that could be adapted to suit the needs of an audience and space. The group, Hale wrote in 1987, performed not only "in hotel rooms for audiences of five hundred," but also "behind boardroom tables for a handful of committee members." Hale said the group's "style and presentation have to be extremely flexible, leaning towards a broad delivery in large spaces and a more subtle performance in confined areas. We take advantage of any opportunity to enrich the presentation with guest artists who can highlight topical issues and enhance our overall mandate towards progressive thinking and action."[28] Member Aida Jordão later commented on how the group worked at "adapting original material and adding or deleting scenes" based on a particular audience's interests. In doing that, she said, the Company of Sirens "adopted the building-block method of play creation. Also with this process, where we stretched and poked each other's work into new shapes, it became unimportant to name one playwright, and collective ownership of the work ensued."

The Company of Sirens experimented with the Forum Theatre approach, creating a scene that called for audience intervention. "At a conference of domestic workers," Jordão noted, "our spectators became spect-actors and we added yet another dimension to our performance and to the pages of our non-recorded script. We also introduced a workshop component into the performance whereby images (or tableaux) created with audience members became new scenes."[29]

The Sirens' *The Working People's Picture Show* provides a clear example of a text that cannot be reduced to a written script. It is not a "play" but a performance as textual praxis. Instead of a driving character narrative that unlocks a social issue, the show worked as a sequence of pointed sketches: "a baseball game of Gains & Losses between Management and Labour, the K-Tel Ad ('Harassments of the 60s, 70s and 80s, all on one exciting video cassette, available in factories, offices and workplaces everywhere!'); and popular songs with reworked lyrics."[30] This is popular theatre not as a forum of instrumental analysis and decision-making but as the occasion and expression of solidarity. As Hale pointed out, many of the group's performances functioned as post-banquet entertainment at conferences (including the Steelworkers' international convention in Florida).

The show was more than trivial entertainment. When performed in the work spaces and working lives of its audience, it exposed the politics of the everyday. When performed in remote communities, or as part of a union's educational campaign or in a labour school, it expanded the web of solidarity in shared spectatorial pleasure, and reinforced the efforts of activists working within unions, ministries, and school boards. Sirens worked in alliance with activists in client organizations, always taking a political position on the issue at hand, pointing to underlying social causes and political solutions. In contrast, popular theatres working in the applied theatre model often did little more than animate policy for training purposes. Such work could be highly effective, but its potential for activist change was restricted. The distinction between the Sirens' approach and the applied theatre model is crucial.

The 1988 production of *Under Broken Wings: A Collective Drama on Family Violence* by the Sherwood Park, Alberta, RCMP detachment, mounted as part of Strathcona County's Family Violence Awareness Campaign, clearly shows this different. In a series of vignettes compiled by Deborah-Kim Hurford, the crime prevention and community relations officer for the RCMP detachment, the play enacts two dozen short scenes and monologues of violence situations, heavily aestheticized with metaphorical modern dance and lyrical songs. The work is positive, affirmative, and optimistic, ending with a rather soft sentiment:

> Ah, everything will be okay.
> Maybe together we can make it that way.
> For if we realize the things we should
> Then violence will be gone from our lives for good.[31]

Like many of the sanctioned sexual-health role-play troupes that are familiar features of modern campus life, this is an animated information delivery system that depoliticizes its subject. It seeks to make change through emotional effect rather than critical analysis. Despite its narrative form and sentimentalization, it is more agitprop than popular education.

The Working People's Picture Show became the Company of Sirens' signature performance – as Jordão said of it, "my bread and butter for four years."[32] It launched Sirens as one of the busiest popular theatres in Canada, and one that never compromised its core commitment to creating activist networks across boundaries of class, gender, race, and institutionality. The show activated an expanding network of potential sponsors, which enabled subsequent projects. The company's 1990–91 season's report of performances revealed a project-based company that managed to create employment for two teams of actors.[33] The shows that year included *Shelter from Assault* (the stories of women who survived domestic violence, framed in a medley of fairy stories – Cinderella, Snow White, Sleeping Beauty – and popular songs) and *Whenever I Feel Afraid*, which looked at violence and sexism in the lives of teenagers. Both of these plays toured the province extensively with funding from the Ontario Women's Directorate and the Ministry of Education during the designated Family Violence Prevention Month in November. In spring 1990, *Shelter from Assault* had engagements in universities, high schools, women's centres, and shelters from Huntsville to Windsor; in the fall a second tour played to more shelters, a mental health centre, and federal government employees, and made a swing tour through Nova Scotia. In that case the performance was the result of advance planning and booking. The company worked with local contacts and networks to sponsor the show.

The next Sirens show, *No Problems Here!*, was commissioned by the Ministry of Citizenship in the provincial Liberal government under David Peterson as an anti-racism instrument for "an audience of business, media, education and racial minority community leaders."[34] According to Grant it "really took off" under the succeeding NDP government, elected in 1990 – when Sirens' political analysis became more compatible with the ministry sponsor. The tour took the show to union locals, schools, corporations (including Consumers' Gas and CIBC), immigrant associations, and boards of education from October through to the following May, travelling as far north as Fort Francis and Rainy River. In that same spring touring season *The Working People's Picture Show* had fourteen performances, mainly in schools and colleges in communities as far apart as Cornwall, Waterloo, and Kirkland Lake. The final show on tour that year was *All the Way (to Equality)*, on the subject of youth sexuality. It had twenty-four performances in Toronto high schools.

By the time Sirens shut down in 1995, when the Harris government's attack on cultural and social service programs devastated both of those sectors, it had played to tens of thousands of people across the province. It was a period when, as Grant explained, "the schools, the workplaces, the communities had money to commit to bringing the Company of Sirens' projects into their settings."[35] Activist cultural organizations were among the first of the Harris targets precisely because they were effective in disseminating social analyses and linking communities. Cuts to arts services and to community social justice organizations destabilized the funding model that sustained popular theatre work.

In a way, then, popular theatre is an index of political health in a democratic society because it enacts the capacity of communities in struggle to organize social justice programs and to reach out in networks. Theatre workers and activists might debate the horizons of radical possibility in this work, but to the hard conservative right there was no doubt whatsoever that a theatre company committed to eradicating inequities of race, gender, and culture, and at the same time creating work and livelihoods for a culturally diverse creative workforce, was the very face of the radical left. Company of Sirens was only one of many companies working in this arena and committed to those principles, but it was always at the front of the struggle. It constantly reminded its peer community in the theatre world that highly trained theatre workers could make a living with professional disciplinary skill and refuse the dominant model of production and its systematized injustices.

The Issue of Radical Sustainability

As a collective formed out of a fracture in a collective theatre, Company of Sirens is an example of a theatre company that never attained, or sought to attain, long-term stability. Its members had other theatre and political ambitions. In that sense it was less a company and more what David Watt and I describe as a "strategic venture," a multi-year project enabled by a not-for-profit corporate structure but subject to change in membership, principle, and method.[36]

This makeup is true of most theatre companies. Those that attain sustainability do so through an institutionalization that integrates them into local economies, captures an audience market, or answers long-term needs (such as delivering sexual health education to school boards). The most successful theatre companies follow this pattern and become economic pumps in their communities. The Stratford Festival offers the clearest example of a theatre company that has become the engine of its city; without the theatre, with its hundreds of jobs and half-million theatregoers every year, the economy of the city would collapse. In metropolitan areas large theatre operations transform urban areas into entertainment districts and become destination sites for cultural tourism.

Many established theatre companies, then, gain stability through physical facilities, funding lines, and a self-perpetuating board. Within these elements, artistic mandates and personnel are subject to negotiation, challenge, and change.

The long-term viability of a theatre company is often less about its artistic mandate and programming than about its own professional or economic niche. The theatres in those niches compete, often passively, for the legitimization that brings larger revenues and, often more importantly, corporate or philanthropic donations. Although there may be a widely held public perception that theatre in Canada is state subsidized, theatre companies eligible for funding receive less than 20 per cent of their revenues from all levels of government cultural grants. The bulk of their budgets is derived from box-office and private-sector sponsorships. Of all the performing arts, theatre receives the smallest percentage of its revenues in public subsidy.[37]

These standard conditions have made it extraordinarily difficult for activist theatre troupes to attain the sustainable institutionality that ensures continuing theatre careers. With a diminishing pool of public sponsorship, coupled with a peer review system that for the most part speaks for the mainstream, small activist troupes work in conditions pressured by critical dismissal, poverty, and uncertainty. Those companies that have managed to find a sustaining organizational model have sought out sponsoring clients for their interventionist work on a scale that enables corporate and personal survival. If there is a benefit to long-term institutional survival (other than the important one of providing secure work for employees), it is in the accumulated knowledge that comes of experience. Canada, fortunately, has some prime examples of success stories in this regard, and among them are three groups that between them have a hundred working years of field-tested knowledge and innovation in applying theatre to social change.

Le Théâtre Parminou: "Theatre for You, with You"

Founded in 1973 as a co-operative, under the official name of Coopérative des travailleuses et travailleurs de Théâtre des Bois-Francs, and originally located in Montreal and Quebec City, Théâtre Parminou has since 1976 been a resident theatre in Victoriaville, Quebec. The core members of the co-op enjoy job security and democratic participation in organizational decision-making and planning. Rare for members of a theatre group in Canada, they also have access to child care and a pension plan. The company also hires theatre workers on union contract for shows, tours, and seasonal work. In its four decades of work Parminou has produced over five hundred shows for audiences totalling more than two million people.

When Parminou began in the early 1970s, it was one more radical theatre in a crowded field in Quebec. For its part, it expressed the Maoist/ Marxist-Leninist platform that was a connective thread in the collectivist and anti-hierarchical *"jeune théâtre"* movement. After relocating in Victoriaville and establishing itself as the major theatre of its region, Parminou received increasing support as a "national theatre centre" from the Quebec government. By the end of the century this backing would be manifested in an architect-designed theatre centre with state-of-the-art production facilities.

As part of its commitment to social justice activism, Parminou worked hard to build connections with the radical theatre community in anglophone Canada. It was an active participant in the steering committee and festivals of the Canadian Popular Theatre Alliance. Unlike many Québécois companies, it did not focus on issues of nationhood and sovereignty in its public agenda, and in its engagement with anglophone Canadians issues of national politics rarely arose. (In part this was because in the sphere of theatrical nationhood, Quebec has always been perceived in anglophone Canada as separate and autonomous.) The anglophone Canadians who met Parminou at festivals and workshops saw clear affinities in subject, method, and style, but were in awe of the troupe's success in building an institutional structure that was not only integrated into the theatre economy and ensured career development but also operated as a democracy and retained a fundamental orientation to activist work. This combination did not seem possible outside of Quebec.

The success at least partly had to do with the support of the Quebec government – a factor that reveals the considerable differences in cultural policy between Quebec and the rest of Canada. Quebec has historically been more proactive in systematizing theatre through the various reformations of the Ministère de la Culture (it was not until 1992 that Quebec established the arms-length Conseil des arts et des lettres du Québec). For the most part, cultural policy in Quebec has been a *national* cultural policy – that is, an affirmation of national presence and autonomy. As a result arts organizations in the province become political footballs in the never-ending competition for influence by federal and provincial interests. That these interests can greatly diverge shows up in Parminou's success in positioning itself as a major theatre in Quebec, while being stripped of its federal funding from the Canada Council.

In 2007–8, with its established stature as a regional theatre, in funding from the Conseil des arts et des lettres du Québec, Parminou ranked sixteen out of seventy-seven supported theatres, with a subsidy of $241,664. That amounted to roughly the same level of funding that the Ontario Arts Council awarded to Tarragon Theatre, the pre-eminent theatre for new play development in Toronto, in that same period ($237,000). The theatre in Ontario that most closely resembles Parminou is Mixed Company in Toronto, a designated Centre for the Theatre of the Oppressed, which does commissioned popular and youth activist theatre. It received $16,000 from the OAC in 2008. In British Columbia, the comparable company, Headlines Theatre, received $30,000 from the provincial arts council that year.[38]

But Parminou's success has also been based on its ability to develop a market demand for its specialty: issue-themed commissioned work for client organizations. The group's approach is much like that of an advertising agency. It works with client groups not just to develop an idea, but also to do the appropriate research, to consult about language, dramaturgy, and style, and to finalize the script. It offers "theatre for you, with you" in one-off performances, workshops, and booking of shows created for touring or public performance. The company's areas of intervention have a remarkable range through abuse of power, poverty, and violence in schools to suicide prevention and drug and nicotine addiction. The areas taken up include women's issues, volunteer work, caregiving, aging (and senior citizens' rights), and violence against women, elders, and children. They cover workplace relations (including violence in the workplace), pay equity, non-traditional occupations, "positive reinforcement," mental illness, Alzheimer's disease, and sexually transmitted diseases – among many other social issues.[39]

In North Bay in 2005, for example, as a follow-up to an international commitment the Sisters of St. Joseph of the Catholic Diocese of Sault Ste.

Marie sponsored *Lost in Traffic,* a theatre forum performance on sex trafficking. The Catholic Diocese reported on the event:

> Theatre Parminou, with game leader Michel Cormier, provided
> participants with a learning experience that was a real eye-
> opener for those in attendance. The cast included Isabelle Cyr,
> Lynne Cooper, and Luc Gauthier. These four actors outlined sev-
> eral aspects of human trafficking – domestics, mail-order brides,
> illegal migrant workers, and the sex trade.
>
> There were moments when the entire audience was spell-
> bound by the moving presentation. Several times during the
> play our game leader, Michel, froze the action and queried the
> audience as to what we would do in the situation presented.
> Once a scenario was determined, the actors "rewound" the
> scene and incorporated our suggestions. These actors were
> amazing in their ability to improvise based on audience input
> and yet still portray the complex problems associated with this
> illegal activity.[40]

Success, yes, but Maureen Martineau, a founding member still with the
co-operative, pointed out in 2004 that the company's organizational survival had entailed a renegotiation of the original vision. In the 1970s the
troupe asserted a militant alliance with the oppressed, which Martineau
described as "don't perform for the bosses, don't perform in English in
Quebec, and don't accept commissions from the private sector." By the
1990s, economic necessity meant that if the members of the co-operative
wanted to make a living through their profession, they needed to market
their services more broadly. This led to what she came to define as ideological incoherence, with the company supporting client groups on topical issues without deeper analysis. An example of this contradiction was
the time the group was "called upon to speak to the question of the health
and safety at General Motors, at the very moment when the factory itself
was threatened with closure because of the effects of the free market."[41]

The "remobilization" of the company came through expanding
international contacts (particularly in Belgium and Africa) and was
fuelled by the polarizing international politics of the Bush era. In 2003
Parminou held the first national festival and meeting of activist theatre
since the end of the Canadian Popular Theatre Alliance in an attempt

to bring the European francophone "*théâtre-action*" movement into dialogue with new world counterparts. The Rencontres Internationales de Théâtre d'Intervention featured performances from Belgium, Quebec, France, Chile, Italy, Mali, and the United States (this last by Bread and Puppet, one of the few interventionist companies that is older than Parminou). It also featured multilingual panels that included a significant cohort of anglophone Canadians, many of them veterans of the CPTA. This reconfirmation of a radical position and analysis provided a more politicized context for Parminou's commissioned work, but after four decades the company was still struggling with the politics and ethics of activist theatre work and asking, "Is it possible to reconcile artistic and ideological integrity with professionalism in our theatre practice?"[42]

Headlines Theatre: Theatre for Living

Like Parminou, Vancouver's Headlines Theatre produces commissioned and partnership productions with a high degree of theatrical disciplinarity and cultural legitimacy (recognized by several local theatre awards). But unlike Parminou it has the freedom to be more selective about its affiliations because it is neither operating a production centre nor securing livelihoods for a tenured membership. Parminou's fifteen core members and their families depend on the organization for their living. Headlines operates with a staff of eight contract employees who are a junction point for a network of communities and activists that reaches across North America and beyond.

Headlines was set up in 1981, and since then it has developed a unique and innovative application of Boal's Theatre of the Oppressed, under the overarching title "Theatre for Living."[43] David Diamond, the artistic director of the company for most of its history, studied under and worked closely for many years with Boal, and his refinements of TO methods have been influential around the world. His adjustments include the basic protocols of theatre forums – he allows the audience to step in and replace not just the oppressed protagonist but other characters, including the oppressor (because the oppressor is in all of us). He has also introduced new workshop methods that extend Boal's "Rainbow of Desire" techniques. In "Rainbow of Desire," as Headlines describes the method, a "series of transformative techniques" leads participants to recognize "how we contain many different desires and fears at any one time." Rather than being yet another case of the "psychoanalysis of an individual," the exercise becomes "an exploration of a metaphor that reflects the group consciousness as the particular relationship offered becomes a symbol for the entire workshop group to investigate blockages around a certain issue." Another Headlines technique, "Your Wildest Dream," employs "Image Theatre and Polaroid photography to help a community do positive visioning."[44]

In B.C. activist campaigns Headlines plays a key role by functioning as a facilitator for community political development and cross-cultural communication. Like Parminou it has produced hundreds of project productions, forums, and workshops alongside its usual mainstage season. Many of those productions have been partnership interventions with cultural minority and First Nations communities on issues ranging from land claims and globalization to drug addiction and violence. Often workshops on related issues over a period of time result in reformulated projects that become the basis of larger public performances.

Headlines does differ from similar companies, such as Parminou and Mixed Company, in that its goals are not just socially instrumental. Diamond, and through him the work of the company, has often expressed a deep affinity with what some critics might dismiss as new age metaphysics. In his book *Theatre for Living: The Art and Science of Community-Based Dialogue*, Diamond speaks of the "living community," explaining that "communities are alive and need to express themselves just like people; if they don't they get sick, just like people."[45] This concept has proven to be an effective political gathering point because it enables Diamond to use theatre as a process of social change that heals by giving communities cultural methods of not just telling, but using, their stories. Issue-centred work can intervene and advocate while sidestepping traditional politically adversarial polarities. Diamond has written that early in his experience with Theatre of the Oppressed he became uncomfortable with the language of oppressed and oppressor, which "created a polarization in community that did not seem relevant to the communities I was being asked to work with."[46] His introduction of a new vocabulary, substituting "Power Plays" for Forum Theatre and "Theatre for Living" for Theatre of the Oppressed, enacted this holistic idea of social change and community health. It also had the benefit of sounding less adversarial to sponsoring partners and granting bodies.

In effect, by establishing itself as a company that produces social dialogue, Headlines can take sides without taking sides. With a project-based structure operating within a theatre economy, Headlines managed to retain the flexibility and mobility to follow its own political agenda and take on controversial subjects, such as the 2006 power play *Palestine, Israel and Me*, a collaboration with Jews for a Just Peace and the Social Justice Committee of the Unitarian Church of Vancouver, with an endorsement by the Canada Palestine Association. The play tackled the one topic that Canadian theatres have found to be so divisive that it triggers threats of censorship.[47]

Diamond's holistic sense of community also resonates with (and is informed by) First Nations understandings of the place of the individual in the community and the land. When Headlines enters into partnerships with communities it does so by understanding and working within the host's patterns of cultural authority and value.

In its "Legislative Theatre" method, in which a popular theatre project works closely with a legal team that develops draft legislation to present to politicians, Headlines found a way to intervene in a social issue with a clear political analysis and yet present the event as non-partisan. The Legislative Theatre model that Headlines developed in its 1999 production *Squeegee* is a form of theatre that produces textualities in three stages: as a process that produces performance; as a forum theatre performance that leads to interventions; and as audience interventions that draft legislation. *Squeegee* began as an employment or training project for street youth, which in turn led to a collectively devised play. As a forum play the show responded to the interventions of its audience, and as an interventionist process of response it was the research phase for a draft legislation prepared by a lawyer who worked as part of the production team.

As Diamond described the process, the theatre company in effect had to become a social service agency, providing work and housing for the youth participants and being answerable to the complex of social welfare funders, inextricably bound in the systematizations of state policy that it sought to change.[48] *Squeegee* also demonstrated the company's commitment to transparency and community knowledge transfer.

As a theatricalization of social policy, *Squeegee* proposed that performances were mechanisms of social change on all of its levels of intervention: in the political sphere, as policy formulation, in its audiences as enacted modelled community, and in its participants as a therapeutic instrument. The theatre thus becomes a social mechanism for producing the model citizen – creative, critically aware, and empowered – at least in the structure of the theatrical event. The more innovative and socially embedded that Headlines becomes in its theatrical democracy, the more its projects work because they are seen to work. The project reveals that political theatre is effective not through representation but through the structures enacted in the task of making theatre – structures that mobilize and activate political relationships. In the 2005 project *Gimme the Keys*, for example, Diamond visited seven communities across the country to seed Theatre for Living techniques by working with local groups on two power plays for youth: one on drinking and driving, the other about racism and violence. The object was to train local facilitators who would take over the projects and continue them with a budget provided by the company. This project built on the company's long-standing commitment to skills transfer, which includes annual summer training courses.

The desire to transform spectating audiences into activist networks led to Headlines' most innovative development of Theatre of the Oppressed – its use of interactive television programs on cable access stations and, later, webcast for theatre forum performances. Between 1989 and 2006 the company took ten of its shows into broadcast and webcast, with "tele-actors" standing to receive telephoned or chat-room instructions for interventions by remote viewers. Diamond estimated that the televised performances on average reached fifteen thousand viewers. The webcasts had the capacity to draw many more and, as Diamond noted, by 2007 had already drawn interventions from spectators around the world.[49] As digital technology and virtual performance change the ways in which we make and watch theatre, Headlines' remote forums have opened up new directions of theatrical activism, by performing in and via the networks the organization helps to create. And, Diamond stated, the work can be done cheaply. Technical support for the television broadcasts was provided by cable access volunteers; the webcasts used computers borrowed from the company and participants. This image of activist performers reaching across the world with borrowed home computers more than anything explains how Headline has managed to survive as an institution while working at the forefront of social change.

Ground Zero Productions:
Industrials for the Social Services

Since 1982 Ground Zero Productions – a company in which I have been involved, even if remotely, as a member of its board of directors – has operated as a hybrid of fringe theatre, activist video maker, and small business. It provides services to client groups and initiates its own artistic projects when arts council funding permits. Although Ground Zero is largely the work of one man, its founder and director Don Bouzek, it is not reducible to that one man because the work has been produced with the collaboration of gifted actors, administrators, puppet-makers, painters, writers, and activists. Ground Zero is neither a theatre nor an individual: it is an ongoing business structure that enables an artist both to make a living and to help others make their livings in the arena of political change.

For most of its history Ground Zero has existed as a small office cum studio crammed with old computers, video editing machines, and boxes of the detritus of theatrical work. It has also been, on occasion, Bouzek's living space. While Ground Zero is in a sense the external identity of Bouzek's theatrical practice, it is also a lasting structure that cannot be personalized. Yet the two identities, of artist and company, are deeply intertwined – and because of this complex Bouzek has been able to succeed, where many others have failed, in establishing a continuing role for theatre work in the social justice and labour movements. Bouzek the artist deploys Ground Zero the company to create work, often with arts council grants, joining together with other artists and building a repertoire of traditional plays, ceilidhs, parades, and processional performances; Ground Zero the company pays Bouzek the artist to undertake video and performance commissions from labour organizations; together both claim a space in the theatrical community, offering opportunities, solidarity, and moral support for artists from marginalized communities.

Like the labour movement that it often works with, Ground Zero can accommodate the dominant ideology even as it challenges it. Its ability to function as a service-providing agency has enabled it to legitimize its presence in the labour and other social justice movements and operate in a network of alliances and coalitions that focus on tactical issues. As Bouzek explained years ago, "We have always worked with different methodologies and communities. It's the fluidity of moving from video to theatre, from what the Australians call 'Contemporary Performance' to Boal, that gives us a lot of the stability to survive as the conditions change."[50]

To manage this fluidity, Bouzek developed an administrative structure for an artist-controlled theatre to operate on a professional basis within a partially subsidized milieu. For Bouzek, the project meant renegotiating the charity model of theatrical organization in Canada, with its volunteer boards "who are ideally people with 'clout,' i.e. well-heeled enough to fundraise. I have great problems with this model, preventing as it does, artists from controlling their own organisations, and reinforcing a cult of volunteerism in Canadian social policy."[51] As Bouzek knew from his own experience with his first company, Penguin Theatre in Ottawa, time and again Canadian arts organizations have seen self-replicating boards exercising creative control by purging the founding artistic creators of the company.

The cult of volunteerism that Bouzek deplored has a long history of disenfranchising artists. After his own bitter experience of being purged by the board of a theatre he founded, he left Ottawa for Toronto and became involved with development education. A gig as an assistant director at the Stratford Festival left him disillusioned with the theatre world. As he later wrote, "I knew I never wanted again to direct a building. The focus on my work in Ottawa was in filling a theatre space with a season. It was not on actually doing each show. I feel theatre companies must look at the models of independent artists working in dance, music and the visual arts."[52] In 1984 he did a series of shows dealing with technology, one of which, *St George/ The Dragon*, on nuclear power workers, brought him into contact with labour activists and a new direction of work. Out of that project he developed a theatrical style that juxtaposed dramatic scenes with multimedia, puppetry, object manipulation, and documentary reportage. As he was building his company, then located in Toronto (although he lived for a time in nearby Peterborough), he developed productive partnerships with culturally specific popular theatres, most notably the Filipino company Carlos Bulosan Cultural Workshop. Ground Zero also provided institutional backup to Company of Sirens and helped arrange the labour bookings for *The Working People's Picture Show.*

After five years of building networks with activist groups and artists, Bouzek had built the artistic track record required to make a bid for funding status as a company. He had also consolidated his artistic methods. In his application for charitable tax status he could write: "We meld live performers, multi-layered soundtracks, projections, video and other elements into shows designed to play spaces like convention centers or community centers at reasonable cost."[53]

In 1997 Bouzek moved the company to Edmonton, where he once again began building a relationship with local labour organizations and connecting with a community of local theatre activists. As an independent production house rather than a repertoire company, Ground Zero developed a hybrid model with a small volunteer board that respected the artist's "right to manage" (to expropriate a current phrase from anti-labour government). It did this by breaking the cycle of dependency on public funding. Its fundamental administrative principle, reiterated annually in grant applications, is that the company does not undertake work on a given project until all financing for it is secured. While it applies for and receives grants, they are earmarked for specific, non-revenue-generating projects or for infrastructural support while the bulk of the work is undertaken as commissions from sponsoring organizations in the labour and social justice movements. Ground Zero is an anomaly in Canadian theatre. In a system that virtually forces arts organizations to engage in deficit-financing, with boards penalizing artists for so doing, it has never run a deficit.

In its theatre work Ground Zero focuses on inexpensive, mobile performances developed in consultation with client and target groups, mainly labour unions and activist coalitions. Its theatrical idioms include site installations, processional events at demonstrations, puppet work, and agitprop. In the years before the move to Edmonton, Ground Zero had become one of the linchpins of activist theatre in Ontario. Its giant puppets and mobile agitprops became familiar icons of the "Days of Protest" in the demonstrations against the Harris government's assault on social and cultural services. The company was a key player in the labour arts and heritage movement.

Ground Zero's theatrical vocabulary is eclectic but invariably reflects Bouzek's early interest in postmodern performance. The techniques of postmodernism – including genre mash-up, decentred character, split focus, and the disruption of image and text – proved to be highly effective and portable. They provided a working method of play development in rehearsal that could draw on the tradition of collective creation that had been so important in the growth of the postcolonial Canadian theatre. They offered a dramaturgical process that escaped the trap of overly familiar social realism that had become conventionalized in "art and working life" theatre throughout the English-speaking world. A typical Ground Zero performance might include quoted documentary text, hand-held puppets, actor-manipulated signs, satiric songs, short dialogue bits, and voice-overs. Usually these elements are exhibited in a show context that sets up and strikes quickly in found space – a union hall, a hospital cafeteria, a parking lot.

Where's the Care? was a show, for instance, that began as a contract to produce a video for the Canadian Union of Public Employees to mobilize health-care workers during the election that brought the NDP to power in 1990. With some trepidation, the union accepted Bouzek's proposal to do a fifteen-minute show (at half the cost) rather than a video. The project was planned as part of the union's internal communication and education program with two complementary objectives: to encourage activism by coalitions expressing local responses to provincial cuts in hospital funding, and to integrate local action with centrally distributed media releases. The performances of the show would take place between August 21 and September 4, 1990, the day of the election, in nine cities.

According to Bouzek, the focus on local mobilization was a crucial aspect. "The organisational process of getting an event to happen for a union is part of the event." To stage a show like this, Bouzek recognized that he would have to rely on the union executive "to be out talking to the members, getting the members out, they've got to figure out the logistics of holding a public meeting, getting the press to it." When Bouzek talked to a union members they told him "that being part of [the show] was as important to them as anything else." Together they built "a network of people who actually had to do media contact, understood it, [and] could then do their own stuff in a local community."[54]

While the show was being researched, Bouzek assembled a team of artists to bring it together quickly. The whole project had to be devised, fitted up, and toured within a forty-day union campaign; the tour was booked before work even started on the show. Bouzek started work simultaneously with two actors (Rhonda Payne and Gwen Baillie), designers Diana and Jerrard Smith, and country musician Washboard Hank: "Essentially the piece was constructed as a storyboard of photo ops. We worked the interview material into the images and added the song to get 15 minutes."[55]

The performance venues varied: a shopping centre in Hamilton, a public library in Windsor, hospitals in London and Peterborough, labour halls in Thunder Bay and Toronto, parks in Kingston and Sudbury. The show had to be quickly erected, performable in adverse conditions, and ready to be picked up and moved in the event of inclement weather. As a tactical agitprop, its effect was variable and hard to assess. But while much activist theatre analysis stresses the value of the community experience of spectatorship, projecting a vision of the theatre as a human space in which meaning is enhanced by the physical act of communication, Ground Zero discovered that an indifferent performance could still be effective propaganda. In one performance, in Windsor, Bouzek said, the union locals were not able to drum up much support.

> There were very few people there, the participation was minimal. But a CBC crew came in and shot it. We heard later from people in the community that the reporter wanted to spike it, he said, "Hey, there's no story here, nobody came." The camera guy said, "No, you've got pictures, you've got great visuals, do it, you've got to do the item." The editor in the station agreed, and they ran the item. At that point the provincial feed for the Saturday night news originated out of Windsor, and so, lo and behold, we drove through Toronto and got back at 11 o'clock that night to Peterborough, turned on the TV and there was the Windsor gig. That was ultimately what it was about, that kind of media game.[56]

As in the case of *Where's the Care?* Ground Zero identifies not just with individual communities but with emergent coalitions of resistance and communities activated by the political moment. Bouzek has worked closely with particular partners – health-care unions, the giant Communications, Energy and Paperworkers Union, Carlos Bulosan Cultural Workshop, Ontario Federation of Labour, Toronto Labour Council, and Alberta Federation of Labour, to name some of his closest partners. The labour movement in particular needs to be addressed not as a political bloc (the "labour community") but as an extremely diverse and culturally plural alliance of local organizations crossing through and reconstituting existing communities.

When Ground Zero relocated to Alberta in 1997, it was for reasons that were both personal for Bouzek and political for the company. The Ontario Harris government's deep cuts to the arts and social services hit Ground Zero hard in a double whammy: both the company's grant revenues and client base were shaken. Once it was re-established in Edmonton, Ground Zero was informed by the Canada Council that its annual funding request had been denied because the company's niche in the local "cultural ecology" was unclear. After that the company rebuilt its funding base, but in 2008 its subsidy of $27,000 still ranked at the bottom of the fifteen theatre operating grants in Alberta.[57]

By its very history Ground Zero challenges the fundamental precepts encoded in the Canada Council's concept of "cultural ecology" – a concept that neatly frames bureaucratic policies in an undifferentiated community served by the arts, and which the arts in turn reflect. The rhetoric of community in cultural policy is closely related to the familiar rhetoric of the cultural "garden," in which the arts sink "roots" in the community that they nourish and that in turn supports the arts. This rhetoric disallows politicized art because the liberal humanist ideology that it articulates sees engaged art as being disruptive of the unifying value of community unless it addresses issues that "bring communities together," as Headlines strives to do. For arts councils, activist art is viable if it has a community to support it. This principle is obviously and easily true of the numerous issues of identity politics; it is less obviously the case in questions of class, which disrupt the fiction of the subsuming national community and locate identity in economic determinants that are not only changing and changeable, but cannot be reduced to narratives of essential identity.

When Ground Zero moved to Alberta it broke away from the fundamental relation of art and community that had governed Canadian arts policies for decades. It revealed the possibility of a theatre being something more than a narrative space that anchors a community by transforming ideology into cultural geography. Instead, Ground Zero's move highlighted the idea of the strategic venture that adapts to the contingencies of the political moment and helps to connect and reconnect communities as they appear, reform, and mobilize in struggle. Like Parminou and Headlines, Ground Zero offers a productive model of how activist theatre workers can appropriate the entrepreneurial models of market capitalism – generating self-employment while enacting a radical politics of community and resistance.

9

Out There

Digital Streets, Chaos Aesthetics, Heritage Guerrillas

Theatrical culture-jamming: George Mougias as Neptune greets
Jason C. McLean as Poutrincourt in *Sinking Neptune*.
Matthias Elsdörfer

It is hard to predict where it is going
next, except to say, "There."
    – David Diamond, Headlines Theatre, 2004

Out "there" is beyond the horizon of the visible, and in activist theatre these days "there" looks less and less like a traditional theatre
performance.[1] The artists and theatre workers who are probing the ways
of navigating the rapidly changing conditions of radical theatre are revising fundamental precepts that have governed the interaction of performers and spectators for the last century.

Today at one end of a spectrum of power and resources, the per-
vasiveness of digital technology enables the state and corporate capital to intrude into every aspect of human life. The state deploys those
same tools to narrow the public spaces in which dissent performs, and it
attempts to force activists into spaces subject to high degrees of surveillance and regulation. At the other end of the spectrum the Internet and
digital media give activists unprecedented tools of their own – instruments of communication and mobilization that bypass boundaries.
Digital technology produces a wider distribution of spectatorship and
participation and enables remote organization and collaboration and the
instantaneous delivery of messages. It blurs the difference between live
and digitally reconstituted bodies.

The Banner–Ground Zero
Collaborations: Video Ballads

Shortly after Don Bouzek moved Ground Zero to Edmonton, an
unexpected development opened up new possibilities that shaped his
subsequent working life and methods.

Towards the close of the 1990s I was working with an Australian colleague, David Watt, on the research for a book on theatre in the labour
movement, and we identified Ground Zero as the subject for a case
study. Meanwhile, in England, Dave Watt met up with Dave Rogers,
a musician, actor, and director who had been performing with a loose
collective known as Banner Theatre in Birmingham for more than thirty
years. Almost inevitably, when Don Bouzek and Dave Rogers came to
know of each other's work, they started to think of ways of working
together. That was the beginning of a transnational collaboration that
would continue through the next decade and more.

Banner has had a curious history on the British left. It has operated almost entirely within the labour movement, with the result that
until recently it was virtually unknown in the theatre world (I have met
theatre professors from Birmingham who have never heard of the company). Almost all of its performance work has been within and for the
left activist community. As Dave Rogers says:

> Mention political theatre and a common response is, "Aren't you
> just preaching to the converted?" Well in some ways maybe we
> do, in so much as we believe in supporting those people who are
> fighting to level the injustices and inequities of our times. Why
> waste energy talking to Tories?[2]

Since Banner began in 1974, its various members – of whom Rogers
has been the constant presence as founder, director, songwriter, and
performer – have moved from front-line agitprops, and the blends of
documentary and clowning that were a common idiom in the 1960s, to
more formalized, theatrically stripped-down shows. Banner's signature
performance method is what they call the "video ballad," inspired by the
celebrated BBC *Radio Ballads* program written and produced by Charles
Parker, Ewan MacColl, and Peggy Seeger between 1958 and 1964.[3]

In the radio ballad Parker created a new form of documentary
that intercut oral history and testimony with song cycles composed for
the program. The introduction of "actuality" – real people being interviewed – rather than using actors was a revolutionary step in documentary production at the time, and would become a core ethical principle
for Banner. The radio ballads had a major impact on the British folk
scene in the early sixties because MacColl and Seeger used musical styles

and vocal techniques that drew on the living archive of the traditional British working-class song. In his songs MacColl composed melodies in traditional styles, with lyrics that used simple evocative metaphors to make their point. Parker decided to try out some of the radio ballad material on stage, and in doing so in 1968 he taught both of those skills to Dave Rogers. That was the beginning of Banner Theatre.

In the video ballad form, as developed by Banner over twenty years, live musical performance and projections work together to produce testimony and analytic commentary. The use of projections arises out of an ethical commitment to follow the radio ballad principle of using the actual voices of the people involved in the issue. This approach is a major reformation of the idea of documentary theatre. As it developed in the twentieth century, from the living newspapers of the 1930s to the "verbatim theatre" form that has had a major revival in this new century (widely performed examples include *My Name Is Rachel Corrie* and *The Laramie Project*), documentary theatre has rarely addressed the blurred ethical boundaries between the subject who speaks and the actor who represents that subjectivity.

The actor's presence has always been a problem for documentary theatre because in the most basic sense we almost always recognize a contradiction between the actuality of the words spoken and the pretence of the actor who speaks them. The actor becomes the agent of authenticity by embodying actuality, but we understand the performance to be a re-created pretence. The performance erases everything that the actor does *not* embody, so that reality collapses into the presence of the actor who stands before us as subject and object, document and documenter; the actor's authority derives simultaneously from the representation and the erasure of actuality. The documentary process seeks typifying figures and moments, a selectively particularized construction of the real, and embodies it as a totality. But the more we experience the performance as the phenomenal reality, the wider the gap between subject and object. Performance threatens to become more "real" than the actuality it enacts. It is not unusual for documentary theatre to offset this dilemma by resorting to the endorsement of the represented subject.

An early example of this practice can be found in the history of the Mummers Troupe, from 1974, when – during the time I was working with them – they spent a summer with tape recorders talking to miners and playing back what they found. The result was a pro-union documentary in the emerging collective style, combining actuality, monologues, comic dialogue, puppets, and clowning. One day while rehearsing in the union hall, the actors were trying to whip up a scene based on the mining company's practice of giving gold watches to men who served twenty-five years. While they were improvising, one of the retired miners who sat in on the rehearsals out of curiosity asked permission to speak. He then delivered the speech he had wanted to deliver, but never had, during his own retirement ceremony. In it he calmly but angrily measured the value of the watch against the lives lost to accident and silicosis. The actors present all dived for the tape recorders, and the entire sequence was imported into the final play exactly as experienced in the rehearsal room. After the show opened and began touring mining towns in Newfoundland and Nova Scotia, the miner showed up at one performance. At the end of the scene he spontaneously stood and announced himself: "Ladies and Gentlemen, I am that man." The drama critic for a national press syndicate was on hand, and he wrote, "And there, in that museum with the walls hung with the picks and hammers of soft-coal miners long gone, with a real miner giving a short impromptu speech, theatre ceased to be an imitation of life and became life itself."[4]

A second example was recorded on film. The template show of the Canadian documentary was Theatre Passe Muraille's 1972 collective creation *The Farm Show*, built out of the experiences of a group of young actors from Toronto who spent a summer in a farmhouse near Clinton, Ontario. It is a hugely entertaining, highly sentimental, and, in hindsight, extremely ethnocentric testament to local culture, inflected with the cultural nationalism of the day and a kind of tepid, romanticized Maoism. It spawned dozens of successors and helped define principles of performance structure, acting technique, theatricality, and dramatic voice at a critical stage in an emergent Canadian theatre culture. A year after the show opened in an Ontario barn, Michael Ondaatje, then a young poet, made a film documenting the remount tour of the show. One of the fascinating treasures of Ondaatje's *The Clinton Special* is its montage of monologues from the show juxtaposed with their actual sources. After an extended sequence that intercuts a farmer talking about his wildlife park and the actor performing the same monologue, the camera returns to the farmer, who comments, "He mimicked me pretty good."[5]

In these moments, and in dozens like them, the actor's claim to authenticity is validated by the authority of the informant. For the actors involved such moments are charged with emotion. At work here is a principle identified in a groundbreaking work, *Cities of the Dead*, by U.S. theatre historian Joseph Roach as *surrogation*, the material displacement of identity in a symbolic exchange.[6] Roach examines the idea of the surrogate as applied to the politics of race and performance in American culture, but his ideas extend far beyond the minstrel shows and slave auctions that he examined. In the surrogate transfer, the performer supersedes actuality and expropriates authenticity. The paradigmatic example is the minstrel show: the point was not that white performers played oppressive stereotypes, but that in their cultural expropriation, they *produced* an authenticity that eradicated the source.

With the best of intentions, most documentary theatre has been a minstrel show. For a documentary theatre to solve this conflict of surrogation and silencing, the centrality of the actor must be reworked. For Banner this meant removing the actors' right to speak – or to appropriate – the words of people in struggle. In the video ballad, digital recording projection enables the people to speak. The actors answer back, in theatrical song. Like the *songspiel* of Bertolt Brecht and Kurt Weill in the 1930s, the performance of theatrical songs against projections is sustained in the conventions of theatre aesthetics: rigorously rehearsed, constituted in spectatorship, driven by narrative and argument.

From the mid-1990s to 2011 Banner produced more than twenty video ballads with an intercultural core group of performers, musicians, and technicians. A typical example is a sequence of video ballads under the group title of *Local Stories/ Global Times*. The series focused on issues of social justice, migration, forced dislocation, and refuge seekers in an embracing political analysis that traces the actual human cost of corporate globalization and militarized imperium. It began in 2001 with *Migrant Voices*, based on the experience of Kurdish and Iraqi refugees in Britain, followed in 2005 by *Wild Geese*, about exile and the forced migration in the global economy of workers from Ireland, the Caribbean, the Middle East, and Asia. The musical vocabulary for the shows moved between and blended traditional folk, rock, reggae, klezmer, Persian, and African styles. In this the company draws its musical decisions out of political analysis.

In fall 1997 Bouzek travelled to England and met Dave Rogers to begin a series of conversations that culminated in 2002 when Rogers spent time in Edmonton workshopping a show on Alberta labour history and a Canadian segment of the *Migrant Voices* project. The collaboration continued with Bouzek working as a director in 2004 on Banner's miners' strike anniversary show, *Burning Issues*, commissioned by the National Union of Mineworkers, and in the following year on *Wild Geese*, which brought Banner performers to Canada.[7]

Both groups learned from this cultural exchange. Ground Zero introduced Banner to the Canadian popular theatre and education processes and contributed a deep experience in negotiating cultural diversity. In return Banner's history in the ballad form provided Ground Zero with a new set of artistic protocols that repositioned the aesthetic traditions of Canadian popular theatre and provided new avenues of release from the disciplinary frame of the theatre profession. Using the video ballads form, Bouzek produced a hybrid that derives from Canadian storytelling, early twentieth-century chautauqua, and working-class concerts, reconsidered through Banner's experience in adapting art to digital video.

The script of *Troublemakers*, a show produced by Ground Zero about working-class history in Alberta, reveals the texture of the video ballad dramaturgy. The show includes songs written and performed by Edmonton singer-songwriter Maria Dunn during her period as artist in residence with the Alberta Federation of Labour in 2002. In performance, Dunn and her fiddler accompanist stand close to the audience, before and to the side of a projection screen that dominates the stage. Although it seems like a concert, her performance has none of the usual ad libs and asides that respond to the concert audience. It is austere and rehearsed. Her songs establish a dialogue with the digital images and voice-overs.

TITLE: 1922

NEWS ITEM (*voice-over*): Coal Miners in the Drumheller Valley yesterday walked off their jobs in defiance of their own union. They claim the union betrayed them by negotiating a contract which reduced their rate of pay. The miners voted to instruct their representative Arthur Evans to use their dues money as strike pay.

> **Slim Evans** (*voice-over*): The United Mine Workers accused me of stealing their dues money. I was arrested for 'fraudulently converting' union funds to feed the starving, instead of sending it to a bunch of business agents in Indianapolis. I was brought up for trial in Calgary. They sentenced me to three years in the Prince Albert penitentiary.

Song:

Drumheller Valley in 1922

And still it's hard, hard times

'Cause that Yankee union chokes off our dues

And leaves us to struggle in the mines

They say One Big Union was one big mistake

We never should have made that choice

But when it comes to righting a wrong

We'll still be raising one big voice.

A capella

Yes I know Slim Evans

Friend of the working miner

And yes I'll sign my name to petition his release

It's the least that I can do for

The man who put the money

Where our hungry mouths were and damn their union fees.[8]

This is the basic theatrical vocabulary of the video ballads: actor-musicians, digital video projection, and audio recordings creating a montage of recorded actuality and performed commentary. Ground Zero has been taking this form further, digging into local history and politics, as in *GWG: Piece by Piece*, a 2009 collaboration with Maria Dunn on the history of garment workers in an Edmonton jeans factory, and a new collaboration with an Edmonton hip-hop group on Sudanese workers in the meat industry in Alberta. The mix of live music, digital video, documentary collage, and news item voice-overs disrupts normative patterns of theatrical reception. It is character-centred, but it is not theatre; neither is it video or musical concert. It does not take the audience on a plot-driven emotional ride with a climactic rush, but it can be intensely engaging. It is the performance of hybridity; forms migrate and reterritorialize across disciplinary, cultural, and national borders. Indeed, Banner and Ground Zero have legitimized each other in adapting a common form that was delegitimized as theatre work. Now, together, they have produced a new historical procedure: their collaboration is a merger of histories and the implementation of new genealogies that are independent of the institutionalized theatre profession.

For Ground Zero and Banner, digital technology has enabled a reformation and adaptation of already established practices. In production, digital recorders and video playback effectively provide not only inexpensive and mobile studio facilities but also the capacity to produce sophisticated visuals, including animation, using only a laptop and an external hard drive. As the technology becomes more accessible and portable, it enables more flexibility in delivering performances. Sequences can be altered and reordered between shows to tailor them to specific audiences. In program development, email and web access means that theatres can work together regardless of distance. The creators can transfer files immediately. With this kind of collaboration, as theatre crosses and sometimes erases borders, it begins to be more and more difficult to define performance work by traditional markers, including national origin. The Ground Zero–Banner collaboration suggests the possibility of the transnational connection in an active disruption of the solidity of national culture as export commodity. What is particularly new is how "transnational" is understood and activated: not as a structure, as it was understood in the 1930s, when the notion of international superseded national in theory but was captured by statism in practice, but as an expanding and decentred activation of the local in the process of reproduction through transference. It is in effect the reclaimed underside of globalization.

Digital media is both the means and the form of the reconstitution of activist theatre: it disrupts and relocates cultural genealogies, reterritorializes artistic traditions, produces new structures. Digitalization is the enabling condition, then, of new theatricalities: it disturbs the traditional narrative structures of national culture. The resulting refusal of the institutionalized theatre models the nation not as an organic structure but as an expanding, always changing, network of interconnected strands, in which theatre culture is just one of many veins. The Banner–Ground Zero collaborations, and countless others, are practising a transnational politics – at the edge that pushes back, *out there*, at the edge where work defines form, audiences define space, and performance maps the connections between them.

Chaos Aesthetics: Viral Theatre

If Ground Zero and Banner provide a historical bridge between the agit-props of the thirties and the wired world, for a new generation of theatre radicals the Internet and digital technology have always been part of the cultural toolkit. Digital technology and the ubiquitous use of digital surveillance by the state and corporations have between them not only created new social play spaces for radical performance but also opened new pathways linking local activists in an expanding network of trails to follow.

For the anarchist and street culture groups that have arisen to enact popular protest, especially in the showcase political summits of the G8 and G20 meetings, the flash-mob capacity of instantaneous communication has vastly multiplied their effect. We can witness the agitprops of the 1930s through a few surviving scripts and photographs, but today's street agitprops and actions cycle endlessly on YouTube and circulate from hand to hand on DVDs. The most commonly used adjective to describe this new generation of agitprop, with its recurring emphases on public disruption and ridicule, is carnivalesque. Rather than propagandizing, the participants seek to reclaim public space, expose operations of power, and disrupt media images of political order. In doing this they follow the traditions of the early twentieth-century futurists and the situationists of the sixties. But the new street theatre activists have relocated their performances, linking streets with digital pathways, and refusing the art paradigm.

In the United Kingdom the Laboratory of Insurrectionary Imagination, a network of artists and activists, has been central in gathering and circulating examples of this work. Their DVD *13 Experiments in Hope* offers a snapshot of the diversity of forms at play.[9] The approaches range from the British phenomenon of the Clandestine Insurgent Clown Army, in which clowns armed with plungers and mops parade to and invade military recruitment centres, to "the vacuum cleaner," a self-described one-person collective who, in the performance on the DVD, offers up prayers to consumer items in Sainsbury's supermarkets. Some of the performers, such as Reverend Billy and his Church of Stop Shopping, have achieved celebrity status as icons of the anti-globalization movement.

Many of these performances are situationist-derived parodies, but some, like the Yomango movement of tactical shoplifting that originated in Spain, take riskier paths. In Barcelona forty "civil weapons inspectors" dressed in white paper coveralls show up at the head offices of a weapons manufacturer. They spread briskly through the building and dismantle computers, piling them up in the lobby before melting away in the crowd as the police arrive. Meanwhile another activist has been careful to stay

outside the building to avoid being charged with trespassing, and when
the office invaders disappear he covers their escape with a speech.

> My name is Bob and to mend my broken heart I have come here
> with my friends to the offices of Indra. We have taken on the role
> of Civil weapons inspectors, and we will dismantle the weapons
> of mass destruction in our midst. As a group of people, for us,
> it is the most normal thing to do. We're not going to play your
> game of violence and aggression. We will show our power and
> our compassion by taking apart your computers, your weapons
> for designing mass destruction. We will show what we can
> achieve together and how we can mend our broken hearts by
> dismantling Indra.[10]

The entire operation manifests militarily precise planning and execu-
tion. Similarly, an Argentine "Yomango Tango" shows elegantly dressed
dancers in a seemingly impromptu tango performance in a high-end
department store at the height of the Argentine banking crisis. As they
dance they shoplift bottles of champagne. They reassemble the next day
in the main hall of a major bank, and as they dance they pop the corks
and drench the interior of the bank. These kinds of actions echo the
situationist tactics of the Vancouver Street Theatre decades earlier (notably, the VST's invasion of a department store at Christmas), but with
considerably more organizational sophistication.

The power of agitprop in this mode is its sudden performance of
invisible organization. It may seem frivolous, but it has a powerful capacity to disturb spectators. I saw this for myself in a class that I taught
on simulation and public-space performance. I asked teams of students
to create events that would transform public space without a literal text.
One group distributed blue cloths and asked the rest of the class to tie
the cloths on their arms. Each team member took a group of class members, who were instructed to remain silent, to the plaza at the centre of
the campus. Each group arrived from a different direction and joined
the others in a large circle, and they all stood silently outside the main
doors of the university's central concourse building. They stood for ten
minutes and then, without a word, faded away.

The effect was startling and, for the students involved, disconcerting. Passers-by were not just visibly curious but also worried and in some

cases alarmed by the presence of an organized, marked group standing in a cryptic formation. The event had no public text or meaning but clearly manifested *something*. Because it had no obvious political valence, some onlookers found it threatening. When we returned to the class, the debrief was heated and intense as students raised the spectre of fascism and debated the ethics of their action. They had tapped into how agit-prop can be much more than representation because it has the power to compel spectatorship and implant images. Bodies in formation are more than bodies in a space.

In Canada one of the most articulate voices arguing for the efficacy of situational interventions as a radical art practice is the playwright and director Darren O'Donnell of Toronto. In his book, or manifesto, *Social Acupuncture*, O'Donnell outlines some of interventions that he developed with his company Mammalian Diving Reflex (whose producer, Naomi Campbell, provides a direct link to the popular theatre movement and Great Canadian Theatre Company agitprops). O'Donnell exemplifies the trajectory of the radical theatre artists who walk away from the canonical theatre. The particular power of theatre under capitalism, he says, is that it cannot be commodified: "It's impossible to duplicate and mass-produce theatre." He offers a distinction between this impossibility and the megamusical industry, in which performances are just part of a larger complex of entertainment experience. But the very trait that has enabled theatre to persist as an uncaptured form also means that it is always a local and therefore isolated phenomenon. Audiences normally watch theatre in groups, but the groups remain separate and unconnected. He concludes, "Information-age capitalism, with its demand that cultural products be digitized and circulated via electronic networks, has left theatre gasping for intelligence, relevance and currency."[11]

For O'Donnell theatre is stuck in a contradiction between its social, democratic potential as a form that brings people together in space, and its practitioners, who are "stuck in some bizarre headspace that keeps us focused on the classical canon with Shakespeare as the gold standard."[12] As playwright he builds in practical requirements that push the theatre work into relevance. His casting note for his play *Pppeeeaaaccceee*, in which three people float in and out of a conversation about revolution, stipulates that the piece can be performed by any three people so long as no more than one of them is white, and no more than one is male.[13] For a playwright to invoke this kind of restriction might risk fewer productions, but it is at the same time a useful example of how theatre workers can manage to change the demographics and the politics of their profession.

As a creative, sceptical artist, O'Donnell is unforgiving about his own motives and past work, and very aware of the danger of solipsism in situationist performance. "Was it really me," he asks himself, "who dressed like a business man and went down to the financial district to dance in the streets, convinced that it had the power to affect the withered souls there?"[14] Mammalian Diving Reflex and its "operatives" have generated new public encounters that take theatricality and participatory performance into unexpected domains. O'Donnell describes staging "Spin the Bottle" kissing parties during the viral SARS scare in Toronto. More recently he coordinated an international instance of "Haircuts by Children," in which people received free haircuts from kids. The work "invites the consideration of children as creative and competent individuals whose aesthetic choices can be trusted. The idea that kids should be allowed to cut our hair evokes the same leap of faith, courage and understanding required to grant children deeper citizenship rights."[15]

Theatre workers who adhere to a canonical tradition of the rehearsable performance, the playing space, and empathic spectatorship might well dismiss this other project as being on the horizon where theatre disappears into and is dissolved by an amorphous notion of "performance art." But "performance" in this sense of the word simply describes an institutional and critical context for provocative or explorative theatricalities. O'Donnell argues that theatre is not about representation and stories but about "generating affect, and that's it."[16]

O'Donnell is not the first radical theatre worker in Canada to turn away from the canonical theatre profession in disgust and anger. In the 1980s, after the collapse of the Mummers Troupe, rather than return to the stage Chris Brookes started a new career as an independent radio producer. In the same decade the most successful and high-profile leftist playwright in Canada, David Fennario, renounced the professional theatre and founded a working-class amateur community theatre in Montreal. In that milieu he created a series of complex, imaginative, and angry agitprop dramas on local history, including a play about Joe Beef.[17] In his plays, monologues, and radical history walking tours since then, Fennario has maintained a deep activist commitment to a socially useful Marxist theatre practice that may at times engage with but is not complicit in the theatre industry.

In each of these cases theatrical refusal sought ways of continuing radical theatre by taking it in directions where it may not resemble theatre any longer. But a risky haircut, a broadcast sound performance, and a walking tour all open up new theatrical possibilities that create new constituencies of spectators.

This intersection of theatrical refusal and digital networking, with its creation of new possibilities for activist theatre workers, shows up in a series of interventions gathered under the title of *Sinking Neptune*. The project is facilitated by Donovan King, a founder and core organizer of the anarchist collective – perhaps theatrical assembly is more accurate – Optative Theatrical Laboratories in Montreal, but the actual author of the play is identified as "the Radical Dramaturgy Unit" of OTL, in a gesture to the organizational rhetoric of the communist left of the 1930s.[18]

King established the company out of his own theorizing about the nature and practice of activist theatre, in which he drew on situationism to construct a model of theatrical efficacy based on "counter-hegemonic playing." His 2004 Master's theatre thesis on "optative theatre" occasioned a bitter controversy at the University of Calgary. In it he stated:

> Optative theatre proposes that by adopting an anti-oppressive foundation to human identity, it is possible to employ theatre activism to challenge oppression in all its forms – by meta-theatrically playing the provocateur, and hence by living in action. With the ability to create instant virtual realities, optative theatre provides both a tool for critical reflection and a theatrical strategy for challenging oppression on personal, cultural, and structural levels of society. Furthermore, as a viral form of theatre, it has the potential to spread rapidly.[19]

The work of the Optative Theatrical Laboratories is in itself an intervention in Canadian theatre history. The OTL uses a variety of media in an interdisciplinary fashion – "live performance, direct action, theatre, video, text, music, internet, installation" – and according to a "Mandate" section on its website it "employs a diversity of cutting-edge activist performance techniques, such as culture-jamming, Viral Theatre, Sousveillance Theatre, meme-warfare, Radical Dramaturgy, Electronic Disturbance Theater, and Global Invisible Theatre."[20] *Sinking Neptune* was devised as a disruptive, culture-jamming response to an event planned for 2006 to mark the four hundredth anniversary of the inaugural European theatrical performance in what is now Canada: Marc Lescarbot's *Le Théâtre de Neptune en la Nouvelle-France*. In 2006, Richard Pinto, a Halifax theatre director, announced plans to seek funding from provincial and federal bodies for a full-scale commemorative re-enactment; Optative responded immediately with its parodistic deconstruction. Pinto's plan did not receive funding, and Optative – which neither sought nor needed funding – instead went on to perform in Annapolis Royal.

Sinking Neptune intersects with critical discussions by theatre historians that identify the original masque as a moment of imperial invasion by spectacle – with the surrogate bodies of indigenous peoples, played by Frenchmen, gifting their land to the king of France.[21] Lescarbot's *Le Théâtre de Neptune* has been narrated over time as a founding moment of Canadian theatre, but we know of it through a series of false authenticities – which is to say, theatricalizations – beginning with C.W. Jefferys's wildly improbable but now canonical drawing of 1942, which shows the "restored" fort of Port Royal on the Bay of Fundy and King Neptune standing in a canoe paddled by Mi'kmaq warriors. In a similar citation of the common imperial motif, the Portuguese Military Museum in Lisbon exhibits an image of Neptune and Tritons unveiling India for Vasco da Gama.

In his moment of racial impersonation and colonial masquerade, Lescarbot had claimed the New World in a new way by enlisting the spectating bodies and appropriated voices of its inhabitants in his imagined theatre. He established the principle that colonialism through spectacle is the necessary precondition of imperial invasion. Writing about his decision to mount an offensive against the planed re-enactment, King compares *Le Théâtre de Neptune* to a minstrel show, arguing that "it signifies the starting point of a cultural genocide against First Nation peoples."[22]

For me, *Le Théâtre de Neptune* is the first instance of a surrogate performance – of performance authenticity feedback – that is a defining and recurring condition of Canadian theatre history.[23] Indeed, because I had written about *Le Théâtre de Neptune* as an instrument of colonial invasion, I became a character in *Sinking Neptune*. The play proceeds as a deliberately sabotaged production of the original text, performed with lampoon and parody, interspersed with documentary quotations – some of them deliberately twisted or changed – from me, CBC news reports, and Richard Pinto, the director who had proposed the re-enactment.

Optative tried when possible to offer the performance with anti-racism workshops and to incorporate local volunteers, who would join the performance to read documentary items that added to the always changing and adaptive script. For that very reason the notes to the published version call it "an adjustable tool for any initiative to challenge racism, imperialism, and oppression."[24]

In his theory, and in the development of practices that derive from the theory, King has often taken a combative stance that accords with the confrontational tactics of the anti-globalization movement. In *Sinking Neptune* this approach becomes a deliberate attempt to subvert normative expectations of theatrical pleasure. "Subvert" is an overworked word in academic left criticism these days, but in this case it is accurate. When I brought the show to perform in Guelph, my students were disconcerted by the actors' apparent lack of interest in theatre craft or polish. It was anarchism at play, and yet, to recall O'Donnell's point, it generated affect.

As an anarchist collective – and I use anarchist in a fairly loose way, as activist dissent unconstrained by ideological program – Optative plays in the interstices of political activism and theatrical reception. Its participants have no performance space, no stable membership, no funding. What they do have is a website and a mutable community of members who take part as they will; the cast is whoever makes it to the show. This has significant theoretical consequences because it is part of a mechanism of deliberate de-professionalism and de-aestheticizing of theatre performance. It highlights one of the most important features of contemporary political activist theatre, which uses digital transmission and web-based organization to create local liveness. *Sinking Neptune* has a viral YouTube presence in which it joins thousands of other interventionist performances, including the Clandestine Insurgent Clown Army phenomenon.

This refusal evidences itself in performance as a deliberate disruption of convention. In this Optative joins one of the enduring traditions of radical political theatre, in which anti-authoritarianism turns against the internal pressures of artistry itself. In the past this approach has often led to an artistic reconceptualization that moves through refusal to counter-disciplinarity and then to a re-engagement with disciplinarity. Such was the case of the first phase of left-wing agitprop in the early 1930s, and with early interventionist groups such as the Mummers Troupe in the

1970s. Dissident refusal played out in disruptive parody, but could not suppress the desire to become "better," which in those cases entailed entering into artistic professionalism. In the 1930s the pressure came from the political left and a need to recapture position in the recuperation of popular nationhood; in the 1970s it came from the increasing possibilities of making careers in theatre.

That pattern seems to be not the case with *Sinking Neptune*. Digital communication, culture-jamming, and a plugged-in global activist community sprawling across the web invest aesthetic refusal with counter-cultural capital and sustain the refusal of disciplinarity as a rejection of cultural hierarchy. This refusal replaces disciplinarity with chaos aesthetics. *Sinking Neptune* reveals this pattern in its caricature and under-rehearsed performance. The opening stage directions provide a sense of theatrical deconstruction:

> The players set up the stage as the audience trickles in. The space is arranged as though for a large and spectacular news conference. A large gaudy banner displaying the words "THE-ATRE OF NEPTUNE IN NEW FRANCE" is hung, and a painted cardboard bow of a ship is attached to a block for an actor to stand on, as though at the helm. USL [upstage left] is a make-up table and mirror, a chair, and a coat rack which holds various costumes. Once the audience is seated, the players take their places.[25]

The rhythm of the performance is casual. Between units, action ceases to give time for the audience to read projected quotations about genocide and indigenous resistance. King as director sits at a table at centre stage with the prompt script because some of the actors may have been integrated into the performance from a workshop only minutes before the performance. The acting is not representational or even demonstrative in the Brechtian sense (in which an actor shows, rather than becomes, the character). Rather, the acting is citational: the acting style and scenography both cite the theatrics of amateur community pageants; performing bad theatre badly to prove that they could perform more professionally but they don't really care.

Again, as Roach argued, in the circum-Atlantic world cultural continuity has been enabled through processes of surrogation, as bodies and spaces are occupied and adapted to fill what he refers to as "actual or perceived vacancies ... in the network of relations that constitutes the social fabric."[26] In the paradigmatic example of the minstrel show, cultural hybridity creates generative performative boundaries of racial categorization, and mimicry becomes experienced as somehow authentic. The surrogate performance enacts an authenticity that confirms ideology in the body by producing knowledge that is felt to be true. Optative refers to minstrelsy overtly with the accusation that *Sinking Neptune* is a "redface" show.[27] This reference explains the deeper purpose of the anti-disciplinarian performance. If *Le Théâtre de Neptune* initiated a history of surrogation and genocide, the racialized body on stage must always be perceived through the lens of this surrogation, even when reclamative, as in the celebrated plays of Thomson Highway. For Optative, the response to surrogation is to efface racialized bodies and replace them with the semiotics of racial difference, indicated, as in *Sinking Neptune*, by costume, makeup, and props. Midway through the play an actor has put on a clichéd "Indian" costume and begins a "cowboys and Indians" whoop. Soon after the stage direction reads: "*Suddenly he stops, and assumes a 'savage' posture. Over the course of four 'Savage' monologues, he becomes more and more scantily clad, 'redfaced' and misrepresentative of First Nations people.*"[28] In this case, to efface is to deface in a double sense: to deface the mask of the surrogate, the "redface," and to deface the propriety of theatrical performance and spectatorship.

Optative staged *Sinking Neptune* again in 2009 as part of the protests against the four hundredth anniversary celebration of the founding of Quebec City. At the same time it continued with its long-standing *Car Stories* project, in which spectators are taken in small groups to theatrical encounters in cars. This had led to a significant development in 2001 at the Montreal Fringe Festival, when an Optative member refused to give the critic of the Montreal *Gazette* a complimentary press ticket to see the performance. In the kerfuffle that followed, Optative became the first play ever to be kicked out of a Fringe Festival. In response King pressured the festival for ten years for box-office monies and fee reimbursements owing to Optative. In 2010, while waiting for a resolution from a new festival management, Optative announced, "The OTL has responded, as promised, with a theatrical campaign to collect the ticket sales and spur social justice." It called the campaign "Collection Agency" and posted the rules on its website.

COLLECTION AGENCY is a piece of Do-It-Yourself theatre whereby those wishing to participate create and assume a theatrical "Collection Agent" character, and proceed to investigate 3 dramatic people or companies to collect what is owed. Using primary documents within a theatrical matrix that includes both the Fringe and the infringement festivals, the first participant to collect from all three people or companies wins a $500.00 prize (or 10% commission on what the fringe owes OTL). To participate, find someone at the Fringe beer tent distributing the instructions and documentation, or download them.[29]

The Infringement Festival was Optative's other response to the growing institutionalization of the Fringe. Since 2004 the Infringement has spread to Hamilton, Buffalo, and Brooklyn as a loosely organized, non-funded festival of self-identified underground theatre, dance, music, and spoken word performance.

Optative's oppositional stance, political energy, and fearlessness are sustained by its refusal to accommodate with the theatre as a profession or a set of cultural and aesthetic values. In that sense it is less a company or a venture than the theatrical branch of an anarchist community that is itself mobile and mutable. In another way it is Donovan King's continuing personal praxis research into the possibilities of activist performance, made possible by its immersion in a wider activist community.

Heritage Guerrillas:
Re-enactment as Right-Wing Agitprop

In the polarizing globalization conflicts of the twentieth century, both sides use streets and public space as performance battlegrounds; when anarchist and activist performers take to the streets, they find that spectatorship itself can be performative – and armed. Nowhere was this more clear than in Toronto in June 2010 at the G20 protests, as one group of environmental activists who had planned for months for a series of performances for the demonstrations found out. Such agitprop performances have been common features of the globalization protests around the world, and have provided the coalitions of dissent with some of their most enduring icons. In the Toronto case, the performers never even had a chance to get started. Having imported thousands of officers from across the country as mercenaries, the state assembled a police presence five times greater than the Canadian army force in Afghanistan. This was a state occupation of public space with paramilitary force. Instead of performing, the protesters found themselves hemmed in and "kettled" – trapped and squeezed between two advancing battalions of armoured police – and detained without charge for twenty-three hours in concentration cages erected for the purpose.

The Queen's Park site where protesters were brutalized by police was the same ground on which mounted police had ridden down the Workers' Theatre eighty years before, but the scale of police militarization and combativeness had increased vastly. Some things had not changed. The police still used informers and undercover agents, but they also infiltrated the digital communication pathways of activist networks. With unprecedented powers and resources, the police effectively directed the flow of the protesters, leading many onlookers to the conclusion that what was reported widely as (a small) anarchist riot was a stage-managed act of performance with planned outcomes. Whether the police anticipated that a small faction of demonstrators would initiate violence – and so the police eased the way of these demonstrators by giving them preset targets – or whether the powers that be just happened to mobilize ten thousand armed police in the wrong place to stop looters – but the right place to trap and overpower peaceful demonstrators – we may never know. But photos of the events show rehearsed (or in military parlance, drilled) formations and placement.

If we think of the police presence in these heavily media-oriented events as a staging of power to command public perception, it is not a reach to think of the outcome as state-produced agitprop. That insight opens up a larger domain of performance that embraces military and paramilitary culture, with its own horizons of disciplinarity between official and irregular formations. This is the domain that is commonly known as re-enactment. A standard case of re-enactment is the guy next door who dresses up in a Civil War or War of 1812 uniform and takes his replica musket off for a weekend of parading. In the summer months such performances are regular fare at historical sites, and most old forts offer staff who impersonate historical figures. In Guelph, on the first of August holiday, the John McCrae Museum – the childhood home of the author of "In Flanders Fields" – invites local re-enactors to set up display booths of uniforms and gear and carry out demonstrations. In 2010 the show included drill and musketry from a squad of 1812 re-enactors, and two men with a small naval cannon from the same period.

Masculinist hero-combat plays

For theatre historians, the "hero-combat" play refers to a dramatic form distributed across cultures in which, as its name suggests, a hero does battle against an evil enemy and triumphs. These are often ceremonially staged, as in village mummers plays that have King George being killed by the Turkish Knight and resurrected by the Doctor's "inky dink white drops of life."[30] More often today these plays are staged at public events, with hobbyists pretending to do battle with lovingly re-created or collected gear.

Like theatre activists, re-enactors have taken to the web as a recruitment, organizational, and communications tool, and "web rings" of re-enactment units around the world link thousands of groups that converge around the events. The happenings can be as local as a parade muster at a fall fair or as immense as an international gathering to restage the Battle of Leipzig with Napoleonic-era cavalry. Or they might be replaying the Battle of Berlin with restored tanks. A brief surf of the web indicates that re-enactment is a growing practice that seeks new sites and objects. If you can think of a period or a military culture, someone is probably re-enacting it.

An example of re-enactment as a form of activist theatre from the right can be seen at the Canadian National Exhibition in Toronto. The CNE sponsors a Warriors' Day, during which military veterans of Canadian and allied forces receive free admission to the grounds and assemble for a parade. The parade continues the Exhibition's long tradition of military commemoration, which began in the late nineteenth century with pyrotechnic pageants of imperial victories, such as the Relief of Lucknow and Siege of Mafeking. At their high point in the early years of the twentieth century, these pageants were immense spectacles that featured casts drawn from militia regiments and Boy Scouts. After the Second World War the pageants gave way to pop-culture grandstand shows, but the annual parade of veterans continues the spectacle of martial pomp. In the 2004 parade the several dozen units that passed in review comprised in the main the pipe bands and colour parties of Royal Canadian Legion branches from across Southern Ontario. They were joined by aged veterans of various units, accompanied in some cases by honour guards from the present complement of the regiments in which they served. The assembly of units provided a cultural map of contemporary Canadian society. Along with veterans from various Canadian regiments and services came African, Polish, Chinese, Korean, and U.S. veterans (but not German, Italian, and Japanese).

In 2004, with Canadian troops once more fighting overseas, the parade was dedicated to a commemoration of the D-Day landings, and pride of place went to the surviving members of the First Canadian Parachute Battalion. They marched proudly, retaining the formation of the young men who had dropped into Normandy on the eve of the invasion sixty years earlier. Before them marched a colour party from the Canadian army, and behind them came the performance ghosts of their younger selves: two dozen younger men kitted in authentic 1944 battle gear. They were members of the First Canadian Parachute Battalion Re-enactment Group, following literally in the footsteps of the men whose uniforms they wore.

In this meeting of veterans and their performative doubles, military re-enactment emerges as both performance and commemoration. While the event is clearly theatrical, it is equally grounded in the structures and protocols of legitimation in military culture. In this moment, theatre and military cultures converge, and that convergence opens the possibility that they are deeply, reciprocally, connected. Re-enactment traditions in the military do more than maintain cultural continuity and invest personnel in the military as a shared community. They have a deeper ideological function, which again points to a complicit relationship to the theatre: they establish a boundary between legitimate and non-legitimate militaries, between the professional estate of the national army and the unprofessional guerrilla. Re-enacted tradition is in this sense the enactment of professional legitimacy. The distinction can be critical, a matter of life and death, because in the modern world most wars are fought not by national armies but by armed populations of people variously known as guerrillas, insurgents, militias, or more recently, in a naming that has been used by the United States to imprison captives without recourse to the protection of the Geneva Convention, "enemy combatants."

In these moments of ceremonial re-enactment, by amateur hobbyists and army reservists, military re-enactment becomes a field in which theatre and army are the same thing. Re-enactment is neither and both:

militarized theatre, theatricalized army, a theatre without playhouses, and an army without power. It is also extraordinarily pervasive and popular, and is clearly emergent as a cultural estate in its own right. At one point it sits within the theatre, as demonstrated by the immense Bolshevik revolutionary spectacles, staged spectacles like *Meet the Navy* and the Edinburgh Tattoo, and indeed by medieval dinner theatres and the jousting tournaments of "renaissance fairs." At another point it sits within the army, in the pomp and circumstance of ceremonial military commemorations.

Most hobbyist re-enactment reproduces periods that have passed from living, if not cultural, memory, and the further they travel in time, the more they enter the realm of fantasy. But as the Canadian paratroopers demonstrate, the re-enactment of modern wars takes place under the eye of the survivors and intersects more clearly with the politics of memory in military culture. In recent years the Second World War has become one of the fastest-growing domains of re-enactment. It began with collectors of militaria, especially vehicles and aircraft, and has now spawned a substantial economy of collector exchanges and an industry of facsimile reproduction. Pictorial Histories, a publishing house in Montana, has produced numerous volumes of illustrated texts that depict in detail the equipment, weapons, uniforms, and insignia for re-enactors and modellers, including a volume on Canadian battle gear. Its series on the German forces, *Soldat*, runs to eleven volumes. The last of these volumes focuses on postwar reproductions designed to alert hobbyists to a growing industry of counterfeits.[31]

Today the hundreds of units that re-create military culture of all periods, from Roman legions to Viet Cong guerrillas, are connected in an expanding network that has produced a growing economy of collectors, restorers, suppliers, traders, craftspeople, and artisans. Increasingly the field includes specialists who market their expertise to film and television. Anyone who has watched the CBC series *Canada: A People's History*, or any of the recent Hollywood blockbuster war films, has seen the re-enactment economy at work. Some six hundred years ago, itinerant and migrating amateur players began a professional economy of theatre work by hiring out their performances. Today a similar process can be seen in an emergent professionalism in re-enactment culture.

Because of the vast diversity of these practices, which cross cultural locations, it may be futile to generalize about the ideological and political meaning of the culture, beyond noting its entrenched masculinism.

While re-enactment cultures offer opportunities for "civilian" portray-
als, their fundamental orientation to history as warfare is a gendering
of history. They mirror not only the masculinism of military culture but
also the centrality of war in the professionalized discipline of academic
history. Re-enactment is characteristically a hetero-masculinist practice,
but the politics of gender, in participation and reception, vary widely. In
Second World War re-enactments women are almost invisible (although
some women's re-enactment groups do exist, and women enter Red
Army re-enactment units as "combatants"). In Civil War re-enactments
women are present in the simulations of civilian life as ancillaries in a
masculinist world.

Although re-enactment units and their members manifest social and
ideological diversity, and frequently condemn "extremism," they exhibit
a general indifference to questions of ethics and history. This is particularly evident and problematic with those units that re-create the Waffen
SS. The ethical questions posed by these units are, however, applicable
to others. For this reason, Paul Fussell, the eminent historian whose book
The Great War and Modern Memory was a formative landmark in the study
of cultural memory, dismisses re-enactors as "weirdos" who indulge "fan-
tasies of heroism." For Fussell, himself a combat veteran, re-enactment
is morally offensive: "Comprehensive as the re-enactors' ambitions to
achieve absolute authenticity are, they neglect certain details, like the
writing of the wounded, their attempts to thrust back into their abdomen
their protruding intestines, and their weeping and calling on Mother."[32]

For many re-enactors, the act of dressing up in military gear and
playing war is simply a pleasant social pastime. But as a performance
field the focus on weaponry, heroics, and tactics reinforces maculinist
and conservative national historiography. It is for this reason that officially established state war museums, like the Canadian War Museum
and the Australian War Memorial, cultivate close relationships with
re-enactment communities – not just because of the value of applied
military history but because of the preservation and reaffirmation of
ideologically invested state pedagogies.

Re-enactment is for the most part an inherently right-wing activist theatre that mirrors contemporary radical left theatre in its distributed performances, digital sprawl, and decentred spectatorship. Does it
hold a capacity for radical dissent, or even critique? I suggest that it
does, but that capacity is not to be found in the culture of historicized

re-enactment but in its unspoken other, in fantasy role play that upsets history and regenders military culture.

The suggestion that fantasy role play is fundamentally depoliticized (or ideologically neutralized) re-enactment would be anathema to participants who consider themselves serious applied historians. But they are all forms of "subjective authenticity role play," and they are all governed by serious purpose, strict regimes of authenticity, and convention. Indeed, a vast number of groups such as the Society for Creative Anachronism, Star Trek fandom, and Cosplay events (that is, re-enactment of costumed moments from famous films), and the many local, one-off LARP (Live Action Role Play) groups, take up this other stream of re-enactment theatre. In the aftermath of the G20 police riots in Toronto, some of the evidence of terrorist weaponry that the Toronto police showed to the media was in fact LARP gear confiscated at Union Station from an uninvolved role player on his way to a scenario game.

A fetish for authenticity is one of the critical bridges between "hardcore" military and subjunctive fantasy re-enactment. To the professional military historian who engages in what Victor Suthren describes as "skinout" authenticity, and to the tributary re-enactor who is deeply invested in cultural memory alike, fantasy role play bears no relation to military reenactment.[33] But as the somatic, felt proof of authenticity, the experience of enacting a Starfleet Marine may be no less "real" than that of a Second World War paratrooper (and conversely, as Fussell argues, they are equally fantasized).

I have, for instance, a friend who is active in Star Trek fan culture. He belongs to a fan club chapter that is organized as a Starfleet vessel, on which he holds officer rank. His chapter – his starship – is part of the worldwide club of Starfleet International, which includes hundreds of fictitious ships, organized in regional fleets, headed by admirals who earn their command. Like his comrades in the organization, he progresses through the ranks by finishing courses offered by the Starfleet Academy. If he wishes, he can join the Starfleet Marine Corps and download hundreds of pages of tactical manuals based on U.S. military publications. He knows this is just play, a re-enactment of a history that exists only in fantasy, but it is based on a vast and growing encyclopedic literature and strict regimes of adherence to the authenticities of the various *Star Trek* series and timelines. At the same time it is more than play because he has an ongoing identity in a growing culture of people who know one another only through this shared experience. The world is fantasy, but its relations, hierarchies, and feelings are very real.

Like all re-enactment groups, Starfleet wages a virtual war with its enemies, the most popular of which is the Klingon Domain and its marine auxiliary, the Klingon Assault Group. Klingon fan culture is somewhat famous – these are the people who go to conventions decked out in full gear and prosthetic makeup. The Klingon Language Institute – consisting of dedicated fans with backgrounds in linguistics – has published a Klingon dictionary and a growing library of translated works, including the *The Klingon Hamlet*.[34]

My friend described to me a ceremony he witnessed several years ago, when a group of Klingons commemorated the death of John Colicos, the Canadian actor who was the first to play a Klingon in the original *Star Trek* series. They gathered in a circle, lifted their heads to the sky, and joined together in the Klingon Death Wail, a group howl that sends a message that a warrior is on his way to wherever dead Klingon warriors are presumed to go. What was interesting about this commemorative moment, my friend tells me, is that it was powerful, emotive, and honestly experienced. It was more than play because these people in their Klingon personas deeply grieved for the man who had first given flesh to the culture in which they invested so much of their identities.

By relocating re-enactment authenticity to invented worlds, fantasy re-enactment enables players to reformulate historical oppressions of race, gender, and class. The Star Trek world is a utopian vision of a society that has conquered sexism, racism, and the money economy (unless players choose to enact racist Klingons or money-obsessed Ferengi); in the Society for Creative Anachronism the entire player population seems to be an aristocrat or a knight. In effect they release re-enactment from its ideological constraints and expose national military re-enactment as one particularly politicized domain of fantasy play. Perhaps the Changing of the Guard on Parliament Hill would be no less authentic if the troops were replaced by a detachment of Star Fleet Marines. If military re-enactors replay a notion of historical fixity, of a pedagogical history that must be inviolate to preserve their understanding of the nation, fantasy re-enactors continue to insist on their right to invent and remake their world, and their capacity to generate spectatorial affect.

Coda

Out There, In Here

A man walked into a city hall with a bouquet of caterpillars. Was that act of radical theatre simply a matter of efficacy? In the end we can never empirically determine how any cultural action contributes to change. In many cases it is the instance of change, or the production of a spectatorial affect, that produces other causalities. By looking at how activists have sought to exercise a capacity to articulate and provoke activism within the changing conditions of spectatorship and theatre economy, we can see a recurring sense of the value of the performance moment and its exposure of the deeper collaborative social processes that have produced it.

As Darren O'Donnell reminds us, theatre is local and isolated.[1] As popular theatre activists demonstrate, it is portable, accessible, and, when demystified, available to everyone as a liberatory communication process. As fantasy gamers reveal, it can invent and share visions of new worlds. As revolutionaries in the thirties proved, and street activists today prove, it can provoke the state into exposing its own theatricality. And as a new generation of activists show, it offers person-to-person methods of creating networks and coalitions that mirror and resist globalizing structures.

In 2003 in my home community of Guelph I saw a play called *The Strong Breast Revolution*, created in 2003 in the cause of "breast freedom" by students in a class on collective creation taught by Kim Renders, a former member of Nightwood Theatre and at the time a colleague of mine. *The Strong Breast Revolution* collective performed the show intermittently at conferences and festivals in Guelph, Toronto, and Windsor between 2003 and 2006, and a redeveloped version by one of the original members with a British cast played the London and Edinburgh Fringe Festivals to enthusiastic reviews in 2008.

In Guelph the performance by a troupe of young women replayed the principles of committed performance, disciplinary refusal, and reconstituted spectatorship that I have been exploring in this book. Watching the play at a benefit performance celebrating the launch of the "Breasts of Canada" calendar, created as a breast cancer awareness project, I experienced my own disconcerted spectatorial moment. I recognize breast freedom as a social and political issue, and one that has had a history in Guelph since 1996, when Gwen Jacobs took off her shirt on a hot summer day on a downtown street. She was charged in a legal proceeding that ended when the Ontario Court of Appeal ruled that because her action did not have a sexual context, it was not indecent. This confirmed a common right to be topless in public, but the social chaos predicted by the press failed to ensue; so too did the streetscapes of bared bosoms.

The Strong Breast Revolution followed the theatrical template of a Company of Sirens show, with songs, comedy, monologues, and manifesto statements on issues ranging from sexuality to breastfeeding, cancer, self-image, adolescence, and sexism. It was also a rediscovery of the power of agitprop. Some of its most powerful sequences replayed the cadence and polyphony of the mass recitation of the 1930s.

> **C**: Our bodies, our breasts speak a language of power, tell a history of oppression.
> **Mel**: Free yourself.
> **L**: Free your breasts!
> **All**: THE STRONG BREAST REVOLUTION!
> **Mel**: Invites
> **L**: Beckons
> **Meg**: Demands
> **C**: Begs
> **All**: Your presence.
> **Mel**: What a powerful way to inspire change through love,
> **C**: Celebration,
> **L**: and reclamation.
> **Meg**: Let your breast see the sun,
> **Meg, C**: feel the wind
> **Meg, C, L**: taste the rain
> **Mel**: Without the secret embarrassment or shame because our boobs are out there flopping around
> **All**: AND IT'S NORMAL!!!!
> **L**: Proudly walking down the street
> **All**: TOPLESS
> **L**: holding hands with friends

L, C: lovers

L, C, Meg: sisters

L, C, Meg, Mel: mothers

All: Come on mom!!

C: Let's unmake our breasts as museum artefacts, rarely seen except on some "special occasion."

Mel: So be proud, not ashamed!

C: Stand up to speak

All: AND BE HEARD! STRONG BREASTS!!![2]

Writing about the performance in the *Guelph Mercury*, Robyn Read said, "While raising serious concerns, the play is performed with humility and humour, persuading the audience to feel comfortable discussing an issue which was previously limited to intimate conversations with a partner or, more likely, the sales assistant at La Senza." She added, "By showing us their breasts and leaving nothing to the imagination, they are not only proud owners of their own bodies, but protectors of the female body image. This is an important message for anyone, of any age or gender."[3]

As they performed, the women – Meagan Timms, Melannie Gayle, Christine Lafazanos, and Laurel Atkinson (directed by Vicki Hambley, with stage management by Jessica Strothard) – transformed the concert hall of the Guelph Youth Music Centre into a radicalized space that compelled reordered ways of seeing. Watching young feminists performing for an hour with bared breasts was disconcerting, not just because I had to relearn how to see these woman, to see and at the same time not see their breasts and to *naturalize* my seeing, but because I knew them as my students. As a male professor in a theatre program in which women students greatly outnumber men, I have trained myself to avert and erase – to *unsee* – body display as much as possible. The performance reversed that mode of seeing. At the same time it required me to see the performers not as students but as women going past their safe comfort zone to play to their community. When I walked into the room they were students; when I walked out, they were activists.

I hold the memory of that show as an instance of what committed interventionist theatre really is. Relatively few people saw the show as it went on its round of performances, but those who did would most likely never forget it. For some it must have been a powerful and helpful public sharing of a very personal matter. It was local, and it generated a meaningful spectatorial event: we were not just audience; we were participants.

In a discussion afterwards nobody spoke about aesthetic value, but many commented on the politics and the fun. From a canonical theatre perspective it was illegitimate performance, but it was one of thousands of similar performances in which the rules break down, propriety dissolves, a woman performs her breasts, transgression compels spectatorship, performance refuses disciplinarity, a man bows and presents caterpillars. That is the point of refusal and the beginning of activist performance.

There is always something happening out there that we cannot see. In theatre that is where the radical plays.

Notes

1 Purposeful Performance and Theatrical Refusals

1. All theatre artists are workers, but not all theatre workers are artists. For this reason I use the term "artist" to refer to creative workers: actors, directors, playwrights, dramaturges, and designers; and "worker" to refer to the inclusive field – including technicians, carpenters, cutters, sewers, stage managers, and the whole range of theatre labour.
2. *Vancouver Province*, 7 June 1919.
3. Brecht, "On Gestic Music," p.104.
4. Kershaw, *Radical in Performance*, p.91.
5. Canada, Royal Commission, *Massey Report*, pp.193, 195–96.
6. Statistics Canada, "Patterns in Culture Consumption and Participation," p.58.
7. Benson and Conolly, *English-Canadian Theatre*, p.113.
8. Robertson Davies, quoted in Canada, Royal Commission, *Massey Report*, p.192.
9. Even if we merely count the not-for-profit theatre organizations funded by the various arts councils, we will always find discrepancies because of differences in funding criteria. It is virtually impossible to identify the number of not-for-profit and fringe theatre "companies." The Canada Council now funds close to three hundred not-for-profit theatre companies that meet its criteria (although "funds" is itself an opaque term that can mean a large seasonal operating grant or a very small one-time project grant).
10. For incomes and ages, see Hill Strategies Research, Inc., *Statistical Profile of Artists in Canada Based on the 2006 Census*, p.9. In Quebec a different contract model for actors enables longer rehearsal periods. But Quebec is a metropolitan theatre culture, in which all theatre artists work within a few hours' drive of one another. In English Canada theatre culture is dispersed across immense distances.
11. Brecht, "Theatre Communist," p.112.
12. Piscator, *Political Theatre* (London: Eyre Methuen,1979), pp.324, vii, 308.
13. Samuel, *Theatres of Memory*. The term "rhizomorphic" enters cultural criticism from the works of the philosophers Gilles Deleuze and Félix Guattari.
14. Schechner, *Performance Studies*, p.28.
15. Boal, *Rainbow of Desire*, p.20; Williams, *Drama from Ibsen to Brecht*, p.14.
16. I include military communication here as a cultural medium because of the immense social and cultural effects of military organization and mobility in Canada during the world wars. In my own family history, my paternal grandfather saw his first radio when he joined the navy, and my maternal grandfather was a signalman in the trenches. My father was a naval telegrapher from Esquimalt who met and married a WREN teletype operator from Toronto. In each case military

organization introduced them to new communications technology and media, and opened the possibility of new relationships, new professions, and unanticipated lives.

2 Class, Spectatorship, and the Unruly: The Nineteenth Century

1. Robertson Davies used to delight in telling his students at the University of Toronto's Graduate Centre for the Study of Drama of the time he spoke with an actor who had spoken with an actor who had spoken with the great early-nineteenth-century superstar Edmund Kean; by telling the story he extended the chain of cultural memory.

2. The Chautauqua Institution was (and still is) a socially progressive summer "assembly" dedicated to popular education. It occupies a legendary place in the shared history of the United States and Canada, because since its founding in 1874 as a Methodist summer educational assembly it has become a de facto university of popularized high culture. For many North Americans in the early twentieth century, their first exposure to new ideas in the liberal arts and sciences, and indeed to Shakespeare, came via travelling chautauqua tent shows.

3. Butsch, *Making of American Audiences*, p.78.

4. Blagrave, "Temperance and the Theatre," p.26.

5. *Labor Advocate*, 10 April 1891.

6. *Guelph Herald*, 5 Nov. 1850.

7. Ogden's Big Spectacular Uncle Tom's Cabin Company, poster, c.1900.

8. *Labor Union*, 19 Feb. 1883.

9. Massey, "Prospects of a Canadian Drama," p.197.

10. Fuller, *H.M.S. Parliament*, pp.158–93.

11. Smith, "Three Political Dramas from New Brunswick," pp.144–47.

12. Doucette, *Drama of Our Past*, pp.33, 40.

13. Ibid., pp.40, 33.

14. "The Legal Trade Union," *The Palladium of Labour*, 10 Nov. 1883.

15. Tait, "Playwrights in a Vacuum," p.13.

16. For a discussion of Mair and Curzon, see Filewod, *Performing Canada*, pp.24–29. For an analysis of Curzon's *Laura Secord*, see Derksen, "Out of the Closet."

17. Candidus, *Female Consistory of Brockville*, p.3.

18. Ibid., p.17.

19. Fuller, *Unspecific Scandal*, p.7.

20. *Toronto Globe*, 9 March 1880.

21. Lawrence, "*H.M.S. Parliament* Dramatic History," p.40.

22. "Debates of Conscience with a Distiller, a Wholesaler Dealer, and a Retailer," p.54.

23. Blagrave, "Temperance and the Theatre," p.30.

24. Cook, *"Through Sunshine and Shadow,"* p.24.

25. The pageant form that spread throughout the British Empire through the efforts of the British director Louis Napoleon Parker began as a kind of Pre-Raphaelite theatrical invocation of pre-industrial community. It circulated a romantic myth of Englishness through the empire and in the United States, where the widespread adoption of the Parker model expressed a myth of classical form. Parker's vocabulary was a conscious reference to a romantic construction of medieval theatre, in which the guilds are narrated as idealized communities that come together as creators of beauty under the guiding hand of the Pageant Master. Parker's followers retained this romantic pastoralism even as they continued his precedent of placing the pageant form at the service of the state.

26. Nelles, "Historical Pageantry and the 'Fusion of the Races.'"

27. Blagrave, "Temperance and the Theatre," p.25. The text was *Scenes and Dialogues entitled Harvest Queen Coronation*

prepared and presented for the Halifax "Cold Water Army" and Intended to Benefit the Cause of Temperance and Intelligence (Halifax: Alex. J. Richie, 1854), p.27.

28. Meek, Young People's Library of Entertainment and Amusement, p.295.

29. Doughty, ed., Selections from the Girl's Own Paper, p.73.

30. High River Self Culture Club, "Second Annual Program,"1908-1909, Glenbow Museum Archives Programs Collection.

31. Davies, ed., At the Mermaid Inn, p.67.

32. Bengough, Bengough's Chalk-Talks, pp.23, 82–83.

33. McClung, Stream Runs Fast. McClung provides a detailed description of the show, framed as fiction, in her novel The Purple Spring.

34. Bird, Redressing the Past, p.69.

35. Ibid., pp.70, 71.

36. Banks, Sir John George Bourinot, p.103; Bourinot, Parliamentary Procedure and Practice.

37. Toronto Globe, 16 March 1900.

38. Toronto Globe, 2 April 1902.

39. Moose Jaw Literary and Debating Society, Mock Parliament Program, 1903, Glenbow Museum Archives Programs Collection.

40. "College Life: The Mock Parliament," OAC Review, April 1908, pp.391–92.

41. "College Life: The Spinster's Convention," OAC Review, April 1908, pp.456–57.

42. Palladium of Labor, 18 Aug. 1883.

43. Labor Realm, 1 Jan. 1910.

44. Labor Advocate, 23 Jan. 1891.

45. Labor Advocate, 10 April 1891.

46. Heron and Penfold, Workers' Festival, p.xv. See also Davis, Parades and Power.

47. The Globe, 24 July 1882.

48. Carnes, Secret Ritual and Manhood in Victorian America, p.144.

49. Stevens, Cyclopaedia of Fraternities.

50. Jenkyns, Sovereign Great Priory of Canada, pp.118–20.

51. Burr, Canada's Victorian Oil Town, p.131.

52. Wagar, ed., Adelphon Kruptos, p.5.

53. Labor Advocate, 20 Feb. 1891. "Calithumpian" (or "callithumpian") was a common North American term for a noisy, boisterous parade. Heron and Penfold, Workers' Festival, p.14, identify such parades as "street theatre" that offered "a unique form of social or political satire aimed at both elites and lower orders, or as light entertainment for official ceremonies and private advertising." In her study of nineteenth-century Petrolia, Canada's Victorian Oil Town, p.151, Burr notes, "In 1878, the Queen's Birthday was celebrated with a Callithumpian procession that paraded the streets of Petrolia banging pots and pans, and in the tradition of anti-authoritarian burlesque ridiculed the traditional social order."

Although commonly associated with such anti-authoritarianism, the loud masculine dissidence of the calithumpian parades could uphold social order as well. Reporting on the Queen's birthday festivities in Elora in 1896, the Guelph Mercury, 28 May 1896, reported, "The calithumpians were busy all morning and about 9.30 mustered at the rink and at 10 were escorted by the Galt band through the principal streets to the grounds. The parade was a very good one. Loyalty was shown by the Queen's picture, decked with flags and maple leaves, being carried at the head of the procession."

54. Firth, Town of York 1814–1834, p.312; Mullaly, "Saint John Theatre Riot of 1845," pp.44–55.

55. Evans, Frontier Theatre, pp.62–64.

56. Ibid., p.77.

57. DeLottinville, "Joe Beef of Montreal," p.195.

58. "Canadian Voyageur," New York Times, 20 Aug. 1881.

59. Montreal by Gaslight, p.116.

60. DeLottinville, "Joe Beef of Montreal," p.193.

61. Story, "Mummers in Newfoundland History," pp.177–79.

3 Mobilized Theatre and the Invention of Agitprop

1. Sandwell, "Annexation of Our Stage," p.23.

2. Massey, "Prospects of a Canadian Drama," p.207.

3. Multicultural History Society of Ontario, *Polyphony*.

4. Skrypnyk, "First Wave of Ukrainian Immigration to Canada."

5. Wynnyckyj, "Ukrainian Canadian Drama," p.30.

6. Krawchuk, *Our Stage*, p.21.

7. Pritz, "Ukrainian Cultural Traditions in Canada," p.31.

8. Ibid., p.25.

9. Krawchuk, *Our Stage*, pp.24, 4.

10. Balan, *Salt and Braided Bread*. Dedicated historians, including Krawchuk, Balan, and Iroida Wynnyckyj, have produced detailed performance calendars that enable us to track the role of performance in community and political organization.

11. Sangster, "Robitnytsia, Ukrainian Communists, and the 'Porcupinism' Debate."

12. Roslin, "Canada's Bolshevist Drama," pp.2–3.

13. Irchan, *Skupar* [The Miser].

14. Irchan, *Pidzemma Halichina* [Undergound Galychyna].

15. Wynnyckyj, "Ukrainian Canadian Drama," pp.121, 133.

16. Wagner, "Canada: Introduction," p.84.

17. For a history of *Le Théâtre de Neptune en la Nouvelle-France*, see Wasserman, *Spectacle of Empire*. For a modern theatrical critique of the play as a "redface" show, see the discussion of *Sinking Neptune* in Wasserman, ch. 20.

18. A wide, multidisciplinary literature exists on white appropriations of indigeneity, and a growing body of work on questions of Aboriginal self-representation; but less writing has been done on the relationship of licensed self-representation and performative dissent.

19. Canada, *Indian Act 1906*, p.47.

20. Canada, Royal Commission on Aboriginal Peoples, "Attacks on Traditional Culture."

21. Bracken, *Potlatch Papers*.

22. Canada, *Indian Act 1906*, p.47.

23. Queen's Own Rifles of Canada, "Semi-Centennial Reunion and Historical Pageant," pp.24–26, 91.

24. Ibid., p.13.

25. Armstrong, *Hiawatha, the Mohawk*, p.9.

26. Ibid., p.2.

27. Godsell, "Red River Pageant."

28. Geller, "'Hudson's Bay Company Indians.'" The official record of the pageant is a photo album now in the possession of the Glenbow Museum; it is the subject of an insightful study by Geller, who examines the politics of Aboriginal performers re-enacting their history to commemorate centuries of colonialism.

29. Godsell, "Red River Pageant."

30. Ibid.

31. Godsell, "Opening Speech by Philip Godsell, at Lower Fort Garry."

32. Hudson's Bay Company, Red River Pageant Photograph Album.

33. Geller, "'Hudson's Bay Company Indians,'" pp.70, 76.

34. Godsell, "Red River Pageant."

35. Baxter, "Birth of the National Theatre," pp.27–29.

36. The Dumbells, "Original Scripts: 1917–1919."

37. Dillon et al., *P.B.I., or, Mademoiselle of Bully Grenay*.

38. Vance, *Death So Noble*, p.80.

39. Charlesworth, "Re P.B.I."

40. Dillon et al., *P.B.I., or, Mademoiselle of Bully Grenay*, p.430.

41. Ibid., pp.430, 432, 434.

42. Ibid., p.435.
43. Dillon et al., *P.B.I., or, Mademoiselle of Bully Grenay*, typescript, Act 2, Scene 1.
44. Dillon et al., *P.B.I., or, Mademoiselle of Bully Grenay*, p.469. Instead of "We've had our fun," the typescript version reads, "Ah, we have our fun," and adds, "To our Empire we'll be true."
45. Newman, *Thrones and Palaces of Babylon and Ninevah*, p.173. Newman was a bishop of the Methodist Episcopal Church; he converted Ulysses S. Grant and delivered Grant's funeral oration. For the Aberhart quotation connecting prophecy and history, see Aberhart, *Outline of Dispensational Truth Fundamental to All Bible Study*, p.1. Aberhart plagiarized this bit of wisdom from Newman's 1876 *Thrones and Palaces of Babylon and Ninevah*.
46. Aberhart and Manning, "Branding Irons of the Anti-Christ," pp.1–9.
47. Elliot and Miller, *Bible Bill*, p.104.
48. Hinton, "Aberhart-Manning Stage Play Terrified Depression-Era Audiences."
49. Bondreau, ed., *Alberta, Aberhart and Social Credit*, p.31.
50. Aberhart, Radio Broadcast, 30 June 1930. The transcription of the broadcast was made manually by the editor of the *United Farmer*, Walter Norman Smith, a long-time Aberhart opponent.
51. *The Alberta Social Credit Chronicle*, 1 Feb. 1935.
52. Quoted in Day, "William Aberhart," p.117.
53. William Aberhart Foundation, "Clifford Willmott's Memory of Aberhart."
54. Lowell, *Mars*.
55. Gernsback, *Ralph 124C41+: A Romance of the Year 2660*.
56. *The Alberta Social Credit Chronicle*, 2 Nov. 1934.
57. Elliot and Miller, *Bible Bill*, p.151; Day, "William Aberhart," p.125; *The Alberta Social Credit Chronicle*, 26 Oct. 1934.

4 Six Comrades and a Suitcase: From Agitprop to "Eight Men Speak"

1. Perhaps the most familiar image of contemporary agitprop is also the simplest: the red clown nose. When superimposed on a business suit in a public space, it conveys dissent, subversion, and ridicule. It is never subject to set procedures. The clown nose is an artifact designed to create instant spectatorship.
2. McDermid Studio Fonds, Glenbow Museum Archives.
3. Kealey and Whitaker, eds., *R.C.M.P. Security Bulletins: The Depression Years*, Part I, pp.58–59. For the photos of this event, see p.60 and front cover here.
4. Piscator, *Political Theatre* (New York: Avon), p.179.
5. Samuel, MacColl, and Cosgrove, eds., *Theatres of the Left*, p.33.
6. Ibid., p.253; Angus, *Canadian Bolsheviks*, p.23.
7. Buchwald, "ARTEF Arbeiter Theatre Verband," p.5.
8. When she married Oscar Ryan, Toby Gordon took his name, and so was known as Toby Ryan; much later in her life she used Toby Gordon Ryan when she published her memoir, *Stage Left*, in 1981. I thus refer to her variously as Toby Gordon Ryan, Toby Gordon, or Toby Ryan.
9. Hart, ed., *American Writers' Congress*, p.182.
10. Workers' Laboratory Theatre, "Open Letter," pp.36–37.
11. Bonn, "Situation and Tasks of the Workers Theatre," p.8; Alfred Saxe, "NEWSBOY – From Script to Performance," pp.12–13, 29.
12. Buchwald, "Prize Winners of the Spartakiade," pp.8–9.
13. Jones, "British Workers Theatre, 1917–1935," pp.132–33.
14. Buchwald, "First International Olympiad of Revolutionary Theatres," p.139.

15. Ibid., p.141.

16. Hart, *American Writers' Congress*, pp.131–32.

17. Bonn, "Dram Buro Report," p.8.

18. Material in this section was previously published in Filewod, "Performance and Memory in the Party."

19. By "professionalized" here I do not refer to the status of the artists but to the discourse of theatre culture as a disciplinary regime with embedded values of art, artistry, training, and stage conventions.

20. Canadian Labour Defence League (CLDL), "Minutes and Reports and Resolutions"; CLDL, Press Release, 15 Nov. 1933. For an account of the Winnipeg ban on *Eight Men Speak*, see Smith, *Joe Zuken*, pp.51–56.

21. Birney, *Down the Long Table*, p.204.

22. Cecil-Smith, "Workers' Theatre in Canada," pp.100–5; Cecil-Smith, "Growing Workers' Theatre Is Means of Dramatising the Class Struggle," p.6.

23. Ryan and Ryan, "Canadian Precedents," p.22.

24. Kealey and Whitaker, eds., *R.C.M.P. Security Bulletins: The Depression Years*, Part II, p.207.

25. Kealey and Whitaker, eds., *R.C.M.P. Security Bulletins: The Early Years*, p.337.

26. Hunter, *Which Side Are You On, Boys*, pp.64, 19.

27. Livesay, *Right Hand Left Hand*, p.74.

28. Kealey and Whitaker, *R.C.M.P. Security Bulletins: The Early Years*, p.331.

29. Ryan, *Tim Buck*, p.271.

30. "Ten Day Campaign," *Masses*, March-April, 1934, p.11.

31. Anecdotal information about Oscar Ryan and Toby Gordon Ryan comes from a series of interviews I had with them in 1987 and 1989. My initial meetings with them were cautious because, as they later told me, they had felt misrepresented by some previous researchers. One result of these interviews was Toby's decision to deposit her papers at the University of Guelph.

32. Cecil-Smith, "Workers' Theatre in Canada," p.103.

33. Samuel, *Theatres of Memory*, p.18.

34. Denning, *Cultural Front*.

35. Endres and Wright, eds., *Eight Men Speak and Other Plays*, p.x.

36. Cowan, "Red Theatre," p.3.

37. Kealey and Whitaker, *R.C.M.P. Security Bulletins: The Depression Years*, Part III, pp.198–99.

38. Ibid., p.195.

39. *Toronto Star*, 3 Dec. 1934.

40. Kealey, *R.C.M.P. Security Bulletins: The Depression Years*, Part I, p.440; *Toronto Daily Star*, 3 Dec. 1934, p.4.

41. Ryan, *Stage Left*, p.22.

42. For an account of Oscar Ryan's career as a drama critic, see Gomez, "In Anger and in Hope," pp.254–67. The account is highly circumspect and avoids any mention of the LPP, or of Oscar Ryan's organizational role in party cultural activities. Gomez identifies the *Tribune* merely as "a labour newspaper" (p.255).

43. Birney, *Down the Long Table*, pp.69–86.

44. Hannant, "'My God, Are They Sending Women?'" p.161.

45. Rifkind, *Comrades and Critics*, analyses the movement of this period in detail.

46. Ryan, *Stage Left*, p.26.

47. For further reading on Herman Voaden, see Wagner, ed., "Worlds of Herman Voaden" website. This extensive website has all of Voaden's dramatic and critical writings, and links to critical writings about his work.

48. Cowan, "Red Theatre," p.3; Thomas, "A Propertyless Theatre for a Property-less Class," pp.77–98.

49. Oscar Ryan, interview, Toronto, August 1990.

50. For "Jesus Chrysler" see Ryan, *Stage Left*, p.35; for "six comrades" see "Workers Theatre Tours Ontario," p.9; *Masses* quoted in Ryan, *Stage Left*, p.34.

51. *Masses*, July/August 1932, p.13.
52. "Theatre – Our Weapon," *Masses*, December 1932, p.5.
53. Bonn, "15-Minute Red Revue," p.306.
54. Canadian Labor Defence League, *Report*, 1933.
55. "Workers Theatre in Action," *Masses*, May-June 1933, p.11.
56. Ryan, *Stage Left*, pp.41-42; "Workers Theatre in Action," *Masses*, May-June 1933, p.11.
57. "Workers' Theatre Tours Ontario," *Masses*, September 1933, p.9.
58. "Workers Theatre in Action," *Masses*, May-June 1933, p.11.
59. Ryan, *Stage Left*, pp.28–29.
60. Ibid., p.44.
61. Ferris, "*Eight Men Speak*," p.30.
62. Quoted in Baetz, "Role of the Working Class in *Eight Men Speak*," p.40. Cecil-Smith's preface is in Ryan et al., *Eight Men Speak*, p.2.
63. Ryan, *Stage Left*, p.44.
64. Ibid., p.44.
65. For an excellent analysis of the gender politics of *Eight Men Speak*, see Rifkind, *Comrades and Critics*, pp.141–47.
66: Ryan et al., *Eight Men Speak*, p.16.
67. Ibid., p.17.
68. "Sing Out 'Red Flag'; Hiss and Boo Anthem," *Toronto Daily Star*, 5 Dec. 1933, p.5.
69. Toronto Police Commission, Minutes, 1933–1934.
70. Dorothy Livesay reprints the full text of the resolution in her memoir. See Livesay, *Right Hand Left Hand*, pp.80–82.
71. Smith, *Joe Zuken*, pp.51–56.
72. "'Eight Men Speak' Drama Is Banned in Winnipeg," *The Worker*, 12 May 1934; "Club Is Denied Use of Civic Auditorium for Protest Meeting," *Winnipeg Free Press*, 12 May 1934, pp.11–12.
73. Smith, *Joe Zuken*, p.55.
74. Wolfe, "Tim Buck, Too."
75. Adams, "Reclaiming Popular Theatre," p.15.

5 Crafting Theatre Work: Mid-Century Radicalism

1. Whittaker, "Un/Disciplined Performance."
2. Bray, "Against All Odds," pp.489–504.
3. Toby Gordon Ryan, interview, April 1988.
4. Odets, *Waiting for Lefty*, p.18, in Toby Gordon Ryan Papers, University of Guelph.
5. Left Book Club Theatre Guild, *Notes on Forming 'Left' Theatre Groups*, pp.1–2.
6. Chambers, *Story of Unity Theatre*, pp.41–42.
7. Postcard note, Clifford Odets Papers.
8. Theatre of Action, "A Theatre in Action," p.1.
9. Ryan, *Stage Left*, pp.90, 101. The New Theatre Group has been documented in some detail, chiefly by Toby Gordon Ryan, whose scrapbooks of reviews, posters, and programs from the productions form the core of her memoir. They are complemented by interviews with participants from Toronto, Montreal, Winnipeg, and Vancouver, which provide rich and detailed information on the histories and memberships of the groups.
10. Theatre of Action, "Five One-Act Plays" program.
11. Ryan, *Stage Left*, p.110.
12. Ibid., p.141.
13. New Theatre Group, Montreal, "Bury the Dead" program.
14. Ryan, *Stage Left*, p.238.
15. Theatre of Action, Minutes Book, 1939–40.
16. Ryan, *Stage Left*, pp.214, 215.
17. Orchard, cited in Ryan, *Stage Left*, p.78.
18. Krawchuk, *Interned without Cause*.
19. Halladay, "Lovely War," p.25.
20. Canadian Armed Forces, "Meet The Navy," souvenir program; Canada,

Department of National Defence, *Army Show*.

21. Canada, Royal Commission, *Massey Report*, p.275.

22. Schwam, "Stratford Festival."

23. The name of the troupes is spelled variously as "Play-Actors," "Play Actors," and "Playactors." In her memoir Toby Gordon Ryan uses "Play Actors," but the troupe's programs and correspondence include the hyphen.

24. Canada, Royal Commission, *Massey Report*, pp.193–94.

25. Rubin, "Creeping Towards a Culture," p.322.

26. Endres and Wright, eds., *Eight Men Speak and Other Plays*, p.25.

27. Benson and Conolly, *English-Canadian Theatre*, p.59.

28. Stewart, "People's Culture Flourishes."

29. Doyle, *Progressive Heritage*, p.189. Doyle documents this work in detail.

30. "Rising Tide of Resistance to U.S. Cultural Invasion," *Canadian Tribune*, 15 April 1952.

31. "War, Culture Cannot Be Separated, Is View of Massey Royal Commission," *Canadian Tribune*, 11 Feb. 1951.

32. "On the Right to Culture," *Canadian Tribune*, 8 May 1950.

33. "Labour Progressive Party," *Canadian Tribune*, 4 May 1953.

34. "They're out to Build a People's Theatre," *Canadian Tribune*, 17 April 1950.

35. "Repeat Performance of No Time to Cry," *Canadian Tribune*, 21 Jan. 1952.

36. Ibid.

37. Bromstein, "Announcing the New Paul Bunyan Drive."

38. McEwan, "Paul Bunyan."

39. Bromstein, Holmes, and Holmes, "Little Paul Bunyan," p.2.

40. Ibid., p.4.

41. Ibid., p.7.

42. Ibid., pp.18–19.

43. Ibid., p.20.

44. Ibid., p.19; "Little Paul Bunyan a Triumph," *Canadian Tribune*, 24 Jan. 1955.

45. Ryan, *Stage Left*, p.132.

46. Typescript found in Toby Gordon Ryan papers.

47. "Cheers Followed Theatre Night," *Canadian Tribune*, 12 May 1952.

48. "The Play Actors, Ethnic Alliance," *Globe and Mail*, 1 May 1954.

49. "Taking up the Tradition of the 30's Theatre of Action," *Canadian Tribune*, 20 April 1953; Play-Actors, "Play-Actors Letter."

50. "The Play-Actors' Debut," *Canadian Tribune*, 11 May 1953.

51. Play-Actors, *Tecumseh* press release, 4 Feb. 1954. For a discussion of the Play-Actors' treatment of Tecumseh, seen in the context of the play's stage history, see Filewod, "National Battles," pp.71–86.

52. Ryan, *Stage Left*, p.222.

53. Michel, "Play-Actors Produce Play That Moved Lawmakers."

54. Ibid.

55. Toby Gordon Ryan, Letter to Herbert Whittaker, 22 May 1954.

56. Penner, "My Life in Art."

57. "Theatre," *Canadian Tribune*, 9 May 1955.

58. Toby Gordon Ryan, Letter to Roland Penner, 4 May 1955.

59. Ibid., p.223.

60. Friedlander, "Survivor: George Luscombe," p.46.

61. MacColl, *Journeyman*, p.208; Littlewood, *Joan's Book*, p.91. MacColl was known as "Jimmy Miller" when Littlewood first met him.

62. Goorney, *Theatre Workshop Story*, p.7.

63. Laban and Lawrence, *Effort*, p.8.

64. Theatre ensembles, like left political collectives, have a tendency to become the reflexive targets of their own critical practice – or, in theatre terms, become the rehearsal of their antiauthoritarian politics.

65. Carson, *Harlequin in Hogtown*, pp.65–66.

66. Halferty, "Theatrical Protest before Gay Liberation," p.29. Cited with permission.
67. Rubin, "Creeping Towards a Culture," p.328; Johnston, *Up the Mainstream*. In fairness, I must admit that I too took a similar position in my writings at the time.
68. Vogt, *Critical Stages*, p.140.

6 Generation Agitprop, with Puppets

1. I define the theatrical sixties broadly, as being from roughly 1964 to 1974. The period begins with the visit of the San Francisco Mime Troupe to Vancouver in 1964 and ends in 1974, the year the Mummers Troupe collaborated with a United Steelworkers local in Buchans to create *Company Town* and George Luscombe produced *Ten Lost Years*. Periodization is always a blunt instrument, but this method locates the "decade" as the period between theatrical stirrings in the new countercultural radicalism and student activism in the peace movement at one end, and the move to solidarity collaboration with labour at the other.
2. By "hippies," I do not mean to reduce generational dissent to a media cliché, but use the term to describe those who would have been seen and described as hippies at the time.
3. "Guerilla Act Didn't Entertain Trustees," *Toronto Telegram*, 8 Feb. 1971, p.15.
4. Brover, "Some Notes in Defense of Combative Theater," p.38.
5. Giap, *People's War, People's Army*, p.104.
6. Palmer, *Canada's 1960s*, p.246.
7. Brookes, Rehearsal Diaries, 1973.
8. Mummers Troupe, "What's That Got to Do with the Price of Fish?" p.1.
9. Brookes, Rehearsal Diaries.
10. Richard and Robertson, *Performance in Canada*, p.96.
11. Bread and Puppet Theater, "Cheap Art Philosophy."
12. "CURSES," *Georgia Straight*, 8-13 April 1971, p.17.
13. Barker, "Alternative Theatre/Political Theatre," p.32.
14. Brookes, "Coronation of Cecil B. DeMille."
15. Brookes, *Public Nuisance*, p.46.
16. *Georgia Straight*, 21-27 May 1969, p.3.
17. Angel, "The Bribe."
18. "Street Theatre Trial," *Vancouver Free Press*, 26 June-2 July 1969, p.8.
19. "Park Players Jailed by Pigs," *Georgia Straight*, 2-15 July 1969, p.1; Angel, "Pigs on Horses and Other Street Marvels of the Sixties," pp.20, 22.
20. Leonard Angel, interview, May 2008.
21. David Anderson, interview, 3 April 2008.
22. Sarah Barker, interview, 10 April 2008.
23. Ibid.
24. Ibid.
25. David Anderson, interview.
26. Great Canadian Theatre Company, Minutes, 7 Feb. 1975; Great Canadian Theatre Company, Board of Management, Minutes, 23 March 1975.
27. Robin Mathews, Letter to the Board of Management, 1 May 1979.
28. The Gaspé Manifesto, "Strange Enterprise," p.302.
29. Ibid., p.304.
30. Robin Mathews, "Letter to the Editor," p.134.
31. Great Canadian Theatre Company, "Members Handbook," 1978.
32. Mathews, "Letter to the Editor," p.134.
33. Great Canadian Theatre Company, "Members Handbook."
34. Macdonald, "Production Notes for The Big Nickel," pp.1–6.
35. Bouzek, "Industrials for the Social Services," p.10.
36. Macdonald, "Production Notes for The Big Nickel."
37. In conversation, Arthur Milner, a playwright and artistic director of

the GCTC from 1991 to 1995, once alluded to this point when discussing the decision to create *Sandinista!* collectively. It was not a decision based on theatrical ideology, but on rehearsal efficiency. The process of collective creation was the shortest way to write, rehearse, and produce a play to a tight deadline.

38. Jackson, "Union Activism Punjabi Theatre in BC," p.11.

39. Ibid.

40. Ibid., p.12

41. Pollock, *STRIKE!* p.19.

42. As is invariably the case today with theatre made by young activists, *STRIKE! The play* was uploaded to YouTube.

43. Pollock, *STRIKE!* pp.6-8.

44. Gabe Pollock, email to the author.

7 A Case of Cultural Sabotage: The Mummers Troupe

1. Kilbourn et al., "Canada Council and Theatre," p.179.

2. Brookes, *Public Nuisance*, p.160.

3. Brookes, his employees, and the Canada Council had conflicting expectations of how the company should operate; it was in no small part because in the theatre the term "company" is a shifting formation that conveys two distinct but overlapping meanings. On the one hand the term is used as it is in business, to describe the corporate entity; on the other the term retains its older theatrical meaning of the troupe of artists engaged in a particular production. Thus in the theatre the company employs the company and the company is employed by the company. The ambivalent referents are always poised to slide into conflict unless contained by clearly defined policies. In the Mummers' case, this conflict was complicated by the use of "troupe" as part of the corporation's operating name.

4. Brookes, Letter to Sabourin, 1972. At the time this material was compiled the papers were privately held.

5. Resource Foundation for the Arts, Articles of Incorporation, 1973.

6. Brookes, *Public Nuisance*, p.71.

7. For an account of the context, rehearsals, and performance of *Gros Mourn*, see Brookes, *Public Nuisance*. His chapter on *Gros Mourn* appears in Brookes, "Seize the Day," in *Popular Political Theatre and Performance*, ed. Salverson, pp.1–13.

8. Chris Brookes, interview, January 1980; Brookes, *Public Nuisance*, p.99.

9. Mummers Troupe, Canada Council Correspondence.

10. Brookes, Letter to Muriel Sherrin, 15 Nov. 1973.

11. Mummers Troupe, Minutes, "Meeting re Proposed Newfoundland Theatre Company."

12. Turnbull, Letter to David Peacock, 6 May 1974.

13. Brookes, *Public Nuisance*, p.160.

14. Canada Council for the Arts, Mummers Troupe Grant Applications, A-75-1066, box 23. The letter continued, "Council is pleased to note your success in bringing in a writer of the calibre of Rick Salutin to work with you. It is exactly this kind of development which it is hoped the increase in your grant will allow you to carry out." Implicit in this statement is the pressure to develop a text-based dramaturgy that valorizes the playwright – that is, the creation of national literature – as the purpose of theatrical work. A writer of "calibre" can only be useful if he or she retools the theatre to produce more writers.

15. Canada Council for the Arts, Mummers Troupe Grant Applications, A-76-0315, box 15.

16. Locke, "Brief History of the LSPU Hall."

17. Mummers Troupe, Minutes, February 1976.

18. Mummers Troupe, Untitled Manifesto, 26 July 1976.

19. Canada Council for the Arts, Mummers Troupe Grant Applications, A-75-1066, box 23.

20. Ibid., A-76-0315, box 15.

21. Ibid.

22. Ibid.

23. Brookes, "Federal Funding Cutbacks to the Arts," November 1978.

24. Canada Council for the Arts, Mummers Troupe Grant Applications, A-77-0133, box 8.

25. The Mummers Troupe was not the only company in Canada to argue that its work had to be judged on its own terms and in its own context: the same argument could be heard throughout the growing community of marginally funded popular theatres that addressed concerns of interest to women, gays and lesbians, ethnic minorities, and the political margins. Nor were these arguments confined to Canada; Brookes' arguments with Canada Council were remarkably parallel to the problems that John McGrath was encountering in Scotland with his political 7:84 Theatre Company at the same time. John McGrath's struggles with the Scottish Arts Council are described in detail in his memoir *The Bone Won't Break: On Theatre and Hope in Hard Times* (1990).

26. For a description and analysis of the production and tour of *They Club Seals, Don't They?* see Filewod, *Performing Canada*, ch.4, "Dissent on Ice: The Mummers Enact the Public Sphere."

27. Rising Tide would later obtain the funding commitments that Brookes could not, eventually securing residency status at the Arts and Culture Centre in St. John's, performing topical collective revues and British and American dramas under the artistic direction of Donna Butt. It went on to develop local playwrights and to stage the annual Seasons in the Bight festival in the historic village of Trinity. Butt was inducted into the Order of Canada in 2004.

28. Learning, Letter to Board of Directors, Kam Lab Theatre, 27 Sept. 1979.

29. Brookes, Letter to Learning, 14 July 1979.

30. Canada Council for the Arts, Mummers Troupe Grant Applications, 241-79-0009, box 35.

31. Learning, Letter to Client Theatres, 13 Dec. 1979; Learning, Letter to Board of Directors, Kam Lab Theatre, 27 Sept. 1979.

32. Sobota, Letter to Brookes, 5 Sept. 1979.

33. Brookes, *Public Nuisance*, p.155.

34. Locke, "Brief History of the LSPU Hall."

35. Lunde, Letter to Brookes, May 1975.

36. Mummers Troupe, Unsigned Motion.

37. Mummers Troupe Ltd., Incorporation papers, 1979.

38. Riggio, Open Letter.

39. Mummers Troupe, Public Meeting, "Possible Motions," 14 Aug. 1979; Jones, Letter to Brookes et al., 15 Aug, 1979.

40. Resource Centre for the Arts, *Annual Report*, 1979.

41. Rhonda Payne was born in Newfoundland but raised primarily in Ontario. She began her theatre career with the Newfoundland Travelling Theatre in 1974 and joined the Mummers in 1975. She was a major voice in the Mummers to the end; despite her occasional difficulties with Brookes (who fired her in 1976 but rehired her in 1978), she eventually succeeded him as artistic director in 1980. Later she had her own company, Riverbank Productions in Peterborough, Ontario. She died in 2002.

8 Powering Structures and Popular Theatre

1. Anderson, Michol, and Silverberg, *Ready for Action*, p.6.

2. Ibid., p.56.

3. Ibid.

4. Prentki and Selman, *Popular Theatre in Political Culture*, p.8.

5. Evans, *In the National Interest*, pp.163–64.

6. Freire, *Pedagogy of the Oppressed*, p.95.

7. For a detailed study of Catalyst's early interactive work, see Filewod, "Interactive Documentary in Canada," pp.133–47.

8. The scenario of "Empty Plates" comes from my own personal notes from the workshop. I kept detailed notebooks, filled in during the workshop, including a typescript of the whole play.

9. In his *Lehrstücke* ("learning plays"), such as *The Measures Taken*, Brecht essentially took agitprop off the streets and into the classroom. The actors model an ideological or political problem in a stylized, highly rhetorical performance. In *He Who Says Yes* and *He Who Says No,* he makes slight changes in the modelling of the ethical problem to produce equally logical but opposite solutions, thereby demonstrating that agitprop is not an ideologically determined form. See Brecht, *Measures Taken and Other Lehrstucke.*

10. Prentki and Selman, *Popular Theatre in Political Culture*, p.78.

11. Canadian Popular Theatre Alliance, "Principles and Objectives." The original draft principles are written by hand in my own notebook from the Bread and Circuses Festival, Kam Theatre Lab, Thunder Bay, Ont., 1981.

12. Ibid.

13. Ground Zero Productions, "Popular Theatre Workers Retreat, Statement of Principles," Peterborough, Ont., 19 July 1992.

14. Salverson, "Popular Theatre Workers Retreat," pp.1–2. The Peterborough draft was compiled by Salverson and not published until 1998 (when a new initiative to restart the CPTA resulted in a briefly lived newsletter).

15. International Theatre of the Oppressed Organization, "Declaration of Principles."

16. Boal, *Theatre of the Oppressed*, p.155. For the Boal quote that opens this section, see Crowder, "Standin' the Gaff," pp.73–75. As Crowder explains, Boal was expressing impatience with the tendency of Canadian participants to worry about hurt feelings in the workshop.

17. McGauley, "Super(stack) Inspiration," p.37.

18. Ibid., p.36.

19. "Are We There Yet?": Using Theatre in Teen Sexuality Education/ Community University Research Alliance, "The Results – Evaluation Research."

20. For overviews, see Beveridge and Johnston, *Making Our Mark*; and *Canadian Theatre Review* 99 (Summer 1999): *Theatre and Labour*. For case studies of Canadian and Australian and British labour theatre projects, see Filewod and Watt, *Workers' Playtime.* The development of labour arts projects in Canada has been well documented, especially in detailed case studies of specific projects by theatre and labour scholars and in overview surveys, such as Beveridge and Johnston, *Making Our Mark*, which includes documentation on ten theatre projects developed in collaboration with unions, and *Canadian Theatre Review*'s 1999 theme issue on Theatre and Labour.

21. O'Neill and Schwartz, "Westray," p.26.

22. Prentki and Selman, *Popular Theatre in Political Culture*, p.78.

23. Barrie, *Straight Stitching*, p.91.

24. Ibid., p.97.

25. Ibid., p.92.

26. Bonn, "Dram Buro Report," p.10; McGrath, *Good Night Out*; Boal, *Theatre of the Oppressed*, p.109; Ryga, Keynote

Address, Bread & Circuses Festival, 1981.

27. Grant, "Still 'Activist' after All These Years?" p.15.
28. Hale, "Ballrooms and Boardroom Tables," pp.31–32.
29. Jordão, "Playwriting in Canadian Popular Theatre," p.100.
30. Hale, "Ballrooms and Boardroom Tables," p.31.
31. Hurford, ed., *Under Broken Wings*, p.60.
32. Jordão, "Playwriting in Canadian Popular Theatre," p.99.
33. Company of Sirens, "Report of Performances 1990-1991."
34. Ibid.
35. Grant, "Still 'Activist' after All These Years?" p.16.
36. Filewod and Watt, *Workers' Playtime*, p.236.
37. Hill Strategies Research, *Finances of Performing Arts Organizations*, 2008.
38. Conseil des arts et des lettres du Québec, *Subventions et bourses accordées aux organismes*; Ontario Arts Council, *Current List Of Grant Recipients*; British Columbia Arts Council, *Annual Report 2007-8*, p.7.
39. Théâtre Parminou, "Intervention Theatre: The Conception and Realization Process"; Théâtre Parminou, "Intervention Theatre: Social Issues."
40. Labelle and Labelle, "Human Trafficking."
41. Martineau, "Théâtre Parminou," p.7.
42. Ibid., p.9; Théâtre Parminou, Rencontres Internationales de Théâtre d'Intervention.
43. Diamond, *Theatre for Living*.
44. Headlines Theatre, "Components of Theatre for Living."
45. Diamond, *Theatre for Living*, p.19.
46. Diamond, "In This Moment," p.10.
47. One example of this chill is the nervousness that theatres have shown about Katharine Viner and Alan Rickman's verbatim documentary play, *My Name Is Rachel Corrie*, based on letters by the young American peace activist killed in an Israeli military operation while volunteering as a human shield for Palestinian civilians. In 2006 the Canadian Stage Company abruptly cancelled an announced production of the play. See Ouzonian, "'Corrie' Canceled in Canada."
48. Diamond, "Squeegee Report," pp.60–82. The final lawyer's report, and Diamond's own report, are posted on the company's website (www.headlinestheatre.com). The site serves as a digital history of the company and may be the most comprehensive online archive of production documentation and evaluation yet produced by a Canadian theatre.
49. Diamond, *Theatre for Living*, pp.287–95.
50. Bouzek, Letter to Alan Filewod, 10 Oct. 1997.
51. Bouzek, Letter to Department of National Revenue, 7 May 1986.
52. Bouzek, Letter to Caroline Lulham, 17 Nov. 1996. This six-page letter outlining his personal history and principles was written as a response to a questionnaire sent to popular theatre workers by a student at Mount Allison University, Sackville, N.B.
53. Bouzek, Letter to Department of National Revenue, 7 May 1986.
54. Bouzek, interview with Scott Duchesne; Bouzek, Letter to Filewod, 26 Oct. 1997.
55. Bouzek, Letter to Alan Filewod.
56. Ibid.
57. Canada Council for the Arts, Ground Zero Production Grant Notification, 1988; Canada Council for the Arts, Searchable Grant Listings: Alberta 2008.

9 Out There: Digital Streets, Chaos Aesthetics, Heritage Guerrillas

1. Diamond, "In This Moment," p.13.

2. Rogers, "Banner Theatre – What Kind of Theatre?"

3. For a study of Charles Parker and the origin of the Radio Ballads, see Watt, "Maker and the Tool," pp.41–66.

4. Filewod, *Collective Encounters*, p.146.

5. *The Clinton Special*, dir. Michael Ondaatje, 1974.

6. Roach, *Cities of the Dead.*

7. Banner Theatre's website <www.bannertheatre.co.uk/> contains detailed information about its history and project.

8. Dunn and Ground Zero Productions, "Troublemakers," 2004. (In this case, because of the historical material, the voiceovers were recorded by actors.)

9. *13 Experiments in Hope*, Laboratory of Insurrectionary Imagination, 2005.

10. For the translation of the speech, see <vacuum.org.uk/drbranson./>.

11. O'Donnell, *Social Acupuncture*, pp.13, 17.

12. Ibid., p.15.

13. O'Donnell, *Pppeeeaaaccceee.*

14. O'Donnell, *Social Acupuncture*, p.13.

15. Mammalian Diving Reflex, "Social Acupuncture."

16. O'Donnell, *Social Acupuncture*, p.19.

17. Fennario, *Joe Beef.*

18. Optative Theatrical Laboratories, Radical Dramaturgy Unit, "Sinking Neptune," pp.202–15.

19. King, "Optative Theatre," p.iii.

20. Optative Theatre Laboratories, "Mandate."

21. See Wasserman, S*pectacle of Empire*, and Filewod, *Performing Canada.*

22. King, "*Sinking Neptune*," pp.199–201.

23. Filewod, *Performing Canada*, p.xvii.

24. Optative, "*Sinking Neptune*," p.202.

25. Ibid., p.203.

26. Roach, *Cities of the Dead*, p.2.

27. King, "*Sinking Neptune*," p.199.

28. Optative Theatrical Laboratories, Radical Dramaturgy Unit, "*Sinking Neptune*," p.210.

29. Optative Theatre Laboratories, "Artists Still Waiting for Box Office Cash." The website contains three downloadable examples of "collections" and a downloadable archive of documents, press reports, and letters.

30. The language of mummers plays is never standard, and always local. The phrase "inky dinky white drops of life" comes from the Mummers Troupe's 1975 Christmas production of its mummers script, cobbled together from various versions remembered in rural Newfoundland.

31. Dorosh, *Canuck*; Lee, *Soldat.*

32. Fussell, *Uniforms*, pp.127, 131.

33. Suthren, "Unlikely Thespians," pp.5–8.

34. Schoen, *Klingon Hamlet.*

Coda: Out There, In Here

1. See O'Donnell, *Social Acupuncture*, and ch.9 here.

2. Atkinson et al., "Strong Breast Revolution," pp.13–14.

3. Read, "Play Launches Calendar for Breast of Canada."

Bibliography

1. Archives and Archival Collections

Archives of Ontario. Attorney Generals Papers.

Chris Brookes Papers. Personal collection, St. John's, Nfld.

Clifford Odets Papers, Billy Rose Collection, New York Public Library.

Glenbow Museum Archives. Calgary.

Great Canadian Theatre Company Archives. L.W. Conolly Theatre Archives, McLaughlin Library, University of Guelph.

Ground Zero Papers. L.W. Conolly Theatre Archives, McLaughlin Library, University of Guelph.

Library and Archives Canada.

Mummers Troupe Papers. Centre for Newfoundland Studies Archives, Memorial University of Newfoundland.

Theatre Passe Muraille Archives. L.W. Conolly Theatre Archives, McLaughlin Library, University of Guelph.

Robert S. Kenny Collection. Thomas Fisher Rare Books Library, University of Toronto.

Toby Gordon Ryan Papers. L.W. Conolly Theatre Archives, McLaughlin Library, University of Guelph.

Toronto Police Archives.

2. Unattributed Articles

"Canadian Tradition Flouted." Editorial. *Toronto Star*, 23 June 1955.

"Cheers Followed Theatre Night." *Canadian Tribune*, 12 May 1952.

"Club Is Denied Use of Civic Auditorium for Protest Meeting." *Winnipeg Free Press*, 12 May 1934, pp.11–12.

"College Life: The Mock Parliament." *OAC Review* 20,7 (April 1908), pp.391–92.

"College Life: The Spinster's Convention." *OAC Review* 20,7 (April 1908), pp.456–57.

"CURSES." *Georgia Straight* (Vancouver), April 8-13, 1971, p.17.

"Debates of Conscience with a Distiller, a Wholesaler Dealer, and a Retailer." In *A Collection of Temperance Dialogues for Divisions of Sons, Good Templar Lodges, Sections of Cadets, Band of Hope, and Other Temperance Societies*, ed. S.T. Hammond. Ottawa: Hunter, Ross and Co, 1869.

"'Eight Men Speak' Drama Is Banned in Winnipeg." *The Worker*, 12 May 1934.

"Guerilla Act Didn't Entertain Trustees." *Toronto Telegram*, 8 Feb. 1971, p.15.

"Labour Progressive Party." *Canadian Tribune*, 4 May 1953.

"The Legal Trade Union." *The Palladium of Labour*, 10 Nov. 1883.

"Little Paul Bunyan a Triumph." *Canadian Tribune*, 24 Jan. 1955.

"On the Right to Culture." *Canadian Tribune*, 8 May 1950.

"Park Players Jailed by Pigs." *Georgia Straight* (Vancouver), 2–15 July 1969, p.1.

"Repeat Performance of No Time to Cry." *Canadian Tribune*, 21 Jan. 1952.

"Rising Tide of Resistance to U.S. Cultural Invasion." *Canadian Tribune*, 15 April 1952

"Sing Out 'Red Flag'; Hiss and Boo Anthem: Standard Theatre Crowd See Satire on Tim Buck's Imprisonment." *Toronto Daily Star*, 5 Dec. 1933, p.5.

"Street Theatre Trial." *Vancouver Free Press*, 26 June-2 July 1969, p.8.

"Taking up the Tradition of the 30's Theatre of Action." *Canadian Tribune*, 20 April 1953.

"Ten Day Campaign." *Masses*, March-April 1934, p.11.

"The Canadian Voyageur: Continuing the Descent of the St. Lawrence. Some Information. Montreal. Joe Beef's Canteen. Bound for Quebec." *New York Times*, 20 Aug. 1881.

"The Dynasts." *Toronto World*, Editorial, 18 Feb. 1916.

"The Play Actors, Ethnic Alliance." *Globe and Mail* (Toronto), 1 May 1954.

"The Play-Actors' Debut." *Canadian Tribune*, 11 May 1953.

"Theatre – Our Weapon." *Masses* 1,7 (December 1932).

"Theatre." *Canadian Tribune*, 9 May 1955.

"They're Out to Build a People's Theatre." *Canadian Tribune*, 17 April 1950.

"War, Culture Cannot Be Separated, Is View of Massey Royal Commission." *Canadian Tribune*, 11 Feb. 1951.

"Workers Theatre in Action." *Masses* 2,9 (May-June 1933).

"Workers' Theatre Tours Ontario." *Masses* 2,10 (September 1933).

3. Articles and Books

Aberhart, William. *An Outline of Dispensational Truth Fundamental to All Bible Study, Section 1: Three Introductory Lectures on God's Great Prophecies.* Calgary: Calgary Prophetic Bible Institute, c. 1925. <www.aberhartfoundation.ca/Pages/Preacher.htm #RadioPropConfDocs>.

Aberhart, William and Ernest Manning. "Branding Irons of the Anti-Christ." In *Aberhart: Outpourings and Replies*, ed. David Elliot. Calgary: Historical Society of Alberta, 1997.

Adams, Rose. "Reclaiming Popular Theatre." In *Popular Political Theatre and Performance*, ed. Julie Salverson. Toronto: Playwrights Canada Press, 2010.

Anderson, Jennifer, Jennifer Michol, and Joshua Silverberg. *Ready for Action: A Popular Theatre Popular Education Manual.* Waterloo, Ont.: Waterloo Public Interest Group (WPIRG), 1994.

Angus, Ian. "A Stalinist and Nationalist View of Art." *Labor Challenge*, 24 Feb. 1975.

_____. *Canadian Bolsheviks: The Early Years of the Communist Party of Canada.* Montreal: Vanguard, 1981.

Armstrong, L.O. *Hiawatha, the Mohawk: The Lake Champlain Tercentenary Pageant, 1909.* Kahnawake, Que.: Kanien'kehaka Raotitiohkwa Cultural Center, 1981.

Baetz, Elaine M. "The Role of the Working Class in *Eight Men Speak*." MA thesis, University of Guelph, 1988.

Balan, Jars. *Salt and Braided Bread: Ukrainian Life in Canada.* Toronto: Oxford University Press, 1984.

Banks, Margaret. *Sir John George Bourinot, Victorian Canadian: His Life, Times and Legacy.* Montreal and Kingston: McGill-Queen's University Press, 2001.

Barker, Clive. "Alternative Theatre/Political Theatre." In *The Politics of Theatre and Drama*, ed. Graham Holderness. London: Macmillan, 1992.

Barrie, Shirley. *Straight Stitching.* In *New Canadian Drama 5: Political Drama*, ed. Alan Filewod. Ottawa: Borealis Press, 1991.

Baxter, Arthur Beverly. "The Birth of the National Theatre." *Maclean's Magazine*, 29 Feb. 1916, pp.27–29.

Bengough, J.W. *Bengough's Chalk-Talks: A Series of Platform Addresses on Various Topics, with Reproductions of the Impromptu Drawings with Which They Were Illustrated.* Toronto: Musson, 1922.

Benson, Eugene and L.W. Conolly. *English Canadian Theatre.* Toronto: Oxford University Press, 1987.

Beveridge, Karl and Jude Johnston. *Making Our Mark: Labour Arts and Heritage in Ontario.* Toronto: Between the Lines, 1999.

Bird, John. "New Changing Guard Ritual Fine for Tourists, but How Canadian Is It?" *Toronto Star,* 1 Aug. 1949, p.7.

Bird, Kym. *Redressing the Past: The Politics of Early English-Canadian Women's Drama, 1880–1920.* Montreal: McGill-Queen's University Press, 2004.

Birney, Earle. *Down the Long Table.* Toronto: McClelland and Stewart, 2004.

Blagrave, Mark. "Temperance and the Theatre in the Nineteenth Century Maritimes." *Theatre History in Canada/Histoire du Théâtre au Canada* 7,1 (1986), pp.23–32.

Boal, Augusto. *Theatre of the Oppressed.* Trans. Charles McBride and Maria-Odilia Leal McBride. New York: Urizen Books, 1979.

———. *The Rainbow of Desire: The Boal Method of Theatre and Therapy.* Trans. Adrian Jackson. London: Routledge, 1995.

Bondreau, Joseph, ed. *Alberta, Aberhart and Social Credit: Canadian History through the Press Series.* Toronto: Holt, Rinehart and Winston of Canada, 1975.

Bonn, John E. "Situation and Tasks of the Workers Theatres of the U.S.A.: A Report to the First National Workers Theatre Conference Held in New York, April 17." *Workers Theatre* 2,3 (June-July 1932), p.8.

———. "15-Minute Red Revue." In *Theatres of the Left 1880-1935: Workers' Theatre Movements in Britain and America,* ed. Raphael Samuel, Ewan MacColl, and

Stuart Cosgrove. London: Routledge and Kegan Paul, 1985.

———. "Dram Buro Report." In "First National Workers Theatre Conference on the Developing Prospects, and Tasks of the Workers Theatre in the United States." *Workers Theatre,* May 1932, pp.8–10.

Bourinot, John George. *Parliamentary Procedure and Practice with an Introductory Account of the Origin and Growth of Parliamentary Institutions in the Dominion of Canada.* Montreal: Dawson Bros, 1884.

Bouzek, Don. "Industrials for the Social Services." *Canadian Theatre Review* 99 (Summer 1999), pp.10–15.

Bracken, Christopher. *The Potlatch Papers: A Colonial Case History.* Chicago: University of Chicago Press, 1997.

Bray, Bonita. "Against All Odds: The Progressive Arts Club's Production of *Waiting for Lefty.*" *Journal of Canadian Studies* 25, 3 (1990), pp.489–504.

Brecht, Bertolt. "On Gestic Music." In *Brecht on Theatre,* ed. John Willett. London: Methuen, 1986.

———. "The Theatre Communist." In *Bertolt Brecht Poems,* ed. John Willett and Ralph Manheim. London: Eyre Methuen, 1976.

———. *The Meaures Taken and Other Lehrstucke.* Trans. Carl R. Mueller et al. London: Eyre Methuen, 1977.

Bromstein, Rube, John Holmes, and Mary Holmes. "Little Paul Bunyan." Transcript with imprint. Toronto: Champion Publishing Association, 1955. Robert S. Kenny Collection, Thomas Fisher Rare Books Library, University of Toronto.

———. "Announcing the New Paul Bunyan Drive." *Champion* 14 Jan. 1956.

Brookes, Chris. "Seize the Day: The Mummer's Gros Mourn." In *Popular Political Theatre and Performance,* ed. Julie Salverson. Toronto: Playwrights Canada, 2010.

_____. *A Public Nuisance: A History of the Mummers Troupe.* St. John's, Nfld.: Institute for Social and Economic Research, 1988.

Brover, Charles. "Some Notes in Defense of Combative Theater." In *Guerilla Street Theater*, ed. Henry Lesnick. New York: Avon, 1973.

Buchwald, Nathaniel. "The Prize Winners of the Spartakiade." *Workers Theatre*, June-July 1932, pp.8–9.

_____. "ARTEF Arbeiter Theatre Verband." *Workers Theatre*, February 1932.

_____. "The First International Olympiad of Revolutionary Theatres." *International Literature 4*, 1933, p.139.

Burr, Christina. *Canada's Victorian Oil Town: The Transformation of Petrolia from a Resource Town into a Victorian Community.* Montreal: McGill-Queen's University Press, 2006.

Butsch, Richard. *The Making of American Audiences: From Stage to Television, 1750–1990.* Cambridge, N.Y.: Cambridge University Press, 2000.

Canada. Army. Canadian Expeditionary Force. *Oh, Canada! A Medley of Stories, Verse, Pictures, and Music Contributed by Members of the Canadian Expeditionary Force.* London: Simpkin, Marshall, Hamilton, Kent and Co., 1917.

Canada. Department of National Defence. *The Army Show.* Program. Glenbow Museum Archives Program Collection.

Canada. Royal Commission on Aboriginal Peoples. "Attacks on Traditional Culture." In *Report*, vol.1, *Looking Forward Looking Back.* Sc. 9.5: <www.collectionscanada.gc.ca/webarchives>.

Canada. Royal Commission on National Development in Arts, Letters and Sciences. *Report [Massey Report].* Ottawa: The King's Printer, 1951.

Canada. *The Indian Act 1906.* Ottawa: The King's Printer, 1920.

Candidus, Caroli. *The Female Consistory of Brockville: A Melo-Drama in Three Acts.* Brockville, Ont.: Printed for the Author, 1856.

Carnes, Mark. *Secret Ritual and Manhood in Victorian America.* New Haven, Conn.: Yale University Press, 1989.

Carson, Neil. *Harlequin in Hogtown: George Luscombe and Toronto Workshop Productions.* Toronto: University of Toronto Press, 1995.

Cecil-Smith, Edward. "Growing Workers' Theatre Is Means of Dramatising the Class Struggle." *The Worker*, 3 March 1934, p.6.

_____. "The Workers' Theatre in Canada." In *Canadian Theatre History: Selected Readings*, ed. Don Rubin. Toronto: Copp Clark, 1996.

Chambers, Colin. *The Story of Unity Theatre.* New York: St. Martin's Press, 1989.

Charlesworth, Hector. "Re P.B.I." *Saturday Night*, 20 March 1920.

_____. "Re The Dynasts." *Saturday Night*, 19 Feb. 1916.

Cook, Sharon. *"Through Sunshine and Shadow": The Woman's Christian Temperance Union, Evangelicalism, and Reform in Ontario, 1874-1930.* Montreal: McGill-Queen's University Press, 1995.

Cowan, Andrew Gillespie. "Red Theatre." *Masses* 1, 3 (June 1932), p.3.

Crowder, Eleanor. "Standin' the Gaff: Assessing Boal." *Canadian Theatre Review* 53 (Winter 1987), pp.73–75.

Davies, Barrie, ed. *At the Mermaid Inn: Wilfred Campbell, Archibald Lampman, Duncan Campbell Scott in The Globe, 1892–93.* Toronto: University of Toronto Press, 1979.

Davis, Susan. *Parades and Power: Street Theatre in Nineteenth-Century Philadelphia.* Berkeley: University of California Press, 1986.

Day, Moira. "William Aberhart: The Evangelist as Subversive Political Dramatist." *Theatre Research in Canada* 11, 2 (Fall 1990), p.117.

DeLottinville, Peter. "Joe Beef of Montreal: Working-Class Culture and the Tavern,

1869-1889." In *Canadian Working Class History,* ed. Laurel MacDowell and Ian Radforth. Toronto: Canadian Scholars Press, 1992.

Denning, Michael. *The Cultural Front: The Laboring of American Culture in the Twentieth Century.* London and New York: Verso, 1996.

Derksen, Céleste. "Out of the Closet: Dramatic Works by Sarah Anne Curzon. Part One, Woman and Nationhood." In *Laura Secord, the Heroine of 1812, Theatre Research in Canada* 15,1 (Spring 1994), pp.3–20.

Diamond, David. "In This Moment: The Evolution of 'Theatre for Living.'" *Canadian Theatre Review* 117 (Winter 2004), pp.10–13.

____. "The Squeegee Report." *Canadian Theatre Review* 103 (Summer 2000), pp.60–82.

____. *Theatre for Living: The Art and Science of Community-Based Dialogue.* Victoria, B.C.: Trafford, 2007.

Dillon, H.R., R.W. Downie, W.L. McGreary, and H.B. Scudamore. *The P.B.I., or, Mademoiselle of Bully Grenay.* In *The Canadian Forum* 11, 12 (September 1921), pp.368–374; 11, 13 (October 1921), pp.400–5; 11, 14 (November 1921), pp.430–36; 11, 15 (December 1921), pp.464–69; also available in typescript, microform, Canadian Drama Collection, Mount Saint Vincent University Library Special Collections.

Doucette, Leonard. *The Drama of Our Past: Major Plays from Nineteenth-Century Quebec.* Toronto: University of Toronto Press, 1997.

Doughty, Terri, ed. *Selections from the Girl's Own Paper, 1810-1907.* Peterborough, Ont.: Broadview, 2004.

Dorosh, Michael. *Canuck: Clothing and Equipping the Canadian Soldier 1939–1945: Battledress, Weapons and Equipment.* Missoula, Mont.: Pictorial Histories Publishing, 1995.

Doyle, James. *Progressive Heritage: The Evolution of a Politically Radical Literary Tradition in Canada.* Waterloo, Ont.: Wilfrid Laurier University Press, 2002.

Elliot, David R. and Iris Miller. *Bible Bill: A Biography of William Aberhart.* Edmonton: Reidmore Books, 1987.

Endres, Robin and Richard Wright, eds. *Eight Men Speak and Other Plays from the Canadian Workers' Theatre.* Toronto: New Hogtown Press, 1976.

Evans, Chad. *Frontier Theatre: A History of Nineteenth Century Theatrical Entertainment in the Canadian Far West and Alaska.* Victoria, B.C.: Sono Nis, 1983.

Evans, Gary. *In the National Interest: A Chronicle of the National Film Board of Canada from 1949 to 1989.* Toronto: University of Toronto Press, 1991.

Fennario, David. *Joe Beef: A History of Pointe Saint Charles.* Vancouver, Talonbooks, 1991.

Ferris, Will. *"Eight Men Speak."* *New Theatre,* July-August 1934, p.30.

Filewod, Alan. "National Battles: Canadian Monumental Drama and the Investiture of History." *Modern Drama* 38, 1 (Spring 1995), pp.71–86.

____. "The Interactive Documentary in Canada: Catalyst Theatre's *It's About Time.*" *Theatre Research in Canada* 6, 2 (1985), pp.133–47.

____. *Collective Encounters: Documentary Theatre in English Canada.* Toronto: University of Toronto Press, 1987.

____. *Performing Canada: The Nation Enacted in the Imagined Theatre.* Kamloops, B.C.: Textual Studies in Canada, 2002.

____. "Performance and Memory in the Party: Dismembering the Workers' Theatre Movement." *Essays in Canadian Writing* 80 (Fall 2003), pp.59–77.

____ and David Watt. *Workers' Playtime: Theatre and the Labour Movement since 1970.* Sydney, New South Wales: Currency Press, 2001.

Firth, Edith. *The Town of York 1814–1834: A Further Collection of Documents of Early Toronto.* Toronto: The Champlain Society, 1966.

Freire, Paulo. *Pedagogy of the Oppressed.* Trans. Myra Bergman Ramos. Harmondsworth, England: Penguin, 1973.

Frick, John W. *Theatre, Culture and Temperance Reform in Nineteenth-Century America.* Cambridge: Cambridge University Press, 2003.

Friedlander, Mira. "Survivor: George Luscombe at Toronto Workshop Productions." *Canadian Theatre Review* 38 (Fall 1983), p.46.

Fuller, William Henry. *The Unspecific Scandal: An Original, Political, Critical and Grittical Extravaganza.* Ottawa: A.S. Woodburn, 1874.

Fuller, William Henry. *H.M.S. Parliament, or, The Lady Who Loved a Government Clerk,* ed. Anton Wagner, in *Canada's Lost Plays,* vol.1, *The Nineteenth Century.* Toronto: CTR Publications, 1978.

Fussell, Paul. *Uniforms: Why We Are What We Wear.* Boston: Houghton Mifflin, 2002.

Gaspé Manifesto, The. "A Strange Enterprise: The Dilemma of the Playwright in Canada." In *Canadian Theatre History: Selected Readings.* ed. Don Rubin. Toronto: Copp Clark, 1996.

Geller, Peter. "'Hudson's Bay Company Indians': Images of Native People and the Red River Pageant, 1920." In *Dressing in Feathers: The Construction of the Indian in American Popular Culture.* ed. Elizabeth Bird. Boulder, Col.: Westview Press, 1996.

Gernsback, Hugo. *Ralph 124C41+: A Romance of the Year 2660.* Boston: Stratford Co., 1925.

Giap, Vo Nguyen. *People's War, People's Army: The Viet Cong Insurrection Manual for Underdeveloped Countries.* Foreword by Roger Hilsman. New York: Frederick A. Praeger, 1962.

Gomez, Mayte. "In Anger and in Hope, Oscar Ryan at the Canadian Tribune, 1955-1988." In *Establishing Our Boundaries: English-Canadian Theatre Criticism,* ed. Anton Wagner. Toronto: University of Toronto Press, 1999.

Goorney, Howard. *The Theatre Workshop Story.* London: Eyre Methuen, 1981.

Grant, Cynthia. "Still 'Activist' after All These Years?" *Canadian Theatre Review* 117 (Winter 2004), pp.14–16.

Hale, Amanda. "Ballrooms and Boardroom Tables." *Canadian Theatre Review* 53 (Winter 1987), pp.31–32.

Halladay, Laurel. "A Lovely War: Male to Female Cross-Dressing and Canadian Military Entertainment in World War II." *Journal of Homosexuality* 46, 3 (2004), p.25.

Hannant, Larry. "'My God, Are They Sending Women?': Three Canadian Women in the Spanish Civil War, 1936–1939." *Journal of the Canadian Historical Association / Revue de la Société historique du Canada* 15, 1 (2004), pp.153–176.

Hardy, Thomas. *The Dynasts.* London: Macmillan, 1977.

Hart, Henry, ed. *American Writers' Congress.* New York: International Publishers, 1935.

Heron, Craig and Steven Penfold. *The Workers' Festival: A History of Labour Day in Canada.* Toronto: University of Toronto Press, 2005.

Hinton, Darcy. "Aberhart-Manning Stage Play Terrified Depression-Era Audiences." *Edmonton Journal,* 18 May 2009.

Hunter, Peter. *Which Side Are You On, Boys: Canadian Life on the Left.* Toronto: Lugus Productions, 1988.

Hurford, Deborah-Kim, ed. *Under Broken Wings: A Collective Drama on Family Violence.* Sherwood Park, Alta.: Sherwood Park RCMP Crime Prevention/ Police Community Relations Unit, 1988.

Irchan, Myroslav. *Pidzemma Halichina* [*Undergound Galychyna*]. Winnipeg: Labour Farmer Press Society, 1926.

____. *Skupar* [*The Miser*]. Winnipeg: Labour Farmer Press Society, 1928.

Jackson, David. "Union Activism Punjabi Theatre in BC." *Fuse* 9, 1-2 (Fall 1985), pp.10–14.

Jenkyns, Michael. *The Sovereign Great Priory of Canada of the United Orders of Malta and of the Temple, 1855-2002: The Supreme Grand Masters*. Nepean, Ont.: Gryphon Jenkyns Enterprises, 2003.

Johnson, Bryan. "Road to Charlottetown Retains Its Earthly Allure." *Globe and Mail*, 10 Nov. 1978, p.15.

Johnston, Denis. *Up the Mainstream: The Rise of Toronto's Alternative Theatres, 1968-1975*. Toronto: University of Toronto Press, 1993.

Jones, Leonard. "The British Workers Theatre, 1917-1935," PhD diss., Karl-Marx Universitat, Liepzig, 1964.

Jordão, Aida. "Playwriting in Canadian Popular Theatre: Developing Plays with Actors and Non-Actors." In *Popular Political Theatre and Peformance*, ed. Julie Salverson. Toronto: Playwrights Canada, 2010.

Kealey, Gregory and Reg Whitaker, eds. *R.C.M.P. Security Bulletins: The Depression Years, Part 1, 1933-1934*. St. John's, Nfld.: Canadian Committee on Labour History, 1993.

____. *R.C.M.P. Security Bulletins: The Depression Years, Part II, 1935*. St. John's, Nfld.: Canadian Committee on Labour History, 1995.

____. *R.C.M.P. Security Bulletins: The Depression Years, Part III, 1936*. St. John's, Nfld.: Canadian Committee on Labour History, 1995.

____. *R.C.M.P. Security Bulletins: The Early Years, 1919-29*. St. John's, Nfld.: Canadian Committee on Labour History, 1994.

Kershaw, Baz. *The Radical in Performance: Between Brecht and Baudrillard*. London and New York: Routledge, 1999.

Kilbourn, William et al. "The Canada Council and Theatre: The Past 25 Years and Tomorrow." *Theatre History in Canada / Histoire du théâtre au Canada* 3, 2 (1982), pp.165–92.

King, Donovan. "Optative Theatre: A Critical Theory for Challenging Oppression and Spectacle." MFA thesis, University of Calgary, 2004.

____. "*Sinking Neptune*: Introduction." In *Theatre Histories*, ed. Alan Filewod. Toronto: Playwrights Canada Press, 2009.

Krawchuk, Peter. *Interned without Cause: The Internment of Canadian Anti-Fascists During World War Two*. Toronto: Kobzar, 1985 <www.socialisthistory.ca/Docs/CPC/WW2/IWC25.htm>.

____. *Our Stage: The Amateur Performing Arts of the Ukrainian Settlers in Canada*. Trans. Mary Skrypnyk. Toronto: Kobzar, 1984.

Laban, Rudolf and F.C. Lawrence. *Effort: Economy of Human Movement*. London: Macdonald and Evans, 1974.

Labelle, Linda and Paul Labelle. "Human Trafficking: Slavery in the New Millennium." *Diocese of/ de Sault Ste. Marie Online Newspaper* <news.diocesessm.org>.

Lascelles, Frank. "*The Dynasts*: A Reading Before the Empire Club of Canada, Toronto, February 10, 1916." In *The Empire Club of Canada Speeches 1915-1916*. Toronto: The Empire Club of Canada, 1917.

Lawrence, Robert. "*H.M.S. Parliament*: Dramatic History." *Canadian Theatre Review* 19 (Summer 1978).

Lee, Cyrus A. *Soldat: The World War II German Army Combat Collector's Handbook*, vol. 11, *The Reproductions – The Postwar Years*. Missoula, Mont.: Pictorial Histories Publishing, 1994.

Left Book Club Theatre Guild. *Notes on Forming 'Left' Theatre Groups*. London: Left Book Club, n.d. [probably 1934]. Unity Theatre Archives, Victoria and Albert Museum.

Littlewood, Joan. *Joan's Book: Joan Little-wood's Peculiar History As She Tells It.* London: Methuen, 1994.

Livesay, Dorothy. *Right Hand Left Hand.* Erin, Ont.: Press Porcepic, 1977.

Locke, Fran. "A Brief History of the LSPU Hall." In *Inventory of the Papers of the Resource Foundation for the Arts (The Mummers Troupe)*, ed. Gail Weir. St. John's, Nfld.: Centre for Newfoundland Studies, 1989.

Lord, Barry. *The History of Painting in Canada: Towards a People's Art.* Toronto: NC Press, 1974.

Lowell, Percival. *Mars.* New York: Houghton, Mifflin and Co. 1895.

MacColl, Ewan. *Journeyman: An Autobiography.* London: Sidgwick and Jackson, 1990.

Marks, Lynne. *Revivals and Roller Rinks: Religion, Leisure and Identity in Late Nineteenth Century Small Town Ontario.* Toronto: University of Toronto Press, 1996.

Martineau, Maureen. "The Théâtre Parminou: Thirty Years of History." *Canadian Theatre Review* 117 (Winter 2004), pp.5–9.

Massey, Vincent. "The Prospects of a Canadian Drama." *Queen's Quarterly* 30 (1922), pp.194–212.

Mathews, Robin. "Letter to the Editor." *Canadian Theatre Review* 24 (Fall 1979), pp.133–34.

McClung, Nellie. *The Stream Runs Fast: My Own Story.* Toronto: Thomas Allen, 1945.

McEwan, Tom. "Paul Bunyan." *Champion* 22 (May 1952).

McGauley, Laurie-Ann. "Super(stack) Inspiration." *Canadian Theatre Review* 53 (Winter 1987), p.37.

McGrath, John. *A Good Night Out.* London: Eyre Methuen, 1981.

____. *The Bone Won't Break: On Theatre and Hope in Hard Times.* London: Methuen, 1990.

Meek, Thomas Sheppard. *Young People's Library of Entertainment and Amusement.* 1903.

Michel, M. "Play-Actors Produce Play That Moved Lawmakers." *Champion*, 23 March 1956.

Mullaly, Edward. "The Saint John Theatre Riot of 1845." *Theatre History in Canada/ Histoire du Théâtre au Canada* 6, 1 (1985), pp.44–55.

Multicultural History Society of Ontario. *Polyphony: Bulletin of the Multicultural History Society of Ontario* 5, 2 (Fall/Winter, 1983).

Nelles, H.V. "Historical Pageantry and the 'Fusion of the Races' at the Tercentenary of Quebec, 1908." *Histoire Sociale/ Social History* 40 (1996), pp.391–415.

Newman, John P. *The Thrones and Palaces of Babylon and Nineveh from Sea to Sea.* New York: Harper and Brothers, 1876.

O'Donnell, Darren. *Pppeeeaaaccceee.* Toronto: Coach House Press, 2003.

____. *Social Acupuncture: A Guide to Suicide, Performance and Utopia.* Toronto: Coach House Press, 2006.

O'Neill, Chris and Ken Schwartz. "Westray: The Long Road Home." *Canadian Theatre Review* 99 (Summer 1999), pp.25–27.

Optative Theatrical Laboratories, Radical Dramaturgy Unit. "Sinking Neptune." In *Theatre Histories.* ed. Alan Filewod. Toronto: Playwrights Canada Press, 2009.

Ouzonian, Richard, "'Corrie' Canceled in Canada: Play Has Potential to Offend Jewish Community." *Variety*, 22 Dec. 2006.

Palmer, Bryan. *Canada's 1960s: The Ironies of Identity in a Rebellious Era.* Toronto: University of Toronto Press, 2009.

Piscator, Erwin. *The Political Theatre: A History 1914-1929.* Trans. Hugh Rorrison. New York: Avon, 1979.

____. *The Political Theatre.* Trans. Hugh Rorrison. London Eyre Methuen, 1979.

Porter, Mackenzie. "Wrong Turn Taken in This Road Show." *Toronto Sun*, 13 Nov. 1978.

Prentki, Tim and Jan Selman. *Popular Theatre in Political Culture: Britain and Canada in Focus*. Oxford: Intellect, 2000.

Pritz, Alexandra. "Ukrainian Cultural Traditions in Canada: Theatre, Choral Music and Dance, 1891–1967." MA thesis, University of Ottawa, 1977.

Queen's Own Rifles of Canada. "Semi-Centennial Reunion and Historical Pageant." Official Program. Toronto, 1910.

Read, Robyn. "Play Launches Calendar for Breast of Canada." *Guelph Mercury*, 4 Oct. 2003.

Richard, Alain-Martin and Clive Robertson. *Performance in Canada: 1970 to 1990*. Quebec and Toronto: Éditions Intervention and Coach House Press, 1991.

Rifkind, Candida. *Comrades and Critics: Women, Literature and the Left in 1930s Canada*. Toronto: University of Toronto Press, 2009.

Roach, Joseph. *Cities of the Dead: Circum-Atlantic Performances*. New York: Columbia University Press, 1996.

Roslin, Charles. "Canada's Bolshevist Drama – Miroslav Irchan, Playwright and Prophet of a Proletarian Revolution." *Saturday Night* 44 (9 Feb. 1929), pp.2–3. Reprinted in John Kolasky, ed., *Prophets and Proletarians: Documents on the History of the Rise and Decline of Ukrainian Communism in Canada*. Edmonton: Canadian Institute of Ukrainian Studies Press, 1990.

Rubin, Don. "Creeping Towards a Culture: The Theatre in English Canada Since 1945." In *Canadian Theatre History; Selected Readings*, ed. Don Rubin. Toronto: Copp Clark, 1996.

Ryan, Oscar. *Tim Buck: A Conscience for Canada*. Toronto: Progress Books, 1974.

____, E. Cecil-Smith, H. Francis, and Mildred Goldberg. *Eight Men Speak: A Political Play in Six Acts*. Toronto: Progressive Arts Club, 1934.

____ and Toby Ryan. "The Canadian Precedents." *Canadian Theatre Review* 22 (Spring 1979), pp.20–33.

Ryan, Toby Gordon. *Stage Left: Canadian Theatre in the Thirties: A Memoir*. Toronto: CTR Publications, 1981.

Salverson, Julie. "Popular Theatre Workers Retreat. Peterborough 1992 – The Hi-Lites." *CPTA News*, Summer 1998, pp.1–2.

Samuel, Raphael. *Theatres of Memory*. London: Verso, 1994.

____, Ewan MacColl, and Stuart Cosgrove, eds. *Theatres of the Left 1880-1935: Workers' Theatre Movements in Britain and America*. London: Routledge and Kegan Paul, 1985.

Sandwell, Bernard K. "The Annexation of Our Stage." *Canadian Magazine* 38 (November 1911), pp.22–26.

Sangster, Joan. "Robitnytsia, Ukrainian Communists, and the 'Porcupinism' Debate: Reassessing Ethnicity, Gender, and Class in Early Canadian Communism, 1922–1930." *Labour/Le Travail* 46 (Fall 2005) <www.historycooperative.org/journals/llt/56/sangster.html>.

Saxe, Alfred. "NEWSBOY– From Script to Performance." *New Theatre*, July-August 1934, pp.12–13, 29.

Schechner, Richard. *Performance Studies: An Introduction*. London: Routledge, 2002.

Schoen, Lawrence. *The Klingon Hamlet*. Flourtown, Penn.: Klingon Language Institute, 2000.

Schwam, Allan. "The Stratford Festival." *Canadian Tribune*, 3 Aug. 1953.

Smith, Doug. *Joe Zuken: Citizen and Socialist*. Toronto: James Lorimer and Son, 1990.

Smith, Mary Ellen. "Three Political Dramas from New Brunswick."

Canadian Drama/ L'art dramatique cana-dienne 12,1 (1986), pp.144–47.

Stevens, Albert. *The Cyclopaedia of Fraternities: A Compilation of Existing Authentic Information and the Results of Original Investigation as to the Origin, Derivation, Founders, Development, Aims, Emblems, Character and Personnel of More than Six Hundred Secret Societies in the United States.* New York, E.B. Treat: 1907; Detroit: Gale Research, 1966.

Stewart, John. "The People's Culture Flourishes." *Canadian Tribune,* 6 Feb. 1950.

Stone, Martin. "Class War in PEI." *Canadian Tribune,* 20 Nov. 1978.

Story, G.M. "Mummers in Newfoundland History: A Survey of the Printed Record." In *Christmas Mumming in Newfoundland: Essays in Anthropology, Folklore, and History,* ed. Herbert Halpert and George Story. Toronto: University of Toronto Press, 1968.

Suthren, Victor. "Unlikely Thespians: The Historical Re-enactors of the Royal George Society." *Canadian Theatre Review* 121 (Winter 2005), pp.5–8.

Tait, Michael. "Playwrights in a Vacuum: English-Canadian Drama in the Nineteenth Century." In *Dramatists in Canada: Selected Essays,* ed. W.H. New. Vancouver: UBC Press, 1972.

Thomas, Tom. "A Propertyless Theatre for a Propertyless Class." In *Theatres of the Left 1880–1935: Workers' Theatre Movements in Britain and America,* ed. Raphael Samuel, Ewan MacColl, and Stuart Cosgrove. London: Routledge and Kegan Paul, 1985.

Vance, Jonathan. *Death So Noble: Memory, Meaning and the First World War.* Vancouver: UBC Press, 1997.

Vogt, Gordon. *Critical Stages: Canadian Theatre in Crisis.* Toronto: Oberon Press, 1998.

Wagar, Samuel, ed. *Adelphon Kruptos: The Secret Ritual of the Knights of Labor.* 2003

reprint of 1886 original <www.sfu.ca/ labour/akword1.pdf>.

Wagner, Anton. "Canada: Introduction." In *The World Encyclopedia of Contemporary Theatre.* Vol. 2. *The Americas,* ed. Don Rubin. London and New York: Routledge, 1996.

Wasserman, Jerry. *Spectacle of Empire: Marc Lescarbot's Theatre of Neptune in New France.* Vancouver: Talon Books, 2006.

Watt, David. "The Maker and the Tool: High Culture, Popular Culture and the Work of Charles Parker." *New Theatre Quarterly* 73 (September 2003), pp.41–66.

Whittaker, Robin. "Un/Disciplined Performance: Nonprofessionalized Theatre in the Professional Era." PhD diss., University of Toronto, 2009.

Williams, Raymond. *Drama from Ibsen to Brecht.* London: Penguin, 1968.

Wolfe, Morris, "Tim Buck, Too." <www.grubstreetbooks.ca/essays/ timbuck3.html>.

Workers Laboratory Theatre. "Open Letter," *Workers Theatre,* February 1932, pp.36–37.

Wynnyckyj, Iroida Lebid. "Ukrainian Canadian Drama from the Beginnings of Immigration to 1942." MA thesis, University of Waterloo, 1976.

4. Documents, Reports, Interviews

"Are We There Yet?": Using Theatre in Teen Sexuality Education/ Community University Research Alliance. "The Results – Evaluation Research." Information Package, University of Alberta, 2010.

Aberhart, William. Radio Broadcast, 30 June 1930. Transcript Walter Norman Smith Fonds, M 1157, Glenbow Museum.

Anderson, David. Interview, 3 April 2008.

Angel, Leonard. Interview, May 2008.

____. "Pigs on Horses and Other Street Marvels of the Sixties: A Memoir." Transcript, n.d.

____. "The Bribe." Transcript, n.d.

Arbitration Report. 4 Sept. 1979. Chris Brookes Papers.

Atkinson, Laurel, Melissa Falcioni, Melannie Gayle, Vicki Hambley, Christine Lafazanos, Meagan Timms, and Jess Strothard. "The Strong Breast Revolution." Typescript, 2003.

Barker, Sarah. Interview, 10 April 2008.

Bouzek, Don. Letter to Caroline Lulham, 17 Nov. 1996. Ground Zero Productions Papers.

____. Letter to Alan Filewod, 10 Oct. 1997.

____. Interview with Scott Duchesne, Toronto, June 1996. Ground Zero Productions Papers, p.69.

____. Bouzek to Alan Filewod, 26 Oct. 1997.

____. Letter to Department of National Revenue, 7 May 1986. Ground Zero Productions Papers.

Bread and Puppet Theater. "Cheap Art Philosophy." <breadandpuppet.org/cheap-art-philosophy>.

British Columbia Arts Council. *Annual Report 2007-8: Awards Listing 2008–9*: 7 <www.bcartscouncil.ca/documents/publicationforms/pdfs>.

Brookes, Chris. Interview, January 1980.

____. "Coronation of Cecil B. DeMille." Transcript notes. Chris Brooks Papers.

____. "The Federal Funding Cutbacks to the Arts and Their Possible Effects upon Future Operations of the Mummers Theatre Troupe: A Brief Analysis." Transcript, November 1978. Chris Brookes Papers.

____. Letter to Learning, 14 July 1979. Chris Brookes Papers.

____. Letter to Lunde, 17 Feb. 1976. Chris Brookes Papers.

____. Letter to Lunde, 9 Feb. 1976. Chris Brookes Papers.

____. Letter to Muriel Sherrin, 15 Nov. 1973. Chris Brookes Papers.

____. Letter to Sabourin, 1972. Chris Brookes Papers.

____. Rehearsal Diaries. Ms., 1973. Chris Brooks Papers.

Canada Council for the Arts. Mummers Troupe Grant Applications. RG 63, NAC. Library and Archives Canada.

____. Ground Zero Production Grant Notification, 1988.

____. Searchable Grant Listings: Alberta 2008. <www.canadacouncil.ca/grants/recipients>.

Canadian Armed Forces. "Meet The Navy." Souvenir program. <www.navy.forces.gc.ca/cms_images/centennial_images/events/meet-thenavy.pdf>.

Canadian Labor Defence League. Press Release, 15 Nov. 1933. Transcript, Robert S. Kenny Collection on Canadian Radicalism.

____. *Report: First National Representative Convention, Toronto July 14-15-16-17, 1933*. Robert S. Kenny Collection on Canadian Radicalism.

____. "Minutes and Reports and Resolutions of the First Plenum of the Canadian Labour Defence League." Transcript, n.d. [1931]. Robert S. Kenny Collection on Canadian Radicalism.

Canadian Popular Theatre Alliance. "Principles and Objectives." Transcript, Thunder Bay, Ont., 1981. Author's papers.

Company of Sirens. "Report of Performances 1990-1991." Spiral-bound promotional brochure, in possession of the author.

Conseil des arts et des lettres du Québec. *Subventions et bourses accordées aux organismes et aux artistes professionnels en 2008–2009.* <www.calq.gouv.qc.ca/calq/$/bourses_subv.htm>.

Davies, Bembo. Letter to Filewod et al., April 1975. Chris Brookes Papers.

Dumbells, The. "Original Scripts: 1917–1919." Toronto Public Library Special Collections.

Dunn, Maria, and Ground Zero Productions. "Troublemakers." Transcript, 2004.

Filewod, Alan. Personal Minutes. Canada Council Collectives meeting, Toronto. 23 Jan. 1980.

Godsell, Philip. "Opening Speech by Philip Godsell, at Lower Fort Garry, May 3rd 1920, Introducing Assembled Tribes to Sir Robert Kindersley, Governor, H.B.C." Transcript, Red River Pageant Photograph Album, Philip H. Godsell Fonds PD 91, Glenbow Museum.

____. "The Red River Pageant." Transcript, 6 Sept. 1956. Red River Pageant Photograph Album, Philip H. Godsell Fonds PD 91, Glenbow Museum.

Great Canadian Theatre Company. "Members Handbook." 1978. Administrative records, 1978–79, GCTC Archives.

____. Board of Management Minutes. 23 March 1975.

____. Minutes. 7 Feb. 1975. Administrative Files 1975-77, GCTC Archives.

Ground Zero Productions. "Popular Theatre Workers Retreat, Statement of Principles." Peterborough, Ont., 19 July 1992. Transcript, author's papers.

Halferty, Paul. "Theatrical Protest before Gay Liberation: John Herbert and *Fortune and Men's Eyes* at the Central Library Theatre." Transcript, 2010.

Headlines Theatre. "Components of Theatre for Living." <www.headlinestheatre.com/theatre_for_living.htm>.

Hill Strategies Research. *A Statistical Profile of Artists in Canada Based on the 2006 Census.* Ottawa: Canada Council for the Arts, 2009. <www.canadacouncil.ca/NR/rdonlyres/BB1FEA67-724A-44FE-A195-9F58F82D2CD5/0/Artists_Canada2006.pdf>.

Hill Strategies Research. *Finances of Performing Arts Organizations in Canada in 2006–07.* Report funded by the Canada Council for the Arts, the Department of Canadian Heritage and the Ontario Arts Council, November 2008.

Hudson's Bay Company. Red River Pageant Photograph Album. Philip H. Godsell Fonds PD 91, Glenbow Museum.

International Theatre of the Oppressed Organization. "Declaration of Principles." <www.theatreoftheoppressed.org/en/index.php?nodeID=23>.

Jones, Andy. Letter to Brookes et al., 15 Aug. 1979. Chris Brookes Papers.

Learning, Walter. Letter to Board of Directors, Kam Lab Theatre. 27 Sept. 1979. Chris Brookes Papers.

Lunde, Lynn. Letter to Brookes, May 1975. Chris Brookes Papers.

McDermid Studio Fonds. Glenbow Museum Archives, NC-6-13068b, NC-6-13068f.

Macdonald, Larry. "Production Notes for The Big Nickel." Performance Files 1978, GCTC Archives.

____. *The Big Nickel.* Performance Files 1978, GCTC Archives.

Mammalian Diving Reflex. "Social Acupuncture: Haircuts by Children New York." <www.mammalian.ca/template.php?content=social_haircutsNY>.

Mathews, Robin. Letter to the Board of Management,1 May 1979. Administrative Files 1975-79, GCTC Archives.

Montreal by Gaslight. Montreal: "Published for the Trade," 1889 (CIHM Microfiche 11210).

Mummers Troupe Ltd. Incorporation papers, 1979. CNSA 2.04.002.

Mummers Troupe. Minutes, 6 Feb. 1975. Chris Brookes Papers.

____. Minutes, 21 May 1975. Chris Brookes Papers.

____. Minutes, 1 Dec. 1975. Chris Brookes Papers.

____. Minutes, February 1976. Chris Brookes Papers.

____. Canada Council Correspondence. CNSA 3.03.001.Centre for Newfoundland Studies Archives, Memorial University of Newfoundland.

____. Minutes. "Meeting re Proposed Newfoundland Theatre Company." N.d. Chris Brookes Papers.

____. Public Meeting. "Possible Motions."
14 Aug. 1979. Chris Brookes Papers.

____. Unsigned Motion. Ms., n.d. Chris
Brookes Papers.

____. Untitled Manifesto. 26 July 1976.
Chris Brookes Papers.

____. "What's That Got to Do with the
Price of Fish?" Transcript, 1976. Mummers Troupe Papers.

New Theatre Group, Montreal. "Bury the
Dead." Program, October 1936. Toby
Gordon Ryan Papers.

Odets, Clifford. *Waiting for Lefty. New Theatre*, February 1935, p.18. With anno-
tations by Toby Gordon Ryan. Toby
Gordon Ryan Papers.

Ogden's Big Spectacular Uncle Tom's
Cabin Company. Poster, n.d. c.1900.
Possession of the author.

Ontario Arts Council. *Current List Of
Grant Recipients.* <www.arts.on.ca/
Page2161.aspx?PageMode=View&date
=01/01/2008>.

Optative Theatre Laboratories. "Mandate."
<www.optative.net/mandate>.

Optative Theatre Laboratories. "Artists Still
Waiting for Box Office Cash – 10 Years
after Being Kicked out of the Fringe!"
Press Release, 16 June 2010. <www.
optative.net/blog/2010/06/20/artists-
still-waiting-for-box-office-cash-10-years-
after-being-kicked-out-of-the-fringe/>.

Penner, Roland. "My Life in Art." Transcript, n.d.

Play-Actors. "The Play-Actors Letter," 5
Feb. 1954. Toby Gordon Ryan Papers.

Play-Actors. *Tecumseh.* Press Release, 4 Feb.
1954. Toby Gordon Ryan Papers.

Pollock, Gabe. *STRIKE! The play.* Transcript, 2007. <www.youtube.com/
watch?v=h-uZTmzjjV4>.

Resource Centre for the Arts. *Annual
Report,* 1979. Chris Brookes Papers.

Resource Foundation for the Arts. Articles
of Incorporation, 1973. Mummers
Troupe Papers.

Riggio, Mike. Open Letter. N.d. Chris
Brookes Papers.

Rogers, Dave. "Banner Theatre –
What Kind of Theatre?"
<www.bannertheatre.co.uk/
what_kind_of_theatre.htm>.

Ryan, Oscar. Interview, Toronto, August
1990.

Ryan, Toby Gordon. Interview, April 1988.

____. Letter to Herbert Whittaker, 22 May
1954. Toby Gordon Ryan Papers.

____. Letter to Roland Penner, 4 May
1955. Toby Gordon Ryan Papers.

Ryga, George. Keynote Address, Bread
and Circuses Festival of Canadian Theatre, Thunder Bay. N.p., 29 May 1981.

Skrypnyk, Mary. "First Wave of Ukrainian
Immigration to Canada, 1891–1914:
Mary Skrypnyk's story."
<www.virtualmuseum.ca/pm_v2.php
?id=story_line&lg=English&fl=0&ex=
464&sl=5501&pos=1>.

Sobota, Michael. Letter to Brookes, 5 Sept.
1979. Chris Brookes Papers.

Statistics Canada, "Patterns in Culture
Consumption and Participation," 2000.
<www.canadacouncil.ca/
NR/rdonlyres/74E41055-65E2-
4338-990D-A0462CF3583C/0/
cult_consumpe.pdf>.

Theatre of Action, "Five One-Act Plays."
Program, n.d. Toby Gordon Ryan
Papers.

Theatre of Action. "A Theatre in Action."
Toronto, n.p., 1935. Toby Gordon
Ryan Papers.

Theatre of Action. Minutes Book, 1939-
1940. Toby Gordon Ryan Papers.

Théâtre Parminou "Intervention Theatre:
Social Issues." <www.parminou.com/
en/social-issues.php>.

____. "Intervention Theatre: The Concep-
tion and Realization Process."
<www.parminou.com/en/conception-
realization.php>.

____. Rencontres Internationales de
Théâtre d'Intervention. Program, 3-6
June 2004.

Toronto Police Commission. Minutes
1933–1934. Toronto Police Archives.

Turnbull, Keith. Letter to David Peacock, 6 May 1974. Chris Brookes Papers.

Wagner, Anton, ed. "The Worlds of Herman Voaden." <www.lib.unb.ca/Texts/Theatre/voaden/default>.

5. Audiovisual Resources

13 Experiments in Hope. The Laboratory of Insurrectionary Imagination. DVD, 2005.

The Clinton Special. Dir. Michael Ondaatje. Canadian Filmmakers Distribution Centre, 1974.

William Aberhart Foundation. "Clifford Willmott's Memory of Aberhart." <qt.lexicom.ab.ca:8000/aberhartfoundation/the_man_memories/clifford_willmott_dreadnaught.mp3>.

Index

Aberhart, William, 61, 87–95; *Homiletics*, 92; "Man from Mars" skits, 92–95

aboriginality, 72; appropriated representation of, 71; erasure of material reality of, 75; impersonation of, 72–73

Aboriginal theatre, 71–79; absence of from Canadian theatre historiography, 72; banning of, 73–74

activism, theatre as, 2, 4, 18–19, 150–51, 173, 175, 202–3, 240; Piscator and, 15, 94; workers' theatre movement and, 110–11, 123, 127

activist community education, 242

actor-centred textualities, 264

actors: claim to authenticity, 288–89; income of, 12–13; number of working, 13; presence of in documentary theatre, 287

ACTRA, 172

actuality, 286–89, 291; fiction and, 172

Adams, Rose, 135

adult education, 242

advocacy: political, 52; public, 46; theatre, 264; theatricals, 30

aesthetics, 13–14, 89, 247, 289; chaos, 97, 292–302; combat, 156; countercultural, 149, 163; cultural, 6; Dadaist refusal of, 178; dissident/radical, 151; formal, dissolution of, 97; formal principles of, 143; machine-gun, 18; modernist, 118, 162; oppositional, 148; and pleasure of performance, 241; political, 111; principles of "good" dramaturgy, 11; proletarian, 103; protocols of, 208; of revolutionary modernism, 122; vanguard, 88

"aesthetic space" (Boal), 20

aesthetic value, 7; destabilization of assumptions of, 6

affaire Tartuffe, 73

African-American oral poetry, 122

African-Canadian playwrights, 13

agitprop, 16, 18, 35, 63, 87–95, 97–98, 142, 143, 169, 176–208, 279, 293, 299; carnivalesque, 293; chaos aesthetics and, 292–302; continuity of practice in, 202; cultural nationalism and, 193–203; deregulating, 178–86; as derivative of mass communication, 204–5; documentary, 171; evolution of, 178; GCTC and, 193–203; Ground Zero and, 281; localist forms of, 104–5, 141; mass communication and, 88; as micropolitical interventions, 194; military shows as, 147; mobile, 115–25; mobile vs. stationary, 100, 102; as mobilization through theatre, 88; Mummers Troupe and, 216–24; Performance (art) and, 183; power of to compel spectatorship, 294–95; pragmatism, 120; as precondition of art, 105; as projection of power, 97; proliferation of, 183; and puppetry, 179, 181, 185–86, 191–93; re-enactment as right-wing, 302–9; regendering of, 181; resituation of in history of popular "folk" art, 104; retreat from, 102, 104, 124; as shifting practice, 88; as solution in struggle, 203; as spatial practice, 183; state-produced, 303; street, 183–84; theatricality and immediacy of, 137;

343